WATER RESOURCES ASSESSMENT—

METHODOLOGY & TECHNOLOGY SOURCEBOOK

WATER RESOURCES ASSESSMENT—

METHODOLOGY & TECHNOLOGY SOURCEBOOK

by

LARRY W. CANTER

Director and Professor
School of Civil Engineering
  and Environmental Science
University of Oklahoma
Norman, Oklahoma

ANN ARBOR SCIENCE
PUBLISHERS INC
P.O. BOX 1425 • ANN ARBOR, MICH. 48106

Copyright © 1979 by Ann Arbor Science Publishers, Inc.
P.O. Box 1425, 230 Collingwood, Ann Arbor, Michigan 48106

Library of Congress Catalog Card Number 79-88942
ISBN 0-250-40320-X

lw
7-21-80

PREFACE

This book summarizes the work performed under Purchase
Order No. DACW39-78-M1603 titled, "Literature Review on
Methods of Environmental Impact Assessments," dated February,
1978, between the U.S. Army Engineer Waterways Experiment
Station (WES) and the author. The research was sponsored by
the Office, Chief of Engineers, U.S. Army, Washington, D.C.,
and directed by the Environmental Laboratory, WES. The
objective was to prepare a comprehensive review and evaluation of methodologies and technologies that are used directly
or that have potential application to environmental impact
assessment and/or impact assessment and alternative evaluation studies for water resources programs and projects.
    The literature was reviewed in accordance with six time
periods: 1960-70, 1971-73, 1974, 1975, 1976, and 1977-78.
The 1960-70 period encompasses pre-NEPA literature, while the
latter five cover the period since NEPA passage. The latter
five periods were chosen so as to limit the reviewed references to no more than 60 in a period. Each reviewed reference was evaluated relative to 12 criteria: interdisciplinary team, assessment variables, baseline studies, impact
identification, critical impacts, importance weighting,
scaling or ranking, impact summarization, documentation,
public participation, and conflict management and resolution.
    A total of 254 references were examined, with 176 meet-
ing one criterion or more. The first section of the book
summarizes the references according to the 12 criteria.
Salient features of references having potential useable
information for water resources assessments are then summarized by time period. The 176 references meeting one or more
of the 12 entrance criteria are summarized in Appendices A
through F according to time period. For example, Appendix A
contains information on the 16 pertinent references from the
1960-70 period, and Appendix B addresses the 37 germain
references from the 1971-73 period. Abstracts of the 78
references not meeting any entrance criteria are in Appendix
G. It should be noted that just because a reference did not
meet any criterion does not mean it has no value in environmental impact assessment. It may simply reflect non-orientation to water resources projects.

This book is intended for use by professionals working on environmental impact studies. Even though the orientation is to water resources, the book is of general value due to the large number of general methodologies and technologies described. The book could also be used in upper division or graduate level courses dealing with environmental impact assessments/statements.

The author expresses his gratitude to the College of Engineering, University of Oklahoma, for its support during the preparation of this book. Special acknowledgement is given to Ms. Sue Richardson and Dr. Stan West of the Environmental Resources Division, WES, for their professional advice in conjunction with the literature survey. In addition, the author acknowledges Mrs. Edna Rothschild, Mrs. Kristi Smith, Ms. Susan Wilkerson and Mrs. Carol Holloway for their typing assistance in the preparation of this manuscript. Special thanks are extended to Ms. Jerry Lawrence for her efforts in the preparation of the author and subject indexes. Finally, the author thanks his wife and three sons for their encouragement in the process of developing this book.

Larry W. Canter

LARRY W. CANTER, P.E., is Director and Professor, School of Civil Engineering and Environmental Science, University of Oklahoma, Norman. Dr. Canter received his PhD in Environmental Health Engineering from the University of Texas, MS in Sanitary Engineering from the University of Illinois, and BE in Civil Engineering from Vanderbilt University. Before joining the faculty of the University of Oklahoma in 1969, he was on the faculty of Tulane University and was a sanitary engineer in the U.S. Public Health Service.

Dr. Canter has published several books, including *Handbook of Variables for Environmental Impact Assessment* (Ann Arbor Science Publishers, 1979), and is the author of numerous papers, research reports and chapters.

His research includes environmental impact assessment, groundwater pollution control, and solid hazardous waste management. Dr. Canter has been project director or co-director of some 20 externally sponsored research projects at the University of Oklahoma, and conducts courses on environmental impact assessment.

To Donna, Doug, Steve, and Greg

LIST OF TABLES

LIST OF FIGURES

CONTENTS

SUMMARY AND CONCLUSIONS

The National Environmental Policy Act (NEPA) requires
Federal agencies to develop methods and procedures for
including environmental concerns in project planning and
decision making along with technical and economic concerns.
Numerous methodologies have been developed for systematically
identifying and evaluating the environmental impacts of
planning alternatives. Technologies for impact prediction
have also been published in response to NEPA. The objective
of this study was to prepare a comprehensive literature review
of methodologies/technologies (M/T) that are used directly or
have potential application in environmental impact assessments
for water resources programs and projects. Of specific
interest were those M/T which could potentially be used in
the Water Resources Assessment Methodology (WRAM) developed
at the U.S. Army Engineers Waterways Experiment Station. The
WRAM is for impact assessment and evaluation of water
resources alternatives studied under the auspices of the
Corps Civil Works program.

The literature was reviewed in accordance with six time
periods: 1960-70, 1971-73, 1974, 1975, 1976, and 1977-78.
The 1960-70 period encompasses pre-NEPA literature, while the
latter five cover the period since NEPA passage. The latter
five periods were chosen so as to limit the reviewed references to no more than 60 in a period. Each reviewed
reference was evaluated relative to 12 criteria shown in
Table S-1. If one criterion or more was met, then the
salient feature(s) of the methodology/technology (M/T) was
identified and evaluated relative to the 6 considerations in
Table S-2. A conclusion was then drawn that (1) the M/T
contains information which is potentially useable in environmental impact assessments prepared in accordance with WRAM,
or (2) the M/T should be considered as a general reference
for WRAM.

A total of 254 references were examined in this literature review. Table S-3 summarizes the references according
to time period and conclusions. A total of 176 references
met one criterion or more, with 89 considered to have potentially useable information for WRAM, and 87 serving as
general references. The 176 references meeting one or more
of the 12 entrance criteria are summarized in Appendices A
through F according to time period. For example, Appendix A
contains information on the 16 pertinent references from the
1960-70 period, and Appendix B addresses the 37 germain
references from the 1971-73 period. Salient features of the
89 references having potentially useable information for WRAM
are summarized in the main body of this report as per the
time period of occurrences; e.g., 1960-70, 1971-73, etc.
Abstracts of the 78 references not meeting any entrance
criteria are in Appendix G. It should be noted that just
because a reference did not meet any criterion does not mean
it has no value in environmental impact assessment. It may

3

TABLE S-1: CRITERIA FOR INCLUSION
OF METHODOLOGY/TECHNOLOGY (M/T)

---

1. Does the M/T provide information on procedures for interdisciplinary team approaches?

2. Does the M/T contain listings of assessment variables for the system of four accounts in water resources projects?

3. Does the M/T provide information on planning/conduction of baseline field studies?

4. Does the M/T address impact identification?

5. Does the M/T provide information on impact prediction?

6. Does the M/T focus on "red-flag" or critical impacts?

7. Does the M/T include procedures for assignment of importance weights to assessment variables?

8. Does the M/T identify scaling or ranking procedures for the impacts of alternatives?

9. Does the M/T encourage impact summarization, assessment and evaluation of trade-offs?

10. Does the M/T suggest approaches for documentation and communication of impact assessment information?

11. Does the M/T include information on public participation techniques?

12. Does the M/T address conflict management and resolution?

---

simply reflect non-orientation to water resources projects or lack of complete description in the cited reference.

REPORT ORGANIZATION

One of the major emphasis in this study was to review the identified references relative to the 12 criteria in Table S-1. These criteria represent desirable characteristics for methodologies or technologies used in environmental impact assessment studies for water resources projects or programs. Table S-4 summarizes the number of methodologies/technologies meeting the 12 criteria per time period. The criteria most frequently met include prediction of changes, impact summarization and assessment, scaling or ranking procedures, and

TABLE S-2: CONSIDERATIONS IN EVALUATING THE
SALIENT FEATURE(S) OF METHODOLOGY/TECHNOLOGY (M/T)

1. Has the M/T been subjected to field studies/applications?

2. Is the M/T practical for use in routine water resources projects?

3. Is the M/T limited to water resources projects of various types and sizes?

4. Are objective (non-judgmental) approaches stressed in lieu of subjective (judgmental) ones?

5. Does the M/T yield reproducible results?

6. Does the M/T have a sound scientific basis?

TABLE S-3: SUMMARY OF REFERENCES REVIEWED IN THIS STUDY

TIME PERIOD	NUMBER OF REFERENCES			
	Meeting One or More Entrance Criteria		Not Meeting Entrance Criteria	Total
	Contains Potentially Useable Information For WRAM	General Reference For WRAM		
1960-70	5	11	5	21
1971-73	11	26	17	54
1974	8	8	15	31
1975	13	14	14	41
1976	25	17	16	58
1977-78	27	11	11	49
TOTALS	89	87	78	254

TABLE S-4: SUMMARY OF RESULTS RELATIVE
TO 12 ENTRANCE CRITERIA

Entrance Criteria	Number of Methodologies/Technologies Meeting Entrance Criteria						
	1960-70	1971-73	1974	1975	1976	1977-78	Total
1. Interdisciplinary team	0	0	1	0	0	4	5
2. Assessment variables	3	11	6	6	9	13	48
3. Field studies	0	2	0	0	4	3	9
4. Impact Identification	1	13	6	6	7	10	43
5. Prediction of changes	1	10	3	19	28	18	79
6. Critical impacts	0	4	0	0	0	1	5
7. Importance weights	11	14	6	4	8	11	54
8. Scaling or ranking procedures	11	17	7	5	5	14	59
9. Impact summarization and assessment	13	21	8	6	13	12	73
10. Documentation	0	0	1	0	0	1	2
11. Public participation	2	1	4	1	4	6	18
12. Conflict management and resolution	0	0	0	1	2	5	8

importance weights; those least frequently met based on this literature review are documentation, interdisciplinary team, conflict management and resolution, and field studies.

Tables S-5 through S-16 list the authors of the reference sources having information on the 12 criteria, respectively. For example, Alden from the 1974 period, and Canter (1978), Duke, et al, Heer and Hagerty, and the U.S. Soil Conservation Service from the 1977-78 period contain information on the interdisciplinary team approach to impact assessment.

If you identify a reference of potential interest from Tables S-5 through S-16, the following steps can be used to find additional information about that reference:

1. Look up the sequential number of the reference according to the time period it was published. Use either Table 5 (1960-70), 9 (1971-73), 15 (1974), 20 (1975), 32 (1976), or 53 (1977-78) in the main body of this report.

2. To determine the complete characteristics of the reference of interest relative to the 12 criteria in Table S-1, take the sequential number from Table 5, 9, 15, 20, 32, or 53, and utilize Table 6, 10, 16, 21, 33, or 54, respectively. These latter tables identify all criteria met by each reference included in the literature review. The salient features of each reference are summarized in either Table 7 (1960-70), 11 (1971-73), 17 (1974), 22 (1975), 34 (1976), or 55 (1977-78). Additional information on the reference can be found in either Appendix A (1960-70), B (1971-73), C (1974), D (1975), E (1976), or F (1977-78).

3. To determine the conclusion regarding a reference in relation to WRAM use either Table 8 (1960-70), 12 (1971-73), 18 (1974), 23 (1975), 35 (1976) or 56 (1977-78). References which contain potentially useable information for WRAM are summarized in this report in the time period of occurrence.

If you are familiar with certain environmental impact assessment methodologies/technologies and want to know if they are addressed in this report you can look up the reference in the alphabetical listing of all 254 selected references beginning on page R-1. If the reference is not cited the author would appreciate being informed of the omission. If it is cited then turn in this report to the time period when it was published and look up the sequential number in either Table 5 (1960-70), 9 (1971-73), 15 (1974), 20 (1975), 32 (1976), and 53 (1977-78). Then follow Steps 2 and 3 above for procurement of additional information on the reference of interest.

TABLE S-5: METHODOLOGIES/TECHNOLOGIES CONTAINING
INFORMATION ON INTERDISCIPLINARY TEAM

1960–70 Period	1976 Period
None	None
1971–73 Period	1977–78 Period
None	U.S. Soil Conservation Service
1974 Period	
Alden	
1975 Period	
None	

TABLE S-6: METHODOLOGIES/TECHNOLOGIES CONTAINING
INFORMATION ON ASSESSMENT VARIABLES

1960–70 Period	1974 Period
Brown et al.	Battelle-Columbus
Dearinger	Laboratories
Leopold	Battelle-Pacific Northwest Laboratories
1971–73 Period	Jain, Urban, and Stacey
	Schaenman and Muller
Bagley, Kroll, and Clark	School of Civil Engineering
Bureau of Reclamation	and Environmental Science
Dee et al. (1972)	and Oklahoma Biological
Dee et al. (1973)	Survey
Jain et al.	Warner et al.
Morrill	
O'Connor	1975 Period
Ortolano	
Pikul	Carstea et al.
Raines	Fitzsimmons, Stuart, and Wolff
U.S. Army Engineer District	Thom and Ott
	U.S. Department of the Army
	Vlachos et al.
	Voorhees and Associates

8

1976 Period	1977-78 Period
Christensen	Boesch
Curran Associates	Canter and Hill
Jain, Urban, and Cerchione	Canter (1977)
Keyes	Canter (1978)
Lower Mississippi Valley	Chalmers and Anderson
Division	Duke et al.
Muller	Dwyer, Hatmaker, and Hewings
Schaenman	Ellis et al.
U.S. Environmental Protection	Flood et al.
Agency	Guseman and Dietrich
Webster et al.	Jain, Urban, and Stacey
	McEvoy and Dietz
	Ott

TABLE S-7: METHODOLOGIES/TECHNOLOGIES CONTAINING
INFORMATION ON FIELD STUDIES

1960-70 Period	1976 Period
None	Colonell
	Schaenman
1971-73 Period	Springer
	Vlachos and Hendricks
Bureau of Reclamation	
Dee et al. (1972)	**1977-78 Period**
1974 Period	Boesch
	Canter (1978)
None	Flood et al.
1975 Period	
None	

TABLE S-8: METHODOLOGIES/TECHNOLOGIES CONTAINING
INFORMATION ON IMPACT IDENTIFICATION

1960-70 Period	1975 Period
Bishop et al.	Bhutani et al.
	Carstea et al.
1971-73 Period	Malone
	Schlesinger and Daetz
Central New York Regional	U.S. Department of the Army
Planning and Development	Voorhees and Associates
Board	
Chen and Orlob	**1976 Period**
Fischer and Davies	
Jain et al.	Boucher and Stover
Kane, Vertinsky, and	Chase
Thomson	Christensen
Leopold et al.	Curran Associates
Manheim et al.	Darnell et al.
Moore et al.	Jain, Urban, and Cerchione
Ortolano	U.S. Environmental Protection
Raines	Agency
Schlesinger and Daetz	
Sorensen	**1977-78 Period**
U.S. Army Engineer District	
	Canter et al.
1974 Period	Canter (1977)
	Canter (1978)
Alabama Development Office	Chalmers
Battelle-Pacific Northwest	Duke et al.
Laboratories	Finsterbusch
Jain, Urban, and Stacey	Jain, Urban, and Stacey
Kruzic	McEvoy and Dietz
Schaenman and Muller	Stinson and O'Hare
Warner et al.	U.S. Soil Conservation Service

TABLE S-9:   METHODOLOGIES/TECHNOLOGIES CONTAINING INFORMATION
ON PREDICTION OF CHANGES

1960-70
  Bishop et al.

1971-73
  Bagley, Kroll, and Clark
  Bromley et al.
  Chen and Orlob
  Environmental Impact
    Center, Inc.
  Hydrologic Engineering
    Center
  Markofsky and Harleman
  Odum
  Swartzman and Van Dyne
  Texas Water Development
    Board
  Thomas, Paul, and
    Israelsen

1974
  Battelle-Columbus
    Laboratories
  Kruzic
  Warner, et al.

1975
  Bella
  Bhutani et al.

Carstea et al.
Christensen, Van Winkle, and
  Mattice
Clark
Fuhriman et al.
Harkness
Haven
Hornberger, Kelly, and Lederman
Malone
Mitchell et al.
Muller
Nelson and LaBelle
Schlesinger and Daetz
Sharma, Buffington, and
  McFadden
Troxler and Thackston
U.S. Department of the Army
Vlachos et al.
Voorhees and Associates

1976
  Adams and Kurisu
  Boucher and Stover
  Christensen
  Coates (a)
  Colonell
  Curran Associates

TABLE S-10:   METHODOLOGIES/TECHNOLOGIES CONTAINING
INFORMATION ON CRITICAL IMPACTS

1960-70 Period

  None

1971-73 Period

  Dee et al. (1972)
  Dee et al. (1973)
  Fischer and Davies
  Schlesinger and Daetz

1974 Period

  None

1975 Period

  None

1976 Period

  None

1977-78 Period

  Duke et al.

11

TABLE S-11: METHODOLOGIES/TECHNOLOGIES CONTAINING
INFORMATION ON IMPORTANCE WEIGHTS

1960-70 Period

Brown et al.
Dalkey
Dean and Nishry
Dearinger
Eckenrode
Falk
Highway Research Section
Miller
Pikarsky
Schimpeler and Grecco
Southeastern Wisconsin
   Regional Planning
   Commission

1971-73 Period

Bagley, Kroll, and Clark
Central New York Regional
   Planning and Development
   Board
Commonwealth Associates
Crawford
Dee et al. (1972)
Dee et al. (1973)
MacCrimmon
O'Connor
Odum et al.
Raines
Schlesinger and Daetz
Stover
U.S. Army Engineer District
Wenger and Rhyner

1974 Period

Burnham
Pendse and Wyckoff
Salomon
School of Civil Engineering
   and Environmental Science
   and Oklahoma Biological
   Survey
Smith
Utah Water Research
   Laboratory

1975 Period

Gann
Malone
Morrison
Toussaint

1976 Period

Canter
Edwards
Engineering Division
Gum, Roefs, and Kimball
Hammond and Adelman
Lower Mississippi Valley
   Division
MacKinnon and Anderson
Ross

1977-78 Period

Canter and Reid
Canter (1977)
Canter (1978)
Canter
Dunne
Finsterbusch
Hammond et al.
Hobbs and Voelker
Paul
Protasel
Voelker

TABLE S-12: METHODOLOGIES/TECHNOLOGIES CONTAINING
INFORMATION ON SCALING OR RANKING PROCEDURES

1960-70 Period

Brown et al.
Dalkey
Dean and Nishry
Dearinger
Falk
Highway Research Section
Leopold
Miller
Pikarsky
Schimpeler and Grecco
Southeastern Wisconsin
  Regional Planning
  Commission

1971-73 Period

Arnold, Young, and Brewer
Bagley, Kroll, and Clark
Bereano et al.
Bureau of Reclamation
Commonwealth Associates
Crawford
Dee et al. (1972)
Dee et al. (1973)
Fischer and Davies
MacCrimmon
O'Conner
Odum et al.
Raines
Schlesinger and Daetz
Stover
U.S. Army Engineer District
Wenger and Rhyner

1974 Period

Adkins and Burke
Alabama Development Office
Alden
Burnham
Salomon
School of Civil Engineering
  and Environmental Science
  and Oklahoma Biological
  Survey
Smith

1975 Period

Fitzsimmons, Stuart, and Wolff
Gann
Morrison
Toussaint
Voorhees and Associates

1976 Period

Canter
Engineering Division
Hammond and Adelman
Liu and Yu
Lower Mississippi Valley
  Division

1977-78 Period

Canter and Reid
Canter and Hill
Canter (1977)
Canter (1978)
Canter
Dee et al.
Duke et al.
Dunne
Finsterbusch
Guseman and Dietrich
Hammond et al.
Hobbs and Voelker
U.S. Soil Conservation
  Service
Von Gierke

TABLE S-13: METHODOLOGIES/TECHNOLOGIES CONTAINING
INFORMATION ON IMPACT SUMMARIZATION AND ASSESSMENT

1960-70 Period

Bishop et al.
Brown et al.
Dalkey
Dean and Nishry
Falk
Highway Research Section
Hill
Leopold
Miller
Orlob et al.
Pikarsky
Schimpeler and Grecco
Southeastern Wisconsin
  Regional Planning
  Commission

1971-73 Period

Bagley, Kroll, and Clark
Bereano et al.
Bureau of Reclamation
Central New York Regional
  Planning and Development
  Board
Commonwealth Associates
Coomber and Biswas
Crawford
Dee et al. (1972)
Dee et al. (1973)
Fischer and Davies
Leopold et al.
MacCrimmon
Manheim et al.
Moore et al.
O'Connor
Odum et al.
Raines
Schlesinger and Daetz
Stover
U.S. Army Engineer District
Wenger and Rhyner

1974 Period

Alabama Development Office
Alden
Battelle-Pacific Northwest
  Laboratories
Bender and Ahmed
Burnham
Salomon
School of Civil Engineering
  and Environmental Science
  and Oklahoma Biological
  Survey
U.S. Bureau of Outdoor
  Recreation

1975 Period

Christensen, Van Winkle, and
  Mattice
Dee et al.
Fitzsimmons, Stuart, and Wolff
Harkness
Sharma, Buffington, and
  McFadden
Voorhees and Associates

1976 Period

Chase
Christensen
Coates (a)
Coates (b)
Curran Associates
Engineering Division
Fennelly et al.
Liu and Yu
McElroy et al.
Reid
Ross
Schaenman
U.S. Environmental Protection
  Agency

14

1977-78 Period

    Canter and Reid
    Canter (1977)
    Canter (1978)
    Canter
    Chalmers and Anderson
    Duke et al.
    Finsterbusch and Wolff
    Finsterbusch
    Heer and Hagerty
    Hobbs and Voelker
    U.S. Soil Conservation
      Service
    Von Gierke

TABLE S-14: METHODOLOGIES/TECHNOLOGIES CONTAINING
INFORMATION ON DOCUMENTATION

1960-70 Period	1975 Period
None	None
1971-73 Period	1976 Period
None	None
1974 Period	1977-78 Period
Alabama Development Office	Duke et al.

TABLE S-15: METHODOLOGIES/TECHNOLOGIES CONTAINING
INFORMATION ON PUBLIC PARTICIPATION

1960-70 Period	1976 Period
Bishop Falk	Case, Edgmon and Renton Clark, Hendee, and Stankey Gum, Roefs, and Kimball
1971-73 Period	Hammond and Adelman
Crawford	1977-78 Period
1974 Period	Canter (1977) Canter (1978)
Alden Burnham Pendse and Wyckoff Utah Water Research Laboratory	Finsterbusch Heer and Hagerty Hobbs and Voelker Protasel
1975 Period	
Bishop	

TABLE S-16: METHODOLOGIES/TECHNOLOGIES CONTAINING
INFORMATION ON CONFLICT MANAGEMENT AND RESOLUTION

1960-70 Period	1976 Period
None	Clark, Hendee, and Stankey Hammond and Adelman
1971-73 Period	
None	1977-78 Period
1974 Period	Baldwin Freeman and Quint Frost and Wilmot
None	Hammond et al. Wehr
1975 Period	
Summers, Ashworth and Feldman-Summers	

STUDY FINDINGS

The substantive findings of this literature review will be primarily presented based on the salient features of the 176 methodologies/technologies (M/T) meeting one or more of the 12 criteria in Table S-1. The findings will be presented in accordance with the following areas:

1. General environmental impact assessment concerns

2. Assessment variables, environmental indices and functional curves

3. Impact prediction for the physical-chemical, biological, aesthetic and socio-economic environments

4. Interaction matrices, descriptive checklists, scaling and ranking checklists and weighting-scaling and weighting-ranking checklists

5. Public participation and conflict resolution

General Environmental Impact Assessment Concerns

Table S-17 summarizes the salient features of M/T's dealing with general environmental impact assessment concerns. The M/T's identified with an asterisk are considered to have potentially useable information for WRAM; accordingly, their salient features are described in this report in accordance with their time period of occurrence.

Battelle-Pacific Northwest Laboratories (1974) contains a good discussion and comparison of numerical versus subjective approaches in environmental impact assessment. Dee et al. (1975), identified 3 reasons for the limited use of impact assessment methodologies in environmental studies: (1) different perspectives on the role of the EIS held by methodology developers and practitioners, (2) limited guidelines related to EIS implementation, and (3) pressures initiated by the political arena. Minimal usage of methodologies was also observed by Warner et al. (1974), when they examined 67 EIS's on water resources projects and found none with identifiable systems of impact assessment. However, in a 1978 study by Canter it was determined that 20 of 28 EIS's on wastewater facility plans prepared in 1977 used an impact assessment methodology. It is anticipated that the use of methodologies will increase since many recently published procedures include ideas from practitioners and are oriented to field office usage. Additionally, the 1978 proposed CEQ Regulations on EIS preparation give considerable emphasis to a systematic comparison of alternatives.

TABLE S-17: METHODOLOGIES/TECHNOLOGIES WITH SALIENT FEATURES
RELATED TO GENERAL ENVIRONMENTAL IMPACT ASSESSMENT CONCERNS

Time Period	Salient Feature(s)
1960-70	
Orlob	Non-monetary and intangible values are expressed in dollars.
1971-73	
Coomber and Biswas	Provides general discussion of systematic evaluation of environmental intangibles.
MacCrimmon	Literature review on multiple objective and multiple attribute decision making.
Ortolano	Discussion of general impacts associated with water resources projects.
1974	
*See Battelle-Pacific Northwest Laboratories under Descriptive checklists.	
Bender and Ahmed	Concept of relating an index of the composite environment (ICE) to economic differences between alternatives.
*See Warner et al., under Descriptive checklists.	
1975	
Bhutani et al.	Qualitative discussion of impacts of water resources projects.
*Dee et al.	Indicates limitations on use of methodologies.

18

Malone	Technique for impact prediction.
*Mitchell et al.	Literature survey on forecasting techniques.

1976

*Coates (a)	Selected impact prediction models are discussed.
*Coates (b)	Survey of some potential methods and techniques useful for impact assessment is presented.
*Wakeland	Simple modeling process for impact prediction.

1977-78

*Canter et al.	Literature survey of impacts from discharging fill material is presented.
Canter (1977)	Comprehensive textbook on impact prediction, assessment and evaluation.
Canter (1978)	Comprehensive state-of-the-art summary of information on impact prediction, assessment, and evaluation.
*Canter	20 of 28 EIS's on wastewater facility plans used an impact assessment methodology.
*Finsterbusch	This is an excellent literature review on techniques for decision making for water resources projects.
Heer and Hagerty	General overview of impact statement preparation.
*Hobbs and Voelker	Summary of multiobjective decision making techniques is presented.

| Stinson and O'Hare | 33 techniques for forecasting energy development impacts are described. |
| U.S. Soil Conservation Service | Discussion of interdisciplinary team; network for an impoundment. |

*Reference contains information pertinent to WRAM; it is summarized in this report.

Useful information on general impact prediction techniques is contained in Mitchell et al. (1975), Coates (1976 a, 1976 b), and Stinson and O'Hare (1977). Mitchell et al. (1975), discussed 12 basic methods suitable for a wide range of technological, economic, social and environmental forecasting in conjunction with water resources projects. Included are time series and projections (trend extrapolation, pattern identification, and probabilistic forecasting), models and simulations (dynamic models, cross-impact analysis and KSIM, input-output analysis, and policy capture), and qualitative and holistic approaches (scenarios and related methods, expert-opinion methods, alternative futures, and values forecasting). Coates (1976 a) reviews the application of formal models in technology assessments, and concludes that their application is most successful in areas related to physical transport in air, water, and terrain. Coates (1976 b) also summarizes some prediction techniques used in technology assessments and potentially useful in EIA's/EIS's. Stinson and O'Hare (1977) discuss 33 models and techniques for forecasting second-order impacts from energy development. The 33 methods are summarized according to employment, population, service impacts and public revenues and expenditures.

Finsterbusch (1977) and Hobbs and Voelker (1978) present literature surveys on decision making techniques useful in project planning. Finsterbusch (1977) reviews and critiques 19 methods for evaluating non-monetary impacts in conjunction with water resources development projects. Included in the 19 methods are the following 8 weighting schemes: consensal weights, formula weights, justified subjective weights, subjective weights, inferred subjective weights, ranking, equal weights, and multiple methods. The social impacts of water resources projects are briefly reviewed and related to the 19 evaluation methods. Hobbs and Voelker (1978) explore the use of multi-objective techniques in power plant site selection, although the techniques discussed are applicable to a much broader range of planning decision including those related

20

to water resources projects and programs. The basic techniques are discussed in accordance with 3 general steps:
(1) choosing and structuring siting factors, (2) desirability
scaling, and (3) amalgamation of decision information.

Assessment Variables, Environmental Indices, and Functional Curves

Assessment variables refer to those descriptors of the
environment used to describe the baseline environmental setting and upon which the impacts of various alternatives may
occur. Assessment variables for water resources projects can
be grouped into those related to the Environmental Quality
(EQ), Social Well-Being (SWB), and Regional Development (RD)
accounts. Table S-18 summarizes the salient features of M/T's
oriented to identifying and describing assessment variables.
Jain, Urban, and Stacey (1977) present information on 49
selected assessment variables (called environmental attributes).
The 49 biophysical and socio-economic variables are described
in terms of measurement units and the collection and evaluation of data. The information presented is similar to that
contained in Jain, Urban, and Cerchione (1976); U.S. Department of the Army (1975); Jain, Urban, and Stacey (1974); and
Jain et al. (1973).
Three reports on assessment variables have been specifically developed in conjunction with the WRAM research
effort, including Canter and Hill (1977), Guseman and
Dietrich (1977), and Dwyer, Hatmaker, and Hewings (1978).
Canter and Hill (1977) presented information on 62 variables
pertinent for the EQ account in water resources planning.
Each selected variable was grouped into either terrestrial,
aquatic, air or human interface categories. The report
addresses each variable in terms of its definition and
measurement of baseline conditions, prediction of impacts,
functional curve (if available or easily developed), and data
sources. Guseman and Dietrich (1977) present similar information for each of 50 variables related to the SWB account.
Each selected variable was grouped into one of the following
categories: real income distribution; life, health and
safety; educational, cultural, and recreational opportunities
and other community services; emergency preparedness; community
cohesion; and other population characteristics. Dwyer,
Hatmaker and Hewings (1978) also present similar information
on each of 37 variables related to the RD account. Nineteen
of the variables are in a regional output category, with 18
associated with a regional development group.
Schaenman and Muller (1974) and Fitzsimmons, Stuart, and
Wolf (1975) contain information on assessment variables for
the SWB and RD accounts. The Schaenman and Muller report
contains 48 variables useful for estimating the impacts of

21

TABLE S-18: METHODOLOGIES/TECHNOLOGIES WITH SALIENT
FEATURES RELATED TO ASSESSMENT VARIABLES

Time Period	Salient Feature(s)
1971-73	
Jain et al.	Extensive consideration of construction phase impacts. Good description of selected assessment variables (called attributes in the methodology).
Morrill	Presentation of hierarchical information on various categories of the environment and their associated variables. Suggested quantitative measures for defining the quality of life.
1974	
Jain, Urban, and Stacey	Good listing of assessment variables for military activities.
*Schaenman and Muller	Good listing of variables and their associated measurement units for many relevant items in the SWB and RD accounts.
1975	
*Fitzsimmons, Stuart, and Wolff	Listing of 389 assessment for SWB account.
*U.S. Department of the Army	Definitions, measurement, and interpretation information is presented on 46 assessment variables (called environmental attributes) primarily associated with EQ account.
Vlachos et al.	Good listing of potential assessment variables for SWB account.

22

1976

*Jain, Urban, and Cerchione Definitions, measurement, and
                              interpretation information is
                              presented on 49 assessment
                              variables (called environmental
                              attributes) primarily asso-
                              ciated with the EQ account.

1977-78

*Canter and Hill   Information on measurement,
                              impact prediction and func-
                              tional curves is included on
                              62 assessment variables for
                              the EQ account.

*Dwyer, Hatmaker and   Information on measurement,
   Hewings   impact prediction and func-
                              tional curves is included on
                              37 assessment variables for
                              the RD account.

*Guseman and Dietrich   Information on measurement,
                              impact prediction and func-
                              tional curves is included on
                              50 assessment variables for
                              the SWB account.

*Jain, Urban, and Stacey   Impact prediction and assessment
                              information is presented on 49
                              assessment variables (called
                              environmental attributes).

---

*Reference contains information pertinent to WRAM; it is
 summarized in this report.

land development on a local jurisdiction. Four variables
deal with the local economy, 8 with the natural (physical-
chemical and biological) environment, 4 with aesthetic features and cultural values, 22 with public and private services,
and 10 with housing and social conditions. Fitzsimmons, Stuart
and Wolf (1975) address 389 variables related to the SWB
account in water resources planning. Each variable is associated with one of the following major components: individual
personal effects; community, institutional effects; area,
socio-economic effects; national, emergency preparedness
effects; and aggregate social effects.

23

Environmental indices refer to empirical relationships used to describe environmental baseline conditions. Indicator variables refer to those descriptors which can be used to represent and assess the general quality of the environment. For example, fecal coliforms are considered as indicator organisms for bacteriological water quality. Finally, functional curves represent empirical relationships between objective measurement of assessment variables and subjective evaluation of the quality (good to bad) of that variable in the environmental setting. Table S-19 summarizes the salient features of M/T's related to environmental indices and functional curves.

Water and air quality indices are described in O'Connor (1972), Thom and Ott (1975), Engineering Division (1976), and Ott (1978). O'Connor (1972) describes the development of two indices for surface water quality, with one for sustaining a fish and wildlife population and the other for a public water supply. Thom and Ott (1975) report on the use of air pollution indices in 33 metropolitan areas in the United States and Canada. The Engineering Division report describes a study conducted in Scotland from 1973-76. A geometric weighted water quality index comprised of 10 variables was developed. Importance weights were assigned to the 10 variables and functional curves are included for each. Ott (1978) documents the current usage of water quality indices in the United States. The National Sanitation Foundation index and Harkins index are the most commonly used.

Biological indices and indicators are described in two bibliographies by Harrison (1976, 1977). The 1976 bibliography contains 189 abstracts relating to the use of micro-organisms, animals, plants and fishes to detect air and water pollution. The 1977 bibliography contains 54 new entries to the previous edition.

Quality curves or functional curves were introduced by Brown et al. (1970), and supplemented by Arnold, Young, and Brewer (1972) and Engineering Division (1976). Several scaling and weighting-scaling checklists to be discussed later also incorporate functional curves in their respective procedures. Dee et al. (1978), described the concepts involved in adapting "national" functional curves to the southwestern region of the United States, namely, New Mexico. Regionally-oriented functional curves were developed for the following EQ account variables: natural vegetation, soil erosion, waterfowl, biochemical oxygen demand, particulates, sulfur dioxide, variety within vegetation types and non-aircraft noise.

24

TABLE S-19: METHODOLOGIES/TECHNOLOGIES WITH SALIENT FEATURES
RELATED TO ENVIRONMENTAL INDICES AND FUNCTIONAL CURVES

Time Period	Salient Feature(s)
1960-70	
Brown et al.	Concepts of water quality index; use of quality curves or functional curves.
1971-73	
Arnold, Young, and Brewer	Provides bases for the development of functional curves for socio-economic variables.
*O'Connor	Two water quality indices.
Pickul	Use of indices to describe environmental setting and assess potential impacts.
*See also Raines under weighting-scaling checklists.	
1975	
*Thom and Ott	Concept of using an empirical index to assess existing air quality and potential impacts.
1976	
*Engineering Division	Good discussion of concepts and development of a water quality index.
*Harrison (Bioindicators)	189 abstracts of bioindicators of pollution are presented.
1977-78	
Boesch	Numerical classification schemes for ecological studies of water pollution are described.
*Dee et al.	Concepts for developing functional curves are summarized.

Ellis et al.	Systematic approaches for describing the biological setting are summarized.
*Harrison	54 new abstracts of bioindicators of pollution are presented.
*Ott	Summary of state-of-the-art of water quality index usage in the United States.

---

*Reference contains information pertinent to WRAM; it
is summarized in this
report.

Impact Prediction for the Physical-Chemical, Biological, Aesthetic and Socio-Economic Environments

The environment which must be addressed in impact
assessments can be divided into natural and man-made categories. The natural category includes physical-chemical,
biological and aesthetic components, while the man-made category encompasses socio-economic components. The EQ account
for water resources projects primarily addresses the natural
environment and thus includes physical-chemical, biological
and aesthetic components; the SWB and RD accounts are oriented
to the man-made environment and thus address socio-economic
components.

Table S-20 summarizes the salient features of M/T's
related to impact prediction for the physical-chemical environment. Grooms (1977), and Lehman (1976...Vols. 1 and 2) contain abstracts of available computer programs and models
addressing water and air quality and environmental noise.
Grooms (1977) includes abstracts of technologies available
for simulation modeling of water quality, thermal pollution,
solid waste disposal, Gaussian plumes, and noise levels. The
Lehman volumes include abstracts on the modeling of eutrophication, nutrient removal, pollutant dispersion, heat dissipation, aquifer water quality and surface runoff quality.
Volume 1 contains 192 abstracts and Volume 2 has 98 abstracts.

Ott (1976) represents a conference proceedings and contains 164 technical papers on modeling efforts in air quality,
air and water pollutant transport processes, water runoff,
water supply, solid waste, ecology, noise and health. Many
of the described models are useful for impact prediction.
Grimsrud, Finnemore, and Owen (1976) is a handbook for water
resources planners and managers. It summarizes procedures

TABLE S-20: METHODOLOGIES/TECHNOLOGIES WITH SALIENT FEATURES
RELATED TO IMPACT PREDICTION FOR THE
PHYSICAL-CHEMICAL ENVIRONMENT

Time Period	Salient Feature(s)
1971-73	
Hydrologic Engineering Center	Mathematical model for reservoir temperature stratification.
Markofsky and Harleman	Thermal stratification model.
Texas Water Development Board	Models plus examples are presented for water quality impact prediction.
Thomas, Paul, and Israelsen	Water quality model for irrigation return flow.
1974	
*See Battelle-Columbus laboratories under Descriptive checklist.	
*See Warner et al., under Descriptive checklist.	
1975	
Clark	Good discussion of quantifying construction impacts.
Fuhriman, et al.	Impact prediction method is presented for salt balance in a lake.
Nelson and LaBelle	Air quality box model and three stormwater runoff models are described.
Troxler and Thackston	Mathematical model for steam temperature is presented.
1976	
Colonell	Field Studies to develop predictive model for thermal stratification are described.

27

*Curran Associates, Inc.	Contains qualitative/quantitative discussion of the primary impacts of channelization projects.
Fennelly et al.	Contains useful information on impact prediction for air and water environments.
*Grimsrud, Finnemore, and Owen	Presents summary information on water quality models for impact predictions.
*Keyes	Contains a good summary of impact prediction and assessment techniques for the physical-chemical and biological environments.
*Lehman (Vol. 1)	192 abstracts of models of the chemical, physical, biological, and hydrological processes important to water quality.
Liu and Yu	Has information for interpretation of air pollutant impacts.
*McElroy et al.	Good summary of available quantitative information on non-point sources of water pollution.
Omernik	Contains information on nutrient runoff data compiled for 473 non-point-source-type drainage areas in the eastern United States.
*Ott	Summary of modeling efforts for impact prediction on the physical-chemical environment.
Springer	Presents information for planning a statistically significant water quality study.
Thornton and Lessem	Sensitivity analysis for water quality model is presented.
Thronson	Provides information on construction phase non-point pollution control.

*U.S. Environmental Protection Agency	Contains qualitative/quantitative discussion of the primary im- pacts of impoundment projects.

1977-78
*Canter and Hill	Summary of impact prediction for 62 important variables in the EQ account.
*Grooms	Abstracts of available computer programs for impact prediction on the physical-chemical environment are described.
Johnson and Cole	Nutrient transport from terrestrial to aquation systems is described.
Omernik	Non-point sources of nutrients from National Eutrophication Survey are summarized.
*Von Gierke	Noise impact prediction and assessment is described.

*Reference contains informa-
   tion pertinent to WRAM;
   it is summarized in
   this report.

for evaluating and selecting water quality models. Canter and
Hill (1977) present information on impact prediction for 62
important assessment variables in the EQ account.

Keyes (1976) is primarily designed for evaluation of land
development projects. Specific information is presented on
prediction and assessment of impacts on air quality, water
quality and quantity, wildlife and vegetation, and noise.
Summaries are provided for several atmospheric dispersion and
water quality models relative to inputs, outputs, and computing
requirements.

Several references include excellent impact prediction
information for specific areas of the physical-chemical
environment. McElroy et al. (1976), is useful for evaluating
the quantity of water pollutants from non-point sources
including agriculture, silviculture, construction, urban areas
and rural roads. Von Gierke (1977) presents guidelines for the
uniform description and assessment of noise impacts. Whenever
feasible and practical, a single-number noise impact characterization based on level-weighted population is recommended.

29

This represents the summation over the total human population
of the product of each residential person times a weighting
factor that varies with yearly day-night average sound level
outside the residence of that person.

Specific information on impact prediction for two categories of water resources projects is found in Battelle-
Columbus Laboratories (1974) and Warner et al. (1974). The
former is oriented to impact prediction for dredging projects.
A total of 84 assessment variables are included, with 18 in
the physical-chemical category, 16 in the ecological category,
and 15 in the social category. Information is provided on
impact prediction for many of the variables, with the most
information provided for those in the physical-chemical category. Warner et al. (1974), presents materials intended for
use by reviewers of EIS's on major water reservoir projects.
The section on water quality impacts contains a detailed comparison of mathematical models for predicting impacts on water
temperature, dissolved oxygen and several chemical constituents.

Two general reports useful for impact prediction on the
physical-chemical environment are U.S. Environmental Protection
Agency (1976) and Curran Associates, Inc. (1976). The EPA
report provides a detailed framework for the review of EIS's
on impoundment projects. The Curran Associates report contains information on the primary impacts of channelization
projects, and it also provides a framework for review of EIS's.

Table S-21 summarizes the salient features of M/T's
related to impact prediction for the biological environment.
Harrison (1976) and Lehman (1976--Vols. 1 and 2) contain
abstracts on ecosystem models. The Harrison bibliography has
76 abstracts of models for marine biology, wildlife, plants,
microorganisms, food chains, limnology, and diseases as

TABLE S-21: METHODOLOGIES/TECHNOLOGIES WITH SALIENT FEATURES
RELATED TO IMPACT PREDICTION FOR THE BIOLOGICAL ENVIRONMENT

Time Period	Salient Feature(s)
1971-73	
Chen and Orlob	Ecosystem models are presented for lakes and estuaries.
*Environmental Impact Center, Inc.	Impact prediction information for certain biological and physical-chemical variables.
Odum, H.T.	Use of energy diagrams to pre-dict ecosystem changes.
Swartzman and Van Dyne	Good discussion of ecological modelling for natural resource planning.

1974
*See Warner et al., under
  Descriptive checklist.

1975
Bella   Basic information on estuarine
                                 benthic systems is presented.

Christensen, Van Winkle   Information is presented on
  and Mattice   impact predication and assess-
                                 ment for the biological
                                 environment.

Haven   Contains information on ecosystem
                                 models for impact prediction.

Hornberger, Kelly and   A mathematical model for pre-
  Lederman   dicting lake eutrophication
                                 is described.

*Sharma, Buffington, and   Good summary of technical and
  McFadden   philosophical state-of-the-art
                                 of biological impact prediction
                                 and assessment.

1976
Adams and Kurisu   Model of pesticide movement from
                                 land is presented.

*Darnell et al.   Good literature survey of con-
                                 struction impacts on wetlands.

*Harrison (Ecosystem Models)   76 abstracts on ecosystem models
                                 are described.

Jameson   Reviews ecosystem models and the
                                 impacts of urbanization on
                                 natural ecosystems.

*See also Keyes in Impact
  prediction-p/c

*See also Lehman (Vol. 1 & 2)
  in Impact prediction-p/c

Reid   Twelve ecological standards are
                                 proposed.

1977-78
*Canter and Hill   Summary of impact prediction for
                                62 important variables in the
                                EQ account.

*Flood et al.   A habitat evaluation procedure
                                for the biological environment
                                is described.
_____

*Reference contains infor-
   mation pertinent to WRAM;
   it is summarized in this
   report.

related to ecosystems. Information contained in Volumes 1 and
2 of Lehman (1976) was previously mentioned for the physical-
chemical environment and is also useful for impact prediction
on the biological environment. Similarly, Keyes (1976) contains practical suggestions and information on impact prediction for the biological environment.
      Flood et al. (1977), describes a habitat evaluation
system for measuring the effects of water development projects
on fish, wildlife and related resources. In the procedure
developed for useage in the Meramec Park Lake Project in
Crawford County, Missouri six groups of animals are characterized
in as many as six habitat types. The animal groups include
forest game, upland game, tree squirrels, terrestrial fur
bearers, aquatic fur bearers, and waterfowl. The habitat types
include bottomland hardwood, upland hardwood, old field, pasture, small grain and row crops, and the Meramec River and
riverine habitat. The system is useful for describing the
biological setting; however, only minimal information is
included on predicting future habitat types and animal groups.
      Sharma, Buffington, and McFadden (1975) contains the
proceedings of a 1975 workshop on the biological significance
of environmental impacts. These proceedings represent the
state-of-the-art for impact prediction techniques and defining
the significance of biological changes. The potential uses of
ecosystem models for biological impact prediction are discussed
and limitations associated with the models are identified.
      Darnell et al. (1976), summarizes an extensive literature
survey of construction impacts on wetlands, and it is particularly useful for impact identification. Construction activities
which may impact wetland environments include floodplain surfacing and drainage, mining, impoundment, canalization, dredging
and channelization, and bank and shoreline construction. The
most environmentally damaging effects in wetland areas, in
order of importance, are: direct habitat loss, addition of
suspended solids, and modification of water levels and flow
regimes.

32

Table S-22 summarizes the salient features of M/T's related to impact prediction for the aesthetic environment. The most comprehensive reference source is Bagley, Kroll, and Clark (1973). Methodologies for measuring or quantifying the aesthetic features of an area are reviewed as well as the state-of-the-art of research for understanding unquantifiable features often comprising the aesthetic environment.

Table S-23 summarizes the salient features of M/T's related to impact prediction for the socio-economic environment. Dwyer, Hatmaker, and Hewings (1978) and Guseman and Dietrich (1977) address impact prediction for the RD and SWB accounts. These reports were developed in conjunction with the WRAM research effort and were previously mentioned under assessment variables.

Two good references on socio-economic impact prediction are Chalmers and Anderson (1977) and Chalmers (1977). Chalmers and Anderson (1977) address population, employment, and income impacts from both the construction and operational phases of water resources projects. Included is a survey of methodologies currently being used for economic and demographic analysis. Based on current practices, published literature, and the professional judgment of the authors, procedural recommen-

TABLE S-22: METHODOLOGIES/TECHNOLOGIES WITH SALIENT FEATURES RELATED TO AESTHETICS

Time Period	Salient Feature(s)
1960-70	
Leopold	Relative uniqueness and categorization of factors; addresses aesthetics with a quantitative approach.
1971-73	
*Bagley, Kroll, and Clark	Describes several approaches for quantifying the aesthetic features of an area.
See Burnham under Public participation	
1975	
Harkness	Annotated bibliography of visual analysis techniques.

*Reference contains information pertinent to WRAM; it is summarized in this report.

33

TABLE S-23: METHODOLOGIES/TECHNOLOGIES WITH SALIENT FEATURES
RELATED TO IMPACT PREDICTION FOR
THE SOCIO-ECONOMIC ENVIRONMENT

Time Period	Salient Feature(s)
1971-73	
Bromley et al.	Procedure for predicting changes in land use over time both with and without a project.
1975	
*Muller	Presentation of fiscal impact prediction technologies.
1976	
Christensen	Good summary of the social impacts of land development projects.
*Muller	Contains a discussion of economic impacts of land development in terms of employment, housing and property values. Information applicable to SWB and RD accounts.
Vlachos and Hendricks	A thorough presentation of the secondary impacts of highway projects.
Webster et al.	Techniques for quantifying the economic impacts of military activities are described.
1977-78	
*Chalmers and Anderson	Economic and demographic impacts from water resources projects are described.
*Chalmers	Construction worker impacts from water resources projects are described.
*Finsterbusch and Wolf	Series of articles on social impact assessment.
1977-78	
*Dwyer, Hatmaker and Hewings	Summary of impact prediction for 37 important variables in the Regional Development account

34

*Guseman and Dietrich   Information on measurement, impact prediction and functional curves is included on 50 assessment variables for the SWB account.

*McEvoy and Dietz   Prediction and assessment of socio-economic impacts.

---

*Reference contains information pertinent to WRAM; it is summarized in this report.

dations are made for conducting economic/demographic assessments for water resources projects. The impact categories of population, employment, and income are further subdivided into impacts on local communities in terms of population, facilities and services, and fiscal characteristics. Chalmers (1977) specifically addresses economic and demographic impacts from water resources project construction activities. A construction worker survey was conducted to assemble empirical information on worker characteristics and provide input data for use in subsequent impact prediction.

Muller (1975, 1976) addresses the prediction of fiscal and economic impacts resulting from land development projects. Although not specifically related to water resources projects, much of the information in these two reports is germain. Land development can exert economic impacts in terms of employment, housing, and property values. Available impact prediction methodologies for fiscal and economic concerns range from simple one-dimensional models to complex and sophisticated econometric approaches.

Two published books focus on socio-economic impacts. McEvoy and Dietz (1977) present a practical overview of the strategies and methods available for predicting and assessing the social consequences of environmental change. Finsterbusch and Wolf (1977) contains articles written by several individuals on various aspects of social impact assessment. Some of the articles address methodologies and technologies for accomplishing impact prediction and assessment.

Interaction Matrices, Descriptive Checklists, Scaling and Ranking Checklists and Weighting-Scaling and Weighting-Ranking Checklists

Numerous environmental impact assessment methodologies have been developed in response to the National Environmental Policy Act. Methodologies can generally be categorized into

interaction matrices or checklists. Interaction matrices
range from simple considerations of project activities and
ehtir impacts on assessment variables to developed networks
which display interrelationships between impacted variables.
Checklists may range from simple listings of assessment
variables to descriptive approaches which include information
on measurement, prediction and interpretation of changes in
identified assessment variables. Checklists may involve the
scaling of impacts of alternatives on assessment variables
through use of numerical scores or letter assignments. In
ranking checklists each alternative is ranked or rated from
best to worst in terms of its potential impacts on each
assessment variable. The most sophisticated checklists are
those involving the assignment of importance weights to weighted
variables and the scale or rank for each alternative.

The WRAM methodology is a weighting-scaling checklist.
Information from several assessment methodologies can be useful in the WRAM approach. For example, an interaction matrix
can be an aid in generating a list of pertinent assessment
variables. Additionally, descriptive checklists can be useful
in providing information on the measurement and interpretation
of data on assessment variables.

Table S-24 summarizes the salient features of M/T's
having information on interaction matrices. One of the first
interaction matrices developed in response to NEPA was Leopold
et al. (1971). This simple matrix provided an organized
approach for identifying and assessing potential impacts from
U.S. Geological Survey projects. Fischer and Davies (1973)
proposed the use of three separate matrix concepts in environmental baseline conditions in terms of a series of assessment
variables and their respective scales of importance, present
condition, and management. Scales ranging from one (low) to
five (high) are used. The second matrix is called an environmental compatibility matrix, and it is similar to the Leopold
matrix in that project actions are shown on the X-axis and
assessment variables on the Y-axis. Impact index values from
+5 to -5 are assigned by the interdisciplinary team. Short-
term and long-term impacts are delineated through using either
a 5 (short-term) or L (long-term). For example, an impact
could be described by -4L or -45. The third matrix is called
a decision matrix. It displays the major environmental impacts
from the environmental compatibility matrix for each alternative. Major impacts are defined as those represented by ±4
or 5 in individual compatibility matrices.

Kruzić (1974) discusses the concept of cross-impact
analysis in environmental impact assessment. The key concept
is the cross-impact matrix which is used to identify the impact
of one variable upon another. Assessment variables are listed
as both row and column headings of a table, and relationships
between changed variables are displayed in the cross-impact
matrix. For example, if assessment variable X is related to

36

TABLE S-24:   METHODOLOGIES/TECHNOLOGIES WITH SALIENT FEATURES
RELATED TO INTERACTION MATRICES

Time Period	Salient Feature(s)
1960-70 Hill	Simple matrix with goals as an element of comparison.
1971-73 Bereano et al.	Use of probability of an impact as an integral part of an interaction matrix.
Central New York Regional Planning and Development Board	Use of interaction matrices to identify impacts and display their relative importance.
*Fischer and Davies	Use of series of three matrices in defining environmental setting, identifying impacts and summarizing the features of alternatives.
Kane, Vertinsky and Thomson	Focuses attention on cross-impacts of water resources development projects.
Leopold et al.	Use of interaction matrix to identify and visually display potential impacts.
Manheim et al.	Use of interaction matrix for identification and visual display of impacts.
Moore et al.	Stepped or linked matrices to display interrelationships between impacted assessment variables.
Schlesinger and Daetz	Compares several matrix approaches for impact assessment.
Sorensen	Presentation of networks (stepped or linked matrices) for impact identification.

1974
  Alabama Development Office   Good ideas for use of simple
                                interaction matrix.

  *Kruzic   A cross-impact simulation tech-
                                nique for impact indetification
                                and prediction is described.

1975
  *Schlesinger and Daetz   Cross-impact matrix procedure
                                form dealing with long-range
                                impacts.

1976
  *Boucher and Stover   Annotated bibliography of 63
                                references on cross-impact
                                analysis.

  Chase   Summarizes several examples of
                                the use of interaction matrices.

  *Ross   Concepts of cross-impact matrix
                                and disruption matrix.

---

*Reference contains informa-
  tion pertinent to WRAM;
  it is summarized in this
  report.

assessment variable Y, this can be shown in the matrix by
using a plus of variable Y is enhanced by changes in variable
X, or a minus where variable Y is undesirably changed by a
change in variable X. Cross-impact matrices can also be
referred to as stepped matrices wherein secondary and tertiary
relationships between variables are displayed.

Boucher and Stover (1976) provide a listing, in chronological order, of English language publications dealing with
cross-impact analysis. A total of 63 abstracts are included
to provide the user with information on the growth, applications, current status, and possible future development or uses
of the technique. An example of the use of cross-impact
matrices is contained in Ross (1976). A basic cross-impact
matrix is shown along with a disruption matrix to indicate the
relative impacts of various alternatives on assessment variables. The disruption level is displayed in terms of four
scale factors as follows: 0 to denote no noticeable disruption, 1 to denote slight disruption, 2 to denote appreciable
disruption, and 3 to denote severe disruption. The disruption
matrix as utilized by Ross (1976) does not include a display

38

of the beneficial impacts of alternatives, however, it could easily be modified to include them.

Schlesinger and Daetz (1975) describe a procedure for forecasting long range environmental impacts of large scale projects. The methodology entails combining a listing of primary environmental impacts with a cross-impact matrix of assessment variable relationships. Each term in the cross-impact matrix relates a change in one variable in one year to a change in another variable the following year by a linear multiplier. A case study involving strip mining of coal is presented to illustrate the concepts.

Table S-25 summarizes the salient features of M/T's characterized as descriptive checklists. Battelle-Pacific Northwest Laboratories (1974), Battelle-Columbus Laboratories (1974), Warner et al. (1974), and Carstea et al. (1975), all provide a descriptive checklist approach for dealing with the impacts of water resources projects. As previously mentioned, the Battelle-Pacific Northwest Laboratories report compares the advantages and limitations of numerical versus subjective approaches. Following consideration of these approaches, the proposed methodology for use on Corps water resources projects in the Columbia River drainage basin in a descriptive check-list. A simple matrix to identify potential impacts and generate the descriptive checklist. This methodology is applicable to any type of water resources project. The Battelle-Columbus Laboratories report is oriented toward dredging projects; it includes 84 assessment variables with each one being described in terms of measurement units and evaluation.

Warner et al. (1974), contains a descriptive checklist for major water reservoir projects. The report addresses the following impacts resulting from reservoir construction and operation: water quality and ecological impacts, and economic, social and aesthetic impacts. The extensive citations to relevant literature on impact assessment are included for each of the substantive areas addressed.

Carstea et al. (1975), presents a methodology for conducting impact assessments for projects requiring Section 404 permits under the Federal Water Pollution Control Act Amendments of 1972 (P.L. 92-500). The methodology is a descriptive checklist which addresses the potential impacts of the following types of actions/projects: riprap placement; bulkheads; groins and jetties; piers, dolphins, mooring piles, and ramp construction; dredging (new and maintenance); outfalls, submerged lines and pipes; and aerial crossings. Potential impacts are described and information presented on impact calculations for the following: erosion, sedimentation, and deposition; flood height and drift; water quality; ecology; air quality; noise; safety/navigation; recreation; aesthetics; and socio-economics.

TABLE S-25: METHODOLOGIES/TECHNOLOGIES WITH SALIENT FEATURES
RELATED TO DESCRIPTIVE CHECKLISTS

Time Period	Salient Feature(s)
1974	
*Battelle-Columbus Laboratories	Good descriptive checklist for dredging projects; some impact prediction information is included.
*Battelle-Pacific Northwest Laboratories	Good descriptive checklist. Good discussion of numerical versus subjective approaches in environmental impact assessment.
*Warner et al.	Good descriptive checklist for reservoir projects; Information is provided on the technical aspects of prediction of water quality and ecological impacts.
1975	
*Carstea et al.	Descriptive checklist for quantifying impacts from small coastal projects.
1976	
*Schaenman	Descriptive checklist with 47 assessment variables for land development projects.
1977-78	
*Chalmers and Anderson	Descriptive checklist for addressing the economic and demographic impacts of water resources projects.

*Reference contains information pertinent to WRAM; it is summarized in this report.

A good descriptive checklist for the economic and demographic impacts of water resources projects is contained in
Chalmers and Anderson (1977). This methodology addresses
environmental impacts in terms of population, employment and
income, and specifically relates these to community population,
community facilities and services, and community fiscal concerns. Schaenman (1976) contains a descriptive checklist for
land development projects. The checklist contains 47 assessment variables along with capsule summaries of the state-of-
the-art of impact evaluation for each of the general impact
areas and assessment variables. Information is included on
the units of measurement for the 47 variables and potential
back-up indicators which can be used in the absence of
necessary data for primary impact estimates.

Table S-26 summarizes the salient features of M/T's
which address scaling and ranking, weighting, and weighting-
scaling and weighting-ranking checklists. Impact scaling can
be accomplished by either using (1) the factor profile concept,
(2) a reference alternative, (3) linear scaling based on the
maximum change, (4) letter or number assignments designating
impact categories, (5) the concept of environmental potential,
(6) functional curves, or (7) the paired comparison technique.

Bishop et al. (1970), contains information on the factor
profile concept for impact scaling. This concept is represented by a graphical presentation of the effects of each
alternative relative to each assessment variable. Each profile scale is expressed on a percentage basis ranging from a
negative to a positive 100 percent, with 100 percent being
the maximum absolute value of the impact measure adopted for
each assessment variable. The impact measure represents the
maximum change, either plus or minus, associated with a given
alternative being evaluated. If the assessment variables are
displayed along with the impact scale from +100% to -100%, a
dotted line can be used to connect the plotted points for each
alternative and thus describe its "profile." The factor profile concept is useful for visually displaying the relative
impacts of a series of alternatives in conjunction with
selected assessment variables, however, the relative importance
of the assessment variables is not reflected.

Salomon (1974) describes a scaling technique for evaluation
of cooling system alternatives for nuclear power plants. In
order to determine scale values, a reference cooling system was
used and each alternative system compared to it. The following
scale values were assigned to the alternatives based on the
reference alternative: very superior (+8), superior (+4),
moderately superior (+2), marginally superior (+1), no difference (0), marginally inferior (-1), moderately inferior (-2),
inferior (-4), and very inferior (-8). Weighting was also used
to account for the relative importance of the identified decision variables.

41

TABLE S-26: METHODOLOGIES/TECHNOLOGIES WITH SALIENT FEATURES
RELATED TO SCALING AND RANKING, WEIGHTING, AND ASSOCIATED
WEIGHTING-SCALING AND WEIGHTING-RANKING CHECKLISTS

Time Period	Salient Feature(s)
1960-70	
*Bishop et al.	Factor profile concept for impact scaling
*Dalkey	Group judgments are elicited.
*Dean and Nishry	Paired comparisons for weighting and scaling.
*Dearinger	Weighting and rating approach.
*Eckenrode	Comparison of 6 methods for collecting the judgments of experts concerning the relative weights of multiple criteria.
Highway Research Section	Weight-scaling technique.
Miller	General information on weighting and scaling procedures.
Pikarsky	Weighting-scaling checklist.
Schimpeler and Grecco	Inclusion of probability along with weighting and scaling.
Southeastern Wisconsin Regional Planning Commission	Weighting-ranking checklist.
1971-73	
*Bureau of Reclamation	Good listing of assessment variables for biological, physical-chemical, esthetic and cultural environments. A quality scale and human influence scale is suggested.
Commonwealth Associates, Inc.	Techniques for weighting and scaling of impacts.
Crawford	Weighting-scaling checklist for evaluation of impacts of alternatives.

42

*Dee et al. (1972)	Weighting-scaling checklist with a good listing of biological, physical-chemical, esthetic and cultural variables.
*Dee et al. (1973)	Weighting-scaling checklist based on relevant matrices and networks. Ranges of scale values. Concepts of "environmental assessment trees" to account for interrelationships among assessment variables.
*Odum, E.P. et al.	This weighting-scaling checklist includes an error term to allow for midjudgment in the assignment of importance weights. Computerization of the methodology enables the conduction of a sensitivity analysis.
*Raines	Weighting-scaling checklists; use of functional curves to translate environmental impact quantities into environmental cost units.
Stover	Weighting-scaling checklist.
*U.S. Army Engineer District, Tulsa, Corps of Engineers	Has good list of variables for EQ, SWB, and RD accounts. Weighting-scaling checklist used for evaluation of alternatives; includes statistical testing of results.
*Wenger and Rhyner	A stochastic computer procedure is used to account for uncertainty in the weighting and scaling checklist procedure for evaluation of solid waste system alternatives.

1974

Adkins and Burke	Scaling checklist with algebraic additions of scaled impacts.
Alden	Ranking checklist; inclusion of descriptive information on ecological relationships.

*Salomon	Weighting scaling checklist; relative scaling based on a reference alternative is used.
*School of Civil Engineering and Environmental Science and Oklahoma Biological Survey	Weighting-scaling checklist, which is similar in concept to the Battelle Environmental System; an error team is included to account for subjective misjudgments.
*Smith	Weighting-scaling checklist for a rapid transit system.

1975

Gann	Weighting-scaling checklist using weighted rankings technique is described.
Morrison	Weighting-scaling checklist using weighted rankings technique is described.
*Toussaint	Weighting and scaling of 14 water pollution parameters was established by the Delphi procedure using two separate groups of 9 experts.
*Voorhees and Associates	Scaling checklist with 80 assessment variables. Guidance is provided on the assignment of "letter-scale" values for impacts on the 80 variables.

1976

Canter	Weighting-scaling checklist using weighted rankings technique is described.
*Edwards	Multi-attribute utility measurement technique for assigning importance weights.
*Lower Mississippi Valley Division	Weighting-scaling checklist using habitat approach is presented.
Mackinnon and Anderson	Computer program for summarizing participants' judgment on importance weights.

| *Ross | Checking procedure for consistency in paired comparison technique for importance weight assignments. |

1977-78
| Canter and Reid | A weighting-scaling technique for evaluating the environmental impact of wastewater treatment process is described. |

| *Duke et al. | Scaling checklist for water resources projects; concept of environmental potential. |

| Dunne | Weighting-scaling checklist for sanitary landfill site selection. |

| Paul | Weighting-scaling checklist used to prioritize potential projects. |

| *Voelker | Nominal Group Process Technique for group assignment of relative importance weights to decision factors. |

---

*Reference contains information pertinent to WRAM;
it is summarized in this
report.

Odum et al. (1971), utilizes a scaling technique in which the actual measures of the assessment variable for each alternative plan are normalized and expressed as a decimal of the largest measure for that variable. This represents linear scaling, and these normalized values are then multiplied by an importance weight to develop an overall evaluation.

A letter scaling system is used in Voorhees and Associates (1975). This methodology incorporates 80 assessment variables and no importance weights are assigned to the individual variables. The methodology is oriented to the types of projects conducted by the Department of Housing and Urban Development in urban areas. It utilizes a simple interaction matrix to delineate potential impacts, and information is provided on exactly how to address the identified impacts. The scaling system consists of the assignment of a letter grade from A+ to C- for the impacts, with the A+ scale representing a major

beneficial impact and the C- scale denoting an undesirable
detrimental change.

Duke et al. (1977), describe a scaling checklist for the
EQ account used in evaluation of water resources projects.
The assessment variables are identified through use of a simple
interaction matrix. Scaling is accomplished following the
establishment of an evaluation guideline for each assessment
variable. The evaluation guideline is based upon concept of
environmental potential. It represents the measure that
determines if any beneficial or adverse changes are significant, and if there are any environmentally sensitive areas.
Specifically, an evaluation guideline is defined as the smallest
change in the highest existing quality in the region that would
be considered significant. For example, assuming that the
highest existing quality for dissolved oxygen in a region is
8 mg/l, if a reduction of 1.5 mg/l is considered as significant, then the evaluation guideline is 1.5 mg/l irrespective
of the existing quality in a given regional stream. Scaling
of impacts is accomplished by quantifying the impact of each
alternative relative to each assessment variable, and if the
net change is less than the evaluation guideline it is
considered to be insignificant. If the net change is greater
than the evaluation guideline and moves the assessment variable
toward its highest quality, then it is considered to be a
beneficial impact; the reverse exists for those impacts that
move the measure of the assessment variable away from its
highest existing quality.

Functional curves can also be used to accomplish impact
scaling for assessment variables. These curves have been
described earlier in conjunction with environmental indices
and indicators. The functional curve is used to relate the
objective evaluation of an assessment variable to a subjective
judgment regarding its quality based on a range from high
quality to low quality. Functional curves are included in
several checklists involving weighting and scaling; for example,
Dee et al. (1972), Dee et al. (1973), School of Civil Engineering and Environmental Science and Oklahoma Biological Survey
(1974), Smith (1974), Toussaint (1975), and Lower Mississippi
Division (1976).

A paired comparison technique can also be used for
assigning scale values to alternatives based on their impact
on assessment variables. The paired comparison technique for
accomplishing scaling is described in Dean and Nishry (1965).
Several other M/T's utilize a paired comparison technique for
assignment of scale values. This technique was used in the
Interim WRAM report issued in February, 1977.

Another major issue in environmental impact assessment
is the assignment of importance weights to assessment variables. It is generally accepted by environmental professionals
that certain assessment variables may be more critical than

46

others in a particular geography setting. Accordingly, in order to reflect this relative importance, a system for assigning importance weights or at least ranking the assessment variables is desirable. Eckenrode (1965), Edwards (1976), Ross (1976), and Voelker (1977) describe techniques which can be used to assign importance weights to assessment variables.

Eckenrode (1965) describes six methods for collecting the judgments of experts concerning the relative value of sets of criteria. The methods included ranking, rating, three versions of paired comparisons and a method of successive comparisons. They were compared based on their reliability and time efficiency. The results indicated that there were no significant differences in the sets of criterion weights derived from collecting the judgment data by any of the methods, however, ranking was the most efficient method. Ranking is increasingly more efficient than paired comparisons as the number of items to be judged increases from 6 to 30.

Edwards (1976) describes ten steps in the multi-attribute utility measurement technique for assignment of importance weights. The technique basically involves ranking the dimensions or assessment variables in order of importance, and then rating them by assigning to the least important variable an importance of 10. The importance weights for increasingly important variables will be greater than 10. The final weight assignment is derived by summing the importance weights for all variables and then dividing by the individual weights by the sum and multiplying them by 100. This technique is simple and useful for public participation activities.

Dean and Nishry (1965) describe a paired comparison technique which is the importance weight assignment approach used in the Interim WRAM report issued in February, 1977. The paired comparison technique has been used for many environmental studies as well as for decision-making within industrial and governmental programs. Ross (1976) describes a procedure for checking the consistency of importance weight assignments through use of the technique. This procedure is discussed in the main body of this report; it is useful for evaluating the consistency of weight assignments by an individual and for assigning importance weights to assessment variables based on public participation input.

Voelker (1977) describes the application of the nominal group process technique (an interactive group technique) to the identification and rating of factors or assessment variables important in siting nuclear power plants. The technique consists of the identification and discussion of assessment variables followed by independent voting on their priority, with the final group decision based on mathematical rank ordering.

Weighting-scaling checklists represent a major group of environmental assissment methodologies examined in this literature review. Examples of these checklists are included in

Dee et al. (1972), Dee et al. (1973), Odum et al. (1971),
Wenger and Rhyner (1972) and Lower Mississippi Valley Division
(1976). Several other M/T's reviewed during this effort also
included weighting-scaling checklists; the above reference
sources serve as representative examples of the technologies
available.

Dee et al. (1972), is a methodology designed for water
resources projects and includes 78 assessment variables defined
within the categories of ecology, environmental pollution,
aesthetics, and human interest. Weighting is accomplished
through use of the ranked pairwise comparison technique, while
scaling is achieved via the use of functional curves. The
methodology provides a systematic procedure for evaluating
alternatives for meeting water resources needs. Dee et al.
(1973), is a weighting-scaling checklist developed for wastewater treatment plants. The concepts are basically the same
as in Dee et al. (1972); however, a distinct difference is the
use of environmental assessment trees. Specifically, the
ranges of 64 assessment variables are aggregated into 19
components through use of 19 environmental assessment trees
which have been constructed to translate the measure for an
individual variable into a measure for a group of variables.
The concept of environmental assessment trees is one which
needs additional development; however, it appears to be quite
useful for water resources programs and projects.

Odum et al. (1971), represents a weighting-scaling checklist developed for highway route alternatives. A significant
feature is the use of a randomly generated error term to
account for variations in both scaling and importance weight
assignments to 56 assessment variables. Wenger and Rhyner
(1972) also address uncertainty in impact assessment. Their
methodology was developed for the selection of a solid waste
system from among several alternatives, and it includes a
stochastic procedure to account for the inherit uncertainty in
quantitative values assigned to subjective judgments (weighting)
and impacts (scaling).

The Lower Mississippi Valley Division method published in
1976 is a weighting-scaling checklist with primary orientation
to the EQ account. The methodology defines six habitat types
in the lower Mississippi Valley area, and describes each in
terms of several descriptive parameters or assessment variables. Functional curves are used to scale impacts and each
variable is assigned a weight which reflects its relative
importance in describing habitat quality. The importance
weights were assigned through a joint effort by 20 biologists
from the Lower Mississippi Valley Division and the Waterways
Experiment Station.

Public Participation and Conflict Resolution

Public participation in environmental decision-making is
becoming increasingly important. The 1973 Council on Environ-

48

mental Quality (CEQ) Guidelines emphasized that public input
should be received during the decision-making process for projects having potential impacts on the environment. The proposed
CEQ Regulations of 1978 strengthen and expand the concept of
public participation. Additionally, conflicts may arise between
groups representative of different "publics", particularly in
relation to large public projects such as those dealing with
water resources. Accordingly, public participation and conflict resolution represent issues that are important in environmental impact assessments for water resources programs and
projects.

Table S-27 summarizes the salient features of M/T's which
focus on public participation and conflict resolution. An
excellent reference describing the features and effectiveness
of public participation techniques is Bishop (1975). Specific
information is included on public forums (public hearings,
public meetings, informal small group meetings, information
and coordination seminars, and forums of other agencies or
groups), community contacts (operating field offices, local
planning visits, and direct community representation), and
interactive group methods (workshops, charettes and special
committees). The effectiveness of several communicatios techniques with various publics is also described and summarized.

Conflict resolution is addressed by Baldwin (1978),
Freeman and Quint (1977), Frost and Wilmot (1978), and Wehr
(1978). Baldwin (1978) summarizes an environmental mediation
conference held in early 1978. Environmental mediation is
discussed in terms of resolving environmental conflicts; the
limitations of this technique for resolving major differences
between public and private interest groups are also described.
Freeman and Quint (1977) represents a manual prepared for
coordinators of U.S. Forest Service public participation programs. One exercise is on resolving conflicting opinions
relative to Forest Service projects. Procedures for accomplishing resolution include the assignment of importance weights
to decision factors based on interactive group discussions of
the factors.

Frost and Wilmot (1978) was written primarily for academic
courses that focus on the conflict process as a part of normal
on-going communication relationships. Of relevance to environmental impact assessment are the following rules and suggestions
for third part intervenors in conflicts: (1) be descriptive
rather than judgmental, (2) encourage specificity (3) deal
with things that can be changed instead of "givens", (4) encourage parties to give feedback when it is requested,
(5) give feedback as close as possible to the behavior being
discussed, (6) encourage feedback whose accuracy can be checked
by others, and (7) speak only for yourself. These practical
suggestions are illustrated through several examples.

TABLE S-27: METHODOLOGIES/TECHNOLOGIES WITH SALIENT FEATURES
RELATED TO PUBLIC PARTICIPATION AND CONFLICT RESOLUTION

Time Period	Salient Feature(s)
1960-70 Bishop	Description of various techniques of public participation.
*Falk	Public participation in relative weight assignments; example includes a weighting-scaling checklist.
1974 Burnham	Public involvement in assigning importance weights to decision factors. Procedure for systematically addressing the aesthetic features of an area.
Pendse and Wyckoff	A public participation study is described.
Utah Water Research Laboratory	Assignment of relative importance weights through public participation is described.
1975 *Bishop	Describes features and effectiveness of various public participation techniques.
*Summers, Ashworth and Feldman-Summers	Study findings indicated that judgmental inconsistency was likely to be a major cause of conflict.
1976 Case, Edgmon and Renton	Public participation concepts are described.
*Clark, Hendee and Stankey	Conceptual framework and procedure for public involvement in environmental decision-making.
*Gum, Roefs, and Kimball	Method of relative importance weight assignments using public participation is described.

*Hammond and Adelman	Public participation for conflict resolution.

1977-78
*Baldwin	Advantages and limitations of mediation for resolving environmental disputes are discussed.
*Freeman and Quint	Practical procedure for conflict resolution.
*Frost and Wilmot	Practical ideas on conflict management and resolution.
*Hammond et al.	Weighting and scaling as a means for conflict resolution is described.
*Protasel	A public participation technique for importance weighting is described.
*Wehr	Comprehensive information on conflict management and resolution.

---

*Reference contains information pertinent to WRAM; it is summarized in this report.

Wehr (1978) is an unpublished manuscript which provides a comprehensive discussion of conflict regulation based on the studies and personal experiences of the author. Models and techniques for conflict regulation are described along with a case study. An appendix in the manuscript contains a list of organizations engaged in conflict regulation training, education and research.

CONCLUSIONS

This literature survey encompassed 254 references dealing with environmental impact assessments. Each reference was reviewed based on 12 desirable criteria for methodologies/ technologies (M/T) for use with water resources programs and projects. Of specific interest were those M/T's that are potentially useable in the Water Resources Assessment Methodology (WRAM) being developed at the U.S. Army Engineers Waterways Experiment Station in Vicksburg, Mississippi. A total of 176 references met one criterion or more, with 89 considered to have potentially useable information for WRAM

and 87 serving as general references for the methodology. One
of the problem issues that arose during the conduction of this
survey is that even though many M/T's utilize similar principles and concepts, the terminology employed is quite different.
Additionally, many M/T's focus only on portions of the environment, thus they do not provide a comprehensive approach which
would allow for a systematic evaluation of alternatives. For
example, several M/T's address the socio-economic environment
but do not focus on the physical-chemical or biological components; the corollary is true for other M/T's.

Extensive information is available for identifying
appropriate assessment variables for environmental impact
assessments on water resources programs and projects. These
variables can be conveniently divided into those related to
the environmental quality (EQ) account, the social well-being
(SWB) account and the regional development (RD) account used
for evaluation of water resources projects. Although some
information is available on environmental indices and indicator variables, additional development is needed to delimit the
number of assessment variables and focus more attention on
important issues and concerns. Numerous impact prediction
models are available for the physical-chemical environment,
and assessment (interpretation) of changes can be judged based
on environmental standards/criteria for water quality, air
quality, and noise. A major gap exists in sound and useable
technologies for predicting impacts on the biological environment, and there are only minimal standards/criteria for
assessing impacts. The aesthetics environment also needs considerable attention since there is a minimal amount of technical
information for dealing with the aesthetic features of an area.
Numerous impact prediction techniques exist for the socio-
economic environment, and by using standards/criteria developed
by national organizations or comparison with area, regional
or national norms, a reasonable basis is available for
assessing impacts.

Many impact assessment methodologies for systematically
comparing alternatives utilize either matrix (simple to cross-
impact) approaches or checklists (descriptive to weighting-
scaling). The concepts involving weighting of assessment
variables and scaling of the impacts of alternatives on those
variables have been utilized for many types of projects, thus
suggesting their validity in the water resources area. This
is important since WRAM is predicated upon weighting and scaling.

Finally, it is noted that the environmental impact assessment field is less than a decade old and represents a dynamic
area of technology. It is anticipated that many useful reference materials will be published in the immediate future, thus
it will be necessary to continue to review the literature to
provide the most current and useable information for practitioners.

INTRODUCTION

Part B of Section 102 of the National Environmental Policy Act (P.L. 91-190) requires Federal agencies to "identify and develop methods and procedures . . . which will insure that presently unquantified environmental amenities and values may be given appropriate consideration in decision-making along with economic and technical considerations". Since the effective date of NEPA (January 1, 1970) many impact assessment methodologies have been developed for systematically comparing alternatives and aiding in selecting a proposed action. Some methodologies incorporating environmental issues, or having the potential for their incorporation, actually precede 1970. Additionally, many technological procedures for impact prediction have been developed in response to NEPA. Therefore, the available literature on both methodologies and technologies is becoming extensive.

In February 1977 an Interim Technical report describing a Water Resources Assessment Methodology (WRAM) for impact assessment and the evaluation of alternatives was issued by the Waterways Experiment Station. The objective of this research effort, which was initiated in late 1975, was to develop an environmental assessment methodology for Corps of Engineers water resources programs and projects. The concept was that the methodology chosen would be based directly or indirectly on existing impact assessment methodologies. Accordingly, a review of 54 existing impact methodologies was made prior to formulating WRAM (Canter, 1976).

Due to the dynamic nature of environmental assessment literature, as well as the continuing development of WRAM, it was decided that the literature review of methodologies and technologies should be re-evaluated and updated to 1978. The objective of the study reported herein was to prepare a comprehensive review and evaluation of methodological techniques that are used directly or that have potential application to environmental impact assessment and/or impact assessment and alternative evaluation studies for water resources programs and projects. This report was written in order to document the study findings and results.

DESCRIPTION OF STUDY

In order to systematically consider the available literature it was decided that six time periods would be used as follows: 1960-70, 1971-73, 1974, 1975, 1976, and 1977-78. The 1960-70 period essentially represents the pre-NEPA period, while the latter five periods are post-NEPA-passage. The five post-NEPA-passage periods were chosen so as to limit the references to manageable subgroups; i.e., no more than 60 references in a period. Additionally, trends and emphases in

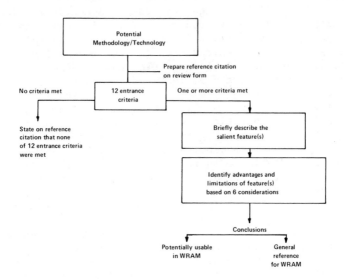

FIGURE 1:   PROCEDURE FOR LITERATURE REVIEW

methodologies and technologies can be examined by time period.
Identified literature sources were first divided into one of
the six time periods and then subjected to the review procedure displayed in Figure 1.   The review form used for each
potential source is shown in Table 1.   A reference citation
with an abstract was prepared for each potential methodology/
technology (M/T).   The 12 entrance criteria used to determine
applicability to WRAM are shown in Table 2.   The criteria were
based on the components of WRAM shown in Table 3 and developed
in conjunction with project personnel at WES.   If one or more
of the 12 criteria were met, a brief description of the salient
feature(s) of the M/T was prepared.   The salient feature(s) was
then subjected to an evaluation based on the six considerations
shown in Table 4.   A conclusion was then drawn regarding the
M/T, with the conclusion being either that (1) the M/T contains
information which is potentially useable in WRAM, or (2) the
M/T should be considered as a general reference supportive of
the WRAM concepts.   All references meeting one or more of the
12 entrance criteria are summarized in Appendices A through F
(Appendix A contains references from the 1960-70 period, B
from the 1971-73 period, C from the 1974 period, D from the
1975 period, E from the 1976 period, and F from the 1977-78
period).   The abstracts of references not meeting any entrance
criteria are listed in Appendix G.

56

TABLE 1:   REVIEW FORM FOR POTENTIAL METHODOLOGY/TECHNOLOGY

Reference:

Abstract:

Entrance Criteria	Yes	No
1. Interdisciplinary team	____	____
2. Assessment variables	____	____
3. Field studies	____	____
4. Impact identification	____	____
5. Prediction of changes	____	____
6. Critical impacts	____	____
7. Importance weights	____	____
8. Scaling or ranking procedures	____	____
9. Impact summarization and assessment	____	____
10. Documentation	____	____
11. Public participation	____	____
12. Conflict management and resolution	____	____

Salient Features:

Considerations for Salient Features:
   1.   Field studies conducted
   2.   Practical for field use
   3.   Applicability for various types/sizes of projects
   4.   Objective vs. subjective approach
   5.   Reproducibility
   6.   Scientifically sound features

Conclusion:
   Potentially useable in WRAM
   General reference for WRAM

RESULTS OF 1960-70 PERIOD

     A total of 21 references on methodologies and technologies
(M/T's) from this period, with the references listed in Table
5.   Table 6 contains a summary of the M/T's reviewed relative
to the 12 entrance criteria in Table 2.   Five M/T's did not
meet any entrance criteria and thus were eliminated from further study; they were Belknap and Furtado, Klein, Lacate,
Lamanna, and McHarg.   Of the 16 M/T's that met one criterion
or more, the following represents the number meeting the stated
criteria:
   1.   Interdisciplinary team --- 0
   2.   Assessment variables --- 3
   3.   Field studies --- 0
   4.   Impact identification --- 1
   5.   Prediction of changes --- 1

6. Critical impacts --- 0
7. Relative importance weights --- 11
8. Scaling or ranking procedures -- 11
9. Impact summarization and assessment --- 13
10. Documentation --- 0
11. Public participation --- 2
12. Conflict management and resolution --- 0

The salient features of the 16 M/T's meeting one more entrance criteria are summarized in Table 7. The advantages and limitations of each of the identified features are summarized in Appendix A along with general information on each of the 16 pertinent M/T's. The reproducibility of each M/T was difficult to evaluate since the references represented single uses.

TABLE 2: ENTRANCE CRITERIA FOR POTENTIAL
METHODOLOGY/TECHNOLOGY

I. Does the methodology/technology (M/T) provide information on procedures or approaches which would:
   A. Aid in the selection of appropriate members of an interdisciplinary team (IDT)?
   B. Aid in the designation of a team leader?
   C. Guide IDT in conduction of study?

II. Does the M/T:
   A. Have a good listing of assessment variables, including measurement units, for one or more of the four accounts or components thereof?
   B. Provide information on procedures or criteria useful for identifying or selecting pertinent assessment variables and associated measurement units?
   C. Reference sources for extant data?
   D. Provide information on interactive influences or cross-impact of variables?
   E. Provide information on procedures for identifying critical variables or fatal flaws?

III. Does the M/T provide information on planning and/or conduction of field studies to gather baseline data.

IV. Does the M/T:
   A. Have a good listing of potential impacts for types of water resources projects?
   B. Provide information on procedures or approaches useful for identifying potential impacts?

V. Does the M/T provide information which will enable prediction of changes in variables (both for short-term as well as long-term) for the no-action alternative and

structural and non-structural alternatives? Changes
can be quantitative, qualitative or relative.

VI. Does the M/T provide information on procedures or criteria useful for identifying "red-flag" or critical
impacts?

VII. Does the M/T provide information on procedures or criteria useful for assigning importance weights (numerical
or qualitative) based on considering both short- and
long-term effects?

VIII. Does the M/T provide information on scaling or ranking
procedures (numerical, letter grading, functional curves,
or qualitative) which can be used to compare the impacts
of each alternative on each assessment variable?

IX. Does the M/T provide information on:
A. Summarization of impacts via numerical systems
(multiplication of weights by scale or rank values),
letter grading systems, or graphical display systems?
B. Procedures or criteria for defining significant
impacts?
C. The sensitivity of the impact findings in terms of
weighting and scaling (i e., which impacts really
make a difference)?
D. How to deal with the probability of impact occurrence?
E. How to deal with the reversibility of impacts?
F. Potential mitigation measures for impacts?

X. Does the M/T provide information on:
A. Communication of impact assessment information
(display of trade-offs of alternatives, etc.) to
various publics in ways that are easily understood?
B. Procedures or approaches for documentation of the
decision processes and information underlying the
decisions?

XI. Does the M/T contain ideas on techniques for involving
various publics in environmental planning and decision-
making?

XII. Does the M/T contain information on conflict management
and resolution within and among:
A. The interdisciplinary team?
B. The agency (interdisciplinary team viewpoints versus
"traditional" agency viewpoints)?
C. Intra-agency relationships?
D. Various publics?

TABLE 3: COMPONENTS OF WRAM

I. Interdisciplinary Team
    A. Selection
        1. Select members of interdisciplinary team.
        2. Designate team leader.
    B. Review and Familiarization
        1. Review study area history.
        2. Visit study area.

II. Assessment Variables
    A. Selection
        1. Assemble list of mandatory* or critical** variables for each of the four national accounts (EQ, NED, SWB, and RD).+
        2. Use criteria questions or weighting portion of weighted rankings technique, along with professional judgment, to select additional relevant variables.
        3. Identify any resulting interactive or cross-inpact variables or categories.
    B. Environmental Inventory
        1. Assemble extant baseline data for selected variables.
        2. Identify variables with data deficiencies.
        3. Use weighted rankings technique and other criteria to allocate manpower and funding resources to data collection effort.
        4. Conduct field studies or assemble information on data-deficient input variables.

III. Impact Prediction, Assessment, and Evaluation
    A. Prediction and Delineation
        1. Predict changes in each variable for each alternative plan and the no-action alternative using available techniques and/or professional judgment.
        2. Delineate potential impacts of alternatives.
        3. Highlight significant impacts and "red flag" any critical issues.
    B. Weighting and Scaling
        1. Use weighted rankings technique to determine relative importance coefficients (RIC) for each variable.
        2. Scale predicted impacts through development of alternative choice coefficients (ACC) or use of function graphs or linear scaling.

C. Evaluation and Interpretation of Results
  1. Multiply RIC's by ACC's to obtain final coefficient matrix. Sum coefficient values for each alternative.
  2. Use values in final coefficient matrix as basis for description of impacts of alternatives and trade-offs between alternatives.
  3. Discuss any critical issues and predicted impacts.

IV. Documentation of Results
  A. Rationale
    1. Describe rationale for selection of decision variables.
    2. Describe procedure for impact identification and prediction, and rationale for weighting, scaling, and interpreting results.
  B. Referencing of Sources of Information
  C. Decision on Environmental Impact Statement

---

*Mandatory = variables required by legislation or regulations.
**Critical = variables that are not mandatory but usually impacted by water resources projects.
+EQ = Environmental Quality
 NED = National Economic Development
 SWB = Social Well-Being
 RD = Regional Development

TABLE 4: CONSIDERATIONS IN IDENTIFYING ADVANTAGES OR LIMITATIONS OF SALIENT FEATURE(S) OF METHODOLOGY/TECHNOLOGY

I. Have field studies been conducted on the M/T? If so, how extensive have they been?
II. Is the M/T practical for use in routine field cases? Some examples of things which would improve practicality are:
  A. Economic costs (manpower and other resources) are feasible.
  B. Can be accomplished in reasonable period of time.
  C. Requirements for pre-use training are minimal.
  D. Few or no unusual skills are required of users.
III. Is applicability of the M/T limited to projects of various types and sizes?
IV. Are objective or non-judgmental approaches stressed as opposed to subjective or judgmental ones?
V. What is the potential for achieving reproducible results?
VI. Are the basic assumptions of the M/T scientifically sound?

TABLE 5:   LIST OF METHODOLOGIES AND TECHNOLOGIES REVIEWED FROM
THE 1960-70 PERIOD

1. Belknap, R. K., and Furtado, J. G., "Three Approaches to
   Environmental Resource Analysis," Nov. 1967, Landscape
   Architecture Research Office, Harvard University, Cambridge,
   Mass.

2. Bishop, A. B. et al., "Socio-Economic and Community Factors
   in Planning Urban Freeways," Sept. 1970, 216 pages, Dept.
   of Civil Engineering Univ., Menlo Park, Cal.

3. Bishop, A. B., "Public Participation in Water Resources
   Planning," IWR Report 70-7, 1970, U.S. Army Engineer
   Institute for Water Resources, Fort Belvoir, Va.

4. Brown, R. M. et al., "A Water Quality Index-Crashing the
   Psychological Barrier," Thomas, W. A. (editor), Indicators
   of Environmental Quality, 1970 pp. 173-182, Plenum Press,
   New York, New York.

5. Dalkey, N. C., "The Delphi Method: An Experimental Study
   of Group Opinion", Memorandum RM-5888-PR, June 1969, The
   Rand Corporation, Santa Monica, California.

6. Dean, B. V. and Nishry, J. J., "Scoring and Profitability
   Models for Evaluating and Selecting Engineering Products,"
   Journal Operations Research Society of America, Vol. 13,
   No. 4, July-Aug. 1965, pp. 550-569.

7. Dearinger, J. A., "Esthetic and Recreational Potential of
   Small Naturalistic Streams Near Urban Areas," April 1968,
   Water Resources Institute, University of Kentucky,
   Lexington, KY.

8. Eckenrode, R. T., "Weighting Multiple Criteria,"
   Management Science, Vol. 12, No. 3, Nov. 1965, pp. 180-192.

9. Falk, E. L., "Measurement of Community Values: The Spokane
   Experiment," Highway Research Record, 1968, No. 229,
   pp. 53-64.

10. Highway Research Section, Engineering Research Division,
    Washington State University, "A Study of the Social,
    Economic and Environmental Impact of Highway Transporta-
    tion Facilities on Urban Communities," 1968, Pullman,
    Washington, (report prepared for Washington State Dept.
    of Highways).

11. Hill, M., "A Method for Evaluating Alternative Plans: The Goals-Achievement Matrix Applied to Transportation Plans," Ph.D. Dissertation, 1966, University of Pennsylvania, Philadelphia, PA.

12. Klein, G. E., "Evaluation of New Transportation Systems," in "Defining Transportation Requirements - Papers and Discussions," 1969, American Society of Mechanical Engineers, New York, New York.

13. Lacate, D. S., "The Role of Resource Inventories and Landscape Ecology in the Highway Route Selection Process," 1970, 198 pages, Dept. of Conservation, College of Agriculture, Cornell University, Ithaca, New York.

14. Lamanna, R. A., "Value Consensus Among Urban Residents," Journal American Institute of Planners, Vol. 30, No. 4, 1964, pp. 317-323.

15. Leopold, L. B., "Quantitative Comparison of Some Aesthetic Factors Among Rivers," Geological Survey Circular No. 620, 1969, 16 pp., U.S. Geological Survey, Washington, D. C.

16. McHarg, I., "A Comprehensive Highway Route Selection Method," pp. 31-41 in Design with Nature, 1969, Natural History Press, Garden City, New York.

17. Miller, III, J. R., Professional Decision-Making: A Procedure for Evaluating Complex Alternatives, 1970, 305 pp., Praeger Publishers, Inc., New York, New York.

18. Orlob, G. T. et al., "Wild Rivers---Methods for Evaluation," Oct. 1970, 106 pp., Water Resources Engineers, Walnut Creek, Cal. (report prepared for U.S. Dept. of the Interior, Washington, D. C.).

19. Pikarsky, M., "Comprehensive Planning for the Chicago Crosstown Expressway," Highway Research Record, 1967, No. 180, pp. 35-51.

20. Schimpeler, C. C. and Grecco, W. L., "Systems Evaluation: An Approach Based on Community Structures and Values," Highway Research Record, 1968, No. 238, pp. 123-152.

21. Southeastern Wisconsin Regional Planning Commission, "Land Use Transportation Study--Forecast and Alternative Plans: 1990", Plan Report 7, Vol. 2, June 1966.

TABLE 6: SUMMARY OF 1960-70 METHODOLOGIES AND TECHNOLOGIES RELATIVE TO ENTRANCE CRITERIA

Criteria	Methodology/Technology*																				
	1	2	3	4	5	6	7	8	9	10	11	12	13	14	15	16	17	18	19	20	21
No entrance criteria met	X											X	X	X		X					
Twelve entrance criteria																					
1. Interdisciplinary team																					
2. Assessment variables				X			X								X						
3. Field studies																					
4. Impact identification		X																			
5. Prediction of changes		X																			
6. Critical impacts																					
7. Relative importance weights				X	X	X	X	X	X	X							X		X	X	X
8. Scaling or ranking procedures				X	X	X	X	X	X	X					X		X		X	X	X
9. Impact summarization and assessment		X		X	X	X	X		X	X	X				X		X	X	X	X	X
10. Documentation																					
11. Public participation			X						X												
12. Conflict management and resolution																					

*The numbers correspond to those listed in Table 5.

64

TABLE 7: SALIENT FEATURES OF 1960-70 METHODOLOGIES/TECHNOLOGIES

Methodology	Feature(s)
Bishop et al.	Factor profile concept for impact scaling.
Bishop	Description of various techniques of public participation.
Brown et al.	Concepts of water quality index; use of quality curves or functional curves.
Dalkey	Group judgments are elicited.
Dean and Nishry	Paired comparisons for weighting and scaling.
Dearinger	Weighting and rating approach.
Eckenrode	Comparison of 6 methods for collecting the judgments of experts concerning the relative weights of multiple criteria.
Falk	Public participation in relative weight assignments; example includes a weighting-scaling checklist.
Highway Research Section	Weight-scaling technique.
Hill	Simple matrix with goals as an element of comparison.
Leopold	Relative uniqueness and categorization of factors; addresses aesthetics with a quantitative approach.
Miller	General information on weighting and scaling procedures.
Orlob	Non-monetary and intangible values are expressed in dollars.
Pikarsky	Weighting-scaling checklist.

Schimpeler and Grecco	Inclusion of probability along with weighting and scaling.
Southeastern Wisconsin Regional Planning Commission	Weighting-ranking checklist.

Table 8 summarizes the conclusions regarding the 16 pertinent references from the 1960-70 period. Five references contain potentially useable information for WRAM, and 11 serve as general references. Potentially useable information from the 5 references is as follows:

Bishop et al.: The key-feature is the use of the community factor profile for analyzing the indirect or community effects of freeway alternatives. The community factor profile is a graphical description of the effects of each proposed freeway location alternative. Figure 2 is a highly simplified and consolidated version of such a profile for four alternative locations numbered 1, 2, 3, and 4. In this figure, each profile scale is on a percentage base, ranging from a negative to a positive 100 percent. One hundred percent, either negative

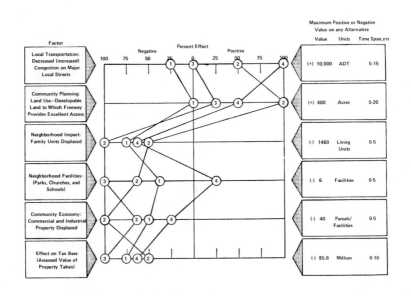

FIGURE 2: COMMUNITY FACTOR PROFILE (AFTER BISHOP ET AL., 1970)

66

or positive, is the maximum absolute value of the measure that is adopted for each factor. Reduction to the percentage base simplifies scaling and plotting the profiles. The maximum positive or negative value of the measure, the units, and the time span are indicated on the right hand side of the profile for reference. For each alternative, the positive or negative value for any factor is calculated as a percent of the maximum absolute value over all alternatives and is plotted on the appropriate abscissa. A broken line connecting the plotted points for each alternative gives its factor profile. For the profiles, factors and measures should be selected which are independent and will adequately describe all important elements of community impact.

The factor profile concept is applicable to WRAM in terms of comparing alternatives and scaling impacts. The relative importance of individual factors are not reflected in factor profiling.

Dalkey: The Delphi technique is a method of eliciting and refining group judgments. In the spring of 1968 a series of experiments were initiated to evaluate Delphi procedures and explore the nature of the information processes occurring in the Delphi interaction. The experiments were conducted using upper-class and graduate students from UCLA as subjects and general information of the almanac type as subject matter. Ten experiments, involving 14 groups ranging in size from 11 to 30 members, were conducted. About 13,000 answers to some 350 questions were obtained.

The two basic issues being examined were (1) a comparison of face-to-face discussion with the controlled-feedback interaction, and (2) a thorough evaluation of controlled feedback as a technique of improving group estimates. The results

TABLE 8: SUMMARY OF CONCLUSIONS REGARDING PERTINENT REFERENCES FROM 1960-70 PERIOD

Potentially Useable in WRAM	General Reference for WRAM
Bishop et al.	Bishop
Dalkey	Brown et al.
Dean and Nishry	Dearinger
Eckenrode	Highway Research Section
Falk	Hill
	Leopold
	Miller
	Orlob et al.
	Pikarsky
	Schimpeler and Grecco
	Southeastern Wisconsin Regional Planning Commission

indicated that, more often than not, face-to-face discussion tended to make the group estimates less accurate, whereas, more often than not, the anonymous controlled feedback procedure made the group estimates more accurate. The experiments thus put the application of Delphi techniques in areas of partial information on much firmer ground.

Of greater long-range significance is the insight gained into the nature of the group information processes. Delphi procedures create a well-defined process that can be described quantitatively. In particular, the average error on round one is a linear function of the dispersion of the answers. The average amount of change of opinion between round one and round two is a well-behaved function of two parameters - the distance of the first-round answer from the group median, and the distance from the true answer.

Another result of major significance is that a meaningful estimate of the accuracy of a group response to a given question can be obtained by combining individual self-ratings of competence on that question into a group rating. Thus result, when combined with the relationship between accuracy and standard deviation mentioned above, opens the possibility of attaching accuracy scores to the products of a Delphi exercise.

Information on the Delphi procedure is important in WRAM since this represents one potential approach for identifying assessment variables, assigning importance weights to those variables, and scaling of anticipated impacts.

Dean and Nishry: A weighting-scaling checklist approach for multiple-criteria decision-making between alternatives is described. The weighting is accomplished by a paired-comparison technique used by the decision team. Alternatives are evaluated relative to the checklist items and choice coefficients are assigned based on a paired-comparison approach. The weighting is subjective while the scaling is more objective.

The Dean and Nishry methodology was one of the conceptual approaches used in the original development of WRAM.

Eckenrode: Six methods for collecting the judgments of experts concerning the relative value of sets of criteria were compared for their reliability and time efficiency. The methods were ranking, rating, three versions of paired comparisons and a method of successive comparisons. The judgment situations used were concerned with the design of a specific air defense system and a general air defense system, and with selecting a personnel subsystem manager for a development program. In each of these three situations six criteria were comparatively evaluated by the judges. The results of these experiments showed that there were no significant differences in the sets of criterion weights derived from collecting the judgment data by any of the methods, but that ranking was by far the most efficient method. A fourth experiment was conducted to develop baseline data on the time required to make comparative judgments vs. number of items to be judged, by the ranking method and by the simplest paired comparisons method.

Ranking is increasingly more efficient than paired comparisons as the number of items to be judged increases from six to 30.

This study is pertinent to WRAM since the assignment of relative importance weights to assessment variables is required. The relative importance weights in WRAM correspond to the relative values in the Eckenrode study; additionally, the assessment variables in WRAM correspond to the criteria in the Eckenrode study.

Falk: This study describes the use of public participation in the assignment of relative importance weights to a series of factors. The pilot study described involved determining the relative importance of four tangible and five intangible factors and identifying a means of applying these measures of importance in selecting the most acceptable one of three hypothetical roadway solutions. The method requires the assumption that frequency of citizen preference for one factor over another is directly related to importance of that factor. An example application using a weighting-scaling checklist is included.

This study is relevant to WRAM in that it describes a simple public participation technique which can be used to assign relative importance weights to assignment variables.

RESULTS OF 1971-73 PERIOD

A total of 54 references on methodologies and technologies (M/T's) were reviewed from this period, with the references listed in Table 9. Table 10 contains a summary of the M/T's

TABLE 9: LIST OF METHODOLOGIES AND TECHNOLOGIES REVIEWED FROM THE 1971-73 PERIOD

1. Arnold, W., Young, J. and Brewer, J., "Constructing Nonlinear Dynamic Models for Socio-Environmental Decision Making: A Methodology", Environmental Quality Series, Oct., 1972, Institute of Governmental Affairs, University of California at Davis, Davis, California.

2. Arthur D. Little, Inc., "Transportation and Environment Synthesis for Action: Impact of National Environmental Policy Act of 1969 on the Department of Transportation", July, 1971, Vol. 3 (Options for Environmental Management), prepared for Office of the Secretary, Department of Transportation, Washington, D. C.

3. Bagley, M. D., Kroll, C. A., and Clark, C., "Aesthetics in Environmental Planning," EPA-600/5-73-009, Nov., 1973, 187 pp., U.S. Environmental Protection Agency, Washington, D. C. (prepared for EPA by Stanford Research Institute, Menlo Park, California).

4. Baker, R. W., and Gruendler, J. D., "Case Study of the Milwaukee-Green Bay Interstate Corridor Location", 1972, paper presented at Highway Research Board Summer Meeting and in "Environmental Considerations in Planning, Design and Construction" Special Report 138, Highway Research Board, Washington, D. C.

5. Bereano, P. L. et al., "A Proposed Methodology for Assessing Alternative Technologies", Technology Assessment, Vol. 1, No. 3, 1973, pp. 179-190.

6. Bromley, D. W. et al., "Water Resources Projects and Environmental Impacts: Towards a Conceptual Model", Feb. 1972, Water Resources Center, University of Wisconsin, Madison, Wisconsin.

7. Bureau of Land Management, "Environmental Analysis", Working Draft, 1973, 126 pages, Bureau of Land Management, Washington, D. C.

8. Bureau of Reclamation, "Guidelines for Implementing Principles and Standards for Multi-objective Planning of Water Resources", Review draft, 1972, Bureau of Reclamation, U.S. Department of the Interior, Washington, D. C.

9. Central New York Regional Planning and Development Board, "Environmental Resources Management", Report No. CNYRPDB-RP-72-HUD-246-06, Oct. 1972, 35 pages, Syracuse, New York (report prepared for Department of Housing and Urban Development, Region 2, New York, New York).

10. Chen, W. W. and Orlob, G. T., "Ecologic Simulation for Aquatic Environments", OWRR-C-2044, December 1972, 156 pp., Office of Water Resources Research, U.S. Dept. of Interior, Washington, D. C. (prepared for OWRR by Water Resources Engineers, Inc., Walnut Creek, California).

11. Commonwealth Associates, Inc., "Environmental Analysis System", Report No. R-1447, 1972, prepared for the Northern States Power Company, Minnesota, by Commonwealth Associates Inc., Jackson, Michigan.

12. Coomber, N. H., and Biswas, A. K., Evaluation of Environmental Intangibles, Genera Press, Bronxville, New York, 1973, 77 pages.

13. Crawford, A. B., "Impact Analysis Using Differential Weighted Evaluation Criteria", 1973, in J. L. Cochrane and M. Zeleny, editors, Multiple Criteria Decision Making, University of South C rolina Press, Columbia, South Carolina.

14. Cross, F. L., "Assessing Environmental Impact", Pollution Engineering, Vol. 5, No. 6, June 1973, pp. 34-35.

15. Dee, N. et al., "Environmental Evaluation System for Water Resources Planning", Final report, 1972 Battelle-Columbus Laboratories, Columbus, Ohio (prepared for the Bureau of Reclamation, U.S. Department of the Interior, Washington, D. C.)

16. Dee, N. et al., "Planning Methodology for Water Quality Management: Environmental Evaluation System", July 1973, Battelle-Columbus, Columbus, Ohio.

17. Ditton, R. B., and Goodale, T. L., editors, "Environmental Impact Analysis: Philosophy and Methods", Proceedings of the Conference on Environmental Impact Analysis, Green Bay, Wisconsin, January 4-5, 1972, Sea Grant Publication Officer, University of Wisconsin, Madison, Wisconsin.

18. Environmental Impact Center, Inc., "A Methodology for Assessing Environmental Impact of Wat r Resources Develop ment", Nov. 1973, PB-226 545, prepared by Environmental Impact Center, Inc., Cambridge, Mass., for U.S. Department of the Interior, Office of Water Resources Research, Washington, D. C.

19. Fabos, J. G., "Model for Landscape Resource Assessment --- Part I of the Metropolitan Landscape Planning Model (METLAND)", February 1973, Department of Landscape Architecture and Regional Planning, University of Massa-chusetts, Amherst, Massachusetts.

20. Fischer, D. W., and Davies, G. S., "An Approach to Assessing Environmental Impacts", Journal Environmental Management, Vol. 1, No. 3, 1973, pp. 207-227.

21. Hetman, F., "Society and the Assessment of Technology", 1973, Organization for Economic Cooperation and Develop-ment, Washington, D. W., pp. 115- 39.

22. Hydrologic Engineering Center, "Reservoir Temperature Stratification Users Manual", January 1972, U.S. Army Engineer District --- Sacramento, Davis, California.

23. Jain, R. K. et al., "Environmental Impact Study for Army Military Programs", Report No. CERL-IR-D-13 December 1973, 170 pages, U.S. Army Construction Engineering Research Laboratory, Champaign, Illinois.

24. Kane, J., Vertinsky, I., and Thomson, W., "KSIM: A Methodology for Interactive Resource Policy Simulation",

Water Resources Research, Vol. 9, No. 1, February 1973,
pp. 65-79.

25. Krauskopf, T. M., and Bunde, D. C., "Evaluation of Environmental Impact Through a Computer Modelling Process"
in Ditton, R., and Goodale, T., (eds.), "Environmental
Impact Analysis: Philosophy and Methods," 1972, pp. 107-
125, University of Wisconsin Sea Grant Program, Madison,
Wisconsin.

26. Leopold, L. B. et al., "A Procedure for Evaluating
Environmental Impact", U.S. Geological Survey Circular
645, 1971, U.S. Geological Survey, Washington, D. C.

27. MacCrimmon, K. R., "An Overview of Multiple Objective
Decision Making", 1973, in J. L. Cochrane and M. Zeleny,
editors, "Multiple Criteria Decision Making", University
of South Carolina Press, Columbia, South Carolina.

28. Manheim, M. L. et al., "Community Values in Highway Location and Design: A Procedural Guide", September, 1971,
Urban Systems Laboratory, Massachusetts Institute of
Technology, Cambridge, Massachusetts (report prepared
for Highway Research Board, Washington, D. C.)

29. Markofsky, M. and Harleman, D. R., "A Predictive Model
for Thermal Stratification and Water Quality in Reservoirs",
EPA-16130-DJII-01/71, Jan. 1971, 286 pp., Massachusetts
Institute of Technology, Cambridge, Massachusetts.

30. McKenry, C. E. et al., "Interstate 75 --- Evaluation of
Corridors Proposed for South Florida", 1971, 62 pages,
University of Miami Center for Urban Studies, Coral
Gables, Florida (report prepared for State of Florida
Department of Transportation).

31. Moore, J. L. et al., "A Methodology for Evaluating Manu-
facturing Environmental Impact Statements for Delaware's
Coastal Zone", June 1973, Battelle-Columbus Laboratories,
Columbus, Ohio (report prepared for State of Delaware).

32. Morrill, R. A., "Comprehensive Resource and Environmental
Management Planning", Research Report, June, 1973, 87
pages, Engineering and Research Center, U.S. Bureau of
Reclamation, Denver, Colorado.

33. National Forest Service, "Interaction Between Resources",
1973, National Forest Service, U.S. Department of Agriculture, Atlanta, Georgia.

34. O'Connor, M. F., "The Application of Multi-Attribute
Scaling Procedures to the Development of Indices of

Value," June 1972, Engineering Psychology Laboratory, University of Michigan, Ann Arbor, Michigan.

35. Odum, E. P. et al., "Optimum Pathway Matrix Analysis Approach to the Environmental Decision Making Process --- Test Case: Relative Impact of Preposed Highway Alternates", 1971, Institute of Ecology, University of Georgia, Athens, Georgia.

36. Odum, H. T., "Use of Energy Diagrams for Environmental Impact Statements", Tools for Coastal Zone Management, Proceedings of the Conference, Washington, D. C., Feb. 1972, pp. 197-213.

37. Ortolano, L., "Analyzing the Environmental Impacts of Water Projects", March 1973, 433 pp., Dept. of Civil Engineering, Stanford Univ., Menlo Park, Cal.

38. Pikul, R., "Development of Environmental Indices", in Pratt, J. W., editor, Statistical and Mathematical Aspects of Pollution Problems, Marcel Dekker Book Company, New York, New York, 1974, pp. 103-121.

39. Raines, G., "Environmental Impact Assessment of New Installations", (paper presented at International Pollution Engineering Congress, Cleveland, Ohio, Dec. 4-6, 1972), Battelle-Memorial Institute, Columbus, Ohio.

40. Rea, R., "Handbook for Assessing the Social and Economic Impacts of Water Quality Management Plans", July 1973, Resource Planning Associates, Inc., Cambridge, Massachusetts (report prepared for Environmental Protection Agency, Washington, D. C.)

41. Rosove, P. E., "A Trend Impact Matrix for Societal Impact Assessment", April 1973, 24 pp., Center for Futures Research, Graduate School of Business Administration, University of Southern California, Los Angeles, California.

42. Schlesinger, B. and Daetz, D., "A Conceptual Framework for Applying Environmental Assessment Matrix Techniques", The Journal of Environmental Sciences, July/August, 1973, pp. 11-16.

43. Sewell, W. R. D., "Broadening the Approach to Evaluation in Resources Management Decision-making", Journal of Environmental Management, Vol. 1, 1973, pp. 33-60.

44. Smith, W. L., "Quantifying the Environmental Impact of Transportation Systems", 1973, Van Doren-Hazard-Stallings-Schnake Consultants, Topeka, Kansas.

45. Sorensen, J., "A Framework for Identification and Control of Resource Degradation and Conflict in the Multiple Use of the Coastal Zone", Master's Thesis, 1971, Department of Landscape Architecture, University of California, Berkeley, California.

46. Stover, Lloyd V., "Environmental Impact Assessment: A Procedure", March 1973, 23 pages, Science Technology Vision, Inc., Pottstown, Pa.

47. Swartzman, G. L., and Van Dyne, G. M., "An Ecologically Based Simulation - Optimization Approach to Natural Resource Planning", in "Annual Review of Ecology and Systematics", Vol. 3, 1972, pp. 347-398.

48. Texas Water Development Board, "Simulation of Water Quality in Streams and Canals, Theory and Description of the AUAL-1 Mathematical Modeling System", EPA-OWP-TEX-128, May 1971, 62 pp., Austin, Texas.

49. Thomas, J. L., Paul, J. and Israelsen, E. R., "A Computer Model of the Quantity and Chemical Quality of Return Flow", OWRR-B-038-UTAH(1), June 1971, 100 pp., Utah Water Research Laboratory, Utah State University, Logan, Utah.

50. Turner, A. K., and Hausmanis, I., "Computer-aided Transportation Corridor Selection in the Guelp-Dundas Area of Ontario", 1972, paper presented at Highway Research Board Summer Meeting and in "Environmental Considerations in Planning, Design and Construction", Special Report 138, Highway Research Board, Washington, D. C.

51. U.S. Army Engineer District, Tulsa, Corps of Engineers, "Matrix Analysis of Alternatives for Water Resource Development", Draft technical paper, July 1972, Tulsa, Oklahoma.

52. Walton, Jr., L. E., and Lewis, J. E., "A Manual for Conducting Environmental Impact Studies", Report No. VHRC 70-R 46, June, 1971, 34 pages, Virginia Highway Research Council, Charlottesville, Virginia (report prepared for Federal Highway Administration, Washington, D. C.)

53. Warner, M. L., "Environmental Impact Analysis: An Examination of Three Methodologies", Ph.D. Dissertation, 1973, 248 pages, Department of Agricultural Economics, University of Wisconsin, Madison, Wisconsin.

54. Wenger, R. B., and Rhyner, C. R., "Evaluation of Alternatives for Solid Waste Systems", Journal of Environmental Systems, Vol. 2, No. 2, June 1972, Pages 89-108.

TABLE 10: SUMMARY OF 1971-73 METHODOLOGIES AND TECHNOLOGIES RELATIVE TO ENTRANCE CRITERIA

Criteria	1	2	3	4	5	6	7	8	9	10	11	12	13	14	15	16	17	18	19	20	21	22	23	24
No entrance criteria met			X	X		X	X						X				X	X	X	X				
Twelve entrance criteria:																								
1. Interdisciplinary team																								
2. Assessment variables				X				X							X	X					X			
3. Field Studies								X							X									
4. Impact identification								X	X										X			X	X	
5. Prediction of changes					X	X			X									X			X			
6. Critical impacts															X	X			X					
7. Relative importance weights				X				X	X	X	X				X	X								
8. Scaling or ranking procedures	X		X		X			X	X	X	X	X			X	X			X					
9. Impact summarization and assessment				X	X			X	X	X	X	X	X	X	X	X			X					
10. Documentation																								
11. Public participation																								
12. Conflict management and resolution			½									X												

*The numbers correspond to those listed in Table 9.

75

reviewed relative to the 12 entrance criteria in Table 2.
Seventeen M/T's did not meet any entrance criteria and thus
were eliminated from further study. The seventeen were
Arthur D. Little, Inc., Baker and Gruendler, Bureau of Land
Management, Cross, Ditton and Goodale, Fabos, Hetman, Krauskopf
and Bunde, McKenry, National Forest Service, Rea, Rosove, Sewell,
Smith, Turner and Hausmanis, Walton and Lewis, and Warner. Of
the 37 M/T's that met one criterion or more, the following
represents the number meeting the stated criteria:

1. Interdisciplinary team --- 0
2. Assessment variables --- 11
3. Field studies --- 2
4. Impact identification --- 13
5. Prediction of changes --- 10
6. Critical impacts --- 4
7. Relative importance weights --- 14
8. Scaling or ranking procedures --- 17
9. Impact summarization and assessment --- 21
10. Documentation --- 0
11. Public participation --- 1
12. Conflict management and resolution --- 0

The salient features of the 37 M/T's meeting one or more
entrance criteria are summarized in Table 11. The advantages
and limitations of each of the identified features are summarized in Appendix B along with general information on each
of the 37 pertinent M/T's. The reproducibility of each M/T
was difficult to evaluate since the references represented
single uses.

Table 12 summarizes the conclusions regarding the 37
pertinent references from the 1971-73 period. Eleven references contain information which is potentially useable in
WRAM, and 26 are general references supportive of the WRAM
concepts. Potentially useable information from the 11 references is as follows:

Bagley, Kroll and Clark: This report addresses the
relationship of aesthetics to environmental planning. The
primary emphasis of the research is on the man/environment
interaction, with the ultimate goal directed toward improving
the understanding of aesthetic concepts and the implication
of using those concepts in research and planning activities.
Methodologies for measuring or quantifying aesthetics are
reviewed, as well as a review of the state of the art of
research in basic theory for understanding the unquantifiable.
Depending upon the geographical and topographical setting,
individual or combinations of methodologies might be appropriate for use in the WRAM methodology.

Bureau of Reclamation: This methodology was one of 8
identified in the interim WRAM report. It has a checklist of
environmental components and categories organized in the same
manner as the Water Resources Council guidelines. The

TABLE 11: SALIENT FEATURES OF 1971-73
METHODOLOGIES/TECHNOLOGIES

Methodology	Feature(s)
Arnold, Young, and Brewer	Provides bases for the development of functional curves for socio-economic variables.
Bagley, Kroll, and Clark	Describes several approaches for quantifying the aesthetic features of an area.
Bereano et al.	Use of probability of an impact as an integral part of an interaction matrix.
Bromley et al.	Procedure for predicting changes in land use over time both with and without a project.
Bureau of Reclamation	Good listing of assessment variables for biological, physical-chemical, esthetic and cultural environments. A quality scale and human influence scale is suggested.
Central New York Regional Planning and Development Board	Use of interaction matrices to identify impacts and display their relative importance.
Chen and Orlob	Ecosystem models are presented for lakes and estuaries.
Commonwealth Associates, Inc.	Techniques for weighting and scaling of impacts.
Coomber and Biswas	Provides general discussion of systematic evaluation of environmental intangibles.
Crawford	Weighting-scaling checklist for evaluation of impacts of alternatives.
Dee et al. (1973)	Weighting-scaling checklist based on relevant matrices and networks. Ranges of scale

77

values. Concepts of "environmental assessment trees" to account for interrelationships among assessment variables.

Environmental Impact Center, Inc.	Impact prediction information for certain biological and physical-chemical variables.
Fischer and Davies	Use of series of three matrices in defining environmental setting, identifying impacts and summarizing the features of alternatives.
Hydrologic Engineering Center	Mathematical model for reservoir temperature stratification.
Jain et al.	Extensive consideration of construction phase impacts. Good description of selected assessment variables (called attributes in the methodology).
Kane, Vertinsky and Thomson	Focuses attention on cross-impacts of water resources development projects.
Leopold et al.	Use of interaction matrix to identify and visually display potential impacts.
MacCrimmon	Literature review on multiple objective and multiple attribute decision making.
Manheim et al.	Use of interaction matrix for identification and visual display of impacts.
Markofsky and Harleman	Thermal stratification model.
Moore et al.	Stepped or linked matrices to display interrelationships between impacted assessment variables.
Morrill	Presentation of hierarchical information on various categories of the environment and

	their associated variables. Suggested quantitative measures for defining the quality of life.
O'Connor	Two water quality indices.
Odum, E. P. et al.	This weighting-scaling checklist includes an error term to allow for misjudgment in the assignment of importance weights. Computerization of the methodology enables the conduction of a sensitivity analysis.
Odum, H. T.	Use of energy diagrams to predict ecosystem changes.
Ortolano	Discussion of general impacts associated with water resources projects.
Pickul	Use of indices to describe environmental setting and assess potential impacts.
Raines	Weighting-scaling checklists; Use of functional curves to translate environmental impact quantities into environmental cost units.
Schlesinger and Daetz	Compares several matrix approaches for impact assessment.
Sorensen	Presentation of networks (stepped or linked matrices) for impact identification.
Stover	Weighting-scaling checklist.
Swartzman and Van Dyne	Good discussion of ecological modelling for natural resource planning.
Texas Water Development Board	Models plus examples are presented for water quality impact prediction.

Thomas, Paul and Israelson	Water quality model for irrigation return flow.
U.S. Army Engineer District, Tulsa, Corps of Engineers	Has good list of variables for EQ, SWB, and RD accounts. Weighting-scaling checklist used for evaluation of alternatives; includes statistical testing of results.
Wenger and Rhyner	A stochastic computer procedure is used to account for uncertainty in the weighting and scaling checklist procedure for evaluation of solid waste system alternatives.

The categories of potential impacts examined deal comprehensively with biological, physical, cultural, and historical resources and with pollution factors, but do not treat social or economic impacts. Impacts are measured in quantitative terms where possible and also are scaled subjectively on quality and human influence. In addition, uniqueness and irreversibility considerations are included where appropriate. Several suggestions for summary tables and bar graphs are offered as communications aids.

Dee et al. (1972): This methodology was one of 8 methodologies identified in the interim WRAM report (Feb., 1977). It is a weighting-scaling checklist methodology. It was designed for major water resource projects, but many parameters used are also appropriate for other types of projects. Seventy-eight specific environmental parameters are defined within the four categories ecology, environmental pollution, aesthetics, and human interest. The approach does not deal with economic or secondary impacts, and social impacts are only partially covered with the human interest category.

Parameter measurements are scaled by converting to a common base of environmental quality units through the use of functional curves. Impacts can be aggregated using a set of pre-assigned weights of relative importance, with the assignments made through use of the ranked pairwise comparison technique. An important idea of the approach is to highlight key impacts via a "red flag" system.

Dee et al. (1973): This methodology of impact assessment can be classified as a weighting-scaling checklist although it also contains elements of matrix and network approaches. Areas of possible impacts are defined by a hierarchical system of 4 categories (ecology, physical/chemical, aesthetic, social), 19 components, and 64 parameters. An interaction matrix is presented to indicate which activities associated with

TABLE 12:   SUMMARY OF CONCLUSIONS REGARDING PERTINENT
REFERENCES FROM 1971-73 PERIOD

Potentially Useable in WRAM	General Reference for WRAM
Bagley, Kroll, and Clark	Arnold, Young and Brewer
Bureau of Reclamation	Bereano et al.
Dee et al. (1972)	Bromley et al.
Dee et al. (1973)	Central New York Regional
Environmental Impact Center, Inc.	Planning and Development Board
	Chen and Orlob
Fischer and Davies	Commonwealth Associates, Inc.
O'Connor	Coomber and Biswas
Odum (E. P.) et al.	Crawford
Raines	Hydrologic Engineering Center
U.S. Army Engineer District, Tulsa, Corps of Engineers	Jain et al.
	Kane, Vertinsky and Thomson
Wenger and Rhyner	Leopold et al.
	MacCrimmon
	Manheim et al.
	Markofsky and Harleman
	Moore et al.
	Morrill
	Odum (H. T.)
	Ortolano
	Pikul
	Schlesinger and Daetz
	Sorensen
	Stover
	Swartzman and Van Dyne
	Texas Water Development Board
	Thomas, Paul, and Israelsen

wastewater treatment projects generally impact which parameters.
The range of parameters used is comprehensive; however, socio-
economic variables are excluded.

Impact measurement incorporates both scaling and weighting.
A set of ranges is specified for each parameter to express
impact magnitude on a scale from zero (worst environmental
quality) to one (best environmental quality). Two examples of
the "range" approach for scaling are shown in Table 13. A
unique part of the methodology is the use of an "environmental
assessment tree". Specifically, the ranges of the parameters
are aggregated into nineteen components with nineteen network
trees which have been constructed to translate the relationship between the good and the bad values on individual parameters into good and bad values for a set of parameters.
Fig. 3 is a reproduction of the Aquatic Species and Populations

TABLE 13: TWO EXAMPLES OF RANGE APPROACH FOR SCALING USED IN
DEE ET AL. (1973)

Dissolved Oxygen

The dissolved oxygen index is

Range	Parameter Measurement (ppm)			Parameter Quality Index
1	0	DO	2	0.0
2	2	DO	5	0.2
3	5	DO	7	0.7
4	7	DO		1.0

Wooded Shoreline Index

The wooded shoreline index is based on the assumption that a shoreline bordered by trees and shrubs is more pleasing than one which is not.

Range	Parameter Measurement	Parameter Quality Index
1	no trees	0.0
2	some trees	0.5
3	half trees	0.8
4	predominantly trees	1.0

Assessment Tree. To obtain the scale value for this component one first determines the range of the vegetation parameter, and then follows the arrow to the next parameter box (water-fowl). The same dichotomy is offered at the next parameter (pests), depending upon the answer to the initial parameter. After following several more branches on the tree, a last branch will intersect the environmental quality scale and provide a score for the component. For example, parameter ratings of 3 in vegetation, 4 in waterfowl, 3 in pests, and 3 in fish may be followed by the dashed lines to an assessment of 0.8 along the tree. The advantages of the assessment tree are that it is simple to use, requires less precise data about individual parameters, and places the single parameter in the context of the real-world interrelationships among similar variables. The disadvantage of the assessment tree approach is the potential loss of information about individual para-meters.

Weighting is accomplished by the interdisciplinary team assigning importance index values based on 100 units to each category and component. An overall score for any alternative can be obtained by multiplying each component scale by its

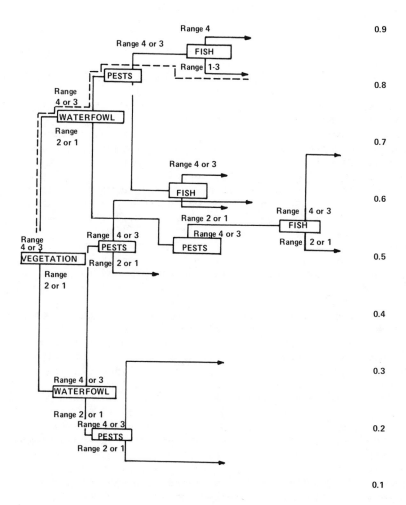

FIGURE 3: BATTELLE AQUATIC SPECIES AND POPULATION ASSESSMENTS
TREE (After Dee, et al, 1973)

83

weight factor and summing across components. Major impacts ("red flags") are defined by a change of two or more ranges, e.g., range 4 to 2, or 3 to 1, or 1 to 3, etc.

Environmental Impact Center, Inc.: This methodology was one of 8 methodologies identified in the interim WRAM report (Feb., 1977). It is a descriptive checklist with no impact weighting or scaling. Environmental impacts of water resource projects are assessed with a dynamic simulation model for forecasting regional economic and demographic changes and their interactions with water supply and water quality over time. Modular sectors were developed to forecast regional population and industrial levels, intra-regional land use patterns, and recreational activities. These are linked to a water sector which models stream flows, water supply withdrawals and consumption, and water quality in terms of dissolved oxygen and carbonaceous and nitrogenous oxygen demand. Water quality is based on both point wasteloads from domestic and industrial sources and dispersed source wasteloads from urban runoff. A final module represents biological activities in a stream, including algal concentrations and fish populations.

Fischer and Davies: This methodology consists of the use of three matrices (environmental baseline, environmental compatibility, and decision). The concepts of the environmental baseline matrix are shown in Table 14. The scale of importance is an arbitrary scale which the interdisciplinary team uses to evaluate the importance of each environmental element to the overall area included. The "importance" factor is thus dependent upon the area included in the analysis and the appraisal of the team. Normally the value on the importance scale will be a consensus derived through team discussion. Rarely will the importance of one element be isolated from other elements. The importance of a group of elements should be decided by an understanding of the linkage combining a group of environmental elements into an environmental unit or bio-cultural linkage. Those environmental elements and their combined linkages (bio-cultural units) receiving an importance rating of 4 or 5 will be carried forward to the next evaluation.

The scale of present condition in Table 14 is an arbitrary measure which the interdisciplinary team uses to evaluate the current quality level of each important environmental element. It is a measure of the existing environmental degradation and is derived by a team consensus from their experiences which are translated into the environmental indices. The final phase of the baseline evaluation comprises an arbitrary scale determining what the management practices and costs would be for maintaining and restoring important environmental elements. Again, judgment is necessary to determine the management requirements and costs for the various important environmental elements and units.

84

TABLE 14:   CONCEPT OF AN ENVIRONMENTAL BASELINE MATRIX AS
            DESCRIBED IN FISCHER AND DAVIES (1973)

Identification	Evaluation		
Environmental Elements/units	Scale of importance 1 2 3 4 5 low high	Scale of present condition 1 2 3 4 5 low high	Scale of management 1 2 3 4 5 low high

Biological:
  flora
  fauna
  ecological relationships
Physical-chemical:
  atmosphere
  water
  earth
Cultural:
  households
  communities
  economy
  communications
Bio-cultural linkages/units:
  resources
  recreation
  conservation			

The second matrix in the Fischer and Davies methodology
is called an environmental compatibility matrix. This matrix
is similar to the Leopold interaction matrix in that introduced
activities (project actions) are shown on the x-axis and environmental elements on the y-axis. To use the environmental
compatibility matrix requires the determination of index values
to be placed in the applicable individual cells. Introducing a
new activity in an area creates a possible impact on the existing environment with its existing activities. Introducing a
new activity may enhance the environment (have positive effects)
or it may degrade the environment (have negative effects).
Index values from +5 to -5 are assigned by the interdisciplinary
team. Short and long term impacts are also important in the
analysis. If the impact is short term (e.g. during construction)
then the suffix S is entered after the number in the cell, say
-4S. If the impact is a long term incompatibility (e.g. inundation) then the suffix L is used, say +4L.
    The final matrix in the Fischer and Davies methodology is
called the decision matrix. This matrix displays the major

environmental impacts (values of +4 or 5) from the environmental compatibility matrices for the alternatives.

O'Connor: Using procedures developed in the study of multidimensional utility analysis, two indices of water quality are developed. One index describes the quality of a surface body of raw water which will be used to sustain a fish and wildlife population. A second index describes the quality of a surface body of raw water which will be treated as is necessary and used as a public water supply. The multi-attribute scaling procedures were applied to this task by assessing, from water quality engineers, (1) judgments about which variables should be included in the index, (2) the type of rule for combining the variables, (3) the relative importance weights of the different variables, and (4) a curve describing the functional relation between water quality and each variable. A modified delphi procedure was used for obtaining consensus among the engineers for each of the indices. Even after the applications of the Delphi procedure, the engineers disagreed on the importance weights, so a sensitivity analysis applied the different indices to actual measurements on samples of river water. This analysis indicated that the disagreement about the weights was not crucial to the measurement of water quality. In fact, a major conclusion of this research is that the multi-attribute scaling procedures are sufficiently robust so that, while great care should be used in determining the purpose for which the index will be used and in selecting variables for inclusion, relatively little time and effort need be invested in resolving small differences among quality functions and among relative weights.

Odum et al.: This methodology is a weighting-scaling checklist of 56 measurable environmental parameters. The actual values of alternative plan impacts on a parameter are normalized and expressed as a decimal of the largest impact (on that one parameter). These represent a scaling procedure. These normalized values are multiplied by a subjectively determined weighting factor, which is the sum of a weight for initial effects plus 10 times a weight for long-term effects. Uncertainty is compensated for by conducting several computer passes and incorporating a randomly generated error variation ·in both actual measurements and weights. This procedure also provides a basis for testing the significance of differences in total impact scores between alternatives. The methodology was used to evaluate highway project alternatives, and the components listed are not suitable for other types of projects. However, appropriate components for water resources projects can be easily included. The procedures for normalizing or scaling measured impacts to obtain commensurability and testing of significant differences between alternatives are notable features of potential value to the WRAM methodology.

Raines: An interaction matrix similar to the Leopold matrix is used to identify impacts of concern. Once the impacts have been identified they are assigned importance weights and scaled for each alternative. Scaling is accomplished through the use of functional curves based on the scientific or technological judgment of professional specialists. A value function (functional curve) essentially expresses the relationship between a set of assessed or calculated environmental impact quantities and the degree of acceptability or desirability of the levels. An example of a value function graph is given in Figure 4 to illustrate the procedure used. Cost to the environment, increasing in the positive direction, is selected for the ordinate axis and an arbitrary scale of 0 to 10 units is used. For convenience the units are designated environment cost units (ECU's), and an ECU value of 10 is defined as indicative of a "clearly unacceptable" environmental cost. The assessed or calculated environmental impact quantity (cost), which is to be translated into ECU's, is placed along the abscissa. Absolute quantities may be used to determine the scale, or as in the figure, the quantities may be normalized with respect to a reference quantity. In either case, the value that would represent a "clearly unacceptable" impact (cost) to the environment must be identified. This reference limit, then, is equivalent to a value of 10 on the ECU scale.

Weighting factors are used to reflect the relative importance of identified impacts. In practice each ECU value obtained from application of the value functions will be multiplied by its weighting factor, and then all products will be summed to arrive at a total environmental cost number. This system has been applied to nuclear reactor site selection.

U.S. Army Engineer District, Tulsa, Corps of Engineers: This methodology can be considered a weighting-scaling checklist although a display matrix is used to summarize and compare the impacts of project alternatives. The approach was developed to deal specifically with reservoir construction projects but could be readily adapted to other project types. This methodology was one of 8 methodologies identified in the interim WRAM report (Feb., 1977).

Potential impacts are identified within three broad objectives: environmental quality, human life quality, and economics. For each impact type identified, a series of factors is described, indicating possible measurable indicators. Impact magnitude is not measured in physical units but by a relative impact system. A score of zero is assigned to the future state of an environmental characteristic without the project; plus five is assigned to the project alternative possessing the greatest positive impact on that characteristic; minus five is given to the alternative exhibiting the greatest negative impact, and all other alternatives are assigned scores between zero and $\pm$ five by comparison. The raw scores thus

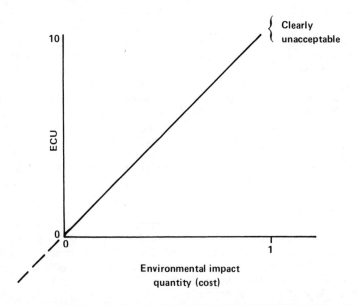

FIGURE 4:   CONCEPT OF VALUE FUNCTION RELATIONSHIP USED IN
            RAINES (1972)

obtained are multiplied by weights determined subjectively by
the impact analysis team. Like the Georgia optimum pathway
matrix approach, the Tulsa methodology tests for the significance of differences between alternatives by introducing error
factors and conducting repeated computer runs.

Wenger and Rhyner: A method is presented which incorporates environmental, social and engineering factors into the
selection of a solid waste system from among several alternatives. The methodology is basically a weighting-scaling
checklist. A stochastic procedure takes account of the inherent uncertainty in the quantitative values assigned to subjective criteria (weighting) and for the uncertainty in impact
values (scaling). This method is similar in concept to the
Odum optimum pathway matrix. It is relevant for consideration
in conjunction with the WRAM methodology due to the way it
deals with uncertainty in weighting and scaling.

RESULTS OF 1974 PERIOD

A total of 31 references were reviewed from the 1974, with
the references listed in Table 15. Table 16 contains a summary
of the methodologies/technologies (M/T's) reviewed relative to
the 12 entrance criteria in Table 2. Fifteen M/T's did not
meet any entrance criteria and thus were eliminated from further study. The fifteen were Agency for International Development, Bennington and Lubore and Pfeffer, Brown, Colston, Curran
Associates, Dickert, Dunst and others, Environmental Protection
Agency, Graf-Webster and Lubore and Pfeffer, Heuting, Peterson
and Gemmell and Schofer, Ross and Spencer and Peterson, U.S.
Bureau of Outdoor Recreation, Viohl and Mason, and Zirkle.
Of the 16 M/T's that met one criterion or more, the following
represents the number meeting the stated criteria:
1. Interdisciplinary team --- 1
2. Assessment variables --- 6
3. Field studies --- 0
4. Impact identification --- 6
5. Prediction of changes --- 3
6. Critical impacts --- 0
7. Relative importance weights --- 6
8. Scaling or ranking procedures --- 7
9. Impact summarization and assessment --- 8
10. Documentation --- 1
11. Public participation --- 4
12. Conflict management and resolution --- 0
The salient features of the 16 M/T's meeting one or more
entrance criteria are summarized in Table 17. The advantages
and limitations of each of the identified features are summarized
in Appendix C along with general information on each of the 16
pertinent M/T's. The reproducibility of each M/T was difficult
to evaluate since the references represented single uses.

89

TABLE 15: LIST OF METHODOLOGIES AND TECHNOLOGIES
REVIEWED FROM THE 1974 PERIOD

1. Adkins, W. G. and Burke, Jr., D., "Social, Economic, and
    Environmental Factors in Highway Decision Making",
    Research Report 148-4, 1974, Texas Transportation Insti-
    tute, Texas A and M University, College Station, Texas
    (report prepared for Texas Highway Department in coopera-
    tion with the Federal Highway Administration, U.S. Depart-
    ment of Transportation, Washington, D. C.)

2. Agency for International Development, "Environmental
    Assessment Guidelines Manual", September 1974, Agency for
    International Development, Department of State, Washington,
    D. C.

3. Alabama Development Office, State Planning Office,
    "Environmental Impact Assessment by Use of Matrix
    Diagram", June 1974, 10 pp., Montgomery, Alabama.

4. Alden, H. R., "Environmental Impact Assessment: A Pro-
    cedure for Coordinating and Organizing Environmental
    Planning", Technical Publication No. 10, December 1974,
    32 pages, Thorne Ecological Institute, Boulder, Colorado.

5. Battelle-Columbus Laboratories, "A Methodology for Assess-
    ing Environmental, Economic, and Social Effects of Dredge
    Spoil Disposal on Marsh and Upland Areas", Draft report,
    1974, Battelle-Columbus Laboratories, Columbus, Ohio
    (report prepared for U.S. Army Engineer Waterways Experi-
    ment Station, Corps of Engineers, Vicksburg, Mississippi).

6. Battelle-Pacific Northwest Laboratories, "Columbia River
    and Tributaries--Environmental Assessment Manual," May
    1974, 429 pages, Richland, Washington (prepared for North
    Pacific Division, U.S. Army Corps of Engineers, Portland,
    Oregon).

7. Bender, M. and Ahmed, S. B., "Index of the Composite
    Environment (ICE): A Basis for Evaluating Environmental
    Effects of Electric Power Generating Plants in Response
    to NEPA", Report No. ORNL TM-4492, Feb. 1974, 77 pages,
    Oak Ridge National Laboratory, Oak Ridge, Tennessee.

8. Bennington, G., Lubore, S., and Pfeffer, J., "Resource and
    Land Investigations (RALI) Program: Methodologies for
    Environmental Analysis, Vol. I, Environmental Assessment",
    MTR-6740, Vol. I, Aug. 1974, The MITRE Corporation, McLean,
    Virginia (report prepared for U.S. Geological Survey,
    Raston, Virginia).

9. Brown, P. J., "Toward a Technique for Quantifying Aesthetic Quality of Water Resources", Report on Contract No. DACW 31-72-C-0060, Oct. 1974, 100 pages, Institute for Water Resources, Fort Belvoir, Va. (prepared for IWP by Utah State University, Logan, Utah).

10. Burnham, J. B., "A Technique for Environmental Decision Making Using Quantified Social and Aesthetic Values", Report No. BNWL-1787, Feb. 1974, Battelle Pacific Northwest Laboratories, Richland, Washington.

11. Colston, Jr., N. V., "Characterization and Treatment of Urban Land Runoff", EPA-670/2-74-096, Dec. 1974, 170 pages, National Environmental Research Center, Environmental Protection Agency, Cincinnati, Ohio.

12. Curran Associates, Inc., Evaluation of Power Facilities: A Reviewer's Handbook, April 1974, 392 pages, U.S. Department of Housing and Urban Development, Washington, D. C., (prepared for HUD by Curran Associates, Inc., Northhampton, Mass.)

13. Dickert, T. G., "Methods for Environmental Impact Assessment: A Comparison", in Dickert, T. G. and Domeny, K. R. (editors), "Environmental Impact Assessment: Guidelines and Commentary", 1974, University Extension, University of California at Berkeley, Berkeley, California.

14. Dunst, R. C. et al., "Survey of Lake Rehabilitation Techniques and Experiences", Tech. Bulletin-75, 1974, 183 pages, Wisconsin Department of Natural Resources, Madison, Wisconsin.

15. Environmental Protection Agency, "Water Quality Management Planning for Urban Runoff", EPA 440/9-75-004, Dec. 1974, 220 pages, Washington, D. C.

16. Graf-Webster, E., Lubore, S., and Pfeffer, J., "Resource and Land Investigations (RALI) Program: Methodologies for Environmental Analysis, Vol. II, Utility Corridor Selection", MTR-6740, Vol. II, Aug. 1974, The MITRE Corporation, McLean, Virginia (report prepared for U.S. Geological Survey, Raston, Virginia).

17. Heuting, R., "A Statistical System for Estimating the Deterioration of the Human Environment", in J. W. Pratt (ed.), Statistical and Mathematical Aspects of Pollution Problems, 1974, Marcel Dekker, Inc., New York, New York, pp. 123-132.

18. Jain, R. K., Urban, L. V., and Stacey, G. S., "Handbook for Environmental Impact Analysis", April 1974, Construction Engineering Research Laboratory, Department of the Army, Champaign, Illinois.

19. Kruzic, P. G., "Cross-Impact Simulation in Water Resource Planning", November 1974, 28 pages, Stanford Research Institute, Menlo Park, California (prepared for U.S. Army Institute for Water Resources, Fort Belvoir, Virginia).

20. Pendse, D. and Wyckoff, J. B., "A Systematic Evaluation of Environmental Perceptions, Optimum Preferences, and Trade-Off Values in Water Resource Analysis", Sept. 1974, 86 pages, Department of Agricultural Economics, Oregon State University, Corvallis, Oregon (prepared for Office of Water Research and Technology, Massachusetts University, Amherst, Massachusetts).

21. Peterson, G. L., Gemmell, R. S., and Schofer, J. L., "Assessment of Environmental Impacts--Multidisciplinary Judgments of Large-Scale Projects", Ekistics, 218, January 1974, pages 23-30.

22. Ross, P. J., Spencer, B. G., and Peterson, Jr., J. H., "Public Participation in Water Resources Planning and Decision-Making Through Information-Education Programs: A State-of-the-Art Study", 1974, 54 pages, Water Resources Research Institute, Mississippi State University State College, Mississippi.

23. Salomon, S. N., "Cost-Benefit Methodology for the Selection of a Nuclear Power Plant Cooling System", paper presented at the Energy Forum, 1974 Spring Meeting of the American Physical Society, Washington, D. C., April 22, 1974.

24. Schaenman, P. S. and Muller, T., "Measuring Impacts of Land Development", URI 86000, November 1974, 93 pages, The Urban Institute, Washington, D. C.

25. School of Civil Engineering and Environmental Science and Oklahoma Biological Survey, "Mid-Arkansas River Basin Study--Effects Assessment of Alternative Navigation Routes from Tulsa, Oklahoma to Vicinity of Wichita, Kansas", June 1974, 555 pages, University of Oklahoma, Norman, Oklahoma (report prepared for U.S. Army Engineer District, Tulsa, Corps of Engineers).

26. Smith, M. A., "Field Test of an Environmental Impact Assessment Methodology", Report ERC-1574, Aug. 1974, Environmental Resources Center, Georgia Institute of Technology, Atlanta, Georgia.

27. U.S. Bureau of Outdoor Recreation, "Handbook: Applications of Remote Sensing and Computer Techniques for Recreation Planning", Vols. 1, 2, 3, and 4, March 1974, Bureau of Outdoor Recreation, Washington, D. C. (report prepared for BOR by University of Wisconsin, Madison, Wisconsin).

28. Utah Water Research Laboratory, "Water Resources Planning Social Goals, and Indicators: Methodological Development and Empirical Test", PRWG-131-1, December 1974, 267 pages, Utah State University, Logan, Utah (prepared for Office of Water Research and Technology, Washington, D. C.).

29. Viohl, Jr., R. C. and Mason, K. G. M., "Environmental Impact Assessment Methodologies: An Annotated Bibliography", Exchange Bibliography 691, November 1974, Council of Planning Librarians, Monticello, Illinois.

30. Warner, M. L. et al., "An Assessment Methodology for the Environmental Impact of Water Resource Projects", Report No. EPA-600/5-74-016, July 1974, Battelle-Columbus Laboratories, Columbus, Ohio (report prepared for Office of Research and Development, U.S. Environmental Protection Agency, Washington, D. C.).

31. Zirkle, J. D., "State of the Art Highway Related Water Quality", June 1974, 13 pages, Washington State Department of Highways, Olympia, Washington.

Table 18 summarizes the conclusions regarding the 16 pertinent references from the 1974 period. Eight references contain potentially useable information for WRAM, and 8 serve as general references. Useable information from the 8 references is as follows:

Battelle-Columbus Laboratories: This methodology is one of 8 methodologies described in the interim WRAM report (February 1977). The primary orientation of this descriptive checklist methodology is toward dredging projects. The methodology includes 84 assessment variables, with 18 in the physical-chemical category, 16 in the ecological category, 16 in the aesthetic category, 19 in the economic category and 15 in the social category. The variables are well described in terms of measurement units and evaluation. Information is

TABLE 16: SUMMARY OF 1974 METHODOLOGIES/TECHNOLOGIES RELATIVE TO ENTRANCE CRITERIA

Criteria	Methodology/Technology																														
	1	2	3	4	5	6	7	8	9	10	11	12	13	14	15	16	17	18	19	20	21	22	23	24	25	26	27	28	29	30	31
No entrance criteria set	X										X	X	X	X	X	X	X				X	X						X	X		X
Twelve entrance criteria																															
1. Interdisciplinary team			X																												
2. Assessment variables					X	X												X						X	X					X	
3. Field studies																															
4. Impact identification					X			X										X	X					X						X	
5. Prediction of changes					X															X										X	
6. Critical impacts																															
7. Relative importance weights										X										X			X	X	X	X					
8. Scaling or ranking procedures			X	X						X													X	X	X						
9. Impact summarization and assessment			X	X		X	X			X																					
10. Documentation			X																	X											
11. Public participation			X							X																	X				
12. Conflict management and resolution																															

94

TABLE 17:   SALIENT FEATURES OF 1974
METHODOLOGIES/TECHNOLOGIES

Methodology/Technology	Feature
Adkins and Burke	Scaling checklist with algebraic additions of scaled impacts.
Alabama Development Office	Good ideas for use of simple interaction matrix.
Alden	Ranking checklist; inclusion of descriptive information on ecological relationships.
Battelle-Columbus Laboratories	Good descriptive checklist for dredging projects; some impact prediction information is included.
Battelle-Pacific Northwest Laboratories	Good descriptive checklist. Good discussion of numerical versus subjective approaches in environmental impact assessment.
Bender and Ahmed	Concept of relating an index of the composite environment (ICE) to economic differences between alternatives.
Burnham	Public involvement in assigning importance weights to decision factors. Procedure for systematically addressing the aesthetic features of an area.
Jain, Urban, and Stacey	Good listing of assessment variables for military activities.
Kruzic	Cross-impact matrix for impact identification and prediction; similar in concept to stepped matrix.
Pendse and Wyckoff	A public participation study is described.

| Salomon | Weighting scaling checklist; relative scaling based on a reference alternative is used. |

Schaenman and Muller — Good listing of variables and their associated measurement units for many relevant items in the SWB and RD accounts.

School of Civil Engineering and Environmental Science and Oklahoma Biological Survey — Weighting-scaling checklist, which is similar in concept to the Battelle Environmental Evaluation System; an error team is included to account for subjective misjudgments.

Smith — Weighting-scaling checklist for a rapid transit system.

Utah Water Research Laboratory — Assignment of relative importance weights through public participation is described.

Warner et al. — Good descriptive checklist for reservoir projects; Information is provided on the technical aspects of prediction of water quality and ecological impacts.

TABLE 18: SUMMARY OF CONCLUSIONS REGARDING PERTINENT REFERENCES FROM 1974 PERIOD

Potentially Useable in WRAM	General Reference for WRAM
Battelle-Columbus Laboratories	Adkins and Burke
Battelle-Pacific Northwest Laboratories	Alabama Development Office
	Alden
	Bender and Ahmed
Kruzic	Burnham
Salomon	Jain, Urban, and Stacey
Schaenman and Muller	Pendse and Wyckoff
School of Civil Engineering and Environmental Science and Oklahoma Biological Survey	Utah Water Research Laboratory
Smith	
Warner et al.	

provided on the technical aspects of impact prediction for many of the 84 assessment variables.

Battelle-Pacific Northwest Laboratories: This report contains a review of environmental assessment methodologies and a good comparison of the advantages and limitations of numerical and subjective approaches. The desirable characteristics of a methodology include that it be comprehensive, concise, understandable, versatile, accurate and economical.

A numerical comparison of environmental effects consists, in general, of

- determining the actual effects for each alternative;

- converting the magnitude of each effect into a numerical value selected from an arbitrary scale of numbers designed to cover all magnitudes from zero to the maximum possible (e.g., a value of 0 might mean no effect, a value of 10 might mean maximum possible effect);

- selecting a second number from another arbitrary scale designed to describe the importance of each type of effect in comparison to all other types of effect (e.g., an effect on salmon might be given a value of 1.0 and an effect on golden eagles might be given a value of 8.0 because it is an endangered species);

- multiplying and/or adding these "magnitude" and "importance" factors to obtain a numerical value indicating the overall merit of each effect; and

- adding the "merit" factors for an alternative to obtain a total numerical value for that alternative. The total numerical values for the several alternatives then are compared to determine which is the best alternative.

A subjective comparison of environmental effects consists of:

- determining the actual effects for each alternative

- converting the effects to common units, if such a method of conversion is available

- comparing subjectively the overall effects of the various alternatives to determine their relative ranking

The advantages and disadvantages of numerical and subjective approaches are summarized in Table 19. Following consideration of these comparisons, the Battelle-Pacific Northwest Laboratories developed a primarily subjective methodology for

TABLE 19: COMPARISON OF NUMERICAL AND SUBJECTIVE ASSESSMENT
METHODS--AFTER BATTELLE-PACIFIC
NORTHWEST LABORATORIES (1974)

Method	Advantages	Disadvantages
Subjective	Simple	Lack of uniformity in subjective analyses
	Results and reasoning processes easily understood	Possible non-uniform consideration of the various types of environmental effects
	Non-rigid procedure permits easy adaption to any size evaluation	
Numerical	Assured uniformity of application and analytical procedures	Higher costs
		Large potential for double counting
	Assured consideration of all identified environmental parameters	Possibility of structured conclusions
		Difficult for public to understand reasoning and results
		Lack of uniformity in subjective analyses

for use in the Columbia River drainage basin. The methodology
uses a matrix to identify potential impacts and generate a
descriptive checklist. An extensive bibliography is included
for specific assessment criteria, data collection, and ata
sources in the Columbia River and Tributaries area.
    Kruzic: KSIM is a simulation procedure for structuring
and analyzing relationships among broadly defined variables
in large socio-economic systems. It was originally developed
to allow decision makers to (1) accommodate a mix of hard data
and intuitive judgment and (2) test alternative planning options
efficiently by:

    - exploring how a range of likely futures may shape a
      plan or, in turn, be subsequently modified by a plan

    - examining how various changes, such as in public
      preference, could affect plans.

The steps in the KSIM procedure are depicted in Figure 5. The key step is the cross-impact matrix to identify the impact of one variable upon another. The variable labels are listed as row and column headings of a table. A basic assumption is that when one variable changes, a second variable may be completely unaffected, or may be encouraged or inhibited. To show this, during the initial phase of KSIM the variables are assigned cross-impact values of (0) for unrelated, (+) for encouraged, or (-) for inhibited. Completing the cross-impact matrix in this way provides the initial structure for the model. Refinements are made by assigning numerical values to these preliminary cross-impact estimates.

In summary, KSIM can be especially helpful in first stage planning, in identifying needs, and in articulating planning objectives. KSIM is also valuable as a future oriented, quantitative technique to display the implications of individual attitudes, orientations, and perceptions of an issue or project at hand.

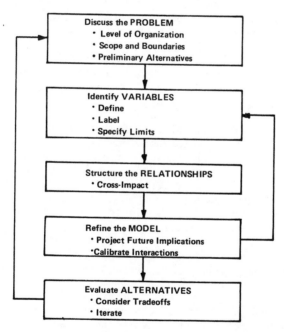

FIGURE 5: STEPS IN THE KSIM PROCEDURE (After Kruzic, 1974)

Salomon: A weighting-scaling checklist methodology is described which will aid in selecting cooling systems for proposed nuclear power plants. Thirteen external socio-economic impacts (consumptive water use, impacts on aquatic life from the intake and discharge of water---this includes mechanical and thermal impacts, environmental costs of chemical pollutants, land requirements and land use impacts, recreation, aesthetics, noise, fogging and other meteorological effects, beneficial uses of heat, materials used, power penalty from loss in efficiency and operation, energy requirements for operation, and uncertainty due to technological innovation) and four direct economic factors (capital costs, annual operation and maintenance, value of lost power per year, and present worth of generating costs) were used in the decision-making process. Information on five alternatives (natural draft towers, wet-dry mechanical draft towers, spray canal, cooling pond, and once-through systems) was assembled for each decision factor.

Usage of the methodology for a particular site involves the assignment of relative weighting factors to each of the 13 external socio-economic impacts. A total of 100 weighting points are divided among the 13 impacts, although no technique for accomplishing this step is described in the Salomon report.

In order to determine scale values a reference cooling system is used. The mechanical draft evaporative cooling tower system was chosen as a reference because the EPA considered this technology as being "the best practicable control technology currently available" relative to PL 92-500. For each external socio-economic impact, an appraisal is made which compares the reference system to the alternative. For a comparative appraisal the following scale values are utilized: very superior (+8), superior (+4), moderately superior (+2), marginally superior (+1), no difference (0), marginally inferior (-1), moderately inferior (-2), inferior (-4), and very inferior (-8).

The final step in the methodology is to multiply the weight factor by the impact scale factor for each of the alternative cooling systems. After the results are summed, the selection of the system with the least impact is made on the basis of the system which has the smallest number. By a comparison with the costs the sum of the external socio-economic impacts can be balanced against the generating cost in arriving at a final decision on which system to choose. This methodology has been used at the site of a large nuclear power plant on Lake Michigan.

Schaenman and Muller: This report outlines an approach to estimating the impacts of land development on a local jurisdiction. The methodology is a descriptive checklist containing 48 factors and indicated units of measurement for each. Four factors deal with local economy, 8 with the natural environment, 4 with aesthetics and cultural values, 22 with public and private services, and 10 with housing and social conditions. The majority of the factors would be associated with the SWB and RD accounts in water resources development projects.

School of Civil Engineering and Environmental Science and Oklahoma Biological Survey: A weighting-scaling checklist methodology was used to evaluate the environmental impacts of 9 alternatives (8 waterway locational routes and the no-action

100

alternative) for extending waterway navigation from Tulsa to Wichita. A total of 102 assessment variables grouped into 6 categories (biology, physical/chemical, regional compatibility, archaeology, aesthetics and climatology) were used. A total of 1000 importance points were distributed to the categories and variables through use of the ranked pairwise comparison technique. Impact scaling was accomplished through the use of functional curves similar in concept to those in the Battelle Environmental Evaluation System (Dee et al., 1972). These functional curves allowed the conversion of information on assessment variables into an environmental quality scale. Composite scores for each alternative were developed by summing the products of the importance points and scale values. A stochastically selected error term was included so as to allow the importance weights to vary by ± 50%. This concept is similar to that used by Odum et al. (1971). The entire methodology was computerized to allow for ease of calculation and the conduction of a sensitivity analysis.

Smith: This weighting-scaling methodology was originally developed for the Georgia Department of Transportation by Battelle-Columbus Laboratories, Columbus, Ohio. The method is similar to the Battelle Environmental Evaluation System (Dee et al., 1972). Smith applied the method to a rapid transit system project in Atlanta. A total of 68 factors are included and grouped into ecological, physical/chemical, aesthetic, and human interest "categories". Functional curves are used and 1000 importance weights (Environmental Quality Units) are assigned to the 68 factors. The Delphi technique was employed to reach a consensus on the optimum distribution of the 1000 units among the factors.

Warner et al.: This methodology was one of 8 methodologies described in the interim WRAM report (February, 1977). This report presents materials intended for use by reviewers of environmental impact statements (EIS's) on major water reservoir projects. The report is prepared as a series of six related but individually referenced discussions of the following major topics:

- reservoir project planning, construction, and operation activities
- water quality impacts of reservoir construction
- ecological impacts of reservoir construction
- economic, social, and aesthetic impacts of reservoir construction
- review criteria for assessing general statement completeness and accuracy
- a review of impact assessment methodologies.

The section on water quality impacts presents a detailed comparison of mathematical models for predicting impacts on water temperature, dissolved oxygen levels, and some chemical constituents of surface waters. The sections dealing with water quality, ecological, and economic-social-aesthetic impacts include extensive citations to relevant literature the impact statement reviewer may wish to consult for further information.

As a part of the review of methodologies for environmental impact assessment, 67 statements were examined for the methodologies used. The statements were distributed as follows: Bureau of Reclamation 15, Army Corps of Engineers 22, Tennessee Valley Authority 14, Soil Conservation Service 13, and Federal Power Commission 3. None of the statements examined employed any identifiable systems of impact assessment. Without exception, the statements utilized techniques that must be characterized as ad hoc, or less frequently, simple checklists.

RESULTS OF 1975 PERIOD

A total of 41 references on methodologies technologies (M/T's) were reviewed from this period, with the references listed in Table 20. Table 21 contains a summary of the M/T's reviewed relative to the 12 entrance criteria in Table 2. Fourteen M/T's did not meet any entrance criteria and thus were eliminated from further study. The fourteen were Bascom and others, Burchell and Listokin, Corwin, Eisler and Wapner, Hellstrom, Jain and Drobny and Chatterjee, Jain and Urban (the 19 methods reviewed by Jain and Urban are covered elsewhere in this report), Lehman, Markley and Bagley, Rote and Wangen, Shaheen, Smith, U.S. Department of Transportation, and Welsh. Of the 27 M/T's that met one criterion or more, the following represents the number meeting the stated criteria:

1. Interdisciplinary team --- 0
2. Assessment variables --- 6
3. Field studies --- 0
4. Impact identification --- 6
5. Prediction of changes --- 19
6. Critical impacts --- 0
7. Relative importance weights --- 4
8. Scaling or ranking procedures --- 5
9. Impact summarization and assessment --- 6
10. Documentation --- 0
11. Public participation --- 1
12. Conflict management and resolution --- 1

The salient features of the 27 M/T's meeting one or more entrance criteria are summarized in Table 22. The advantages and limitations of each of the identified features are summarized in Appendix D along with general information on each of the 27 references. The reproducibility of each M/T was difficult to evaluate since the references represented single uses.

TABLE 20: LIST OF METHODOLOGIES AND TECHNOLOGIES REVIEWED
FROM THE 1975 PERIOD

---

1. Bascom, S. E. et al., "Secondary Impacts of Transportation
   and Wastewater Investments: Research Results", EPA/600/
   5/75-013, July 1975, 225 pages, U.S. Environmental Protection Agency, Washington, D. C. (prepared for EPA by
   Environmental Impact Center, Inc., Newton, Mass.).

2. Bella, D. A., "Tidal Flats in Estuarine Water Quality
   Analysis", EPA/660/3-75/025, June 1975, 200 pages, National
   Environmental Research Center, U.S. Environmental Protec-
   tion Agency, Corvallis, Oregon (prepared for EPA by Dept.
   of Civil Engineering, Oregon State University, Corvallis,
   Oregon).

3. Bhutani, J. et al., "Impacts of Hydrologic Modification
   on Water Quality", EPA-600/2-75-007, April 1975, U.S.
   Environmental Protection Agency, Washington, D. C.

4. Bishop, A. B., "Structuring Communications Programs for
   Public Participation in Water Resources Planning", IWR
   Contract Report 75-2, May 1975, 125 pages, U.S. Army
   Engineer Institute for Water Resources, Fort Belvoir,
   Virginia (prepared for IWR by Utah State University,
   Logan, Utah).

5. Burchell, R. W. and Listokin, D., "The Environmental
   Impact Handbook", 1975, Center for Urban Policy Research,
   Rutgers - The State University of New Jersey, New Brunswick,
   New Jersey.

6. Carstea, D. et al., "Guidelines for the Environmental
   Impact Assessment of Small Structures and Related Activities in Coastal Bodies of Water", MTR-6916, Rev. 1, August
   1975, The MITRE Corporation, McLean, Virginia (prepared
   for U.S. Army Corps of Engineers, New York District).

7. Christensen, S. W., Van Winkle, W. and Mattice, J. S.,
   "Defining and Determining the Significance of Impacts--
   Concepts and Methods", 1975, 71 pages, Oak Ridge National
   Laboratory, Oak Ridge, Tennessee.

8. Clark, J. R., "Environmental Assessment of Construction
   Activities", Unpublished MS Thesis, 1975, 192 pages,
   School of Civil Engineering and Environmental Science,
   University of Oklahoma, Norman, Oklahoma.

9. Corwin, R. et al., Environmental Impact Assessment, 1975, 277 pages, Freeman, Cooper and Company, San Francisco, California.

10. Dee, N. et al., "An Assessment of the Usage of Environmental Assessment Methodologies in Environmental Impact Statements", DMG-DRS Journal (published by Design Methods Group, University of California, Berkeley, California), Vol. 9, No. 1, March 1975.

11. Eisler, R. and Wapner, M., "Second Annotated Bibliography on Biological Effects of Metals in Aquatic Environments", EPA-600/3-75-008, October 1975, 399 pages, Environmental Research Laboratory, U.S. Environmental Protection Agency, Narragansett, Rhode Island.

12. Fitzsimmons, S. J., Stuart, L. I., and Wolff, P. C., "Social Assessment Manual--A Guide to the Preparation of the Social Well-Being Account", July 1975, 279 pages, Bureau of Reclamation, Denver, Colorado (prepared for Bureau of Reclamation by Abt Associates, Inc., Cambridge, Mass.).

13. Fuhriman, D. K. et al., "Water Quality Effect of Diking a Shallow Arid-Region Lake", EPA/660/2-75-007, April 1975, 243 pages, Brigham Young University, Provo, Utah.

14. Gann, D. A., "Thermal Reduction of Municipal Solid Waste", 1975, 91 pages, Master's Thesis, School of Civil Engineering and Environmental Science, University of Oklahoma, Norman, Oklahoma.

15. Harkness, T., "Visual Analysis Techniques: Outfitting Your Tool Box", Proceedings of Conference on Environmental Impact Analysis: Current Methodologies, Future Directions, University of Illinois, Urbana-Champaign, Illinois, 1975.

16. Haven, K. F., "A Methodology for Impact Assessment in the Estuarine/Marine Environment", UCRL-51949, October 1975, 43 pages, Lawrence Livermore Laboratory, Livermore, Cal. (prepared for U.S. Energy Research and Development Administration, Washington, D. C.)

17. Hellstrom, D. I., "A Methodology for Preparing Environmental Statements", AFCEC-TR-75-28, August 1975, 217 pages, U.S. Air Force Civil Engineering Center, Tyndall Air Force Base, Florida (prepared for U.S. Air Force by A. D. Little, Inc. of Cambridge, Massachusetts).

18. Hornberger, G. M., Kelly, M. G., and Lederman, T. C., "Evaluating a Mathematical Model for Predicting Lake Eutrophication", VPI-WRRC-Bull.-82, Sept. 1975, 102 pages, Water Resources Research Center, Virginia Polytechnic Institute and State University, Blacksburg, Virginia.

19. Jain, R. K., Drobny, N. L., and Chatterjea, S., "Procedures for Reviewing Environmental Impact Assessments and State-ments for Construction Projects", Report No. CERL-TR-E-73, August 19 5, 24 pages, Construction Engineering Research Laboratory, U.S. Army, Champaign, Illinois.

20. Jain, R. K. and Urban, L. V., "A Review and Analysis of Environmental Impact Assessment Methodologies", Report No. CERL-TR-E-69, June 1975, 23 pages, Construction Engineering Research Laboratory, U.S. Army, Champaign, Illinois.

21. Lehmann, E. J., "Preparation and Evaluation of Environ-mental Impact Statements (A Bibliography with Abstracts)," NTIS/PS-75/717, Sept. 1975, National Technical Information Service, Springfield, Virginia.

22. Malone, D. W., "An Introduction to the Application of Interpretive Structural Modeling", in Baldwin, M. M. (editor), Portraits of Complexity: Applications of Systems Methodologies to Societal Problems, 1975, Battelle Memorial Institute, Columbus, Ohio.

23. Markley, O. W. and Bagley, M. D., "Minimum Standards for Quality of Life", Report No. EPA-600/5-75-012, May 1975, U.S. Environmental Protection Agency, Washington, D. C. (report prepared for EPA by Stanford Research Institute, Menlo Park, California).

24. Mitchell, A. et al., "Handbook of Forecasting Techniques", IWR Contract Report 75-7, Dec. 1975, 316 pages, U.S. Army Engineer Institute for Water Resources, Fort Belvoir, Virginia (prepared for IWR by Center for Study of Social Policy, Stanford Research Institute, Menlo Park, California).

25. Morrison, T. H., "Sanitary Landfill Site Selection by the Weighted Rankings Method", 1974, 31 pages, Master's Thesis, School of Civil Engineering and Environmental Science, University of Oklahoma, Norman, Oklahoma.

26. Muller, T., "Fiscal Impacts of Land Development", URI 98000, 1975, 68 pages, The Urban Institute, Washington, D. C.

27. Nelson, K. E. and LaBelle, S. J., "Handbook for the Review of Airport Environmental Impact Statements", ANL/ES-46, July 1975, 159 pp., Argonne National Laboratory, Argonne, Illinois.

28. Rote, D. M. and Wangen, L. E., "A Generalized Air Quality Assessment Model for Air Force Operations", AFWL-TR-74-304, Feb. 1975, 168 pages, Air Force Weapons Laboratory, Kirtland Air Force Base, New Mexico.

29. Schlesinger, B. and Daetz, D., "Development of a Procedure for Forecasting Long-Range Environmental Impacts, Report to the Resource and Land Investigations (RALI) Program, U.S. Geological Survey", Report No. USGS-LI-75-007, August 1975, Department of Industrial Engineering, Stanford University, Stanford, California (report prepared for U.S. Geological Survey, Raston, Virginia).

30. Shaheen, D. G., "Contributions of Urban Roadway Usage to Water Pollution", EPA-ROAP-21 ASY-005, April 1975, 358 pages, Environmental Protection Agency, Washington, D. C.

31. Sharma, R. K., Buffington, J. D., and McFadden, J. T., ed tors, Proceedings of the Conference on the Biological Significance of Environmental Impacts, NR-CONF-002 (Conference held at the University of Michigan, Ann Arbor, Michigan, June 4-6, 1975), U.S. Nuclear Regulatory Commission, Washington, D. C.

32. Smith, M. F., "Environmental and Ecological Effects of Dredging (A Bibliography with Abstracts)", NTIS/PS-75/755, October 1975, National Technical Information Service, Springfield, Virginia.

33. Summers, D. A., Ashworth, C. D., and Feldman-Summers, S., "Judgment Processes and Interpersonal Conflict Related to Societal Problem Solutions", unpublished paper, 1975, Human Affairs Research Center, University of Washington, Seattle, Washington.

34. Thom, G. C. and Ott, W. R., "Air Pollution Indices---A Compendium and Assessment of Indices Used in the United States and Canada", Dec. 1975, 164 pages, Council on Environmental Quality, Washington, D. C.

35. Toussaint, C. R. "A Method for the Determination of Regional Values Associated with the Assessment of Environmental Impacts", 1975, 219 pages, Ph.D. Dissertation, School of Civil Engineering and Environmental Science, University of Oklahoma, Norman, Oklahoma.

36. Troxler, Jr., R. W. and Thackston, E. L., "Effect of Meteorological Variables on Temperature Changes in Flowing Streams", EPA/660/3-75-002, Jan. 1975, 86 pages, Department of Environmental and Water Resources Engineering, Vanderbilt University, Nashville, Tennessee.

37. U.S. Department of the Army, "Handbook for Environmental Impact Analysis", DA Pamphlet No. 200-1, April 1975, 155 pages, Headquarters, Department of the Army, Washington, D. C.

38. U.S. Department of Transportation, "Environmental Assessment Notebook Series", 6 volumes, 1975, U.S. Department of Transportation, Washington, D. C.

39. Vlachos, E. et al., "Social Impact Assessment: An Overview", IWR Paper 75-P7, December 1975, 117 pages, U.S. Army Engineer Institute for Water Resources, Fort Belvoir, Virginia (prepared for IWR by Colorado State University, Fort Collins, Colorado).

40. Voorhees, A. M. and Associates, "Interim Guide for Environmental Assessment: HUD Field Office Edition", June 1975, Washington, D. C. (report prepared for U.S. Department of Housing and Urban Development, Washington, D. C.)

41. Welsh, R. L., "User Manual for the Computer-Aided Environmental Legislative Data System", CERL-TR-E-78, November 1975, 62 pages, Construction Engineering Research Laboratory, U.S. Department of the Army, Champaign, Illinois.

Table 23 summarizes the conclusions regarding the 27 pertinent references from the 1975 period. Thirteen references contain potentially usable information for WRAM and 14 serve as general references. Potential usable information from the 13 references is as follows:

Bishop: This report is directed toward describing methods and techniques for planner-citizen communication which will enhance the level of public participation in the planning process and will permit citizens and planners to work effectively together in arriving at planning decisions which affect multiple local, state, and federal jurisdictions. Specific information is included on public forums (public hearings, public meetings, informal small group meetings, information and coordination seminars, and forums of other agencies or groups), community contacts (operating field offices, local planning visits, and direct community representation), and interactive group methods (workshops, charettes, and special committees). Table 24 summarizes the effectiveness of various communications techniques with various publics.

TABLE 21: SUMMARY OF 1975 METHODOLOGIES/TECHNOLOGIES RELATIVE TO ENTRANCE CRITERIA

METHODOLOGY/TECHNOLOGY*

CRITERIA	1	2	3	4	5	6	7	8	9	10	11	12	13	14	15	16	17	18	19	20	21	22	23	24	25	26	27	28	29	30	31	32	33	34	35	36	37	38	39	40	41
No entrance criteria set	X				X				X		X						X	X	X	X	X		X					X	X	X		X						X			X
Twelve entrance criteria																																									
1. Interdisciplinary team																																									
2. Assessment variables						X						X																													
3. Field studies																																		X		X		X	X	X	
4. Impact identification				X		X																X							X									X		X	
5. Prediction of changes				X	X	X	X	X						X	X			X				X	X			X	X	X	X	X	X					X		X	X	X	
6. Critical impacts																																									
7. Relative importance weights														X								X			X										X						
8. Scaling or ranking procedure												X		X										X											X				X		
9. Impact summarization and assessment									X			X			X																X									X	
10. Documentation																																									
11. Public participation					X																																				
12. Conflict management and resolution																																	X								

*The numbers correspond to those in Table 20.

108

TABLE 22:   SALIENT FEATURES OF 1975 METHODOLOGIES/TECHNOLOGIES

Methodology/Technology	Feature(s)
Bella	Basic information on estuarine benthic systems is presented.
Bhutani et al.	Qualitative discussion of the impacts of water resources projects.
Bishop	Describes features and effectiveness of various public participation techniques.
Carstea et al.	Descriptive checklist for quantifying impacts from small coastal projects.
Christensen, Van Winkle and Mattice	Information is presented on impact prediction and assessment for the biological environment.
Clark	Good discussion of quantifying construction impacts.
Dee et al.	Indicates limitations on use of methodologies.
Fitzsimmons, Stuart, and Wolff	Listing of 389 assessment variables for SWB account.
Fuhriman et al.	Impact prediction method is presented for salt balance in a lake.
Gann	Weighting-scaling checklist using weighted rankings technique is described.
Harkness	Annotated bibliography of visual analysis techniques.
Haven	Contains information on ecosystem models for impact prediction.
Hornberger, Kelly and Lederman	A mathematical model for predicting lake eutrophication is described.

Malone	Technique for impact prediction.
Mitchell et al.	Literature survey on forecasting techniques.
Morrison	Weighting-scaling checklist using weighted rankings technique is described.
Muller	Presentation of fiscal impact prediction technologies.
Nelson and LaBelle	Air quality box model and three stormwater runoff models are described.
Schlesinger and Daetz	Cross-impact matrix procedure for dealing with long-range impacts.
Sharma, Buffington, and McFadden	Good summary of technical and philosophical state-of-the-art of biological impact prediction and assessment.
Summers Ashworth and Feldman-Summers	Study findings indicated that judgmental inconsistency was likely to be a major cause of conflict.
Thom and Ott	Concept of using an empirical index to assess existing air quality and potential impacts.
Toussaint	Weighting and scaling of 14 water pollution parameters was established by the Delphi procedure using two separate groups of 9 experts.
Troxler and Thackston	Mathematical model for stream temperature is presented.
U.S. Department of the Army	Definitions, measurement, and interpretation information is presented on 46 assessment variables (called environmental attributes) primarily associated with EQ account.

| Vlachos et al. | Good listing of potential assessment variables for SWB account. |
| Voorhees and Associates | Scaling checklist with 80 assessment variables. Guidance is provided on the assignment of "letter-scale" values for impacts on the 80 variables. |

TABLE 23: SUMMARY OF CONCLUSIONS REGARDING PERTINENT REFERENCES FROM 1975 PERIOD

Potentially Usable in WRAM	General Reference for WRAM
Bishop	Bella
Carstea et al.	Bhutani et al.
Dee et al.	Christensen, Van Winkle and
Fitzsimmons, Stuart, and	Mattice
Wolff	Clark
Mitchell et al.	Fuhriman et al.
Muller	Gann
Schlesinger and Daetz	Harkness
Sharma, Buffington, and	Haven
McFadden	Hornberger, Kelly and Lederman
Summers, Ashworth, and	Malone
Feldman-Summers	Morrison
Thom and Ott	Nelson and LaBelle
Toussaint	Troxler and Thackston
U.S. Department of the Army	Vlachos et al.
Voorhees and Associates	

Carstea et al.: This methodology was specifically developed for conducting impact assessments for certain projects requiring Section 404 permits. The purpose is to describe the probable environmental impacts (physical, biological, and socio-economic) of representative structures and common activities performed in coastal waters of the northeastern United States. The following actions/projects are addressed: riprap placement; bulk-heads; groins and jetties; piers, dolphins, mooring piles, and ramp construction; dredging (new and maintenance); outfalls, submerged lines and pipes; and aerial crossings. For each of the actions/projects considered, the following areas of environmental impact are summarized: erosion, sedimentation, and deposition; flood heights and drift; water quality; ecology; air quality; noise; safety/navigation; recreation; esthetics; and socio-economics.

This methodology can be defined as a descriptive checklist. Usage involves identification of the type of structure

TABLE 24: VARIOUS "PUBLICS" USING DIFFERENT MEDIA
(AFTER BISHOP, 1975)

Publics	Public Hearings and Meetings	Printed Brochures	Radio Programs and News	TV Programs and News	Newspaper Articles	Magazine Articles	Direct Mail and Newsletters	Motion Picture Film	Slide-Tape Presentation	Telelecture
Individual Citizens	M	L	H	H	H	L	L	M	M	L
Sportsmen Groups	M	M	M	M	M	H	H	H	H	M
Conservation-Environment Groups	M	M	M	M	M	H	H	H	H	M
Farm Organizations	M	M	M	M	M	H	H	M	M	M
Property Owners and Users	M	L	H	H	H	L.	L	M	M	L
Business-Industrial	L	L	M	M	M	M	H	M	M	L
Professional Groups and Organizations	L	L	M	M	M	M	H	M	M	L
Educational Institutions	M	L	L	L	M	M	H	M	M	M
Service Clubs and Civic Organizations	L	L	M	M	M	M	L	H	H	M
Labor Unions	L	L	M	M	M	L	L	M	M	L
State-Local Agencies	H	M	L	L	L	M	H	H	H	H
State-Local Elected Officials	H	M	L	L	L	L	H	H	H	H
Federal Agencies	H	M	L	L	L	L	H	M	M	M
Other Groups and Organizations	H	M	M	M	M	M	H	H	H	M

H = Highly Effective
M = Moderately Effective
L = Least Effective

112

or activity to be considered. Referral is then made to a discussion of the specific activities associated with the typical
structure or activity under consideration.

Dee et al.: In 1975 the authors identified three reasons
for the general non-use of environmental impact assessment
methodologies. The cited reasons were: (1) different perspectives on the role of EIS's held by the methodology developers
and practitioners, (2) the limited direction provided by
administrative guidelines related to EIS implementation, and
(3) the pressures initiated by the political arena. The
authors perceive that methodologies will be incorporated into
the EIS process when they are (1) responsive to the needs of
the preparer, (2) perceived by the EIS actors such as CEQ and
proponent agencies to yield more superior information, and
(3 required by CEQ or the proponent agencies.

Fitzsimmons, Stuart and Wolff: This methodology is basically a scaling checklist for the SWB account in water resources
development projects. The structure of the SWB account is
shown in Table 25, and a total of 389 variables are included.
Assessment of existing or baseline conditions involves comparison of the measured variable with appropriate regional or
national data and assigning a rating as follows: AA---above
average; A---average; and BA---below average.

The authors stress that in order to rate an impact as good
or bad, something must be known about the present-day characteristics of the communities themselves. For example, in one
community, a more urban one, residents value growth highly.
They desire more industry and new people to expand the community
and its capacity to support more services. For this community
the effect of more industrial employment can be rated as quite
positive. In the second community, residents are very rural-
oriented in their values and lifestyles and wish no growth of
this type. From the perspective of this community, the same
impact, the rise in industrial employment, can be rated as a
negative effect. One of the following five values is assigned
to each social effect:
    ++ Very Positive
    + Positive
    0 Neutral
    - Negative
    -- Very Negative
These ratings are not viewed as additive across evaluation
categories. They do, however, provide an important and direct
way of comparing social impacts for the same variable across
plans.

Mitchell et al.: This study for the Corps of Engineers
examined 150 forecasting techniques and selected and discussed
12 basic methods suitable for a wide range of technological,
economic, social and environmental forecasting. The general
characteristics of the 12 methods are compared in Tables 26

113

TABLE 25: STRUCTURE OF THE SOCIAL WELL-BEING ACCOUNT
(AFTER FITZSIMMONS, STUART, AND WOLFF, 1975)

Components	Evaluation Categories
Individual, Personal Effects	Life, Protection, and Safety (A) Health (B) Family and Individual (C) Attitudes (D) Environmental Considerations (E) Other (specify) (F)
Community, Institutional Effects	Demographic (A) Education (B) Government Operations and Services (C) Housing and Neighborhood (D) Law and Justice (E) Social Services (F) Religion (G) Culture (H) Recreation (I) Informal Organization Groups (J) Community and Institutional Viability (K) Other (specify) (L)
Area, Socio-Economic Effects	Employment and Income (A) Welfare and Financial Compensation (B) Communications (C) Transportation (D) Economic Base (E) Planning (F) Construction (G) Other (specify) (H)
National, Emergency Preparedness Effects	Water Supplies (A) Food Production (B) Power Supplies (C) Water Transportation (D) Scarce Fuels (E) Population Dispersion (F) Industrial Dispersion (G) Military Preparedness (H) International Treaty Obligations (I) Other (specify) (J)

Aggregate Social Effects	Quality of Life (A)
	Relative Social Position (B)
	Social Well-Being (C)
	Other (d)

---

through 29. Brief descriptions of the 12 methods are as follows:

1. Trend Extrapolation

Trend extrapolation describes a variety of mathematical methods all of which project future values for a single variable through some process of identifying a relationship valid for the past values of the variables. Although the technique is generally useful for only a single variable, this variable may be highly complex in that it may reflect numerous trends.

2. Pattern Identification

Forecasting methods based on pattern identification seek to recognize a developmental pattern in historical data and to use this often obscure pattern as the basis of forecasting future events. The method is useful both for time-series data, where more direct extrapolating methods do not work, and for interpreting numerous social trends.

3. Probabilistic Forecasting

Many phenomena for which forecasts are needed appear to change randomly within limits. Probabilistic forecasting methods use mathematical models of such phenomena. Numerical odds are assigned to every possible outcome or combination of outcomes. On the basis of such assigned odds, predictive statements are made about the future behavior of the phenomenon studied.

4. Dynamic Models

Dynamic models of complex, nonlinear systems are extremely useful for forecasting futures resulting from interacting events. The simulation model, which is usually numeric, reveals the evolution of systems through time under specified conditions of feed-back. By changing equations or adding interacting trends, a large number of possible futures can be explored in computer runs. Dynamic models are also helpful in gaining qualitative insight into the interactions of system elements.

TABLE 26: TYPE OF FORECAST (AFTER MITCHELL ET AL., 1975)

Nature of Results	Time Series and Projections			Models and Simulations					Qualitative and Holistic			
	Trend Extrap-olation	Pattern Identi-fication	Probabi-listic Fore-casting	Dynamic Models	Cross-Impact Analysis	KSIM	Input-Output Analysis	Policy Capture	Scenarios and Related Methods	Expert-Opinion Methods	Alter-native Futures	Value Fore-casting
Quantitative	X	X	X	X		X	X			X	X	X
Qualitative		X		X	X	X		X	X	X	X	X
Normative		X			X	X		X	X	X	X	X

116

TABLE 27: AREAS OF ANALYSIS (AFTER MITCHELL ET AL., 1975)

Focus of Forecast	Time Series and Projections			Models and Simulations					Qualitative and Holistic			
	Trend Extrapolation	Pattern Identification	Probabilistic Forecasting	Dynamic Models	Cross-Impact Analysis	KSIM	Input-Output Analysis	Policy Capture	Scenarios and Related Methods	Expert-Opinion Methods	Alternative Futures	Value Forecasting
Economic	X	X	X	X			X		X	X	X	
Technological		X	X	X			X		X	X	X	
Social	X	X	X	X	X			X	X	X	X	X
Environmental	X	X	X	X	X	X		X	X	X	X	X
Values		X			X	X		X	X	X	X	X
Institutional					X			X	X	X	X	X

117

TABLE 28: QUALITIES OF FORECASTS (AFTER MITCHELL ET AL., 1975)

Quality of Forecast	Time Series and Projections			Models and Simulations					Qualitative and Holistic			
	Trend Extrap-olation	Pattern Identi-fication	Probabi-listic Fore-casting	Dynamic Models	Cross Impact Analysis	KSIM	Input-Output Analysis	Policy Capture	Scenarios and Related Methods	Expert Opinion Methods	Alter-native Futures	Values Fore-casting
Level of detail (fine, medium, gross)	all	all	all	medium-gross	medium-gross	gross	fine	gross	medium-gross	all	gross	medium-gross
Span of forecast (short, medium, long)	short-medium	medium-long	medium-long	medium-long	medium-long	long	short-medium	medium-long	medium-long	all	medium-long	medium-long
Time to make forecast (days, weeks, months, year)	days	weeks	weeks	months	weeks	weeks	months-years	days	weeks-months	days-weeks	weeks-months	weeks-months
Cost of making forecast (low, medium, costly)	low	medium-costly	medium	costly	low-medium	low-medium	costly	low-medium	medium	low-medium	medium-costly	medium-costly
Number of variables forecast (one, several, many)	one	several-many	several	several	several	several	many	several	many	all	many	many
General understand-ability of forecast (low, medium, high)	high	medium	medium	medium-high	medium-high	medium-high	low	high	high	high	medium-high	medium
Versatility of method (narrow, medium, broad)	all	medium	medium	medium-broad	medium-broad	medium-broad	narrow-medium	broad	broad	broad	broad	narrow
Ease of applying method (easy, medium, difficult)	easy	diffi-cult	diffi-cult	medium-diffi-cult	medium-diffi-cult	medium-diffi-cult	medium-diffi-cult	easy	easy-medium	easy-medium	medium-diffi-cult	medium-diffi-cult
Assistance needed to make forecast (none, routine, sophisticated)	none-routine	routine-sophis-ticated	routine-sophis-ticated	sophis-ticated	none-sophis-ticated	routine-sophis-ticated	sophis-ticated	sophis-ticated	none-sophis-ticated	none-sophis-ticated	none-sophis-ticated	none-routine
Type of comparisons (single events, many events, interactions)	single	single-many	single-many	inter-actions	inter-actions	inter-actions	inter-actions	inter-actions	many-inter-actions	single-many	many-inter-actions	many

TABLE 29: RESOURCES NEEDED TO USE THE TECHNIQUES (AFTER MITCHELL ET AL., 1975)

Type of Resource	Time Series and Projections			Models and Simulations					Qualitative and Holistic			
	Trend Extrapolation	Pattern Identification	Probabilistic Forecasting	Dynamic Models	Cross-Impact Analysis	KSIM	Input-Output Analysis	Policy Capture	Scenarios and Related Methods	Expert-Opinion Methods	Alternative Futures	Values Forecasting
Data												
Historical	X	X	X	X	X	X	X					
Public opinion						X		X				X
Expert opinion				X	X	X		X		X	X	X
Imagination/speculation					X	X	X	X	X	X	X	X
Personnel												
Generalists				X	X	X		X	X		X	
Methodologists				X	X	X	X	X		X		X
Subject experts		X		X	X	X	X	X	X	X	X	X
Mathematicians/statisticians	X	X	X	X		X	X					
Writers/communicators									X			
Literature searchers									X		X	
Computer programmers		X	X	X	X	X	X				X	X
Questionnaire and survey experts										X		X
Physical												
Computers	X	X		X	X	X	X					
Programmable hand calculators	X											
Existing computer programs	X							X				
Statistical packages	X	X	X	X	X	X	X	X				
Data banks	X		X				X					

5. Cross-Impact Analysis

Cross-impact analysis strives to identify interactions among events or developments by specifying how one event will influence the likelihood, timing, and mode of impact of another event in a different but associated field. Cross-impact analysis is used not only to probe primary and secondary effects of a specified event, but to improve forecasts.

6. KSIM

KSIM is a cross-impact simulation technique used to better forecast and assess long-range requirements and impacts of water resource development alternatives. The technique provides a tool to interface broad planning issues with detailed dynamic models so that more effective use can be made of planning resources. Both qualitative and quantitative data can be used-- a unique characteristic. KSIM combines a small group workshop procedure with a mathematical forecasting model and a computer program to generate changes over time in a few significant planning variables.

7. Input-Output Analysis

Input-output (I-0) analysis is a means of interrelating industry inputs and outputs in a single model, showing the consequences to all other sectors of a specified change in one. Different models deal with the nation, with regions, with specific industries, and so on. I-0 analyses are of great value in quantifying changes in a region's or subregion's commodity flows and likely industrialization patterns resulting from specific projects.

8. Policy Capture

"Policy capture" involves building a model that, given the same information the individual has, will accurately reproduce his judgments and hence his "policies". The goal is not simply to predict or reproduce judgments accurately; rather policy capture seeks to generate descriptions of the judgmental behavior that are helpful in identifying characteristic differences between individuals. It is felt that the judgmental process can be described mathematically with a reasonable amount of success.

9. Scenarios and Related Methods

Scenarios and related methods depend upon logical, plausible, and imaginative conjectures that are most properly regarded as descriptions of potential futures rather than as probabilistic forecasts of actual futures. Such methods, like all other qualitative methods, are most often used in conjecturing about complex, little-understood social phenomena for which more rigorous quantitative forecasting methods do not exist.

10. Expert-Opinion Methods

Expert-opinion methods include the use of panels, surveys of intentions and attitudes, and Delphi polls. It is emphasized that the definition of expertise as well as the limits to its use for forecasting purposes can be considered in terms of three aspects: topic, sponsor, and other eventual users of the study's end-product. Expert-opinion methods may be used either for actual forecasts or to make conjectural explorations of potential futures.

11. Alternative Futures

Alternative futures methods of forecasting emphasize what may plausibly happen rather than what is predicted to happen. Study of an array of alternative futures is helpful in setting organizational long-term goals and policies, in charting primary strategies, and in developing contingency plans. It is pointed out that a given potential development may or may not occur; if it occurs, it may happen at any of many different times, and may have any of many different potential impacts. Each unique combination of these and other variables constitutes a different alternative future. The techniques are best adapted to mid- and long-term planning.

12. Values Forecasting

Of all the techniques for looking ahead, values forecasting perhaps holds the greatest promise while to date it has yielded the fewest practical results. People's values (priorities, opinions, attitudes, and so on) are of crucial importance in judging what public actions and policies they will support. Data on these matters can be collected through survey methods. Forecasts of changing values usually involve clustering values into a typology and forecasting on the basis of demographic shifts or broad societal scenarios.

Muller: This report addresses the fiscal impacts of private development. It attempts to answer the question "will the developments generate revenues in excess of needed public expenditures or vice versa?" Fiscal impact techniques applied in studies reviewed range from simple, one-dimensional methods to complex econometric models. The determination of which technique to select depends on study objectives and available resources. Given the limited state of knowledge, the most effective approach is to estimate, directly by the use of surveys or indirectly from secondary sources, the likely demographic and income characteristics of new recipents by type of housing. These data can be applied to estimate both revenues expected to accrue and anticipated demand for public services.

Schlesinger and Daetz: This report presents a procedure for forecasting long-range environmental impacts of large scale projects. The term "long-range" refers to fifteen or more years, and "large scale projects" are major construction, mining, or other industrial or municipal undertakings with significant regional impacts. The procedure entails combining a schedule of primary environmental impacts expected as a result of future activities with a matrix of environmental factor relationships. Each term in this "cross-impact" matrix relates a change in one factor in one year to a change in another factor the following year by a linear multiplier. An extended version of the matrix is proposed that contains additional terms to reflect the impact of several environmental factors changing at the same time. A case study involving strip mining of coal in the northern great plains region of the United States is used to test the procedure's concept and formulation.

Sharma, Buffington, and McFadden: This report contains the proceedings of a 1975 Workshop dealing with the biological significance of environmental impacts. The summary addresses both general and assessment perspectives as follows:

1. GENERAL PERSPECTIVES

    (a) Definition of Biological Significance of Environmental
         Impacts

         The significance of environmental impacts can be defined in a biological as well as in a socio-economic context. In the biological context, those impacts can be termed significant which, on being imposed on naturally occurring changes in the ecosystem, modify the dynamics or hasten succession in the communities. As such, all impacts resulting in measurable changes in indicator parameters of community dynamics and succession (such as abundance, functional integrity, species diversity, etc.) can be termed significant. Therefore, it follows that an impact is significant if it results in a change that is measurable in a statistically sound sampling program and if it persists, or is expected to persist, more than several years at the population, community, or ecosystem level. Costs and benefits to society are taken into consideration when a decision is made as to whether an impact is acceptable or unacceptable in the social context.

122

(b) Objectives and Quality of Information

Despite current emphasis on the ideal of collection of ecological data which are relevant in impact analysis, much of the research and monitoring being carried out today produce data that are only marginally related to the evaluation of expected impacts. More information does not necessarily mean better assessment.

(c) Time Frame and Spatial Constraints

The duration of preoperational and operational studies should reflect the variability of data and expected intensity of response due to impact. More time is needed to get a better pulse of the system where data variability is high. Similarly, more observations are needed to detect low-level chronic impacts as opposed to catastrophic changes. The longer the time frame, the more reliable the decision; however, the time frame and spatial limitations should be decided on a site-by-site basis. Relatively much more effort usually is allocated to data collection than to data interpretation. It is important that adequate time and effort be allocated to the latter, as well.

(d) Role of Statistics

Changes in parameters of less than 50% often may not be detectable. Also, ideal statistical designs are not always applicable to impact-evaluation studies. Care should be exercised in biological interpretation or results obtained from statistical analyses. A clear definition of which parameters are relevant and what studies are necessary to detect changes is needed.

(e) The State-of-the-Art and Standardization of Techniques

In areas such as quantitative sampling gear, interpretation of indicator parameters, and assessment of assimilative capacity of ecosystems, the state-of-the-art needs substantial improvement. In other areas such as characterization of ecosystems, identification of indicator parameters, and design of impact studies, current state-of-the-art is adequate but there is not a high degree of uniformity in the approach.

2. ASSESSMENT PERSPECTIVES

(a) Species Lists and Diversity Indices

Detailed static descriptions of ecosystems such as species lists have very little value in impact assessment; however, they provide a mechanism for crude comparisons of before-and-after situations. The use of indicator species in impact assessment should be encouraged, but additional work is necessary to permit their most efficacious use. Diversity indices should be used with caution; they are not equivalent to an ultimate synthesis of information on the state of a system.

(b) Functional Stability of Communities

Insults to functional integrity of communities are likely to result in significant impacts. Qualitative changes up to a certain extent may not be significant if functional integrity is not impaired; however, it is not then certain how many species can be replaced without risking collapse of a community. Replacement of one fish species by another with similar functional value may be important in a social context because of perceived socio-economic values.

(c) Assimilative Capacity and Compensatory Responses

Assimilative capacity is a function of inertia, resiliency, and elasticity of impacted communities. Inertia is defined as the ability of a community or ecosystem to resist displacement or disequilibrium in regard to either structure or function. Resiliency is defined as the number of times a system can snap back after displacement. And elasticity is defined as an ecosystem's ability to recover following displacement of structure and/or function to a steady state closely approximating the original. Assimilative capacity of a community should be considered and factored into the impact analysis. Compensatory responses may be limited to the species population or may be spread over the community impacted. Compensatory responses are difficult to document on large systems (such as the Great Lakes) and, as such, less, certain generalizations can be included in the analysis, e.g. for a given cohort, impacts at early stages of life history before compensatory mechanisms have a chance to operate are less significant than are impacts at later life-history stages.

(d) Simulation Models

Use of simulation models is important in terms of provision of sharp focus on expected impacts and collection of relevant information in analysis of impacts. The predictive models can evaluate assumptions where no hard data are available, provide synthesis, and predict future impacts. Validity of assumptions used in the models is important. However, what is important biologically is not always mathematically tractable, and long-term predictions can be very unrealistic.

(e) Before v. After, Controlled v. Impacted

All ecosystems are dynamic and change naturally in time. Therefore, any before-and-after comparisons should evaluate changes as being superimposed on naturally occurring changes. Where before-and-after comparisons are not possible, parameter or indicator values at disturbed sites and at similar but undisturbed sites can be compared.

Summers, Ashworth, and Feldman-Summers: This paper describes an application of multidimensional scaling to judgments about potential solutions to the overpopulation problem. The airs of the research were twofold: (a) to identify the manner in which individuals make judgments about the acceptability of potential solutions to the overpopulation problem, and (b) to ascertain the source of conflict (if any) between individuals when making such judgments.

The findings related to interpersonal conflict were in substantial agreement with previous findings--derived from quite different judgment tasks--concerning the components of interpersonal conflict in judgment situations. Specifically, it was found that disagreement between randomly selected pairs was largely the result of inconsistency in the execution of judgment policy, rather than actual policy difference. That is, participants tended to use the dimensions in much the same manner in making their judgments, but failed to do so in a perfectly consistent fashion. Under such conditions, conflict is inevitable--even though participants may hold identical beliefs. These findings suggest that the disputes which arise in connection with proposed solutions to some of our most pressing problems may reflect not only different belief systems, but also our cognitive limitations; i.e., our inability to exercise full control over our judgement policies in complex judgment situations.

Thom and Ott: This report presents the findings of a detailed survey of air pollution indices that are presently utilized or available. Of the 55 metropolitan air pollution control agencies surveyed in the United States, 33 routinely used some form of short-term air quality index. However, it was found that nearly all of the indices had different mathematical formulations and different meanings to the public. In terms of environmental impact assessment air quality indices can be useful for assessing existing conditions and potential impacts.

Toussaint: This study was concerned with a determination of the applicability of a decision-making technique to the value judgment-based decisions inherent in environmental impact assessment. The decision-making technique employed was the Delphi method of estimating. Fourteen water pollution parameters from the Battelle Environmental Evaluation System (Dee et al., 1972) were investigated for the proposed Aubrey Reservoir project in northern Texas. Eighteen environmental experts, from the region established regional values for the two judgment-based decisions currently used in environmental impact assessment. These two decisions were referred to as the weighting (determination of the relative emphasis or degree of importance each parameter is to be assigned in the assessment) and scaling (determination of the magnitude of effect resulting from a change in a parameter measure) process. The Delphi procedure was used to reach a consensus of opinion.

U.S. Department of the Army: This handbook presents recommended procedures for use by Army personnel in the preparation and processing of environmental impact assessments (EIA) and statements (EIS). The methodology basically consists of using an interaction matrix to identify potential impacts and generate a descriptive checklist. Representative Army actions that might have a significant environmental impact are grouped into nine functional areas: construction; operation; maintenance and repair; training; mission change; real estate; procurement; industrial activities; research, development, test and evaluation; and administration and support. Forty-six environmental attributes (assessment variables) are included in the methodology and listed in Table 30. Information is provided on the measurement and interpretation of the 46 attributes along with functional curves where available.

Voorhees and Associates: An extensive scaling checklist approach, which also incorporates the concept of an interaction matrix to identify potential impacts, has been developed for the Department of Housing and Urban Development. Potential projects are subjected to an initial screening for the purpose of directing the evaluators to potential problem areas and highlighting the potential benefits. Higher level tests would be applied only in potential problem areas; in most cases, these tests will demand particular professional expertise. The components and subcomponents of the environment which are included in this methodology are delineated in Table 31. Following the identification of potential impacts, the HUD methodology provides additional information on exactly how to address particular identified impacts. The scaling system consists of the assignment of a letter grade from A(+) to C(-). Specific information is provided on the 80 assessment variables in terms of standards/criteria/guidelines which could serve as the basis for assigning scale values.

TABLE 30: ENVIRONMENTAL ATTRIBUTE LISTING
(AFTER U.S. DEPARTMENT OF THE ARMY, 1975)

Category	No.	Attribute	No.	Attribute
Air	1	Diffusion factor	6	Carbon monoxide
	2	Particulates	7	Photochemical oxidants
	3	Sulphur oxides	8	Hazardous toxicants
	4	Hydrocarbons	9	Odor
	5	Nitrogen oxide		
Water	10	Aquifer safe yield	17	Biochemical oxygen demand
	11	Flow variations	18	Dissolved oxygen (DO)
	12	Oil	19	Dissolved solids
	13	Radioactivity	20	Nutrients
	14	Suspended solids	21	Toxic compounds
	15	Thermal pollution	22	Aquatic life
	16	Acid and alkali	23	Fecal coliform
Land	24	Erosion	26	Land use patterns
	25	Natural hazard		
Ecology	27	Large animals (wild and domestic)	31	Field crops
			32	Threatened species
	28	Predatory birds	33	Natural land vegetation
	29	Small game	34	Aquatic plants
	30	Fish, shell fish, and water fowl		
Sound	35	Physiological effects	38	Performance effects
	36	Psychological effects	39	Social behavior effects
	37	Communication effects		
Human	40	Life styles	42	Physiological systems
	41	Psychological needs	43	Community needs
Economic	44	Regional economic stability	46	Per capita consumption
	45	Public sector revenue		

127

TABLE 31:   COMPONENTS AND SUBCOMPONENTS OF THE ENVIRONMENT
(AFTER VOORHEES AND ASSOCIATES, 1975)

PHYSICAL	SOCIAL
1. Geology	7. Energy
1.1 Unique Features	7.1 Energy Requirements
1.2 Mineral Resources	7.2 Conservation Measures
1.3 Slope Stability/ Rockfall	7.3 Environmental Signi- ficance
1.4 Depth to Impermeable Layers	8. Services
1.5 Subsidence	8.1 Education Facilities
1.6 Consolidation	8.2 Employment
1.7 Weathering/Chemical Release	8.3 Commercial Facilities
1.8 Tectonic Activity/ Vulcanism	8.4 Health Care/Social Services
	8.5 Liquid Waste Disposal
	8.6 Solid Waste Disposal
2. Soils	8.7 Water Supply
2.1 Slope Stability	8.8 Storm Water Drainage
2.2 Foundation Support	8.9 Police
2.3 Shrink-Swell	8.10 Fire
2.4 Frost Susceptibility	8.11 Recreation
2.5 Liquefaction	8.12 Transportation
2.6 Erodibility	8.13 Cultural Facilities
2.7 Permeability	
	9. Safety
3. Special Land Features	9.1 Structures
3.1 Sanitary Landfill	9.2 Materials
3.2 Wetlands	9.3 Site Hazards
3.3 Coastal Zones/ Shorelines	9.4 Circulation Conflicts
3.4 Mine Dumps/Spoil Areas	9.5 Road Safety and Design
3.5 Prime Agricultural Land	9.6 Ionizing Radiation
	10. Physiological Well-Being
4. Water	10.1 Noise
4.1 Hydrologic Balance	10.2 Vibration
4.2 Ground Water	10.3 Odor
4.3 Ground Water Flow Direction	10.4 Light
4.4 Depth to Water Table	10.5 Temperature
4.5 Drainage/Chennel Form	10.6 Disease
4.6 Sedimentation	11. Sense of Community
4.7 Impoundment Leakage and Slope Failure	11.1 Community and Organi- zation
4.8 Flooding	11.2 Homogeneity and Diversity
4.9 Water Quality	

5. Biota
    5.1 Plant and Animal
        Species
    5.2 Vegetative Community
    5.3 Diversity
    5.4 Productivity
    5.5 Nutrient Cycling

6. Climate and Air
    6.1 Macro-Climate Hazards
    6.2 Forest and Range
        Flins
    6.3 Heat Balance
    6.4 Wind Alteration
    6.5 Humidity and Preci-
        pipitation
    6.6 Generation and Dis-
        persion of
        Contaminants
    6.7 Shadow Effects

11.3 Community Stability
     and Physical Char-
     a teristics

12. Psychological Well-Being
     12.1 Physical Threat
     12.2 Crowding
     12.3 Nuisance

13. Visual Quality
     13.1 Visual Content
     13.2 Area and Structure
          Coherence
     13.3 Apparent Access

14. Historic and Cultural
     Resources
     14.1 Historic Structures
     14.2 Archaeological Sites
          and Structures

RESULTS OF 1976 PERIOD

A total of 58 references on methodologies/technologies
(M/T's) were reviewed from this period, with the references
listed in Table 32. Table 33 contains a summary of the M/T's
reviewed relative to the 12 entrance criteria in Table 2.
Sixteen M/T's did not meet any entrance criteria and thus were
eliminated from further study. The sixteen were Allen and
others, Babcock and Nadja, Bayley and others, Bransma and
Divoky, Chow and Yen, Clark and Van Horn, Greer and Blome and
Jones, Hall and Westerdahl and Eley, Kemp, Kibby and Hernandez,
Lincor and Haynes and Klein, Naval Environmental Support Office,
Riggins and Novak, Rosen, Schanche and others, and U.S. Bureau
of Census. Of the 42 methodologies/technologies that met one
criterion or more, the following represents the number meeting
the stated criteria:

1. Interdisciplinary team --- 0
2. Assessment variables --- 9
3. Field studies --- 4
4. Impact identification --- 7
5. Prediction of changes --- 28
6. Critical impacts --- 0
7. Relative importance weights --- 8
8. Scaling or ranking procedures --- 5
9. Impact summarization and assessment --- 13
10. Documentation --- 0
11. Public participation --- 4
12. Conflict management and resolution --- 2

129

TABLE 32: LIST OF METHODOLOGIES AND TECHNOLOGIES
REVIEWED FROM THE 1976 PERIOD

1. Adams, R. T. and Kurisu, F. M., "Simulation of Pesticide Movement on Small Agricultural Watersheds", EPA/600/3-76/066, Sept. 1976, 344 pages, ESL, Inc., Sunnyvale, CA.

2. Allen, H. L. et al., "Public Law 92-500, Water Quality Analysis and Environmental Impact Assessment", NCWQ-75/100-1, April 1976, National Commission on Water Quality, Washington, D. C.

3. Babcock, Jr., L. R. and Nadga, N. L., "Popex--Ranking Air Pollution Sources by Population Exposure", EPA/600/2-76-063, March 1976, 345 pages, University of Illinois Medical Center, Chicago, Illinois.

4. Bayley, S. et al., "Energetics and Systems Modeling: A Framework Study for Energy Evaluation of Alternative Transportation Modes in Comparison with Traditional Economic Evaluation", June 1976, Dept. of Environmental Engineering Sciences, University of Florida, Gainesville, Florida (submitted to U.S. Army Corps of Engineers under Contract DACW 17-75-0075).

5. Boucher, W. I. and Stover, J. G., "An Annotated Bibliography on Cross-Impact Analysis," Report 128-01-14, April 1972 (revised September 1976), The Futures Group, Glastonbury, Connecticut.

6. Brandsma, M. G. and Divoky, D. J., "Development of Models for Prediction of Short-Term Fate of Dredged Material Discharged in the Estuarine Environment", WES-CR-D-76-5, May 1976, 297 pages, Tetra Tech, Inc., Pasadena, California (prepared for Dredged Material Research Program, U.S. Army Engineer Waterways Experiment Station, Vicksburg, Mississippi).

7. Canter, L. W., "Supplement to Facility Plan Report for Houma-Terrebonne Regional Sewerage Facilities", August 1976, 62 pages, report submitted to GST Engineers, Houma, Louisiana.

8. Case, P. J., Edgmon, T. D., and Renton, D. A., "Public A Procedure for Public Involvement", Range Science Series No. 22, June 1976, 138 pp., Range Science Department, Colorado State University, Fort Collins, Colorado.

9. Chase, G. H., "Matrix Techniques in the Evaluation of Environmental Impacts", Ch. 10 in Blissett, M. (editor), "Environmental Impact Assessment", 1976, Engineering Foundation, New York, New York, pp. 131-151.

10. Chow, V. T. and Yen, B. C., "Urban Stormwater Runoff: Determination of Volumes and Flowrates", EPA/600/2-76/116, May 1976, 253 pages, Dept. of Civil Engineering, University of Illinois, Urbana, Illinois.

11. Christensen, K., "Social Impacts of Land Development", URI 15700, Sept. 1976, 144 pages, The Urban Institute, Washington, D. C.

12. Clark, E. M. and Van Horn, A. J., Risk-Benefit Analysis and Public Policy: A Bibliography", BNL-22285, Nov. 1976, 81 pages, Brookhaven National Laboratory, Upton, New York,

13. Clark, R. N., Hendee, J. C., and Stankey, G. H., "Codinvolves A Tool for Analyzing Public Input to Resource Decisions," Ch. 8 (pp. 145-165) in Pierce, J. C. and Doerksen, H. R., Water Politics and Public Involvement, 1976, Ann Arbor Science Publishers, Inc., Ann Arbor, Michigan.

14. Coates (a), J. F., "The Role of Formal Models in Technology Assessment", Technological Forecasting and Social Change, Vol. 9, 1976, pp. 139-190.

15. Coates, J. F., "Some Methods and Techniques for Comprehensive Impact Assessment", Ch. 9 in Blissett, M. (editor), "Environmental Impact Assessment", 1976, Engineering Foundation, New York, New York, pp. 103-130.

16. Colonell, J. M., "Field Evaluation of a Predictive Model for Thermal Stratification in Lakes and Reservoirs", OWRT-B-201-MASS(2), January 1976, 215 pages, Water Resources Research Center, University of Massachusetts, Amherst, Massachusetts.

17. Curran Associates, Inc., "Guidelines for Review of Environmental Impact Statements---Vol. IV, Channelization Projects", July 1976, Northampton, Mass. (submitted to U.S. Environmental Protection Agency, Washington, D. C.)

18. Darnell, R. M. et al., "Impacts of Construction Activities in Wetlands of the United States", EPA-600/3-76-045, April 1976, 392 pages, U.S. Environmental Protection Agency, Washington, D. C. (prepared for EPA by Tereco Corporation, College Station, Texas).

19. Edwards, W., "How to Use Multi-Attribute Utility Measurement for Social Decision Making," SSRI Research Report 76-3, August 1976, 67 pp., Social Science Research Institute, University of Southern California, Los Angeles, California (prepared for Advanced Research Projects Agency, U.S. Department of Defense, Arlington, VA).

20. Engineering Division, Scottish Development Department, "Development of a Water Quality Index", Report No. ARD 3, December 1976, 62 pages, Edinburgh, Scotland.

21. Fennelly, P. F. et al., "Environmental Assessment Perspectives", EPA-600/2-76-069, March 1976, 238 pages, U.S. Environmental Protection Agency, Research Triangle Park, North Carolina (prepared for EPA by GCA Corporation, Bedford, Massachusetts).

22. Greer, K. H., Blome, D. A., and Jones, Jr., J. E., "A Directory of Computerized Environmental Information Resources", IMMR 23-GR3-76, October 1976, 46 pages, Institute for Mining and Minerals Research, University of Kentucky, Lexington, Kentucky.

23. Grimsrud, G. P., Finnemore, E. J., and Owen, H. J., "Evaluation of Water Quality Models: A Management Guide for Planners", EPA/600/5-76/004, July 1976, 186 pages, Systems Control Inc., Palo Alto, California (prepared for EPA by Systems Control, Inc.).

24. Gum, R. L., Roefs, T. G., and Kimball, D. B., "Quantifying Societal Goals: Development of a Weighting Methodology", Water Resources Research, Vol. 12, No. 4, August 1976, pp. 617-622.

25. Hall, R. W., Westerdahl, H. E., and Eley, R. L., "Application of Ecosystem Modeling Methodologies to Dredged Material Research", WES-TR-76-3, June 1976, 72 pages, U.S. Army Engineer Waterways Experiment Station, Vicksburg, Mississippi.

26. Hammond, K. R. and Adelman, L., "Science, Values, and Human Judgment," Science, Vol. 194, October 22, 1976, pp. 389-396.

27. Harrison, E. A., "Bioindicators of Pollution (A Bibliography with Abstracts)", NTIS/PS-76/0868/OWP, November 1976, 194 pages, National Technical Information Service, Springfield, Virginia.

28. Harrison, E. A., "Ecosystem Models, Vol. 2, November 1975-November 1976", NTIS/PS-76/0904, November 1976, National Technical Information Service, Springfield, Virginia.

29. Jain, R. K., Urban, L. V. and Cerchione, A. J., "Handbook for Environmental Impact Analysis", Interim Environmental Planning Bulletin 11, June 1976, U.S. Department of the Air Force, Washington, D. C. (prepared for USAF by the U.S. Army Construction Engineering Research Laboratory, Champaign, Illinois).

30. Jameson, D. L., "Ecosystem Impacts of Urbanization Assessment Methodology", EPA-600/3-76-072, July 1976, 249 pages, Corvallis Environmental Research Laboratory, U.S. Environmental Protection Agency, Corvallis, Oregon (prepared for EPA by the Institute of Ecology, Utah State University, Logan, Utah).

31. Kemp, H. T., "National Inventory of Selected Biological Monitoring Programs, Summary Report of Current or Recently Completed Projects, 1976", ORNL/TM-5792, October 1976, 711 pages, Oak Ridge National Lab., Tenn.

32. Keyes, D. L., "Land Development and the Natural Environment: Estimating Impacts", URI 13500, April 1976, 128 pages, The Urban Institute, Washington, D. C.

33. Kibby, H. and Hernandez, D. J., "Environmental Impacts of Advanced Wastewater Treatment at Ely, Minnesota", EPA-600/3-76-082, August 1976, 30 pages, U.S. Environmental Protection Agency, Corvallis, Oregon.

34. Lehman, E. J., "Water Quality Modeling, Hydrological and Limnological Systems, Vol. 1, 1964-1974 (A Bibliography with Abstracts)", NTIS/PS-76/0443/2ST, June 1976, 197 pages, National Technical Information Service, Springfield, Virginia.

35. Lehmann, E. J., "Water Quality Modeling, Hydrological and Limnological Systems, Vol. 2, 1975-June 1976 (A Bibliography with Abstracts)", NTIS/PS-76/0444/0 ST, June 1976, 103 pages, National Technical Information Service, Springfield, Virginia.

36. Lincor, J. L., Haynes, M. E., and Klein, M. L., "The Ecological Impact of Synthetic Organic Compounds on Estuarine Ecosystems", EPA-600/3-76-075, Sept. 1976, 354 pages, Environmental Research Laboratory, U.S. Environmental Protection Agency, Gulf Breeze, Florida (prepared for EPA by Mote Marine Laboratory, Sarasota, Florida).

133

37. Liu, B. and Yu, E. S., "Physical and Economic Damage Functions for Air Pollutants by Receptors", EPA-600/5-76-011, September 1976, 160 pages, U.S. Environmental Protection Agency, Washington, D. C. (prepared for EPA by Midwest Research Institute, Kansas City, Missouri).

38. Lower Mississippi Valley Division, "A Tentative Habitat Evaluation System (HES) for Water Resources Planning", November 1976, U.S. Army Corps of Engineers, Vicksburg, Mississippi.

39. MacKinnon, W. J. and Anderson, L. M., "The SPAN III Computer Program for Synthesizing Group Decisions: Weighting Participants Judgments in Proportion to Confidence," Behavior Research Methods and Instrumentation, Vol. 8, No. 4, 1976, pp. 409-410.

40. McElroy, A. D. et al., "Loading Functions for Assessment of Water Pollution from Nonpoint Sources", EPA/600/2-76/151, May, 1976, 444 pages, U.S. Environmental Protection Agency, Washington, D. C. (prepared for EPA by Midwest Research Institute, Kansas City, Missouri).

41. Muller, T., "Economic Impacts of Land Development: Employment, Housing, and Property Values", URI 15800, September 1976, 148 pages, The Urban Institute, Washington, D. C.

42. Naval Environmental Support Office, "Data Sources for Environmental Impact Assessments (EIA's) and Environmental Impact Statements (EIS's)", NESO 20.2-015, November 1976, 223 pages, Naval Construction Battalion Center, Port Hueneme, CA (prepared for NESO by ManTech of New Jersey Corporation, San Diego, California).

43. Omernik, J. M., "The Influence of Land Use on Stream Nutrient Levels", EPA-600/3-76-014, Jan. 1976, 105 pages, Corvallis Environmental Research Laboratory, U.S. Environmental Protection Agency, Corvallis, Oregon.

44. Ott, W. R., Proceedings of the EPA Conference on Environmental Modeling and Simulation, Held at Cincinnati, Ohio on April 19-22, 1975, EPA/600/9-76-016, June 1976, 861 pages, Office of Research and Development, U.S. Environmental Protection Agency, Washington, D. C.

45. Reid, G. W., "Research to Develop Ecological Standards for Water Resources", July 1976, 304 pages, Bureau of Water and Environmental Resources Research, University of Oklahoma, Norman, Oklahoma (prepared for U.S. Office of Water Resources Research, Dept. of the Interior, Washington, D. C.)

46. Riggins, R. and Novak, E., "Computer-Aided Environmental Impact Analysis for Mission Change, Operations and Maintenance, and Training Activities: User Manual", CERL-TR-E-85, Feb. 1976, 101 pages, Construction Engineering Research Laboratory, U.S. Dept. of the Army, Champaign, IL.

47. Rosen, S. J., <u>Manual for Environmental Impact Evaluation</u>, Prentice-Hall, Inc., Englewood Cliffs, New Jersey, 1976, 232 pages.

48. Ross, J. H., "The Numeric Weighting of Environmental Interactions," Occasional Paper No. 10, July 1976, Lands Directorate, Environment Canada, Ottawa, Canada.

49. Schaenman, P. S., "Using an Impact Measurement System to Evaluate Land Development", URI 15500, Sept. 1976, 106 pages, The Urban Institute, Washington, D. C.

50. Schanche, G. W. et al., "Pollution Estimation Factors", CERL TR-N-12, Nov. 1976, 26 pages, Construction Engineering Research Laboratory, U.S. Army, Champaign, IL.

51. Springer, M. D., "Research for the Development of Guidelines for Conducting and Analyzing an Environmental Water Quality Study to Determine Statistically Meaningful Results", Pub-37, OWRT-A-033-ARK(1), 1976, 173 pages, Water Resources Research Center, Univ. of Arkansas, Fayetteville, Arkansas.

52. Thornton, K. W. and Lessem, A. S., "Sensitivity Analysis of the Water Quality for River-Reservoir Systems Model", WES-MP-Y-76-4, Sept. 1976, 53 pages, U.S. Army Engineer Waterways Experiment Station, Vicksburg, Mississippi.

53. Thronson, R. E., "Nonpoint Source Control Guidance, Construction Activities", December 1976—122 pages, Office of Water Planning and Standards, Environmental Protection Agency, Washington, D. C.

54. U.S. Bureau of the Census, "Environmental/Socioeconomic Data Sources (Supplement to TAB A-1, Environmental Narrative", October 1976, 169 pages, Subscriber Services Section (Publications) Washington, D. C.

55. U.S. Environmental Protection Agency, "Guidelines for Review of Environmental Impact Statements, Vol. 3, Impoundment Projects", Interim Final Report, July 1976, 147 pages, Washington, D. C. (prepared for EPA by Curran Associates, Inc., Northampton, Mass.)

56. Vlachos, E. and Hendricks, D. W., "Secondary Impacts and Consequences of Highway Projects", DPT/TST-77/24, October 1976, 332 pages, U.S. Department of Transportation, Washington, D. C. (prepared for DOT by Departments of Civil Engineering and Sociology, Colorado State University, Ft. Collins, Colorado).

57. Wakeland, W., "QSIM2: A Low-Budget Heuristic Approach to Modeling and Forecasting," Technological Forecasting and Social Change, Vol. 9, 1976, pp. 213-229.

58. Webster, R. D. et al., "The Economic Impact Forecast System: Description and User Instructions", CERL-TR-N-2, June 1976, 36 pages, Construction Engineering Research Laboratory, U.S. Army, Champaign, Illinois.

The salient features of the 42 M/T's meeting one or more entrance criteria are summarized in Table 34. The advantages and limitations of each of the identified features are summarized in Appendix E along with general information on each of the 42 pertinent M/T's. The reproducibility of each M/T was difficult to evaluate since the reference represented single uses.

Table 35 summarizes the conclusions regarding the 42 pertinent references from the 1976 period. Twenty-five references contain potentially useable information for WRAM and 17 serve as general references. Potential useable information from the 25 references is as follows:

Boucher and Stover: This bibliography provides a listing, in chronological order, of English-language publications on cross-impact analysis. The bibliography provides the user with information on the growth, applications, current status, and possible future development or uses of the technique. A total of 63 abstracts are included.

Clark, Hendee and Stankey: This paper describes a public participation program called Codinvolve developed by the U.S. Forest Service in 1972. Five main processes are a part of any public involvement effort: issue definition, public input collection (several techniques should be used), analysis, evaluation and decision implementation. The relationships of these processes are shown in Figure 6.

Codinvolve is the name given to the orderly and systematic transfer of information from any type of written input to a form that is easy to summarize for review. The steps in Codinvolve are shown in Figure 7. Codinvolve has been used in over 75 studies to analyze more than 100,000 public inputs.

Coates (a): This paper reviews the application of formal models to each of the ten principal elements in a technology assessment. The ten elements are shown in Figure 8. A model

TABLE 33: SUMMARY OF 1976 METHODOLOGIES/TECHNOLOGIES RELATIVE TO ENTRANCE CRITERIA

CRITERIA	METHODOLOGY/TECHNOLOGY*																																																										
	1	2	3	4	5	6	7	8	9	10	11	12	13	14	15	16	17	18	19	20	21	22	23	24	25	26	27	28	29	30	31	32	33	34	35	36	37	38	39	40	41	42	43	44	45	46	47	48	49	50	51	52	53	54	55	56	57	58
No entrance criteria set	X	X	X				X			X			X									X			X	X					X		X	X		X						X					X	X			X				X				
Twelve entrance criteria																																																										
1. Interdisciplinary team																																																										
2. Assessment variables											X							X											X			X						X				X						X	X			X		X	X		X	
3. Field studies																	X																																		X				X	X	X	X
4. Impact identification				X				X			X						X	X											X								X																	X			
5. Prediction of changes	X						X				X			X			X	X			X		X					X	X	X		X	X	X	X		X				X	X	X	X				X	X			X	X	X	X	X	X	X
6. Critical impacts																											X																																
7. Relative importance weights							X													X	X				X	X											X											X											
8. Scaling or ranking procedure							X													X						X												X	X	X																		
9. Impact summarization and assessment	X								X		X			X	X		X			X	X		X									X			X			X	X		X		X	X	X			X	X				X	X			
10. Documentation																																																										
11. Public participation							X				X														X	X																																	
12. Conflict management and resolution											X															X																																	

*The numbers correspond to those in Table 32.

137

TABLE 34: SALIENT FEATURES OF 1976 METHODOLOGIES/TECHNOLOGIES

Methodology/Technology	Salient Feature(s)
Adams and Kurisu	Model of pesticide movement from land is presented.
Boucher and Stover	Annotated bibliography of 63 references on cross-impact analysis.
Canter	Weighting-scaling checklist using weighted rankings technique is described.
Case, Edgmon and Renton	Public participation concepts are described.
Chase	Summarizes several examples of the use of interaction matrices.
Christensen	Good summary of the social impacts of land development projects.
Clark, Hendee and Stankey	Conceptual framework and procedure for public involvement in environmental decision-making.
Coates (a)	Selected impact prediction models are discussed.
Coates (b)	Survey of some potential methods and techniques useful for impact assessment is presented.
Colonell	Field Studies to develop predictive model for thermal stratification are described.
Curran Associates, Inc.	Contains qualitative/quantitative discussion of the primary impacts of channelization projects.
Darnell et al.	Good literature survey of construction impacts on wetlands.
Edwards	Multi-attribute utility measurement technique for assigning importance weights.

138

Engineering Division	Good discussion of concepts and development of a water quality index.
Fennelly et al.	Contains useful information on impact prediction for air and water environments.
Grimsrud, Finnemore, and Owen	Presents summary information on water quality models for impact predictions.
Gum, Roefs, and Kimball	Method of relative importance weight assignments using public participation is described.
Hammond and Adelman	Public participation for conflict resolution.
Harrison (Bioindicators)	189 abstracts of bioindicators of pollution are presented.
Harrison (Ecosystem Models)	76 abstracts on ecosystem models are described.
Jain, Urban, and Cerchione	Definitions, measurement, and interpretation information is presented on 49 assessment variables (called environmental attributes) primarily associated with the EQ account.
Jameson	Reviews ecosystem models and the impacts of urbanization on natural ecosystems.
Keyes	Contains a good summary of impact prediction and assessment techniques for the physical-chemical and biological environments.
Lehman (Vol. 1)	192 abstracts of models of the chemical, physical, biological, and hydrological processes important to water quality.
Lehman (Vol. 2)	98 abstracts of models of the chemical, physical, biological, and hydrological processes important to water quality.

Liu and Yu	Has information for interpretation of air pollutant impacts.
Lower Mississippi Valley Division	Weighting-scaling checklist using habitat approach is presented.
MacKinnon and Anderson	Computer program for summarizing participants' judgment on importance weighting.
McElroy et al.	Good summary of available quantitative information on non-point sources of water pollution.
Muller	Contains a discussion of economic impacts of land development in terms of employment, housing and property values. Information applicable to SWB and RD accounts.
Omernik	Contains information on nutrient runoff data compiled for 473 non-point-source-type drainage areas in the eastern United States.
Ott	Summary of modeling efforts for impact predication on the physical-chemical environment.
Reid	Twelve ecological standards are proposed.
Ross	Concepts of cross-impact matrix and disruption matrix; checking procedure for consistency in paired-comparison technique for importance weight assignments.
Schaenman	Descriptive checklist with 47 assessment variables for land development projects.
Springer	Presents information for planning a statistically significant water quality study.

Thornton and Lessem	Sensitivity analysis for water quality model is presented.
Thronson	Provides information on construction phase non-point pollution control.
U.S. Environmental Protection Agency	Contains qualitative/quantitative discussion of the primary impacts of impoundment projects.
Vlachos and Hendricks	A thorough presentation of the secondary impacts of highway projects.
Wakeland	Simple modeling process for impact prediction.
Webster et al.	Techniques for quantifying the economic impacts of military activities are described.

---

is taken to be any systematic interrelationship of elements and components into a system which is intended to parallel in structure, form and function some real world system. Obviously this definition includes mental models, but it is intended primarily to focus on physical, social, biological, organizational and institutional models. The paper concludes that the application of formal models to technology assessment has been the most successful in those areas where formal models have already been developed for other reasons, for example, for understanding physical transport in air, water, and terrain. Formal modelling of physical systems, economic modelling in terms of engineering costs and economics, benefit/cost evaluations, and macroeconometric modelling are likely to continue to be central to most assessments. Coates concludes that little or no use has been made of formal biological, phychological, or social science models.

Coates (b): This report also summarizes some methods and techniques used in technology assessments and potentially useful in EIA's/EIS's. Methods and techniques which are briefly described include Delphi, cross-impact analysis, trend extrapolation, checklists, morphological analysis, decision and relevance trees, economic techniques, systems analysis, similation, modeling, physical modeling, scenarios and games, moot courts, participation techniques and technologies, survey techniques, decision theory, scaling, brainstorming, graphics, and judgment theory. Examples of studies making use of these methods and techniques are included.

TABLE 35:   SUMMARY OF CONCLUSIONS REGARDING PERTINENT
REFERENCES FROM THE 1976 PERIOD

Potentially Useable in WRAM	General Reference for WRAM
Boucher and Stover	Adams and Kurisu
Clark, Hendee and Stankey	Canter
Coates (a)	Case, Edgmon and Renton
Coates (b)	Chase
Curran Associates, Inc.	Christensen
Darnell et al.	Colonell
Edwards	Fennelly et al.
Engineering Division	Jameson
Grimsrud, Finnemore, and	Liu and Yu
Owen	MacKinnon and Anderson
Gum, Roefs, and Kimball	Omernik
Hammond and Adelman	Reid
Harrison (Bioindicators)	Springer
Harrison (Ecosystem Models)	Thornton and Lessem
Jain, Urban, and Cerchione	Thronson
Keyes	Vlachos and Hendricks
Lehman (Vol. 1)	Webster et al.
Lehman (Vol. 2)	
Lower Mississippi Valley	
Division	
McElroy et al.	
Muller	
Ott	
Ross	
Schaenman	
U.S. Environmental Protection	
Agency	
Wakeland	

Curran Associates, Inc.: This report contains a descriptive presentation of information on the primary impacts of
channelization projects. It was written to provide a detailed
framework for EPA's review of channelization project EIS's.
It would be useful to preparers of channelization project EIS's
as a descriptive checklist methodology.

Darnell et al.: This report contains an extensive literature survey of construction impacts on wetlands. It is a useful document as an aid to impact identification. The primary
types of construction activity which severely impact wetland
environments of the United States include: floodplain surfacing and drainage, mining, impoundment, canalization,
dredging and channelization, and bank and shoreline construction. Each type of construction activity is attended by an
identifiable suite of physical and chemical alterations of

142

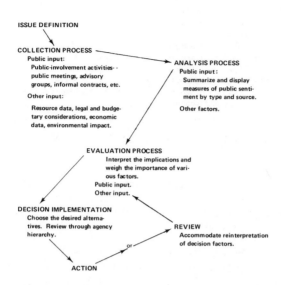

FIGURE 6: BASIC PROCESSES OF PUBLIC INVOLVEMENT AND THEIR
SEQUENTIAL RELATIONSHIP TO ONE ANOTHER. (After
Clark, Hendee and Stankey, 1976)

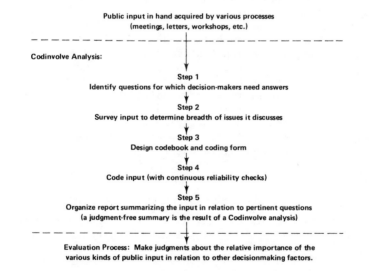

FIGURE 7: FLOW DIAGRAM FOCUSING ON A CODINVOLVE ANALYSIS
(After Clark, Hendee and Stankey, 1976)

143

```
 1. Examine problems statements.
 2. Specify systems alternatives.
 3. Identify possible impacts.
 4. Evaluate impacts.
 5. Identify the decision apparatus.
 6. Identify action options for decision apparatus.
 7. Identify parties at interest.
 8. Identify macro system alternatives (other routes to goal).
 9. Identify exogenous variables or events possibly having effect on 1-8.
10. Conclusions (and recommendations).
```

FIGURE 8:   ELEMENTS OF A COMPREHENSIVE TECHNOLOGY ASSESSMENT
            (After Coates, 1976a)

the wetland environment which may extend for many miles from
the site of construction and may persist for many years. In
turn, each type of physical and chemical modification has been
shown to induce a derived set of biological effects, many of
which are predictable, in general, if not in specific detail.
The most environmentally damaging effects of construction
activities in wetland areas, in order of importance, are:
direct habitat loss, addition of suspended solids, and modification of water levels and flow regimes. Major construction-
related impacts also derive from altered water temperature,
pH, nutrient levels, oxygen, carbon dioxide, hydrogen sulfide,
and certain pollutants such as heavy metals, radioactive
isotopes, and pesticides.

    Edwards: The thrust of this paper is that a public value
is a value assigned to an outcome by a public, usually by means
of some public institution that does the evaluating. This
amounts to treating "a public" as a sort of organism whose
values can be elicited by some appropriate adaptation of the
methods already in use to elicit individual values. Multi-
attribute utility measurement can spell out explicitly what the
values of each participant (decision-maker, expert, pressure
group, government, etc.) are, show how much they differ, and in
the process can frequently reduce the extent of such differences.
The ten steps in the multi-attribute utility measurement technique include:

    Step 1: Identify the person or organization whose utili-
ties are to be maximized. If, as is often the case, several
organizations have stakes and voices in the decision, they
must all be identified.

    Step 2: Identify the issue or issues (i.e., decision)
to which the utilities needed are relevant.

    Step 3: Identify the entities to be evaluated. Formally,
they are outcomes of possible actions. But in a sense, the

distinction between an outcome and the opportunity for further
actions is usually fictitious.

Step 4: Identify the relevant dimensions of value for
evaluation of the entities. As has often been noted, goals
ordinarily come in hierarchies. But it is often practical and
useful to ignore their hierarchical structure, and instead to
specify a simple list of goals that seem important for the
purpose at hand. It is important not to be too expansive at
this stage. The number of relevant dimensions of value should
be modest, for reasons that will be apparent shortly.

Step 5: Rank the dimensions in order of importance.
This ranking job, like Step 4, can be performed either by an
individual or by representatives of conflicting values acting
separately or by those representatives acting as a group.

Step 6: Rate dimensions in importance, preserving ratios.
To do this, start by assigning the least important dimension
an importance of 10. Now consider the next-least-important
dimension. How much more important (if at all) is it than the
least important? Assign it a number that reflects that ratio.
Continue up the list, checking each set of implied ratios as
each new judgment is made. Thus, if a dimension is assigned
a weight of 20, while another is assigned a weight of 80, it
means that the 20 dimension is ¼ as important as the 80 dimension, and so on. By the time you get to the most important
dimensions, there will be many checks to perform; typically,
respondents will want to revise previous judgments to make
them consistent with present ones.

Step 7: Sum the importance weights, divide each by the
sum, and multiply by 100. This is a purely computational step
which converts importance weights into numbers that, mathematically, are rather like probabilities. The choice of a 1-to-
100 scale is, of course, completely arbitrary.

Step 8: Measure the location of each entity being evaluated on each dimension. The word "measure" is used rather
loosely here. There are three classes of dimension: purely
subjective, partly subjective, and purely objective. The
purely subjective dimensions are perhaps the easiest; you simply get an appropriate expert to estimate the position of the
entity on that dimension on a 0-to-100 scale, where 0 is defined as the minimum plausible value and 100 is defined as the
maximum plausible value. Note "minimum and maximum plausible"
rather than "minimum and maximum possible." The minimum plausible value often is not total absence of the dimension. A
partly subjective dimension is one in which the units of
measurement are objective, but the locations of the entities

145

must be subjectively estimated. A purely objective dimension is one that can be measured non-judgmentally, in objective units, before the decision. For partly or purely objective dimensions, it is necessary to have the estimators provide not only values for each entity to be evaluated, but also minimum and maximum plausible values, in the natural units of each dimension.

Step 9: Calculate utilities for entities. The equation is:

$$U_i = \sum_j w_j u_{ij},$$

remembering that $\sum_j w_j = 100$. U_i is the aggregate utility for the ith entity. w_j is the normalized importance weight of j dimension of value, and u_{ij} is the rescaled position of the ith entity on the jth dimension. Thus, w_j is the output of Step 7 and u_{ij} is the output of Step 8. The equation of course, is nothing more than the formula for a weighted average.

Step 10: Decide. If a single act is to be chosen, the rule is simple: maximize U_i. If a subset if i is to be chosen, then the subset for which $\sum_i U_i$ is maximum is best.

Engineering Division: A study was conducted in Scotland from 1973 to 1976 to examine the possibility of improving river water quality classification systems. A water quality index comprised of 10 parameters was developed. Six different formulations for developing an index were considered, with the geometric weighted index being the one of choice. The 10 parameters include DO, BOD, NH_3, pH, total oxidized N, PO_4 (ortho), SS, temperature, conductivity and Escherichia coli. Importance weights on a relative basis were assigned to the 10 parameters, and functional curves are included for each. The functional curves are used to determine a water quality rating of from 0 to 100 for each parameter.

Gum, Roefs, and Kimball: Water resource use is related to "social goals" in the Techcom methodology. Techcom is a multi-objective planning methodology developed by a technical committee of the water resource centers of 13 western states. In the context of this system a weighting methodology is described to measure preferences regarding the attainment of postulated societal goals.

The Metfessel general allocation test was used to assign importance weights to social indicators. The test utilities as a basis the assignment of 100 points: the subject, either actually or symbolically, manipulates units of the ratio scale or cardinal numbers, so that his manipulation of the cardinal

146

numbers expresses his judgments of quantitative relations among the items of a given dimension.

The results of a survey of 2500 persons each in Arizona and New Mexico indicated that societal goals can be quantified in a manner which provides useful information to decision makers. By developing hierarchical goals, subgoal structures and measures of the lowest level subgoals, preference weights can be developed and used to provide measures of the attainment of all goals and subogals within the hierarchical structure. The estimation of preference weights for the general public and groups of the public is possible by the use of the Metfessel general allocation test to obtain measures of the preference for improvement in subgoals.

Hammond and Adelman: This paper describes a technique for integrating social value judgments and scientific judgments in decision-making. Social value judgments involving "policy capturing" are used for assigning relative importance weights to decision factors, while scientific judgments are used for scaling each alternative relative to each decision factor. Importance weights are elicited from the general public. Scaling is accomplished via functional curves. The degree of acceptability of each alternative is equal to the summation of the produce of the importance weights and scale values.

A case study involving use of the technique for conflict resolution is described. The specific case involved the selection of handgun ammunition by the Denver Police Department.

Harrison (bioindicators): This bibliography cites 189 abstracts relating to the use of microorganisms, animals, plants, and fishes to detect air and water pollution. Some of the organisms discussed are algae, bacteria, aquatic plants, oysters, snails, clams, insects, annelida, amphibians, beaver and fungi.

Harrison (Ecosystem Models): This bibliography cites 76 abstracts relating to the development and use of ecosystem models. Models for marine biology, wildlife, plants, water pollution, microorganisms, food chains, radioactive substances, limnology, and diseases as related to ecosystems are included.

Jain, Urban, and Cerchione: This publication is very similar to U.S. Department of the Army DA Pamphlet 200-1 (April 1975). The methodology basically consists of using an interaction matrix to identify potential impacts and generate a descriptive checklist. The 49 environmental attributes (assessment variables) included in the method are shown in Table 36. Information on measurement and interpretation is included for each assessment variable, and functional curves are shown for many of the variables.

Keyes: This report, designed primarily for developers, planners, and others involved in the evaluation of land developments, presents specific information on how to predict and assess impacts on air quality, water quality and quantity,

147

TABLE 36: ENVIRONMENTAL ATTRIBUTE LISTING (AFTER JAIN, URBAN, AND CERCHIONE, 1976).

Major Category	Subcategory	No.	Attribute
Natural Environment	Earth Characteristics	1	Erosion
	Water Characteristics	2	Aquifer Safe Yield
		3	Flow Variation
		4	Oil
		5	Radioactivity
		6	Suspended Solids
		7	Thermal Pollution
		8	Acid and Alkali
		9	Biochemical Oxygen Demand
		10	Dissolved Oxygen (DO)
		11	Dissolved Solids
		12	Nutrients
		13	Toxic Compounds
		14	Aquatic Life
		15	Fecal Coliform
	Air Characteristics	16	Diffusion Factor
		17	Particulates
		18	Sulphur Oxides
		19	Hydrocarbons
		20	Nitrogen Oxides
		21	Carbon Monoxide
		22	Photochemical Oxidants
		23	Hazardous Toxicants
		24	Odors

Biotic Environment (Plants, Animals) Characteristics	Natural Land Vegetation	25
	Aquatic Plants	26
	Field Crops	27
	Threatened and Endangered Species	28
	Large Animals	29
	Predatory Birds	30
	Small Game and Song Birds	31
	Fish, Shellfish, and Waterfowl	32
Resources Characteristics	Fuel Resources	33
	Nonfuel Resources	34
Natural Hazards Characteristics	Natural Hazards	35
Human Environment		
Demographic Characteristics	Psychological Needs	36
	Physiological Systems	37
Economic Characteristics	Regional Economic Stability	38
	Public Sector Revenue	39
	Per Capita Consumption	40
Institutional Characteristics	Life Styles	41
	Community Needs	42
Activity Systems and Plans	Land-Use Patterns	43
	Aesthetics	44
	Physiological Effects (Sound)	45
	Psychological Effects (Sound)	46
	Communications Effects (Sound)	47
	Performance Effects (Sound)	48
	Social Behavior Effects (Sound)	49

149

wildlife and vegetation, and noise. Table 37 contains a comparison of atmospheric dispersion models while Tables 38 and 39 are related to water quality models. The author recommends that local jurisdictions establish specific criteria for impact assessment.

Lehman (Vol. 1 and 2): These bibliographics cite abstracts relating to Federally-sponsored studies on models used to describe water quality. This covers models of the chemical, physical, biological, and hydrological processes important to water quality. Included are studies on the modeling of eutrophication, nutrient removal, pollutant dispersion, stream flow, heat dissipation, limnological factors, aquifer water quality, and water runoff quality. Volume 1 contains 192 abstracts and Volume 2 contains 98 abstracts.

Lower Mississippi Valley Division: This is one of the 8 methodologies mentioned in the interim WRAM report issued in February, 1977. The methodology is a weighting-scaling checklist with primary orientation to the EQ account. The methodology defines 6 habitat types in the Lower Mississippi Valley Division area, these are: freshwater stream, freshwater lake, bottomland hardwood forest, upland hardwood forest, open (non-forest) lands, freshwater river swamp, freshwater non-river swamp. Each habitat type is described in terms of several descriptive parameters as shown in Tables 40 through 45.

A critical component of the system is the use of functional curves for each of the identified parameters. Each parameter is assigned a weight which accounts for its relative importance in describing habitat quality. The habitat types, parameters, functional curves and importance weights were identified and assigned in a joint study effort between about 20 biologists from the Lower Mississippi Valley Division and the Waterways Experiment Station. The product of the quality index and importance weight yields a weighted score for each parameter. These scores are summed and a final value is calculated which represents the quality of that particular habitat. This procedure is repeated to arrive at an estimate of the quality of each major habitat type occurring within the project area for each alternative plan. The effects of various alternative plans of development can then be compared by applying the final values to the acreages of habitats for each alternative considered.

McElroy et al.: Methods for evaluating the quantity of water pollutants generated from non-point sources including agriculture, silviculture, construction, mining, runoff from urban areas and rural roads, and terrestrial disposal are developed and compiled for use in water quality planning. The loading functions, plus in some instances emission values, permit calculation of non-point source pollutants from available data and information. Table 46 summarizes the available information in the report.

150

TABLE 37: COMPARISON OF ATMOSPHERIC DISPERSION MODELS (After Keyes, 1976)

NAME	CO	SOx	NOx	HC	Ox	Part.	Point	Stationary area	Mobile area	Line	Averaged[a]	Inputs	Outputs	Computing Requirements	Cost	Accuracy
	Pollutants Modeled						Sources Modeled									
Rollforward Model	x	x	x[b]	x[b]	x[b]	x					x	Current average ambient concentrations, total emissions (for entire community or subareas) and future emissions. For more complex versions, wind speed, wind direction, and average stack heights	(1) Average ambient concentration for one or a few representative points in the community (2) Any averaging time period	Manual	Low	Unvalidated
Miller/ Holzworth Model		x	x			x					x	Average community-wide emission rate, average wind speed throughout the mixing layer, mixing depth, community size (along wind length of the urbanized area)	(1) Average ambient concentration for the community as a whole (2) Hourly or annual averages	Manual (essentially referencing of tables)	Low	Good (r > 0.8 for SO_2 and NO_x for the test application
Hanna/ Gifford Model	x	x	x[c]	x[c]		x	x	x				Emission rates for area and certain point sources and wind speed (and direction for short-term averages)	(1) Average ambient concentrations for areas as small as 1 square mile. (if the areas are numerous enough, isopleths can be drawn for the community) (2) Any averaging time period	Manual	Low (approximately 1/2 hour of calculations for 150 subareas in Chicago plus the cost of emissions data collection)	Good for *nonreactive version* (r ≥ 0.7), less satisfactory for reactive version based on one application (r = 0.05–0.97)
California Highway Model	x									x		Vehicle speeds, volumes, and mixes; average wind speed, wind direction, and atmospheric stability (joint frequencies), highway elevation	(1) Average ambient concentrations as a function of distance from the highway (up to 1000 feet away) (2) Annual averages	Manual (helpful to computerize some meteorological data)	Low	Unvalidated
ERT/MARTIK Model	x	x	x	x		x	x		x	x		Average wind speed, wind direction atmospheric stability (joint frequencies); emission rates for all sources, background emissions	(1) Average ambient concentrations for areas as small as 1/2 square mile; isopleths can be drawn (2) Seasonal or annual averages	Digital computer	Presumably high (probably tens of thousands of dollars)	Initial validation results were mediocre
TASSIM	x	x	x	x		x	x		x			See ERT/MARTIK for point sources and Hanna/Gifford for area sources. Distribution of trips and speeds by zone for line sources.	(1) Average ambient concentrations for areas as small as 1/2 square mile; isopleths can be drawn (2) Averages by hour, day, year	Digital computer with 156,000 bytes of storage	Presumably High	Good (r = 0.7–0.9) for the various pollutants

TABLE 37 CONTINUED

	Pollutants Modeled					Sources Modeled								
NAME	CO	SO$_x$	NO$_x$	HC	O$_x$	Part.	Point	Stationary area	Mobile area	Line	Averaged[a]	Inputs	Outputs	Computing Requirements	Cost	Accuracy
CDM		X				X	X	X	X			Emission rates for point and area sources; joint wind speed, wind direction and atmospheric stability frequencies; average mixing depth	(1) Average ambient concentrations at an unlimited number of locations (2) Annual averages	Digital computer	Presumably High	Good (r ≅ 0.8)
APRAC	X					X				X		Vehicle speed and volume per link, average hourly cloud cover, temperature, atmospheric stability and mixing depth	(1) Average ambient concentrations at up to 625 locations from which isopleths can be drawn (2) Hourly or annual averages	Digital computer, 45,000 words of storage (program modification needed for computers except CDC 6400 and IBM 360/50)	Presumably High	Mediocre (r ≅ 0.25- 0.7)

a. Emissions from all types of sources are averaged together.   b. The application of the model to these pollutants has been very limited.   c. These pollutants are modeled by the more complex "reactive" version.

TABLE 38: ASSESSMENT OF WATER QUALITY MODELS (After Keyes, 1976)

NAME	TYPE OF WATER BODY	POLLUTANTS MODELED	COMPUTING REQUIREMENTS	INPUT	COST	OUTPUT	ACCURACY AND COMMENTS
Streeter-Phelps	Streams and reservoirs	DO-BOD	Hand calculations although a computer can greatly expand number of locations at which values are calculated	Effluent content of point sources, velocity of flow, and ambient DO concentrations	Very low if used manually	DO concentrations as a function of distance downstream from source	Low due to the simplifying assumption used in the calculations
EPA's Simplified Model	Streams and estuaries	Chloride, dissolved solids, total P, bacteria suspended solids, DO-BOD	Hand calculations	Effluent content of point sources, average and low flow velocity, general type of flow, channel geometry and slope, ambient water quality	Fairly low	Pollutant and indicator values as a function of location in stream/estuary	Less than for computerized models (EPA cautions against its use by those unfamiliar with water quality analysis)
Auto-Qual	Streams and elongated estuaries	DO-BOD based on both carbon and N compounds, suspended solids, temperature, chloride	Central core storage requirements are 105,000–115,000 bytes; has been run on IBM 370	Flow and velocity, channel configuration at each junction, effluent content of point sources, water temperature, rates of DO uptake by sediments, and production by photosynthesis	No figures available	Pollutant and indicator values as a function of location in stream/estuary and of time	Theoretically higher than the simple methods, although complex and rare events, such as storm surges, not represented well
HSP, water quality	Streams, lakes, impoundments	Dissolved solids, temperature, bacteria, DO-DOB based on both carbon and N compounds, phytoplankton, zooplankton, benthal organisms, various forms of N and P	See HSP Table 2-6	Effluent content of point sources. (See Table 2-4 for a description of the HSP non-point source component.) See HSP Tables 2-4 and -6 for other input requirements	Approximately $10/acre for small watersheds, less for large ones in addition to cost of the other HSP components	Pollutant and indicator values as a function of stream estuary location and of time	Subjectively estimated as ''reasonable'' and from theoretical point of view, relatively high; HSP is a comprehensive program so this submodel can be coupled with surface runoff and hydrologic submodels

153

NAME	POLLUTANTS MODELED	COMPUTING REQUIREMENTS	INPUT	COST	OUTPUT	ACCURACY
Hydrocomp Simulation Program (HSP), water quality (surface runoff component)[a]	BOD, COD,[b] organic N, phosphate, total solids	Same as for HSP, Table 2-4 (970,000 word core storage required to run all hydrologic and quality modules)	See HSP in Table 2-4, initial dust and dirt loadings on pervious and impervious areas and upper loading limits	No values available	Runoff pollutant concentration during all runoff events as simulated continuously by HSP	No reported data on accuracy of pollutant concentrations
Storage treatment overflow, runoff model (STORM)[c]	Suspended solids, settleable solids, soluble P, Total N, BOD	Program available for IBM 360/50, UNIVAC 1108, and CDC 6600 or 7600 machines, core storage of 35,000 words required plus 1–5 additional tape/disk units	Hourly rainfall for 10–30 years, land use type, percent imperviousness, runoff storage and treatment characteristics, initial dust and dirt loads and upper loading limits	No values available	Runoff pollutant concentration during storm events (pollutographs) simulated from rainfall records; also, quality of runoff after storage and possible treatment if applicable	No reported data on accuracy of pollutant concentrations
Storm water management model (SWMM)[d]	BOD, suspended solids, settleable solids, BOD, N, P and grease	Core storage of 350,000 bytes is required plus additional tape/disk units; has been used on IBM 360/70, UNIVAC 1108, and CDC 6400/6600	Hourly rainfall for many years, subbasin characteristics (area, width, slope, ground cover) storm sewerage (slope, length, roughness and storage capacity) initial dust and dirt loadings and upper loading limits	Effort for input data preparation has been described as "moderate" and, although computing time is 2–3 times longer than for similar models, computing cost is less than $10 per run[e]	Runoff pollutant concentrations during storm events (pollutographs) for the whole basin or at specific points therein	Very low accuracy for suspended solids reported in one test![f] No other data available

154

a. Hydrocomp, Inc., Hydrocomp Simulation Programming, *Mathematical Model of Water Quality Indices in Rivers and Impoundments* (Palo Alto, California: Hydrocomp, Inc., n.d.).

b. Chemical Oxygen Demand. This is an alternative but not exactly equivalent measure for BOD.

c. Water Resources Engineers, Inc., Corps of Engineers (Hydrologic Engineering Center), and City of San Francisco (Department of Public Works), *A Model for Evaluating Runoff Quality in Metropolitan Master Planning* (New York: American Society of Civil Engineers, April, 1974); and Hydrologic Engineering Center, *Urban Storm Water Runoff* "STORM," Generalized Computer Program, 723-58-12520 (Davis, California: Army Corps of Engineers, May, 1974).

d. W. C. Huber, et al., *Storm Water Management Model User's Manual*, vol. II (Cincinnati, Ohio: EPA, Office of Research and Development, March, 1975).

e. D. P. Heeps and R. G. Mein, "Independent Comparison of Three Urban Runoff Models," *Journal of the Hydraulics Division, Proceeding of the American Society of Civil Engineers* 100 (HY7) (1974): 995–1009; and J. Marsalek, et al., "Comparative Evaluation of Three Urban Runoff Models," *Water Resources Bulletin* 11 (2), (1975): 306–28.

f. N. V. Colston, Jr., *Characterization and Treatment of Urban Land Runoff* (Cincinnati, Ohio: EPA, Office of Research and Development, December, 1974).

155

TABLE 40: FRESHWATER STREAM (AFTER LOWER MISSISSIPPI VALLEY DIVISION, 1976)

Parameter	Primary Characteristic	Secondary Characteristic
Sinuosity	Meander pattern	Habitat diversity, aesthetic value, flow characteristics
Dominant centrarchid	Dominant predatory fishes	Water quality history, sport fishing potential, aesthetic value, community structure
Mean low water width	Stream size	Aesthetic values, faunal composition, carrying capacity
Turbidity	Light penetration	Primary productivity, species composition, sport fish production, aesthetic values, water quality, recreation potential
Total dissolved solids	Dissolved solids concentration	Primary productivity, fish production
Chemical type	Prevalent dissolved salts	Primary productivity, water quality, species composition, fish production
Diversity of fishes	Community structure	Water quality history, habitat diversity, recreational potential, aesthetics, population balance
Diversity of benthos	Community structure	Water quality history, habitat diversity, aesthetic and recreational values, population balance

156

TABLE 41: FRESHWATER LAKE (AFTER LOWER MISSISSIPPI VALLEY DIVISION, 1976)

Parameter	Primary Characteristic	Secondary Characteristics
Mean depth	Mean depth	Productivity potential, species composition, littoral habitat availability, macrophyte potential
Turbidity	Light penetration	Primary productivity, species composition, sport fish production, aesthetic values, water quality, recreation potential
Total dissolved solids	Dissolved solids concentration	Primary productivity, fish production
Chemical type	Prevalent dissolved salts	Primary productivity, water quality, species composition, fish production
Shore development	Shoreline irregularity	Littoral habitat availability, habitat diversity, fish productivity, aesthetic values, recreation potential
Spring flooding	Water fluctuation	Sport fish production, fish population balance, largemouth bass year class strength, littoral habitat quality, water quality, aesthetic values, primary productivity
Standing crop of fishes	Total population size	Aquatic productivity, water quality
Standing crop of sport fishes	Population size	Sport fishing potential, population balance, water quality history, aquatic productivity
Diversity of fishes	Community structure	Water quality history, habitat diversity, recreational and aesthetic values, population balance
Diversity of benthos	Community structure	Water quality history, habitat diversity, recreational and aesthetic values, population balance

TABLE 42: BOTTOMLAND HARDWOOD FOREST (AFTER LOWER MISSISSIPPI VALLEY DIVISION, 1976)

Parameter	Primary Characteristic	Secondary Characteristics
Species association	Community structure	Habitat capability to support diverse mix of wildlife species, aesthetic values
Percent of mast-bearing trees	Mast production	Habitat carrying capacity, esthetics, recreation potential
Percent of ground covered by understory	Browse production	Wildlife habitat carrying capacity, cover potential
Understory diversity	Community structure	Year-round food and cover production, esthetics
Percent of ground covered by groundcover	Browse production	Wildlife habitat carrying capacity, cover potential, erosion control
Groundcover diversity	Community structure	Year-round food and cover production, esthetics
Number of trees per acre $\geq$ 18 in. dbh	Habitat maturity	Value to game and non-game wildlife, recreation value, esthetics
Percent of trees $\geq$ 18 in dbh	Habitat maturity	Value to game and non-game wildlife, recreation value, esthetics
Frequency of flooding	Forest vigor	Primary productivity, carrying capacity for wildlife, plant successional pattern, edaphic conditions.
Quantity of edge	Habitat diversity	Browse production, wildlife carrying capacity, esthetic values, wildlife diversity, recreation potential
Mean distance to edge	Habitat diversity	Browse production, wildlife carrying capacity, esthetic values, wildlife diversity, recreation potential

TABLE 43: UPLAND HARDWOOD FOREST (After Lower Mississippi Valley Division, 1976)

Parameter	Primary Characteristic	Secondary Characteristics
Species association	Community structure	Habitat capability to support diverse mix of wildlife species, aesthetic values
Percent of mast-bearing trees	Mast production	Habitat carrying capacity, esthetics, recreation potential
Percent of ground covered by understory	Browse production	Wildlife habitat carrying capacity, cover potential
Understory diversity	Community structure	Year-round food and cover production, esthetics
Percent of ground covered by groundcover	Browse production	Wildlife habitat carrying capacity, cover potential, erosion control
Groundcover diversity	Community structure	Year-round food and cover production, esthetics
Number of trees per acre $\geq$ 16 in. dbh	Habitat maturity	Value to game and non-game wildlife, recreation value, esthetics
Percent of trees $\geq$ 16 in. dbh	Habitat maturity	Value to game and non-game wildlife, recreation value, esthetics
Quantity of edge	Habitat diversity	Browse production, wildlife carrying capacity, esthetic values, wildlife diversity, recreation potential
Mean distance to edge	Habitat diversity	Browse production, wildlife carrying capacity, esthetic values, wildlife diversity, recreation potential

TABLE 44: FRESHWATER RIVER SWAMP (AFTER LOWER MISSISSIPPI VALLEY DIVISION, 1976)

Parameter	Primary Characteristic	Secondary Characteristics
Species association	Community structure	Habitat diversity, capability to support diverse wildlife populations, esthetic values, recreation potential
Percent woody forest cover	Habitat diversity	Productivity, habitat diversity, edge availability, recreation potential, esthetics, wildlife diversity
Percent of area flooded annually	Ecosystem vigor	Primary productivity, wildlife carrying capacity, habitat diversity, successional stages, wildlife diversity, edaphic conditions, water quality
Groundcover diversity	Community structure	Year-round food and cover production, esthetics
Percent of area covered by groundwater	Browse production	Wildlife habitat carrying capacity, cover potential, erosion control
Days subject to river overflow	Ecosystem vigor	Primary productivity, aquatic productivity, wildlife carrying capacity, habitat diversity, successional stages, water quality, aquatic community structure, edaphic conditions, fish and wildlife diversity

160

Parameter	Primary Characteristic	Secondary Characteristics
Species association	Community structure	Habitat diversity, capability to support diverse wildlife populations, esthetic values, recreation potential
Percent woody forest cover	Habitat diversity	Productivity, habitat diversity, edge availability, recreation potential, esthetics, wildlife diversity
Percent of area flooded annually	Ecosystem vigor	Primary productivity, wildlife carrying capacity, habitat diversity, successional stages, wildlife diversity, edaphic conditions, water quality
Groundcover diversity	Community structure	Year-round food and cover production, esthetics
Percent of area covered by groundwater	Browse production	Wildlife habitat carrying capacity, cover potential, erosion control
		OPEN LANDS
Land use	Dominant cover	Wildlife food and cover potential, carrying capacity, esthetics
Diversity of land use	Crop pattern	Wildlife habitat diversity, esthetics
Quantity of edge	Density of ecotones	Carrying capacity, habitat diversity
Mean distance to edge	Frequency of ecotones	Availability of ecotones

161

TABLE 46: SOURCE – POLLUTANT MATRIX[a] (AFTER MCELROY ET AL., 1976)

Source	Sediment	Nutrient matter N, P	Organic matter BOD	Pesticides H, I, F	Salinity TDS	Heavy Metals	Radioactivity	Coliform	Other
Agriculture	3	4	4	5		8			
Irrigation return flow					6				
Silviculture	3	4	4	5		8			
Mining	3					8	8		Acid mine drainage-7
Construction	3					8			
Urban runoff	9	9	9	9	9	9		9	
Highways	9	9	9		9	9			
Feedlots	10	10	10					10	Suspended solids-10
Terrestrial disposal		11[b]	11		11	11			
Background	12	12	12		12	12	12	12	

a/ Numbers in table indicate section numbers in McElroy et al. (1976).
b/ Nitrogen only.

162

Natural background was considered to be a source and loading functions were presented to estimate natural or background loads of pollutants. Loading functions/values are presented for average conditions, i.e., annual average loads expressed as metric tons/hectare/year (tons/acre/year). Procedures for estimating seasonal or 30-day maximum and minimum loads are also presented. The report also presents an evaluation of limitations and constraints of various techniques which will enable the user to employ the functions realistically.

Muller: The information in this report represents a descriptive checklist methodology for predicting and assessing economic impacts from land development. Land development can exert economic impacts in terms of employment, housing, and property values. Employment impact assessment involves estimating the number of jobs created by new development and the share of jobs taken by local residents; and consideration of unemployment and underemployment, employment from the regional perspective, secondary employment effects and future levels and types of employment.

Ott: This report contains 164 technical papers on environmental modeling efforts in air quality management, air and water pollutant transport processes, water runoff, water supply, solid waste, environmental management and planning, environmental economics, environmental statistics, ecology, noise, radiation, and health. The conference where these papers were presented was the first of its kind to cover the state-of-the-art of mathematical and statistical models in the air, water, and land environments. Many of the described models are useful for impact prediction.

Ross: This report has two aspects relevant to the WRAM methodology. A component interaction matrix is shown in Figure 9, and a disruption matrix is in Figure 10. The second aspect is a procedure for checking the consistency of importance weight assignments using paired comparisons. The consistency procedure is described as follows:

When using this technique, an individual who has been requested to assess a number (N) of objects is presented with every possible combination of these objects, and asked to make judgments as to which of each pair is favored. His decisions are recorded in a paired-comparison matrix. An entry (C_{ij}) of "I" in this matrix denotes that the row object i (row stimulus) was judged as being better, or more desirable, than the column stimulus j. Once all possible pairs have been compared, and the decisions recorded in the matrix, the ranking of stimuli can be readily ascertained by summing the rows of the matrix. The stimuli are ranked in order of these row sums. An example comparison matrix is presented in Table 47.

		1	2	3	4	5	6	7	8	9	10	11	12	13	14	15	16	17	18	19	20	21
CURRENTS	1		1																			
WIND	2						1															
WATER TEMPERATURE	3	1	1		1																	
LIGHT	4																					
INTERTIDAL VEGETATION	5	1		1	1																	
UPLAND VEGETATION	6				1			1	1									1	1	1		1
BACTERIA	7			1		1	1		1	1	1	1	1	1	1	1	1	1	1	1	1	1
INSECTS	8	1	1	1		1	1	1														
LARVAE	9	1		1		1		1				1	1	1	1	1						
SHELL FISH	10	1		1		1		1														
CRABS	11			1		1				1	1		1	1	1							
OTHER CRUSTACEANS	12			1		1		1	1	1	1	1		1	1							
PELAGIC FISH	13			1					1	1												
BOTTOM FISH	14			1		1			1	1	1	1	1	1								
WATERBIRDS	15					1			1	1	1	1	1	1	1							
BIRDS OF PREY	16						1		1			1	1	1	1	1		1	1	1		1
SONG BIRDS	17						1		1		1		1	1	1							
MARSH & SHORE BIRDS	18						1		1			1	1	1	1							
UPLAND GAME BIRDS	19						1		1													
AQUATIC & MARINE MAMMALS	20											1	1	1	1	1						
UPLAND MAMMALS	21						1					1	1	1				1		1		

Note: A (1) in any cell indicates that the row component
is dependent on the column component.

FIGURE 9: NANAIMO COMPONENT INTERACTION MATRIX (After Ross, 1976)

The correct ordering of the stimuli in this case is 5, 6, 1, 3, 2, and 4. When the paired-comparison matrix is permuted according to the ranking derived, a characteristic pattern appears in which the upper right portion of the matrix is observed to be composed of 1's, and the lower left portion of 0's (see Table 48).

In the foregoing example, the individual making the comparisons, hereafter termed the judge, has been perfectly consistent in his judgments. It reveals that he has a clear idea of the stimuli, and that he has a good

TABLE 47: EXAMPLE COMPARISON MATRIX (AFTER ROSS, 1976)

Stimulus	1	2	3	4	5	6	Row Sum
1	-	1	1	1	0	0	3
2	0	-	0	1	0	0	1
3	0	1	-	1	0	0	2
4	0	0	0	-	0	0	0
5	1	1	1	1	-	1	5
6	1	1	1	1	0	-	4

TABLE 48: PERMUTED EXAMPLE COMPARISON MATRIX (AFTER ROSS, 1976)

Stimulus	5	6	1	3	2	4	Row Sum
5	-	1	1	1	1	1	5
6	0	-	1	1	1	1	4
1	0	0	-	1	1	1	3
3	0	0	0	-	1	1	2
2	0	0	0	0	-	1	1
4	0	0	0	0	0	-	0

decision rule to follow while making the individual paired
comparisons. Such is often not the case. Inconsistent
judgments are revealed by the presence of 1's below the
diagonal in the permuted matrix. In Table 49, for example, the preference of the judge for 4 over 5, 5 over 1,
and 1 over 4 (generally denoted 4 5, 5 1, 1 4, and termed
an intransitive triad) is revealed. It is clearly a case
of inconsistent judgment and may indicate an unclear
understanding of the stimuli, or a confused or poor decision rule. It might also indicate that one attribute of
stimulus 1 was so far superior to that of stimulus 4 that
it became the sole determinant of the choice made in that
particular comparison. The paired-comparison technique
permits and identifies inconsistencies that would be lost
in more traditional ranking approaches.

FIGURE 10: NANAIMO DISRUPTION MATRICES (After Ross, 1976)

Columns (1–21): CURRENTS, WIND, WATER TEMPERATURE, LIGHT, INTERTIDAL VEGETATION, UPLAND VEGETATION, BACTERIA, INSECTS, LARVAE, SHELL FISH, CRABS, OTHER CRUSTACEANS, PELAGIC FISH, BOTTOM FISH, WATERBIRDS, BIRDS OF PREY, SONG BIRDS, MARSH & SHORE BIRDS, UPLAND GAME BIRDS, AQUATIC & MARINE MAMMALS, UPLAND MAMMALS

Each cell contains four values arranged as a 2×2 block corresponding to the four alternatives.

	1	2	3	4	5	6	7	8	9	10	11	12	13	14	15	16	17	18	19	20	21
1 CURRENTS	0 0 / 0 0																				
2 WIND					0 1 / 1 1																
3 WATER TEMPERATURE	1 1 / 1 1	2 1 / 1 1			3 1 / 2 1																
4 LIGHT																					
5 INTERTIDAL VEGETATION	3 1 / 2 1		2	1 1 / 1 1	3 3 / 3 3																
6 UPLAND VEGETATION				0 3 / 3 3			0 1 / 1 1	0 1 / 1 1								0 1 / 1 1	0 1 / 1 1	0 1 / 1 1	0 1 / 1 1		0 1 / 1 1
7 BACTERIA	0 0 / 0 0	1 1 / 1 1		1 1 / 1 1	2 2 / 2 1	0 2 / 2 2		1 1 / 1 1	1 1 / 1 1	1 1 / 1 1	1 1 / 1 1	1 1 / 1 1	1 1 / 1 1	1 1 / 1 1	1 1 / 1 1	1 0 / 1 1	0 1 / 1 1	1 1 / 1 1	1 1 / 1 1	1 1 / 1 1	0 1 / 1 1
8 INSECTS	0 0 / 0 0	1 1 / 1 1	1 1 / 1 1		1 1 / 1 1	0 1 / 1 1	1 1 / 1 1														
9 LARVAE	2 2 / 2 2		2 2 / 2 2		3 3 / 3 3	2 2 / 2 2				2 2 / 2 2	2 1 / 1 0	2 2 / 2 2	2 2 / 2 2	2 2 / 2 2							
10 SHELL FISH	2 2 / 2 2		2 2 / 2 2		3 3 / 3 3	2 2 / 2 2															
11 CRABS			2 0 / 2 0		2 0 / 2 0			2 0 / 2 0	2 0 / 2 0			2 0 / 2 0	1 0 / 1 0	2 0 / 2 0							
12 OTHER CRUSTACEANS			2 2 / 2 2		2 2 / 2 2		1 1 / 1 1	1 1 / 1 1	2 1 / 2 2	2 2 / 1 0	1 0		1 1 / 1 1	1 1 / 1 1							
13 PELAGIC FISH			2 2 / 2 2				2 2 / 2 2	3 3 / 3 3													
14 BOTTOM FISH			2 2 / 2 2		2 2 / 2 2		2 2 / 2 2	3 3 / 3 3	1 0 / 1 0	1 0 / 0 3	3 3 / 3 3	2 2 / 2 2									
15 WATERBIRDS			3 1 / 2 1				1 0 / 1 0	2 0 / 0 1	2 1 / 1 0	2 0 / 2 0	2 0 / 2 0	2 1 / 1 2	1 0 / 1 0								
16 BIRDS OF PREY			0 3 / 3 3			0 1 / 1 1			1 0 / 0 1	0 1 / 0 1	1 1 / 1 1	1 0 / 0 c	1 1 / 2 1		0 2 / 2 2	1 0 / 0 1	0 1 / 1 1		0 2 / 2 2
17 SONG BIRDS			0 3 / 3 2			1 3 / 3 2		1 0 / 0 0			2 1 / 3 1	1 1 / 1 0	1 1 / 1 1								
18 MARSH & SHORE BIRDS			0 2 / 2 2			0 1 / 1 0		1 0 / 1 0	1 0 / 0 2	2 2 / 2 2	1 1 / 1 1	3 3 / 1 1								
19 UPLAND GAME BIRDS			0 3 / 3 3			0 1 / 1 1														
20 AQUATIC & MARINE MAMMALS							1 1 / 1 0	2 2 / 2 0	2 2 / 2 2	2 2 / 2 2	2 2 / 2 2									
21 UPLAND MAMMALS						0 3 / 3 3			2 2 / 2 2	0 1 / 0 0	0 3 / 3 3					0 1 / 1 1		0 1 / 1 1		

ALTERNATIVE

ALTERNATIVE 1 = INNER HARBOUR
ALTERNATIVE 2 = JACK POINT
ALTERNATIVE 3 = DUKE POINT (A)
ALTERNATIVE 4 = HARMAC SOUTH

DISRUPTION LEVEL

0 - NO NOTICEABLE DISRUPTION
1 - SLIGHT DISRUPTION
2 - APPRECIABLE DISRUPTION
3 - SEVERE DISRUPTION

166

TABLE 49:   PERMUTED EXAMPLE COMPARISON MATRIX
(AFTER ROSS, 1976) (INCONSISTENT)

Stimulus	5	6	1	3	2	4	Row Sum
5	-	1	1	1	1	0	4
6	0	-	1	1	1	1	4
1	0	0	-	1	1	1	3
3	0	0	0	-	1	1	2
2	0	0	0	0	-	1	1
4	1	0	0	0	0	-	1

The degree to which the judge has been consistent
can be determined by calculating the coefficient of consistency (K) as follows:

$$K = 1 - \frac{24d}{n^3 - n} \quad \text{if n is an odd number}$$

$$\text{or . } K = 1 - \frac{24d}{n^3 - 4n} \quad \text{if n is an even number}$$

where n = the number of stimuli and,
where d = the number of intransitive triads observed

The value of K equals 1.0 when d takes a value of
0.0 (i.e., when there are no intransitive triads), and
declines to 0.0, as d approaches the maximum number possible. The number of intransitive triads (d) can be
determined by inspecting each of the n(n-1) (n-2)/6
triads individually, but in general, it is best to compute its value from the equation:

$$d = \frac{T \text{ max} - T}{2}$$

where T = the sum of the squared deviations of the
row sums from their theoretically expected
values, and,
T max = the maximum possible T = $\frac{n^3 - n}{12}$

The expected number of 1's in each row of the matrix,
assuming that the judgments are made randomly, is (n-1)/2.
We can now extend Table 49 as shown in Table 50.

167

Therefore $d = \dfrac{17.5 - 9.5}{2} = 4$

$k = 1 - \dfrac{96}{192} = .5$

The interpretation of K is often difficult. Inspection of the permuted comparison matrix, Table 1 reveals that only one "1" is out of place, yet the number of incorrect judgments this involves (4), is high enough to bring the coefficient of consistency well down. The statistical significance of K must be assessed by comparing d to its expected distribution. A table for this comparison developed for n<8 reveals that d = 4 is significant only at the .792 level.

The chi square distribution, to which the distribution of d tends as n increases, is used to determine the probability of finding as few as d intransitive triads in a matrix where n>7. Chi square is found from the equation:

$$x^2 = 8/(n-4)\left|\tfrac{1}{4}\{(n(n-1)\ (n-2)/6)\}-d+\tfrac{1}{2}\right| \pm V$$

where $\quad v = \{n(n-1)\ (n-2)\}/(n-4)^2$

In this case, the probability of x^2 is the probability that an equal, or higher value of d would be found at random, rather than the inverse - as is usually the case.

The single-judge paired-comparison matrix may be extended to a multi-judge situation by summing the comparison matrices of a number of single judges to yield a group comparison matrix (see Table 51). In such a case, one could hardly expect the level of unanimity to be as perfect as with a single judge matrix. However, this very fact later permits us to convert the ranking into a metric scale, in which the stimuli are given real values rather than ranks.

Schaenman: The methodology presented in this report is basically a descriptive checklist which contains 47 assessment variables shown in Table 52. The report contains capsule summaries of the state-of-the-art of impact evaluation for each impact area listed in Table 52. Information is included in the report on the methodology usage in Pheonix, Arizona, Indianapolis, Indiana, and Montgomery County, Maryland.

  U.S. Environmental Protection Agency: This report contains a descriptive presentation of information on the primary impacts of impoundment projects. It was written to provide a detailed framework for EPA's review of impoundment project

TABLE 50:   THE CALCULATION OF T (AFTER ROSS, 1976)

Stimulus	Row Sum	Expected	D viation	Deviation
5	4	2.5	1.5	2.25
6	4	2.5	1.5	2.25
1	3	2.5	.5	.25
3	2	2.5	.5	.25
2	1	2.5	1.5	2.25
4	1	2.5	1.5	2.25
				T = 9.50

TABLE 51:   PERMUTED EXAMPLE GROUP COMPARISON MATRIX
(n = 100) (AFTER ROSS, 1976)

Stimulus	1	2	3	4	5	6	Row Sum
1	–	80	95	97	100	100	472
2	20	–	75	85	95	100	375
3	5	25	–	60	70	90	250
4	3	15	40	–	70	80	208
5	0	5	30	30	–	75	140
6	0	0	10	20	25	–	55

EIS's. It would be useful to preparers of impoundment project
EIS's as a descriptive checklist methodology.
    Wakeland: The QSIM2 model serves primarily as a peda-
gogical or heuristic device to facilitate brainstorming and
experimentation with hypothesis. The modeling process makes
use of a FORTRAN program called QSIM2, which is inexpensive
to execute, operates in a conversational mode, and has many
features which give non-computer-oriented people the ability
to easily create, exercise, modify and store the models that
they design. The user is required to conceptualize: (1) a set
of variables which describe the system; and (2) a collection of

TABLE 52: SUGGESTED IMPACT MEASURES (After Schaenman, 1976)

IMPACT AREA AND SUBAREAS — Preferred Measures	Fallback Measures	USUALLY APPLICABLE TO EVALUATING[1] — Comprehensive Plans, Cumulative Effects, Large Rezonings	Small to Medium — Residential Rezoning	Small to Medium — Commercial-Industrial Rezoning	BASES FOR ESTIMATES[2]	REFERENCES[3]
I. Local Economy						
Public Fiscal Balance						
1. Net change in government fiscal flow (revenues less expenditures).		x			*Public revenues:* expected household incomes by residential housing type; added property values. *Public expenditures:* analysis of new service demand; current costs; available capacities by service.	M
Employment						
2. Change in numbers and percent employed, unemployed, underemployed, by skill level.	2a. Number of net new long-term and short-term jobs provided to local area.	x		x	Direct from new business; or estimated from floor space, local residential patterns, expected immigration, current unemployment profiles.	
Wealth						
3. Change in land values.		x	x	x	Supply and demand of similarly zoned land, environmental changes near property.	
II. Natural Environment						
Air Quality						
Health						
4. Change in air pollution concentrations by frequency of occurrence and number of people at risk.[4]	4a. Change in air pollutant concentrations relative to standards. 4b. Change in pollutant emissions relative to emission "budgets"[5] or targets.	x		x	Current ambient concentrations, current and expected emissions, dispersion models, population maps.	K

Nuisance

5. Change in occurrence of visual (smoke, haze) or olfactory (odor) air quality nuisances, and number of people affected.[6]

5a. Changes in the likelihood that air quality nuisances (qualitative judgment) will occur or vary in severity.

Water Quality

6. Changes in permissible or tolerable water uses and number of people affected--for each relevant body of water.

6a. Change in water pollutant concentrations (relative to standards), for each water pollutant.

6b. Change in amount discharged into body of water relative to effluent "budgets" for each pollutant.[5]

Noise

7. Change in noise levels and frequency of occurrence, and number of people bothered.[6]

7a. Changes in traffic levels, sound barriers, and other factors likely to affect noise levels and perceived satisfaction.

Wildlife and Vegetation

8. Change in diversity and population size (abundance) of wildlife and vegetation (including trees) of common species.[7]

8a. Changes in amount and quality of (a) habitat by animal type; (b) green space, or (c) number of mature trees.

9. Change in numbers of rare or endangered species.

9a. Same as 8a.

Item				Measurement	Code
5a.	x		x	Baseline citizen survey, expected industrial processes, traffic volumes.	K,C
6a.	x		x	Current and expected effluents, current ambient concentrations, water quality model.	K
6b.		x			
7a.	x	x	x	Changes in nearby traffic or other noise sources, and in noise barriers; noise propagation model or nomographs relating noise levels to traffic, barriers, etc.; baseline citizen survey of current satisfaction with noise levels.	K,C
8a.	x	x	x	Wildlife and vegetation inventory; expected removal of cover or changes to habitats.	K
9a.	x	x	x	Same as 8a.	K

171

TABLE 52 CONTINUED

IMPACT AREA AND SUBAREAS		USUALLY APPLICABLE TO EVALUATING[1]				BASES FOR ESTIMATES[2]	REF-ER-ENCES[3]
		Comprehensive Plans, Cumulative Effects, Large Rezonings	Small to Medium				
Preferred Measures	Fallback Measures		Residential Rezoning	Commercial-Industrial Rezoning			
Natural Disasters							
10. Change in number of people and value of property endangered by: flooding, earthquakes, landslides, mudslides, and other natural disasters, by frequency of occurrence.	10a. Change in flooding frequency. 10b. Change in percent of land with impermeable cover relative to "budgeted" levels.[8]	x	x	x		Flood plain and other hazard maps; changes in local topography and sewering; change in percent permeable cover; stream flow and hydraulic models.	K
III. Aesthetics and Cultural Values							
Attractiveness							
11. Change in number and percent of citizens who are satisfied with neighborhood appearance.	11a. Disturbance of physical conditions currently considered attractive; removal/improvement of conditions currently rated unattractive.	x	x	x		Baseline citizen survey of ratings of current attractiveness and identification of problems and assets; visual simulation of proposed development using retouched photos, drawings or 3-D models for assessing future preferences using a sample of citizens.	C
View Opportunities							
12. Change in number or percent of citizens satisfied with views from their homes (or businesses).	12a. Number of households (or businesses) whose views are blocked, degraded, or improved.	x	x	x		Baseline citizen survey; geometric analysis of structures to identify view opportunities before and after development.	C
Landmarks							
13. Number and perceived importance of cultural, historic, or scientific landmarks to be lost, made less accessible, or made more accessible.	13a. Rarity of landmark and distance to nearest similar examples of landmarks to be lost (or made more accessible).	x	x	x		Inventory and importance ranking of landmarks; survey of citizens and scholars regarding importance.	C

172

IV. Public and Private Services

Drinking Water

Availability

Item					Data needs	
14. Change in frequency duration and severity of water shortage incidents, and number of people affected.	14a. Change in likelihood of increased water shortages, and number of people likely to be affected.	x	x	x	Current usage, expected new demand; projected supplies.	K

Quality

Item					Data needs	
15. Change in salinity and other indices of drinking water quality and safety, and number of people affected.[9]	15a. Changes in effluents or purification processing likely to affect taste or other qualities of drinking water.	x	x	x	Expected effluents from new development; purification process used; current and expected usage; profile of underground water system.	K

Hospital Care

Emergency Care Availability

Item				Data needs
16. Change in number of citizens beyond x minutes travel time from emergency health care.	x	x	x	Maps of population distribution and emergency facilities; number of emergency vehicles (if any), expected calls, and dispatch policy.

Availability/Crowdedness

Item				Data needs
17. Change in potential bed need versus bed supply of area hospitals, by type of clinical service (medical, surgical, pediatric, obstetrical).	x	x	x	Current patient hospital bed days per 1000 population by sex-age group and medical service; available bed capacities; expected population by sex-age group.

Crime Control

Crime Rate

Item					Data needs
18. Change in rate of crimes in existing community.	18a. Expert rating of change in crime hazard.	x	x	x	Current crime rates and case histories of similar neighborhood changes; changes in community lighting, sightlines, hiding places, people mix.

173

TABLE 52 CONTINUED

IMPACT AREA AND SUBAREAS — Preferred Measures	Fallback Measures	USUALLY APPLICABLE TO EVALUATING[1] — Comprehensive Plans, Cumulative Effects, Large Rezonings	Small to Medium — Residential Rezoning	Small to Medium — Commercial-Industrial Rezoning	BASES FOR ESTIMATES[2]	REFERENCES[3]
Feeling of Security						
19. Change in percent of people feeling a lack of security from crime.	19a. Change in people mix, police patrolling, and physical conditions (lighting, sightlines, potential hiding places, etc.) likely to affect feelings of security.	x	x	x	Baseline citizen survey plus the data above.	C
Fire Protection						
20. Change in fire incidence, property loss, and casualty rates.	20a. Expert ratings of change in likelihood of fires, fire spread, rescue hazards.	x	x	x	Incidence rates by occupancy types; people mix; available water supply; available fire suppression equipment and manning; likely building materials; site plan if available.	
Recreation—Public Facilities[10] *Overall Satisfaction*						
21. Change in number and percent of households satisfied with public recreation opportunities.	21a. Measure 23 (change in accessibility) and changes in other physical conditions (noise, air quality, hazards, crowdedness) likely to affect satisfaction, and number of households potentially affected.	x	x	x	Baseline citizen surveys, and expected changes in facilities and environment (noise, air quality, dangers).	C
22. Change in number or percent of households using facilities (viewed relative to nominal capacity), by facility.[11]	22a. Same as above.	x	x	x	Citizen survey.	C

Measure				Data sources	
Accessibility 23. Change in number and percent of households with access to various types of recreation facilities within x minutes travel, by type of facility and mode of travel.11	x	x	x	Maps of facilities and distribution of population; citizen survey of travel mode.	C
Recreation—Informal Settings *Overall Satisfaction* 24. Change in number or percent of households satisfied with recreation in informal outdoor spaces in neighborhood. 24a. Measure 25 (availability) and change in other physical condition likely to affect satisfaction and number of households potentially affected.	x	x		Baseline citizen survey and observation of current usage patterns; physical environment changes expected.	C
Availability 25. Change in availability of informal physical settings for recreation and number of people affected.	x	x		Changes in open space and physical environment expected.	C
Education *Accessibility/Convenience* 26. Change in number and percent of households satisfied with accessibility of schools. 26a. Change in location of schools, and physical conditions around schools or along routes to schools that are likely to affect satisfaction with accessibility.	x	x		Citizen survey; changes in available path, nearby traffic conditions en route to schools.	C
27. Change in number and percent of students within x minutes, by type of school and travel mode.	x	x		Map of school and population distribution; busing records.	C

175

TABLE 52 CONTINUED

IMPACT AREA AND SUBAREAS — Preferred Measures	Fallback Measures	USUALLY APPLICABLE TO EVALUATING[1] — Comprehensive Plans, Cumulative Effects. Large Rezonings	Small to Medium — Residential Rezoning	Small to Medium — Commercial-Industrial Rezoning	BASES FOR ESTIMATES[2]	REFERENCES[3]
28. Number and percent of students having to switch schools or busing status.		x	x		Relation of capacity to expected demands, and school board policy.	
Crowdedness						
29. Change in school crowdedness indicators; e.g., student-teacher ratios, number of shifts.		x	x		Citizen survey; expected change in noise, traffic hazard, air quality, other hazards.	
Transportation—Mass Transit						
Satisfaction						
30. Change in number and percent of households satisfied with mass transit service.	30a. Expected changes in scheduling, routing, or crowdedness, and number of households likely to be affected.	x			Citizen survey, expected service changes, expected change in factors affecting satisfaction.	C
	30b. For retrospective studies: changes in number and percent of (a) households and (b) trips using public transit.	x			Usage levels, from fares and surveys.	C
Accessibility						
31. Change in number and percent of citizens residing (or working) within x feet of public transit stop.		x	x	x		C

Transportation–Pedestrians					
Satisfaction/Accessibility					
32. Change in number and per cent of households satisfied with walking conditions and walking opportunities in their neighborhood.[12]					
32a. Change in physical conditions (sidewalks, noise, etc.) affecting current satisfaction or dissatisfaction with walking conditions, and number of households likely to be affected.	x	x	x	Baseline citizen survey, estimated changes in physical walking conditions; additions or removals of desired destinations.	C
Safety					
See measures 33 and 34 below.					
32b. The group of measures of accessibility to shopping, schools (27), recreation (23), public transit (31).	x	x	x	N/A	
Transportation–Private Vehicles					
Safety					
33. Change in number and per cent of households satisfied with traffic safety (vehicle and pedestrian).					
33a. Change in physical conditions (e.g., traffic volumes, sidewalk width, barriers from traffic) likely to affect perceived safety, and number of households likely to be affected.	x	x	x	Baseline citizen survey, changes in traffic and traffic controls; circulation patterns.	C
34. Change in number and severity of accidents per 1,000 persons by pedestrians and riders.					
34a. Change in number and severity of traffic hazards created (may include changes in traffic volume and speed, sightlines, traffic controls), and number of people potentially affected.	x	x	x	Accident frequency and causation data; changes in traffic and traffic controls, circulation patterns, expected traffic volumes.	
Travel Time					
35. Change in vehicular travel times between selected origins and destinations, by time of day and day of week.					
35a. Change in "level of service" for selected roads and intersections, by time of day.[13]	x	x	x	Current traffic volumes; changes in street layout, width and traffic controls; estimated net new vehicle trips.	

TABLE 52 CONTINUED

IMPACT AREA AND SUBAREAS		USUALLY APPLICABLE TO EVALUATING[1]			BASES FOR ESTIMATES[2]	REF-ER-ENCES[3]
Preferred Measures	Fallback Measures	Comprehensive Plans, Cumulative Effects, Large Rezonings	Small to Medium			
			Residential Rezoning	Commercial-Industrial Rezoning		
Parking Availability						
36. Change in average time needed to find acceptable parking space within x feet of residence (or desired destinations) in neighborhood of development, by time of day and day of week.	36a. Change in the ratio of demand for parking spaces to supply of spaces within x distance of destinations in neighborhood of development, by type of space (metered, all-day, sheltered, etc.)	x	x	x	Current spaces available; new demand and supply; math model for estimating parking times (not needed for 36a).	C
37. Percent of drivers finding neighborhood parking satisfactory.	37a. Same as 36a.	x	x	x	Baseline citizen survey; expected changes in supply and demand for spaces.	C
Shopping[14]						
38. Change in number and percent of households satisfied with shopping opportunities.	38a. Change in variety, accessibility, and physical conditions of shopping areas.	x	x	x	Baseline citizen survey; change in physical conditions around shopping areas.	C
39. Change in number and percent of households within x minutes travel time to shopping, by type store and mode of travel.		x	x	x	Map showing location of stores and population, before and after development.	C
Energy Services						
40. Change in the frequency and duration of energy shortages, and the number of people affected, by fuel type.	40a. Expected energy usage per unit area of floor space or per unit of production, relative to standards for usage, by type of buildings and land use.	x	x[15]	x	Current and expected usage and supply in community; design and construction of buildings; type of manufacturing activity expected.	

178

Housing

41. Change in number and percent of housing units that are substandard and the number of people living in them.		x	x	x		Current housing stock conditions, number to be removed or improved.
42. Change in number and percent of housing units relative to need, by type of housing (price, owner/rental, number of bedrooms, style, etc.).						
42a. Change in number of units by type, viewed relative to number of families in various income groups in the community.		x	x	x		Current profile of housing stock units added or destroyed; past housing chain effects in distribution of population by income level, indicators of latent demand for housing.

V. Other Social Impacts (in addition to those included above)[16]

People Displacement

43. Number of residents (or workers) displaced by development, and whether satisfied with move.						
43a. Number of persons displaced.		x	x	x	C	Number of persons living in building to be destroyed; special survey of them.

Special Hazards

44. Number of children physically at risk from "special" hazards created by development (e.g., machinery, junk, unguarded deep water).		x	x	x	C	Physical outdoor changes expected.

Sociability/Friendliness[17]

45. Change in social interaction patterns (e.g., frequency of neighboring, community activities).						
45a. Identification of changes in people mix, settings for social activities, and physical barriers to social interactions.		x	x	x	C	Baseline survey of current neighboring and community activity patterns; changes in availability of community and small group meeting places; changes in physical barriers (e.g., highways, fences, heavy traffic, buildings which hinder access from one area of a neighborhood to another or footbridges or removal of barriers linking the areas); changes in people mix.

TABLE 52 CONTINUED

IMPACT AREA AND SUBAREAS		USUALLY APPLICABLE TO EVALUATING[1]				BASES FOR ESTIMATES[2]	REF-ER-ENCES[3]
		Comprehensive Plans, Cumulative Effects, Large Rezonings	Small to Medium				
Preferred Measures	Fallback Measures		Residential Rezoning	Commercial-Industrial Rezoning			
Privacy							
46. Change in number and percent of households satisfied with privacy in outdoor areas around home.	46a. Change in sightlines, pedestrian volumes, or other conditions likely to affect satisfaction, and number of households potentially affected.	x	x	x		Citizen survey; geometric analysis of sightlines; changes in sight and sound barriers.	C
Overall Contentment with Neighborhood							
47. Change in number and percent of citizens satisfied with their residential (or work) neighborhood.	47a. Degree of change to neighborhood elements that citizens express most satisfaction or dissatisfaction with.	x	x	x		Citizen survey using data from other measures.	C

NOTES:

1. Most measures are directly applicable at one time or another to all types of development.

2. The "bases for estimate" column presents a simplified, brief listing of key data and models (if any) needed for the preferred measure. A subset of the data is needed for the backup measures unless otherwise indicated. For retrospective studies, other, more direct measurement procedures are often feasible. Data collection procedures for the measures are outlined in P.S. Schaenman and T. Muller, *Measuring Impacts of Land Development*, Washington, D.C., The Urban Institute, 1974. A more detailed discussion of data collection and analysis may be found in the references.

3. Reference codes:

   M = Muller, *Fiscal Impacts of Land Development: A Critique of Methods and Review of Issues*, The Urban Institute, Washington, D.C., 1975.

180

C = Christensen, *Social Impacts of Land Development: An Initial Approach for Estimating Impacts on Neighborhood Usages and Perceptions*, The Urban Institute, Washington, D.C., 1976.

K = Keyes, *Land Development and the Natural Environment: Estimating Impacts*, The Urban Institute, Washington, D.C., 1976.

4. Measure 4 could be expanded, where appropriate, to reflect damage to vegetation and materials as well as to people's health.

5. "Emission budgets" would be maximum amounts of additional pollutants that could be added in a year. They would be based on desirable or tolerable ambient concentrations of each pollutant. The "budgets" should be revised periodically as part of comprehensive planning.

6. Citizen satisfaction with air quality and noise levels is "built into" Measures 5 and 7, respectively, via local calibration of what constitutes annoying levels for people to be affected. However, for retrospective studies, a separate measure of "percent of citizens satisfied with neighborhood air quality (or noise) levels" might also be desirable.

7. Diversity is measured by the number of species present or by "diversity index scores"—see Keyes, op. cit.

8. Similar to the emission budgets (see note 5), a budget for the net additional amount of land that can have impermeable ground cover before flooding becomes a likely hazard that can be specified based on the relation between impermeable cover, stormwater runoff, stream flow, and flood levels for individual watersheds.

9. Measure 6 is complementary to Measure 15; it reflects changes in quality of bodies of water from which drinking water is drawn, which may or may not affect water quality at the tap.

10. The recreation measures are worded for residential development, but can be restated for commercial/industrial development to indicate the number or percent of affected employees or shoppers; e.g., to estimate the availability and pleasantness of parks for lunch-time use.

11. Measures 22 (usage) and 23 (accessibility) are in part proxies for Measure 21 (satisfaction). But because citizen expectations affect satisfaction so much, the more "objective" measures are also important to consider, especially when there is considerable population turnover.

12. This measure of pedestrian satisfaction is related to other measures which may reflect walking conditions—measures of traffic safety (33,34), air quality (4,5), noise (7), aesthetics (11-13), and measures of accessibility of services (23,27,31). It also reflects changes in the availability of sidewalks, traffic lights, pedestrian bridges, crowdedness of streets, etc., and accessibility of destinations not listed in other measures, such as houses of friends. Satisfaction with walking opportunities might also be reflected by a measure of "changes in amount of walking activity" (number of people walking to destinations in neighborhood at least x times per week).

TABLE 52 CONTINUED

13. The six "levels of service" are: free flow traffic, stable flow in the upper speed range, stable flow, approaching unstable flow, unstable flow, and forced flow. Each category allows a range of traffic speeds and thus travel times, and describes congestion of the road or inter-section. Definitions for each level are given in: *Highway Capacity Manual*, Special Report 87, Highway Research Board, Washington, D.C., 1965.

14. An additional measure, "number and percent of households using existing stores, by type of store," is needed as a baseline for prediction, and may be useful in its own right for retrospective studies.

15. Although individual developments are unlikely to cause noticeable shortages, energy consumption relative to the type of land use—that is, expected efficiency of energy usage—may be maintained on an on-going basis.

16. Because of likely synergistic effects in assessing social impacts on a neighborhood, it seems important to view neighborhood perceptions, service opportunities, and environmental changes together. This cross-cut view of the measures (all those with a "C" in the reference column) is elaborated in Christensen, op. cit.

17. The "change in the percent of citizens perceiving their neighborhood as friendly (or cohesive)" might also be considered for retrospective studies, but seems difficult to forecast with current knowledge. We have not identified a satisfactory proxy for it, and therefore do not include it. Eventually, as data from before-and-after studies are accumulated (or reliable social models are developed), it may be possible to use this measure of a community attribute important to many people.

General note: For brevity, some fallback measures are included in the exhibit to summarize points raised in the detailed reports, even though they are not designated as measures in those reports.

functional relationships (entered as tables) which describe
how each variable is affected by each of the other variables.
Given their initial values, projections for the future values
of the variables can be made by entering and running the model
on a computer.

The specific modeling process involves the following
eight steps:

Step One. Defining the problem to be solved, e.g., improving a transportation system.

Step Two. Brainstorming the pertinent variables and
establishing temporal and spatial system boundaries.

Step Three. Reducing the number of variables to a manageable size by elimination and aggregation.

Step Four. Identifying the variables which affect each
variable. The concept of an interaction matrix (1) is useful,
with rows representing the affected variables and columns
representing the affecting variables. An "X" is placed in the
matrix to indicate which of the interactions are significant.
In a group effort, majority vote or consensus can be used.
When in doubt, an "X" is written, since the magnitude of the
interaction can be made slight when it is entered in Step Eight.

Step Five. Identifying auxiliary variables. Thus far in
this process it has not been necessary to distinguish between
state and auxiliary variables. To simplify the construction
of a preliminary model, one may disregard this distinction and
proceed directly to step six, delaying the consideration of
auxiliary variables until subsequent model refinements.

(There are several distinctions between state and auxiliary variables. The value of state variable is indirectly
influenced by the values of other variables (by means of their
impact on its rate of change), whereas the value of an auxiliary variable is directly influenced by the values of other
variables. In order to determine the value of a state variable
at some point in time its value at previous times is required.
This is not true of auxiliary variables. State variables cannot change their values instantaneously, whereas auxiliary
variables can. State variables are primary and fundamental;
auxiliary variables are functions of state variables.)

Step Six. Assigning the "initial values" and "base rates"
for the state variables. As previously mentioned, state variables are not analytic functions of the variables checked in
(1). Their values are obtained by numerical integration of
their derivatives. In the QSIM2 implementation, the Euler
approximation is used: $x(t+\Delta 7) = x(t)+\Delta Tx(t)$, where x is a
state variable, ΔT = a short time period, and $x(t)$ is the
derivative of x. $x(t)$ is the sum (or product, if desired) of
the base rate and several terms.

Step Seven. Specifying the functional form of the auxiliary variables identified in Step Five (if any). Auxiliary
variables can be either a polynomial of other variables or an

183

extension of such a polynomial. For computational reasons, the auxiliary variables must be ordered in such a fashion that each depends only on state variables and previously specified auxiliary variables.

Step Eight. Obtaining the "interaction functions". Each interaction function is a detail of an interaction specified by an "X" in the 1-matrix. If data is available, it may be possible to use statistics to get these interaction functions. Otherwise, Step Eight involves extracting the appropriate relationships from the mental models. That is, lacking data, an intuitive approach is acceptable for defining interaction functions in a heuristic model.

RESULTS OF 1977-78 PERIOD

A total of 49 references on methodologies/technologies (M/T's) were reviewed from this period, with the references listed in Table 53. Table 54 contains a summary of the M/T's reviewed relative to the 12 entrance criteria in Table 2. Eleven M/T's did not meet any criteria and thus were eliminated from further study. The eleven were Bockrath, Brown, Cheremisinoff and Morresi, Erickson, Fitzpatrick and others, Kahneman and Tversky, Pease and Smardon, Phillips and Kaune, Slovic, Sorensen and others, and Struss and Mikucki. Of the 38 M/T's that met one criterion or more, the following represents the number meeting the stated criteria:

1. Interdisciplinary team --- 4
2. Assessment variables --- 13
3. Field studies --- 3
4. Impact identification --- 10
5. Prediction of changes --- 18
6. Critical impacts --- 1
7. Relative importance weights --- 11
8. Scaling or ranking procedures --- 14
9. Impact summarization and assessment --- 12
10. Documentation --- 1
11. Public participation --- 6
12. Conflict management and resolution --- 5

The salient features of the 38 M/T's meeting one or more entrance criteria are summarized in Table 55. The advantages and limitations of each of the identified features are summarized in Appendix F along with general information on each of the 38 pertinent M/T's. The reproducibility of each M/T was difficult to evaluate since the references represented single uses.

Table 56 summarizes the conclusions regarding the 38 pertinent references from the 1977-78 period. Twenty-seven references contain potentially useable information for WRAM and 11 serve as general references. Useable information from the 27 references is as follows:

TABLE 53: LIST OF METHODOLOGIES AND TECHNOLOGIES
REVIEWED FROM THE 1977-78 PERIOD

1. Baldwin, P., "Environmental Mediation: An Effective Alternative?", Proceedings of Conference Held in Reston, Virginia, January 11-13, 1978, 1978, RESOLVE, Center for Environmental Conflict Resolution, Palo Alto, California.

2. Bockrath, J. T., Environmental Law for Engineers, Scientists and Managers, McGraw-Hill Book Company, Inc., New York, New York, 1977, 359 pages.

3. Boesch, D. F., "Application of Numerical Classification in Ecological Investigations of Water Pollution," EPA/600/3-77/033, March 1977, 127 pages, Corvallis Environmental Research Laboratory, U.S. Environmental Protection Agency, Corvallis, Oregon (prepared for EPA by Virginia Institute of Marine Science, Gloucester Point, Virginia).

4. Brown, L. R., "Estimate of Maximum Level of Oil Innocuous to Marina Biota as Inferred from Literature Review", CGR/DC-9/77, April 1977, 20 pages, Mississippi State University, Starkville, Mississippi.

5. Canter, L. W. et al., "An Assessment of Problems Associated with Evaluating the Physical, Chemical and Biological Impacts of Discharging Fill Material", Technical Report D-77-29, December 1977, 236 pages, U.S. Army Corps of Engineers, Waterways Experiment Stations, Vicksburg, Mississippi (prepared for WES by School of Civil Engineering and Environmental Science, University of Oklahoma, Norman, Oklahoma).

6. Canter, L. W. and Reid, G. W., "Environmental Factors Affecting Treatment Process Selection", paper presented at Oklahoma Water Pollution Control Federation Annual Meeting, 1977, Stillwater, Oklahoma.

7. Canter, L. W. and Hill, L. G., "Variables for Environmental Quality Account, Oct. 1977, 187 pages, Norman, Oklahoma (report submitted to U.S. Army Engineers Waterways Experiment Station, Vicksburg, Mississippi).

8. Canter, L. W., Environmental Impact Assessment, 1977, 331 pages, McGraw-Hill Book Company, New York, New York.

9. Canter, L. W., "Supplement to Environmental Impact Assessment", 1978, 1062 pages, Canter Associates, Inc., Norman, Oklahoma.

10. Canter, L. W., "Environmental Impact Statements on Municipal Wastewater Program", May 1978, Canter Associates, Inc., Norman, Oklahoma, (draft report submitted to Information Resources Press, Washington, D. C.)

11. Chalmers, J. A. and Anderson, E. J., "Economic/Demographic Assessment Manual: Current Practices, Procedural Recommendations, and a Test Case," November 1977, Engineering and Research Center, U.S. Bureau of Reclamation, Denver, Colorado, (prepared for Bureau of Reclamation by Mountain West Research, Inc., Tempe, Arizona).

12. Chalmers, J. A., "Bureau of Reclamation Construction Worker Survey," October 1977, Engineering and Research Center, U.S. Bureau of Reclamation, Denver, Colorado (prepared for Bureau of Reclamation by Mountain West Research, Inc., Tempe, Arizona).

13. Cheremisinoff, P. N. and Morresi, A. C., Environmental Assessment and Impact Statement Handbook, 1977, 438 pages, Ann Arbor Science Publishers, Inc., Ann Arbor, Michigan.

14. Dee, N. et al., "Literature Review to Identify Rationale for Developing Functional Relationships between Environmental Parameters and Environmental Quality," February 1978, 79 pages, Battelle-Southern Operations and Columbus Laboratories, Atlanta, Georgia (report to U.S. Army Corps of Engineers Waterways Experiment Station, Vicksburg, Mississippi).

15. Duke, K. M. et al., "Environmental Quality Assessment in Multiobjective Planning," November 1977, Final Report to U.S. Bureau of Reclamation, Denver, Colorado (prepared for BuRec by Battelle-Columbus Laboratories, Columbus, Ohio).

16. Dunne, N. G., "Successful Sanitary Landfill Siting: County of San Bernadino, California", SW-617, 1977, U.S. Environmental Protection Agency, Cincinnati, Ohio.

17. Dwyer, J. F., Hatmaker, M. L., and Hewings, G. J. D., "Profile and Measurement of Regional Development Indicators for Use in the Evaluation of Water and Related Land Management Planning", May 1978, 140 pages, University of Illinois, Urbana, Illinois (prepared for U.S. Army Waterways Experiment Station, Vicksburg, Mississippi).

18. Ellis, S. L. et al., "Guide to Land Cover and Use Classification Systems Employed by Western Governmental Agencies," FWS/OBS-77/05, March 1978, 183 pages, Ecology Consultants, Inc., Fort Collins, Colorado (prepared for Western Energy

and Land Use Team, Office of Biological Services, U.S.
Fish and Wildlife Service, Fort Collins, Colorado).

19. Erickson, L. E., "Approach to Valuing Visual Pollution
    from Western Electricity Production," BNWL-2103, February
    1977, 76 pages, Battelle Pacific Northwest Labs.,
    Richland, Washington.

20. Finsterbusch, K. and Wolf, C. P., The Methodology of
    Social Impact Assessment, 1977, Dowden, Hutchinson and
    Ross Publishing Co., Stroudsberg, Pennsylvania.

21. Finsterbusch, K., "Methods for Evaluating Non-Market Im-
    pacts in Policy Decisions with Special Reference to Water
    Resources Development Projects," IWR Contract Report 77-78,
    November 1977, 46 pages, U.S. Army Engineer Institute for
    Water Resources, Fort Belvoir, VA (prepared for IWR by
    University of Maryland, College Park, Maryland).

22. Fitzpatrick, M. S. et al., "Manual for Evaluating Secondary
    Impacts of Wastewater Treatment Facilities", EPA-600/5-78-
    003, February 1978, 175 pages, U.S. Environmental Protec-
    tion Agency, Washington, D. C., (prepared for EPA by Abt
    Associates, Inc., Cambridge, Massachusetts).

23. Flood, B. S. et al., "A Handbook for Habitat Evaluation
    Procedures", Resource Publ. 132, 1977, 77 pages, U.S.
    Fish and Wildlife Service, Washington, D. C.

24. Freeman, D. M., and Quint, J., "Coordinator's Manual ---
    The Analysis of Social Well-Being: Procedures for Com-
    paring Social Impacts of Proposed Resource Management
    Alternatives", October 1977, Department of Sociology,
    Colorado State University, Fort Collins, Colorado.

25. Frost, J. H., and Wilmot, W. W., Interpersonal Conflict,
    1978, Wm. C. Brown Company Publishers, Dubuque, Iowa.

26. Grooms, D. W., "A Directory of Computer Software Applica-
    tions - Environmental, 1977", PB-270 018/5WP, Sept. 1977,
    189 pages, National Technical Information Service, Spring-
    field, Virginia.

27. Guseman, P. K. and Dietrich, K. T., "Profile and Measure-
    ment of Social Well-Being Indicators for Use in the
    Evaluation of Water and Related Land Management Planning",
    Misc. Paper Y-78-2, June 1978, 112 pages, U.S. Army
    Engineers Waterways Experiment Station, Vicksburg,
    Mississippi (prepared for WES by Texas Transportation
    Institute, Texas A and M University, College Station, Texas.

187

28. Hammond, K. R. et al., "Social Judgment Theory: Applications in Policy Formation", in Kaplan, M. F., and Schwartz, S. (editors), Human Judgment and Decision Processes in Applied Settings, 1977, Academic Press, New York, New York.

29. Harrison, E. A., "Bioindicators of Pollution (A Bibliography with Abstracts)", NTIS/PS-77/0993, November 1977, 243 pages, National Technical Information Service, Springfield, Virginia.

30. Heer, Jr., J. E., and Hagerty, D. J., Environmental Assessments and Statements, 1977, 382 pages, Van Nostrand Reinhold Company, Florence, Kentucky.

31. Hobbs, B. F. and Voelker, A. H., "Analytical Multiobjective Decision-Making Techniques and Power Plant Siting: A Survey and Critique", ORNL-5288 Special, February 1978, Oak Ridge National Laboratory, Oak Ridge, Tennessee.

32. Jain, R. K., Urban, L. V., and Stacey, G. S., Environmental Impact Analysis, 1977, 340 pages, Van Nostrand Reinhold Company, Florence, Kentucky.

33. Johnson, D. W. and Cole, D. W., "Anion Mobility in Soils: Relevance to Nutrient Transport from Terrestrial to Aquatic Systems", EPA-600/3-77-068, June 1977, 28 pages, U.S. Environmental Protection Agency, Corvallis, Oregon.

34. Kahneman, D. and Tversky, A., "Intuitive Prediction: Biases and Corrective Procedures", Special Issue of Management Science on Forecasting Methodologies and Applications, in press.

35. McEvoy, III, J. and Dietz, T., Handbook for Environmental Planning, 1977, John Wiley and Sons, New York, New York.

36. Omernik, J. M., "Nonpoint Source - Stream Nutrient Level Relationships: A Nationwide Survey", EPA-600/3-77-105, September 1977, 151 pages, U.S. Environmental Protection Agency, Corvallis, Oregon.

37. Ott, W. R., "Water Quality Indices: A Survey of Indices Used in the United States", EPA-600/4-78-005, January 1978, 128 pages, U.S. Environmental Protection Agency, Washington, D. C.

38. Paul, B. W., "Subjective Prioritization of Energy Development Proposals Using Alternative Scenarios", (paper presented at the Joint National ORSA/TIMS Meeting,

San Francisco, Cal., May 1977), Engineering and Research
Center, U.S. Bureau of Reclamation, Denver, Colorado.

39. Pease, J. R. and Smardon, R. C., "Environmental Impact
    Assessment Project---Final Report, Analysis and Evalua-
    tion", Special Report 481, April 1977, Oregon State
    University Extension Service, Corvallis, Oregon.

40. Phillips, R. D. and Kaune, W. T., "Biological Effects of
    Statis and Low-Frequency Electromagnetic Fields: An Over-
    view of United States Literature", BNWL-2262, April 1977,
    40 pages, Battelle Pacific Northwest Labs., Richland,
    Washington.

41. Protasel, G. J., "Evaluating Natural Resource Planning,"
    September 1977, Department of Political Science, Oregon
    State University, Corvallis, Oregon (report submitted to
    U.S. Soil Conservation Service, Washington, D. C.)

42. Slovic, P., "Judgment, Choice, and Societal Risk Taking",
    paper presented at Symposium on Judgment and Choice in
    Public Policy Decisions, Annual Meeting of the American
    Association for the Advancement of Science, Denver,
    Colorado, February, 1977 (author's address is Decision
    Research, A Branch of Perceptronics, 1201 Oak Street,
    Eugene, Oregon.

43. Sorensen, D. L. et al., "Suspended and Dissolved Solids
    Effects on Freshwater Ciota: A Review", EPA-600/3-77-042,
    April 1977, 65 pages, U.S. Environmental Protection Agency,
    Corvallis, Oregon (prepared for EPA by Utah State Univer-
    sity, Logan, Utah).

44. Stinson, D. S. and O'Hare, M., "Predicting the Local
    Impacts of Energy Development: A Critical Guide to Fore-
    casting Methods and Models", May 1977, 98 pages, Laboratory
    of Architecture and Planning, Massachusetts Institute of
    Technology, Cambridge, Massachusetts.

45. Struss, S. R. and Mikucki, W. J., "Fugitive Dust Emission
    from Construction Haul Roads", Special Rep. N-17, February
    1977, 53 pages, Construction Engineering Research Labora-
    tory, U.S. Army, Champaign, Illinois.

46. U.S. Soil Conservation Service Environmental Assessment
    Guidelines in the Federal Register, Vol. 42, No. 152,
    Monday, August 8, 1977, pages 40127-40128.

47. Voelker, A. H., "Power Plant Siting: An Application of
     the Nominal Group Process Technique", ORNL/NUREG/TM-81,
     February 1977, Oak Ridge National Laboratory, Oak Ridge,
     Tennessee (prepared for U.S. Nuclear Regulatory Commission,
     Washington, D. C.)

48. Von Gierke, H. E., "Guidelines for Preparing Environmental
     Impact Statements on Noise", June 1977, 131 pages, National
     Research Council, Washington, D. C.

49. Wehr, P., <u>Conflict Regulation</u>, 1978, manuscript to be
     published by Westview Press, Boulder, Colorado.

Baldwin: This report summarizes an Environmental Mediation
Conference held in early 1978. Seven selected case histories
are summarized. The important general points discussed during
the Conference are summarized as follows:

- Environmental mediation and related techniques offer
  promising new approaches to environmental decision-making.

- Environmental mediation is not a panacea. While in some
  cases mediation and related techniques may prevent protracted and expensive litigation, these methods will
  certainly not supplant litigation entirely. They represent a new addition to the decision-making tool kit,
  not a substitution for other processes.

- Environmental mediators can learn much from the experience of labor mediators, but there are important
  differences which preclude a wholesale transfer of
  methodologies.

- Conflict resolution is not an end in itself; rather, it
  is a means to sound environmental decision-making.
  Conflict is often healthy in a democratic society, and
  the most difficult conflicts may produce the most
  creative solutions.

Canter et al.: This report contains a state-of-the-art
survey of the physical, chemical, and biological impacts
resulting from the discharge of fill material. Fill materials
can be natural (soil, rock, or sand) or man-altered (dredged
material, solid wastes, or residues), with projects involving
useage including property protection, causeway/roadfills, and
site development. Potential environmental impacts are regulated by permits based on Section 404 of PL 92-500. A paired
comparison technique was used to prioritize technical needs in
terms of impact identification, prediction, and assessment.

TABLE 54: SUMMARY OF 1977-78 METHODOLOGIES/TECHNOLOGIES RELATIVE TO ENTRANCE CRITERIA

METHODOLOGY/TECHNOLOGY*

CRITERIA	1	2	3	4	5	6	7	8	9	10	11	12	13	14	15	16	17	18	19	20	21	22	23	24	25	26	27	28	29	30	31	32	33	34	35	36	37	38	39	40	41	42	43	44	45	46	47	48	49
No entrance criteria set	X	X											X					X				X												X					X	X			X		X			X	
Twelve entrance criteria																																																	
1. Interdiciplinary team																														X														X					
2. Assessment variables				X					X	X	X			X	X			X	X				X				X						X		X														
3. Field studies				X						X													X														X												
4. Impact identification									X	X			X	X	X						X											X		X										X					
5. Prediction of change					X				X	X	X	X				X										X	X		X	X		X	X	X	X	X								X			X		
6. Critical impacts															X																																		
7. Relative importance weights								X	X	X	X					X					X							X			X							X		X	X				X				
8. Scaling or ranking procedure								X	X	X	X			X	X	X					X						X	X			X							X								X			
9. Impact summarization and assessment								X	X	X	X			X						X	X									X	X														X		X		
10. Documentation														X																																			
11. Public participation									X	X											X									X	X										X								
12. Conflict management and resolution			X																					X	X		X			X																			X

*The numbers correspond to those listed in Table 53.

191

TABLE 55: SALIENT FEATURES OF 1977-78
METHODOLOGIES/TECHNOLOGIES

Methodology/Technology	Salient Feature(s)
Baldwin	Advantages and limitations of mediation for resolving environmental disputes are discussed.
Boesch	Numerical classification schemes for ecological studies of water pollution are described.
Canter et al.	Literature survey of impacts from discharging fill material is presented.
Canter and Reid	A weighting-scaling technique for evaluating the environmental impacts of wastewater treatment processes is described.
Canter and Hill	Information on measurement, impact prediction and functional curves is included on 62 assessment variables for the EQ account.
Canter (1977)	Comprehensive textbook on impact prediction, assessment and evaluation.
Canter (1978)	Comprehensive state-of-the-art summary of information on impact prediction, assessment, and evaluation.
Canter	20 of 28 EIS's on wastewater facility plans used an impact assessment methodology.
Chalmers and Anderson	Descriptive checklist for addressing the economic and demographic impacts of water resources projects.
Chalmers	Economic and demographic impacts from water resources project construction are described.

Dee et al.	Concepts for developing functional curves are summarized.
Duke et al.	Scaling checklist for water resources projects; concept of environmental potential.
Dunne	Weighting-scaling checklist for sanitary landfill site selection.
Dwyer, Hatmaker and Hewings	Summary of impact prediction for 37 important variables in the Regional Development account.
Ellis et al.	Systematic approaches for describing the biological setting are summarized.
Finsterbusch and Wolf	Series of articles on social impact assessment.
Finsterbusch	This is an excellent literature review on techniques for decision-making for water resources projects.
Flood et al.	A habitat evaluation procedure for the biological environment is described.
Freeman and Quint	Practical procedure for conflict resolution.
Frost and Wilmot	Practical ideas on conflict management and resolution.
Grooms	Abstracts of available computer programs for impact prediction on the physical-chemical environment are described.
Guseman and Dietrich	Information on measurement; impact prediction and functional curves is included on assessment variables for the SWB account.
Hammond et al.	Weighting and scaling as a means for conflict resolution is described.

Harrison	54 new abstracts of bioindicators of pollution are presented.
Heer and Hagerty	General overview of impact statement preparation.
Hobbs and Voelker	Summary of multiobjective decision-making techniques is presented.
Jain, Urban, and Stacey	Impact prediction and assessment information is presented on 49 assessment variables (called environmental attributes).
Johnson and Cole	Nutrient transport from terrestrial to aquation systems is described.
McEvoy and Dietz	Prediction and assessment of socio-economic impacts.
Omernik	Nonpoint sources of nutrients from National Eutrophication Survey are summarized.
Ott	Summary of state-of-the-art of water quality index usage in the United States.
Paul	Weighting-scaling checklist used to prioritize potential projects.
Protasel	A public participation technique for importance weighting is described.
Stinson and O'Hare	33 techniques for forecasting energy development impacts are described.
U.S. Soil Conservation Service	Discussion of interdisciplinary team; network for an impoundment.
Voelker	Nominal Group Process. Techniques for group assignment of relative importance weights to decision factors.

Von Gierke   Noise impact prediction and
                               assessment is described.

Wehr   Comprehensive information on
                               conflict management and reso-
                               lution.

TABLE 56:   SUMMARY OF CONCLUSIONS REGARDING PERTINENT
            REFERENCES FROM THE 1977-78 PERIOD

Potentially Useable in WRAM   General Reference for WRAM

Baldwin   Boesch
Canter et al.   Canter and Reid
Canter and Hill   Canter (1977)
Canter (May, 1978)   Canter (1978)
Chalmers and Anderson   Dunne
Chalmers   Ellis et al.
Dee et al.   Heer and Hagarty
Duke et al.   Johnson and Cole
Dwyer, Hatmaker, and Hewings   Omernik
Finsterbusch and Wolf   Paul
Finsterbusch   U.S. Soil Conservation Service
Flood et al.
Freeman and Quint
Frost and Wilmot
Grooms
Guseman and Dietrich
Hammond et al.
Harrison
Hobbs and Voelker
Jain, Urban, and Stacey

Potential physical impacts include changes in infiltration
and flow regimes, destruction/alteration of natural or man-made
habitats, and creation of habitats. Chemical impacts result
from the release of suspended solids, organics, nutrients and
toxic substances. Biological impacts range from physical barriers to fish migration to complete "smothering" of entire
wetland areas. The effects of leachates on aquatic biota are
complex and diverse, ranging from no measurable changes to
acute toxicity.

Canter and Hill: This report contains a comprehensive
list of variables to be used in the EQ account associated with
water resources planning. Each selected variable was grouped
into either terrestrial, aquatic, air or human interface categories. To select pertinent variables, a master list of 189
potential ones was assembled following a review of several

195

environmental assessment methodologies and related reports. A total of 62 variables were included in the final selection, and the report contains information on each in terms of definition and measurement of baseline conditions, prediction of impacts, functional curve (where one was available or easily developed), general remarks, and data sources. Figure 11 displays the categories of the selected variables.

Canter (May, 1978): This report describes a comprehensive study of 28 EIS's on wastewater facility 201 plans. The EIS's were primarily prepared in late 1976 and 1977. Twenty EIS's utilized an impact assessment methodology in selecting the proposed action from the alternatives which were studied. Four descriptive checklists, 4 ranking checklists, 6 scaling checklists, 1 weighting-ranking checklist and 5 weighting-scaling checklists were used. For the 8 EIS's in which no selection methodology was identified it is possible that they were described in the Facility Plans, but not included in the EIS's.

Chalmers and Anderson: This report is focused on the problems associated with projecting the population, employment, and income impacts of both the construction and the operation phases of water resource development projects. The manual consists of three sections as follows:

1. Survey of Current Practices. A large number of environmental assessments and planning reports are reviewed. Methods currently being used for economic and demographic analysis are described.

2. Procedural Recommendations. Based partly on current practices and partly on the professional social science literature, a set of procedural recommendations are made for carrying out economic/demographic assessments. Important methodological options are identified and evaluated as they apply to the different steps in the projection and assessment process.

3. Test Case. The procedural recommendations are demonstrated by applying them to a proposed desalting plant near LaVerkin, Utah. The organization of the assessment follows the procedural recommendations and illustrates the way in which many of the practical problems of an actual assessment can be met.

Each of the three major sections of the manual is organized around a seven-step procedure for carrying out an economic/ demographic assessment. The seven-step procedure is shown in Figure 12.

Chalmers: This study is focused on the problems associated with estimating the economic and demographic impacts arising out of project construction activities. The

196

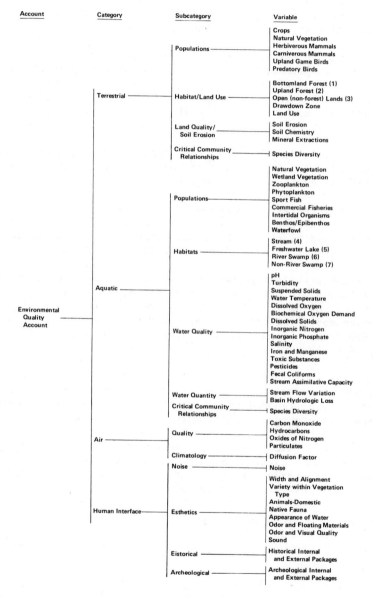

Account	Category	Subcategory	Variable

Account

Category

Subcategory

Variable

Terrestrial

Populations
- Crops
- Natural Vegetation
- Herbiverous Mammals
- Carniverous Mammals
- Upland Game Birds
- Predatory Birds

Habitat/Land Use
- Bottomland Forest (1)
- Upland Forest (2)
- Open (non-forest) Lands (3)
- Drawdown Zone
- Land Use

Land Quality/Soil Erosion
- Soil Erosion
- Soil Chemistry
- Mineral Extractions

Critical Community Relationships
- Species Diversity

Aquatic

Populations
- Natural Vegetation
- Wetland Vegetation
- Zooplankton
- Phytoplankton
- Sport Fish
- Commercial Fisheries
- Intertidal Organisms
- Benthos/Epibenthos
- Waterfowl

Habitats
- Stream (4)
- Freshwater Lake (5)
- River Swamp (6)
- Non-River Swamp (7)

Water Quality
- pH
- Turbidity
- Suspended Solids
- Water Temperature
- Dissolved Oxygen
- Biochemical Oxygen Demand
- Dissolved Solids
- Inorganic Nitrogen
- Inorganic Phosphate
- Salinity
- Iron and Manganese
- Toxic Substances
- Pesticides
- Fecal Coliforms
- Stream Assimilative Capacity

Water Quantity
- Stream Flow Variation
- Basin Hydrologic Loss

Critical Community Relationships
- Species Diversity

Air

Quality
- Carbon Monoxide
- Hydrocarbons
- Oxides of Nitrogen
- Particulates

Climatology
- Diffusion Factor

Noise
- Noise

Human Interface

Esthetics
- Width and Alignment
- Variety within Vegetation Type
- Animals-Domestic
- Native Fauna
- Appearance of Water
- Odor and Floating Materials
- Odor and Visual Quality
- Sound

Eistorical
- Historical Internal and External Packages

Archeological
- Archeological Internal and External Packages

Environmental Quality Account

FIGURE 11: STRUCTURE OF THE ENVIRONMENTAL QUALITY ACCOUNT (After Canter and Hill, 1977)

FOOTNOTES TO FIGURE 11

(1)   Bottomland forest represents a composite consideration of the following 11 parameters: species associations, percent mast-bearing trees, percent coverage by understory, diversity of understory, percent coverage by groundcover, diversity of groundcover, number of trees > 16 in. (or 18 in.) dbh per acre, percent of trees > 16 in. (or 18 in.) dbh, frequency of inundation, edge (quantity) and edge (quality).

(2)   Upland forest represents a composite consideration of the following 10 parameters: species associations, percent mast-bearing trees, percent coverage of understory, diversity of understory, percent coverage of groundcover, diversity of groundcover, number of trees $\geq$ 16 in. dbh/acre, percent of trees $\geq$ 16 in dbh, quantity of edge and mean distance to edge.

(3)   Open (non-forest) lands represent a composite consideration of the following 4 parameters: land use, diversity of land use, quantity of edge, mean distance to edge.

(4)   Stream represents a composite consideration of the following 8 parameters: sinuosity, dominant centrarchids, mean low water width, turbidity, total dissolved solids, chemical type, diversity of fishes and diversity of benthos.

(5)   Freshwater lake represents a composite consideration of the following 10 parameters: mean depth, turbidity, total dissolved solids, chemical type, shore development, spring flooding above vegetation line, standing crop of fishes, standing crop of sport fish, diversity of fishes, and diversity of benthos.

(6)   River swamp represents a composite consideration of the following 6 parameters: species associations, percent forest cover, percent flooded annually, groundcover diversity, percent coverage by groundcover, and days subject to river overflow.

(7)   Non-river swamp represents a composite consideration of the following 5 parameters: species associations, percent forest cover, percent flooded annually, groundcover diversity and percent coverage by groundcover.

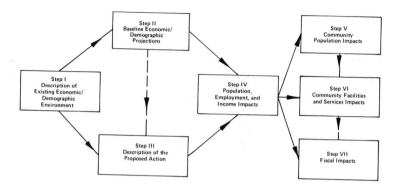

FIGURE 12:   STEPS IN ECONOMIC/DEMOGRAPHIC ASSESSMENT PROCESS
(After Chamers and Anderson, 1977)

construction worker survey is an attempt to obtain empirical
observations on key characteristics of Bureau of Reclamation
construction workers.   A survey was conducted during the summer
of 1977 and was designed to determine the characteristics of
construction workers and their families; the distribution of
the construction force between local and nonlocal workers; the
extent to which nonlocal workers were accompanied by their
families; the way in which the local residences of the nonlocal
workers were distributed; and, finally, to investigate the
previous employment status of local workers.

Dee et al.:   This study focused on the adaptation of
"national" functional curves to the southwestern portion of
the United States, namely, New Mexico.   A procedure for developing functional curves included 7 steps as follows: (1) define
the variable, (2) define measurement units, (3) obtain specific
data points, (4) calibrate selected data points, (5) derive
functional relationship, (6) test relationship, and (7) prepare
a post-project audit.   Regionally-oriented functional curves
were developed for natural vegetation, soil erosion, waterfowl,
biochemical oxygen demand, particulates, sulfur dioxide, variety
within vegetation types, and non-aircraft noise.

Duke et al.:   This scaling checklist methodology is
addressed to the EQ account used in evaluation of water resources
programs and projects.   A flow diagram of the methodology is in
Figure 13.

The environmental factors for the analysis are identified
through use of an interaction matrix (called an environmental
activity matrix similar to the Leopold matrix.   Table 57 contains a list of potential assessment variables for water
resources projects.

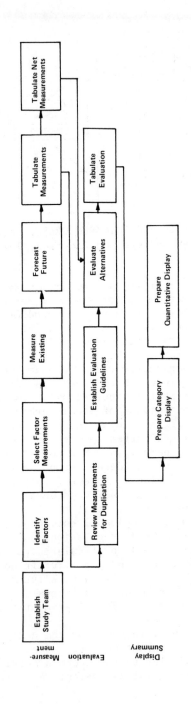

FIGURE 13: FLOW DIAGRAM OF ENVIRONMENTAL QUALITY ASSESSMENT METHODOLOGY (After Duke, et al. 1977)

200

TABLE 57: LIST OF COMPONENTS, CATEGORIES, AND FACTORS FOR
THE ENVIRONMENTAL QUALITY ACCOUNT (AFTER DUKE ET AL., 1977)

ECOLOGICAL COMPONENT

Biological Resources Category
  Aquatic Flora
  Trees
  Grasses and Shrubs
  Aquatic Animals
  Terrestrial Animals
  Endangered and Threatened Species
  Unique Biota
  Educational and Scientific Value
  Legal and Administrative Protection
Ecological Systems Category
  Ecosystem Type
  Ecosystem Quality
  Uniqueness
  Educational and Scientific Value
  Legal and Administrative Protection
Estuarine and Wetland Areas Category
  Estuarine Areas
  Wetland Areas
  Water Quality
  Productivity
  Uniqueness
  Educational and Scientific Value
  Legal and Administrative Protection
Wilderness, Primitive and Natural Areas Category
  Size
  Significant Topographic Features
  Significant Water Features
  Educational and Scientific Values

PHYSICAL COMPONENT

Water Quality Category
  Water Quality Standards
  Nonpoint Source Problems
  Constraints by Water Quality Problems
Air Quality Category
  Conformance with Air Quality Standards
  Extent of Environmental Degradation
  Adverse Impacts on Flora
  Air Quality Problems Attributable to Human Activity
Sound Quality Category
  Critical Sound Levels
  Temporal Distribution of Sound Problems
  Institutional Mitigation Measures

Visual Quality Category
  Scale
  Variety
  Naturalness
  Human Usage
Land Quality Category
  Land Use
  Land Degradation
  Land Use Regulations
Geological Resources Category
  Processes and Formations
  Fossil Beds
  Uniqueness
  Educational and Scientific Value
  Legal and Administrative Protection

CULTURAL COMPONENT

Historical and Archaeological Resources Category
  Sites
  Level of Investigation
  Educational Value
  Symbolic Land Features
  Extent Used by Public
  Protection of Significant Sites

RECREATIONAL COMPONENT

Streams and Stream Systems Category
  Amount of Significant Land/Water Features
  Degree of Flow Regularity
  Type of Flow
  Stream Use for Recreation
  Potential for Designation as a National/State River
Beaches and Shores Category
  Availability for Recreation
  Susceptibility to Adverse Impacts
  Physical Acceptability of Beaches
  Projected Beach/Shoreline Use
  Development Controls
Lakes and Reservoirs Category
  Number of Lakes
  Area of Lakes
  Water Quality
  Productivity
  Uniqueness
  Recreation
  Legal and Administrative Protection

Open Space and Greenbelts Category
    Sufficiency of Open Space
    Diversity of Land Uses Classified as Open Space
    Extent to Which Open Space Can Be and is Being Used
    Diversity of Public Use Facilities Available
    Extent of Development Controls in Area

The critical element in the evaluation phase is the establishment of evaluation guidelines. The guidelines will be specific to the project setting and will enable the user to determine the magnitude and direction of each environmental effect. The evaluation guidelinesis based upon the concept of environmental potential. Each environmental factor measurement describes an element of the environment which has an optimal environmental quality. The differences between the existing quality and this optimal level is defined as the environmental potential (Figure 14). An environmental effect is defined as the difference between the future with and the future without a project plan. If the change is toward the optimum, it is beneficial (Figure 15); and if it is away from the optimum, it is adverse (Figure 16). What is defined as the optimal level of environmental quality for an environmental factor measurement varies among regions of the western United States. In some cases, the maximum quality may also be the optimal while in others it is not. The evaluation guideline is the standard that determines if the beneficial or adverse changes are significant and if there are any environmental sensitive areas (flags).

Specifically, an evaluation guideline is defined as the smallest change in the highest existing quality in the region that would be considered significant. The highest existing quality is defined as the best environmental quality for that factor measurement that currently exists in the region. For example, assume that the highest existing quality for dissolved oxygen in the region is 8 mg/l. If a reduction of 1.5 mg/l in that stream would be considered significant, then the evaluation guideline is 1.5 mg/l. A schematic diagram of the evaluation guideline is provided in Figure 17.

A three-step process can be used to develop evaluation guidelines for each factor measurement. It is suggested that more than one individual be involved in the development process. A consensus producing approach like the Delphi Technique might be valuable in this process.

Step 1. Identify the highest existing quality in the region.

Step 2. Determine the change in the highest existing quality that would be considered significant. The estimate can be based on professional judgment or the use of prediction techniques combined with professional judgment.

203

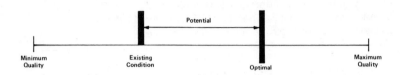

FIGURE 14:   ENVIRONMENTAL POTENTIAL (After Duke, et al, 1977)

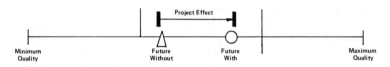

FIGURE 15:   BENEFICIAL PROJECT EFFECT (After Duke, et al, 1977)

FIGURE 16:   ADVERSE PROJECT EFFECT (After Duke, et al, 1977)

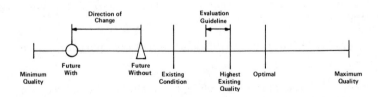

FIGURE 17:   EVALUATION GUIDELINE (After Duke, et al, 1977)

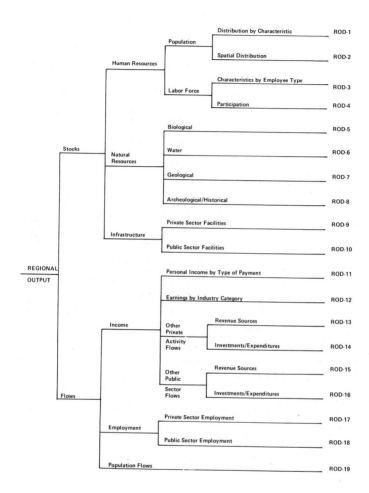

FIGURE 18:   REGIONAL OUTPUT DISAGGREGATION (After Dwyer, Hatmaker,
and Hewings, 1978)

incorporate elements of the stock and flow breakdown. These
direct changes are subjected to the income multiplier analysis
within the framework of Figure 18 to produce total changes in
stock variables and flows such as income.

The relationship between Figures 18 and 19 is illustrated
by Figure 20. In step I the stock and flow variables which
were outlined in the regional output disaggregation (ROD)

205

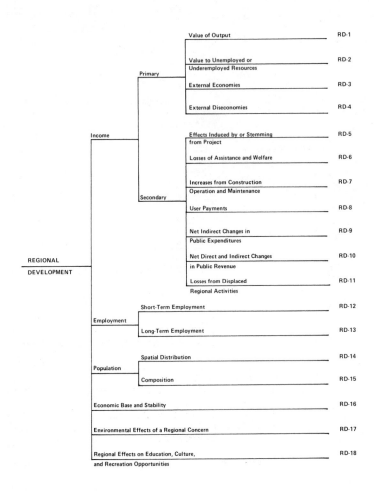

			Value of Output	RD-1
			Value to Unemployed or Underemployed Resources	RD-2
		Primary	External Economies	RD-3
			External Diseconomies	RD-4
	Income		Effects Induced by or Stemming from Project	RD-5
			Losses of Assistance and Welfare	RD-6
		Secondary	Increases from Construction Operation and Maintenance	RD-7
			User Payments	RD-8
			Net Indirect Changes in Public Expenditures	RD-9
REGIONAL DEVELOPMENT			Net Direct and Indirect Changes in Public Revenue	RD-10
			Losses from Displaced Regional Activities	RD-11
	Employment	Short-Term Employment		RD-12
		Long-Term Employment		RD-13
	Population	Spatial Distribution		RD-14
		Composition		RD-15
	Economic Base and Stability			RD-16
	Environmental Effects of a Regional Concern			RD-17
	Regional Effects on Education, Culture, and Recreation Opportunities			RD-18

FIGURE 19:   REGIONAL DEVELOPMENT ACCOUNT (After Dwyer, Hatmaker, and Hewings, 1978)

The WRAM framework (Figure 19) provides a "balance sheet" approach to regional accounting. However, its elements cannot be projected as entities in themselves; they must be aggregated from projections of the stock and flow variables in the regional output disaggregation (Figure 18). For example, the component of the WRAM framework "income increases from induced or stemming activities," cannot be estimated directly. Rather, direct project impacts are used as changes in projection models that

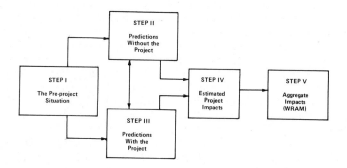

FIGURE 20:   RELATIONSHIP BETWEEN ROD AND WRAM MODELS (After
Dwyer, Hatmaker and Hewings, 1978)

Step 3.   Document the rationale for the selection of the
highest existing quality and the selection of the guideline.

Impact display involves preparing a category display and
quantitative display.   The purpose of the category display is
to provide an overview of the evaluation results.   The entries
in a summary table are the number of environmental factor measurements that meet each of the five evaluation possibilities
for each alternative:
1.   No significant effect
2.   Significant beneficial effect
3.   Significant adverse effect
4.   Beneficial flag
5.   Adverse flag
Dwyer, Hatmaker, and Hewings: The system presented in
this report includes both regional output disaggregation and
a regional development account.   A regional output disaggregation of the regional development (RD) account is presented in
Figure 18.   The regional output disaggregation shows the economic, social, and environmental variables that are elements
of regional output or have an influence on that output.   It
provides a convenient framework for inventorying the readily-
available information on stock and flow variables that are of
significance to regional development and output.   Stock variables are those that are measured at a point in time, while
flow variables are those measured over an interval of time.
The regional output disaggregation (Figure 18) is designed to
display several variations of the incidence of impacts and
combinations of impacts.   Consequently, some impacts occur more
than once in the model but in different forms.   For example,
both government revenues and expenditures are shown because
each may be critical to the evaluation of a project's regional
impact.   For the same reasons, direct income is considered in
terms of three categories: value of output, income by sources,
and income by type.

207

model are estimated for the pre-project situation. Predictions
of these variables under conditions without the project are
developed in step II. In step III the stocks and flows are
predicted for conditions with the project. Estimates for with
and without the project are compared to develop estimates of
project impacts (step IV). In the last step, project impacts
are aggregated into the WRAM framework. Thus there is not a
direct or 1 to 1 correspondence between the ROD and WRAM frameworks; rather, it is an elaborate linkage of procedures.

The primary focus of the report is on the 37 variables
listed in Figures 18 and 19. Each of the variables is defined
and described. Procedures for measurement and prediction are
also outlined, and selected data sources and references are
presented. For those variables that cannot be measured in
pecuniary terms, an illustrative hypothesized functional
relationship between the variable and a quality index is presented. The hypothesized functional relationship is intended
to operationalize some of the concepts presented in the discussion of the variables.

Finsterbusch and Wolf: This book contains a series of
articles written by different persons on various subjects
related to social impact assessment. Several articles address
methodologies and technologies for accomplishing impact prediction and assessment.

Finsterbusch: This report reviews and critiques 19
methods for evaluating non-market (non-monetary) impacts in
conjunction with water resources development projects. The
methods are listed in Table 58. In the second section of the
report the social impacts of water resources projects are
briefly reviewed and related to the 19 evaluation methods.

Flood et al.: This handbook report describes the concepts
of a habitat evaluation system for measuring the effects of
water development projects on fish, wildlife and related resources. The handbook was specifically written for the Meramec
Park Lake project site in Crawford County, Missouri. In the
handbook six groups of animals are categorized in as many as
six habitat types. They are composed principally of animals
whose habitat requirements are well known, easily found in
literature, and occur in the project area. Animals with similar requirements were grouped in the following manner: Forest
Game, Upland Game, Tree Squirrels, Terrestrial Furbearers,
Aquatic Furbearers, and Waterfowl. Marsh birds, raptors,
songbirds, small mammals, reptiles, and amphibians inhabit the
Meramec area but habitat criteria have not yet been developed
for these groups. Habitat Types include Bottomland Hardwood,
Upland Hardwood, Old Field, Pasture, Small Grain and Row Crops,
and Meramec River and Riverine Habitat. An Old Field is an
uncultivated or ungrazed tract; Pasture, a grazed grassland;
any cultivated field is classified as Small Grain and Row

TABLE 58: ALTERNATIVE EVALUATION FRAMEWORKS FOR COMPARING
NON-MARKET VALUES (AFTER FINSTERBUSCH, 1977)

A. Common Metrics
    1. Objective Metrics
    2. Subjective Metrics

B. Weighting Schemes
    1. Consensual Weights
    2. Formula Weights
    3. Justified Subjective Weights
    4. Subjective Weights
    5. Inferred Subjective Weights
    6. Ranking
    7. Equal Weight
    8. Multiple Methods

C. Discrete Dimensions Evaluation
    1. Balance Sheet
    2. Lexicographic Pruning
    3. Minimum Criteria Analysis

D. Methods Which Utilize Public or Political Evaluations
    1. Public Choice
    2. Advisory Committee Choice
    3. Political Process Outcome

E. Methods Which Obviate Evaluation
    1. Standardize Costs or Benefits
    2. Minimize Negative Effects
    3. Compensation and Mitigation

Crops; and River and Riverine Habitat is the association of
water, beach, and bank.

The handbook format is the same for each animal group
(Evaluation Element): requirements; preferred food list;
cavity-forming tree list if applicable; references; and field
forms for each relevant habitat type. Exhaustive life-histories
are not given; rather habitat needs (seral stages, food, cover,
and reproductive requirements) are discussed. Plants are listed
in decreasing order of importance as a food source for a particular species.

From one to eight habitat characteristics are shown on
each field form. These differ among habitat types, but relate
to food, cover, and reproductive requirements. Criteria for
scoring and ranges of scores are given for each habitat characteristic. The most important characteristics are scored on a

1 to 10 scale. Less important characteristics are scored on
a 1 to 5 scale, permitting the weighting of characteristics.

Freeman and Quint: This manual was prepared for coordinators of U.S. Forest Service public participation programs. One
exercise is focused on resolving conflicting opinions relative
to Forest Service projects. Procedures for accomplishing resolution involve the assignment of importance weights to decision
factors and group discussions.

Frost and Wilmot: This book is written primarily for
academic courses that focus on the conflict process as part of
normal, ongoing communication relationships. Persons interested
in small groups, communication in organizations, marriage communication, male and female communication, management, counseling, and organizational development will find this book
helpful as a primary text or supplement to another text. Of
interest in terms of WRAM are some suggestions for third party
intervenors in conflicts. The third party should intervene in
the communication process itself when it is apparent that the
participants are not listening to each other, or that they need
help in understanding one another. Some of the rules that
might be appropriate to follow are:

1. Be descriptive rather than judgmental. Describe
behavior in terms of what your reaction is to it, rather than
pinning a label on the other person. For instance, try to get
participants to say, "This is the fifth time we've tried to
find a solution" instead of this is a "totally uncooperative
group." Describe in terms of observable behavior instead of
"mindraping" the other person by saying, "I know what you're
thinking."

2. Encourage specificity. Feedback is more effective
when it describes specific instances instead of general feelings. For instance, instead of letting people say, "I'm sure
that's not going to be acceptable to some people," encourage
them to be specific by saying "I'm almost certain that Sam will
say no to that. And we need his cooperation." When dealing
with painful feelings, there is a tendency to be abstract.
People flounder when they are unsure. Encourage them by saying,
"Could you tell the group of an instance that illustrates when
you get resentful of Sam's directions?" Try to avoid the use
of such phrases as "most people," "they say," "it seems we"
or "one might think" (Brammer 1973). If a statement is worth
making, it is worth making specifically so its full power can
be felt.

3. Deal with things that can be changed instead of
"givens." Feedback is most effective when it concerns descriptions that are not inherent characteristics of persons or
situations. Saying, "Mary just bugs me. There's nothing I

210

can do to change that" is not very helpful. The leader could call a foul on such statements, asking for the participants to deal with issues that are at issue. Concentrating on things that cannot be changed is a waste of time and emotional energy.

4. Encourage parties to give feedback when it is requested. If Mary says, "I'm not sure how John feels. He never tells me," the third party might say, "Do you want to check that out? You could ask him to tell you." Or the intervention agent can ask parties to give feedback to each other when they need it, even if the need has not been articulated.

5. Give feedback as close as possible to the behavior being discussed. Feedback sometimes serves as a kind of "instant replay" to a behavioral pattern that has been observed by the third party. But it loses its effectiveness if someone says, "I was angry at your suggestion at our last staff meeting. I thought about it all week." The feedback would have more power closer to the triggering event.

6. Encourage feedback whose accuracy can be checked by others. In a group situation, sometimes people are unaware of their own word choices and behavior. A high school principal made a statement once at a workshop about wanting the facilitator to "make the faculty have more respect for each other." When the third party fed back that statement to the principal, he denied that he had said anything implying coercion. One of the teachers spoke up and said, "Mr.____, when you talk about 'making' us do something, it makes me feel like a third grader. I feel resentment." He was able to understand her feelings since other people were able to corroborate the statement he had made earlier.

7. Speak only for yourself. Encourage persons in conflicts to not speculate what other people think, and to say, "I think," or "I feel" often. Especially, check out coalitions by saying, "Mr. Jones has said you all agree with him. I'd like to check that out with the rest of you. Mr. Rogers, what are your feelings on the matter?" Often, coalition members will say, "Yes, I agree, except," and then give a substantially different statement from the one made by a team leader or high power person.

Grooms: This directory contains abstracts of technologies available for impact prediction on the physical-chemical environment. Software for simulation modeling of automobile emissions, Gaussian plumes, noise levels, radioactive hazards, water quality, solid waste disposal, thermal pollution, and other environmental conditions are included in this directory.

211

Guseman and Dietrich: This report defines the specific
concerns of the social well-being objective of water resources
planning by presenting a listing of variables that are relevant
for social well-being impact assessment of a water project.
The listing of variables and their categorization are shown in
Figures 21 through 26. The following information is included
in the report for each listed variable: definition and measurement of baseline conditions, prediction of impacts, idealized
functional curve and rationals, remarks, data source and references. A total of about two pages is devoted to each variable
in the report.

Hammond et al.: Techniques for conflict resolution involving weighting and scaling are described. For example, a
case study involving the reduction of conflict in labor-
management negotiations is as follows:

1. Description of the Study. Six negotiators (three
from labor and three from management) who recently had been
involved in a long bitter strike at a major chemical company
agreed to reenact their negotiations. Both sides agreed that
the reenactment should begin with the situation as it stood
one week prior to the settlement. Both sides also agreed that
four issues remained at that point: (a) contract duration,
(b) wage increases, (c) number and use of certain "special
workers," and (d) number of strikers to be recalled. Judgment
analysis was employed to determine whether the cognitive
aspects of the situation had contributed to the dispute and
whether cognitive feedback might have shortened the strike.

Profiles depicting 25 contracts that included differing
magnitudes on four dimensions representing the four issues were
presented to each negotiator, who (a) rated each of the contracts in terms of its acceptability to him, (b) indicated the
weight that he thought he had placed on each of the four dimensions, and (c) predicted the weight that his counterpart placed
on each dimension. Subsequently, four of the six negotiators
received cognitive feedback that displayed their weights and
function forms on the four dimensions, as well as the weights
and function forms of their counterparts (two of the six negotiators served as a "control" pair and did not receive
feedback).

2. Summary of Results. Self-understanding on the part
of the negotiators was poor before cognitive feedback; estimation of the weights they placed on the four issues were
inaccurate. The implication of such misunderstanding for
negotiation is important: inaccurate understanding of one's
own negotiating policy is conflict-producing; it leads to the
unwitting communication of misleading information.

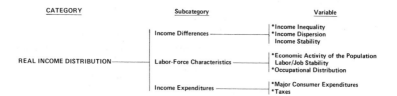

FIGURE 21: STRUCTURE OF THE REAL INCOME DISTRIBUTION CATEGORY
(After Guseman and Dietrich, 1978)

FIGURE 22: STRUCTURE OF THE LIFE, HEALTH AND SAFETY CATEGORY
(After Guseman and Dietrich, 1978)

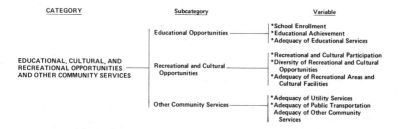

FIGURE 23: STRUCTURE OF THE CATEGORY OF EDUCATIONAL, CULTURAL
AND RECREATIONAL OPPORTUNITIES AND OTHER COMMUNITY
SERVICES (After Guseman and Dietrich, 1978)

213

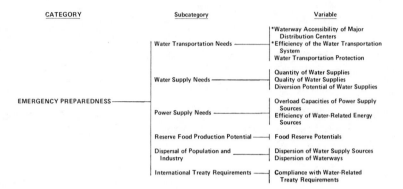

FIGURE 24: STRUCTURE OF THE EMERGENCY PREPAREDNESS CATEGORY
(After Guseman and Dietrich, 1978)

FIGURE 25: STRUCTURE OF THE COMMUNITY COHESION CATEGORY
(After Guseman and Dietrich, 1978)

FIGURE 26: STRUCTURE OF THE OTHER POPULATION CHARACTERISTICS
CATEGORY (After Guseman and Dietrich, 1978)

214

Understanding of others was poor before cognitive feedback; neither side was able to predict the judgments of the other with any significant degree of accuracy, despite the fact that all negotiators expressed prior confidence that they understood their counterpart's judgment policies very well.

Intraunion and intramanagement uniformity varied before cognitive feedback; the three union negotiators were highly uniform in their policies, but the management negotiators were not. The union negotiators, therefore, did not face a uniform management negotiating policy. This situation was not apparent to either side.

Change in policy on the part of the two management negotiators was affected by the use of cognitive feedback (provided by an interactive computer terminal). Cognitive feedback clarified and rectified the above circumstances and led to change in policy that in turn led to increased agreement. After a second rating of the 25 contracts, union and management negotiators found a number of contracts acceptable. In short, the evidence suggests that judgment analysis and cognitive feedback could have shortened this dispute to a fraction of the time required by customary negotiation procedures in which the cognitive sources of conflict are ignored.

Harrison: This bibliography from 1964 to November 1977 cites 243 abstracts relating to the use of microorganisms, animals, plants, and fishes to detect air and water pollution. Some of the organisms discussed are algae, bacteria, aquatic plants, oysters, snails, clams, insects, annelida, amphibians, beaver and fungi.

Hobbs and Voelker: This report explores the use of multi-objective techniques in power plant site selection. Although special emphasis is placed on power plant siting, the techniques discussed are applicable to a much broader range of planning decisions and are commonly employed in other fields such as water resource planning. The discussion of the contents of this report will be in accordance with 3 sections or general steps: (1) choosing and structuring siting factors, (2) desirability scaling, and (3) amalgamation of siting factors.

1. Choosing and structuring Siting Factors. Alternative sites can be described in terms of factors created from a number of plant impact and site characteristics (I&C's). Three general rules can assist in selecting and organizing I&C's in any particular siting study. They are:
- organize I&C's into logical hierarchical groups,
- eliminate unimportant I&C's, and
- consider only those I&C's that differ between alternative sites.

215

2. Desirability Scaling. Many alternative techniques
exist for transforming a physically measured I&C into a factor
measured in units of desirability or site suitability. This
report groups these techniques into four categories, based on
the level of measurement of the resulting desirability. The
four levels of measurement are:

- Categorical: Sites are assigned to categories such as
  acceptable or unacceptable (often called "nominal" in
  the literature).

- Ordinal: Sites are rank ordered. No arithmetic operations are allowed with factors scaled in this way.

- Interval: Sites are assigned values from a continuous
  scale without a fixed zero point, wherein the differences
  between values are meaningful. Values on this scale can
  be added, subtracted, and weighted only.

- Ratio: Sites are assigned values from a continuous
  scale with a fixed zero point, wherein the differences
  between numbers are meaningful. All arithmetic operations with the site values are allowed. The zero point
  is nonarbitrary; therefore, the type of statement "X is
  so many times as much as Y" becomes meaningful.

3. Amalgamation of Siting Factors. Once each I&C has been
transformed into a siting factor expressed in terms of desirability, it is necessary to determine the suitability of each
site by combining a number of desirabilities (a suitability
vector). Formal techniques for determining relative suitability
from a vector of desirabilities are known as amalgamation techniques. Several of the more popular amalgamation techniques
are as follows:

- Exclusion screening is a technique that uses factors
  scaled categorically as acceptable and unacceptable.
  All factors can be considered at once, or the alternatives can be screened one factor at a time until the
  remaining set of sites is deemed sufficiently small.
  The basic problem with exclusionary screening is that
  only rarely are sites either acceptable or unacceptable;
  there is usually a gradation among sites. By limiting
  the site selection process to this method, important
  trade-offs between factors and subtle degrees of differences among sites will be ignored.

- The conjunctive-ranking approach is a method that
  screens out all unacceptable sites in every factor
  except one. The last factor (an ordinally scaled

216

factor) is then used to rank the remaining sites. The
highest ranked site is selected.

- The weighting-summation technique evaluates sites by
  use of the following formula:

$$\text{site suitability} = \sum_{i=1}^{n} W_i F_i,$$

where W_i is the weight for factor i (F_i).

A few important assumptions underlie this method. All
factors must be intervally or ratio scaled, and each
weight must be ratio scaled and represents the relative
importance of change in its factor.

There are a number of methods for selecting weights, some
more theoretically valid than others. These methods fall into
two categories:

- client explicated, which queries the various groups
  concerned with the site selection decision for inter-
  factor value judgments to derive weights, and

- observer derived, which uses multiple regression to
  calculate weights. Factor levels for each site are
  regressed against the overall evaluation of each site
  supplied by various groups.

Jain, Urban, and Stacey: This guide to EIA/EIS methodology
covers the whole spectrum of environmental characteristics -
intangible areas such as sociology, economics and aesthetics -
as well as the more obvious areas of air and water quality and
ecology. The book shows how to determine which environmental
attributes will be affected by a project, and how to identify
and measure in advance the impact on the attributes. Forty-nine
biophysical and socio-economic parameters are described in terms
of their importance, magnitude and overall relationship to the
environment. For each attribute the book discusses the activities that affect it, measurement of variables, collection and
evaluation of data, special conditions and limitations, and
possible secondary effects. The information contained in this
book is similar to U.S. Department of the Army (1975) and Jain,
Urban and Cerchione (1976).

McEvoy and Dietz: This book presents a practical overview
of the strategies and methods available for predicting and
assessing the social consequences of environmental change. The
book examines such topics as legal requirements for impact
analysis; population estimation and projection techniques; land
use impacts; transportation impacts; sociocultural impacts;

217

economic methods for impact analysis; and the organization and presentation of impact information. Included in the volume are introductory discussions of available data sources, analysis techniques ranging from the simple to the complex, examinations of case studies and hypothetical examples, and checklists for impact identification.

Ott: This study documents the extent to which water quality indices currently are being uses in the United States. One-fifth of the State and interstate agencies (12 out of 60 agencies) were classified as users of water quality indices. Of the 51 State agencies (including the District of Columbia), 10 states (20 percent) were classified as index users. The National Sanitation Foundation Index was the most commonly used index, accounting for 7 of the 12 index users. The remaining agencies use Harkins' index or various user-developed indices.

Protasel: This paper describes both theory and methodology associated with measuring public preferences and priorities relative to water resources projects. The Q methodology of rank ordering of individual preferences is described. This can be used to assign importance weights to assessment variables.

Stinson and O'Hare: This report summarized 33 models and techniques for forecasting second-order impacts from energy development. The models and techniques vary in their methodology, output, assumptions, and quality. As a rough dichotomy, they either simulate community development over time or combine various submodels providing community "snapshots" at selected points in time. Using one or more methods--input/output models, gravity models, econometric models, cohort-survival models, or coefficient models--they estimate energy-development-stimulated employment, population, public and private service needs, and government revenues and expenditures at some future time (ranging from annual to "average year" predictions) and for different governmental jurisdictions (municipal, county, state, etc.). The 33 projection methods (techniques) are summarized according to employment (basic and secondary), population (total and sub-groups), service impacts (housing, education services, water and sewerage, other public services and retail services), and public revenues (taxes and expenditures).

Voelker: The application of interactive group processes to the problem of facility siting is examined by this report. Much of the discussion is abstracted from experience gained in applying the Nominal Group Process Technique, an interactive group technique, to the identification and rating of factors important in siting nuclear power plants. The Nominal Group Process Technique (NGT) was developed by Delbecq and Van deVen in 1968. It was derived from social-psychological studies of decision conferences, management-science studies of aggregating group judgments, and social-work studies of problems surrounding citizen participation in program planning. It has gained wide acceptance in health, social service, education, industry, and government organizations. Basically, it consists of four steps: (1) nominal (silent and independent) generation of ideas in writing by a panel of participants, (2) round-robin listing of ideas generated by participants on a flip chart in a serial discussion, (3) discussion of each recorded idea by the group for the purpose of clarification and evaluations, and (4) independent voting on priority ideas, with group decision determined by mathematical rank-ordering. This report concludes that the application of interactive group process techniques to planning and resource management will effect the consideration of social, economic, and environmental concerns and ultimately lead to more rational and credible siting decisions.

Von Gierke: Guidelines are proposed for the uniform description and assessment of various noise environments. In addition to general, audible noise environments, the report covers separately high-energy impulse noise, special noises such as ultrasound and infrasound, and the environmental impact of structure-borne vibration. Whenever feasible and practical, a single-number noise impact characterization is recommended, based on the new concept of level-weighted population: i.e., the summation over the total population of the produce of each residential person times a weighting factor that varies with yearly day-night average sound level outside the residence of that person. A sound-level weighting function for general impact and environmental degradation analysis is proposed, based on the average annoyance response observed in community response studies; this weighting function is supplemented by an additional weighting function at higher noise environments to quantify the potential of noise-induced hearing loss and general health effects.

Wehr: This manuscript provides a comprehensive discussion of conflict regulation based on the studies and personal experiences of the author. Chapter 2 summarizes models and techniques for conflict regulation. Chapter 6 is specifically oriented to regulating environmental conflict based on an actual case study in Colorado. Appendix A contains a list of organizations engaged in conflict regulation training, education and research.

COMPOSITE LIST OF REFERENCES

Adams, R. T. and Kurisu, F. M., "Simulation of Pesticide Movement on Small Agricultural Watersheds", EPA/600/3-76/066,
September 1976, 344 pages, ESL, Inc., Sunnyvale, California.

Adkins, W. G. and Burke, Jr., D., "Social, Economic, and Environ-
mental Factors in Highway Decision Making", Research Report
148-4, 1974, Texas Transportation Institute, Texas A and
M University, College Station, Texas (report prepared for
Texas Highway Department in cooperation with the Federal
Highway Administration, U.S. Department of Transportation,
Washington, D. C.)

Agency for International Development, "Environmental Assessment
Guidelines Manual", September 1974, Agency for International
Development, Department of State, Washington, D. C.

Alabama Development Office, State Planning Office, "Environmental Impact Assessment by Use of Matrix Diagram", June
1974, 10 pages, Montgomery, Alabama.

Alden, H. R., "Environmental Impact Assessment: A Procedure
for Coordinating and Organizaing Environmental Planning",
Technical Publication No. 10, December 1974, 32 pages,
Thorne Ecological Institute, Boulder, Colorado.

Allen, H. L. et al., "Public Law 92-500, Water Quality Analysis
and Environmental Impact Assessment", NCWQ-75/100-1,
April 1976, National Commission on Water Quality,
Washington, D. C.

Arnold, W., Young, J. and Brewer, J., "Constructing Nonlinear
Dynamic Models for Socio-Environmental Decision Making:
A Methodology", Environmental Quality Series, October
1972, Institute of Governmental Affairs, University of
California at Davis, Davis, California.

Arthur D. Little, Inc., "Transportation and Environment Synthesis for Action: Impact of National Environmental Policy
Act of 1969 on the Department of Transportation", July
1971, Vol. 3 (Options for Environmental Management),
prepared for Office of the Secretary, Department of
Transportation, Washington, D. C.

Babcock, Jr., L. R. and Nadga, N. L., "Popex---Ranking Air
Pollution Sources by Population Exposure", EPA/600/2-76-
063, March 1976, 345 pages, University of Illinois Medical
Center, Chicago, Illinois.

220

Bella, D. A., "Tidal Flats in Estuarine Water Quality Analysis",
EPA/660/3-75/025, June 1975, 200 pages, National Environ-
mental Research Center, U.S. Environmental Protection
Agency, Corvallis, Oregon (prepared for EPA by Department
of Civil Engineering, Oregon State University, Corvallis,
Oregon).

Bender, M. and Ahmed, S. B., "Index of the Composite Environment
(ICE): A Basis for Evaluating Environmental Effects of
Electric Power Generating Plants in Response to NEPA",
Report No. ORNL TM-4492, February 1974, 77 pages, Oak Ridge
National Laboratory, Oak Ridge, Tennessee.

Bennington, G., Lubore, S. and Pfeffer, J., "Resource and Land
Investigations (RALI) Program: Methodologies for Environ-
mental Analysis, Vol. I, Environmental Assessment", MTR-
6740, Vol. I, August 1974, The MITRE Corporation, McLean,
Virginia (report prepared for U.S. Geological Survey,
Raston, Virginia).

Bereano, P. L. et al., "A Proposed Methodology for Assessing
Alternative Technologies", Technology Assessment, Vol. I,
No. 3, 1973, pages 179-190.

Bhutani, J. et al., "Impacts of Hydrologic Modification on
Water Quality", EPA-600/2-75-007, April 1975, U.S. Environmental Protection Agency, Washington, D. C.

Bishop, A. B., Oglesby, C. H., Bishop, G. and Willeke, G. E.,
"Socio-Economic and Community Factors in Planning Urban
Freeways," September 1970, 216 pages, Department of Civil
Engineering University, Menlo Park, California.

Bishop, A. B., "Public Participation in Water Resources Planning," IWR Report 70-7, 1970, U.S. Army Engineer Institute
for Water Resources, Fort Belvoir, Virginia.

Bishop, A. B., "Structuring Communications Programs for Public
Participation in Water Resources Planning", IWR Contract
Report 75-2, May 1975, 125 pages, U.S. Army Engineer
Institute for Water Resources, Fort Belvoir, Virginia
(prepared for IWR by Utah State University, Logan, Utah).

Bockrath, J. T., Environmental Law for Engineers, Scientists
and Managers, McGraw-Hill Book Company, Inc., New York,
New York, 1977, 359 pages.

Boesch, D. F., "Application of Numerical Classification in
Ecological Investigations of Water Pollution," EPA/600/3-
77/033, March 1977, 127 pages, Corvallis Environmental
Research Laboratory, U.S. Environmental Protection Agency,

221

Corvallis, Oregon (prepared for EPA by Virginia Institute
of Marine Science, Gloucester Point, Virginia).

Bagley, M. G., Kroll, C. A. and Clark, C., "Testhetics in
Environmental Planning," EPA-600/5-73-009, November 1973,
187 pages, U.S. Environmental Protection Agency, Washington,
D. C. (prepared for EPA by Stanford Research Institute,
Menlo Park, California).

Baker, R. W. and Gruendler, J. D., "Case Study of the Milwaukee-
Green Bay Interstate Corridor Location", 1972, paper
presented at Highway Research Board Summer Meeting and in
"Environmental Considerations in Planning, Design and
Construction," Special Report 138, Highway Research Board,
Washington, D. C.

Baldwin, P., "Environmental Mediation: An Effective Alternative?", Proceedings of Conference Held in Reston, Virginia,
January 11-13, 1978, 1978, RESOLVE, Center for Environmental Conflict Resolution, Palo Alto, California.

Bascom, S. E. et al., "Secondary Impacts of Transportation and
Wastewater Investments: Research Results", EPA/600/5/75-
013, July 1975, 225 pages, U.S. Environmental Protection
Agency, Washington, D. C. (prepared for EPA by Environmental Impact Center, Inc., Newton, Massachusetts).

Battelle-Columbus Laboratories, "A Methodology for Assessing
Environmental, Economic, and Social Effects of Dredge Soil
Disposal on Marsh and Upland Areas", Draft report, 1974,
Battelle-Columbus Laboratories, Columbus, Ohio (report
prepared for U.S. Army Engineer Waterways Experiment Sta-
tion, Corps of Engineers, Vicksburg, Mississippi).

Bayley, S. et al., "Energetics and Systems Modeling: A Frame-
work Study for Energy Evaluation of Alternative Transpor-
tation Modes in Comparison with Traditional Economic
Evaluation", June 1976, Department of Environmental
Engineering Sciences, University of Florida, Gainesville,
Florida (submitted to U.S. Army Corps of Engineers under
Contract DACW 17-75-0075).

Belknap, R. K. and Furtado, J. G., "Three Approaches to Envi-
ronmental Resource Analysis," November 1976, Landscape
Architecture Research Office, Harvard University,
Cambridge, Massachusetts.

Boucher, W. I. and Stover, J. G., "An Annotated Bibliography on
Cross-Impact Analysis", Report 128-01-14, April 1972 (re-
vised September 1976), The Futures Group, Glastonbury,
Connecticut.

Brandsma, M. G. and Divoky, D. J., "Development of Models for
Prediction of Short-Term Fate of Dredged Material Dis-
charged in the Estuarine Environment", WES-CR-D-76-5,
May 1976, 297 pages, Tetra Tech., Inc., Pasadena, California
(prepared for Dredged Material Research Program, U.S. Army
Engineer Waterways Experiment Station, Vicksburg,
Mississippi).

Bromley, D. W. et al., "Water Resource Projects and Environmental Impacts: Towards a Conceptual Model", February
1972, Water Resources Center, University of Wisconsin,
Madison, Wisconsin.

Brown, L. R., "Estimate of Maximum Level of Oil Innocuous to
Marina Biota as Inferred from Literature Review", CGR/DC-
9/77, April 1977, 20 pages, Mississippi State University,
Starkville, Mississippi.

Brown, P. J., "Toward a Technique for Quantifying Aesthetic
Quality of Water Resources", Report on Contract No. DACW
31-72-C-0060, October 1974, 100 pages, Institute for
Water Resources, Fort Belvoir, Virginia (prepared for IWP
by Utah State University, Logan, Utah).

Brown, R. M. et al., "A Water Quality Index-Crashing the Psychological Barrier," Thomas, W. A. (editor), Indicators
of Environmental Quality, 1970, pages 173-182, Plenum
Press, New York, New York.

Burchell, R. W. and Listokin, D., "The Environmental Impact
Handbook", 1975, Center for Urban Policy Research, Rutgers-
The State University of New Jersey, New Brunswick, New
Jersey.

Bureau of Land Management, "Environmental Analysis", Working
Draft, 1973, 126 pages, Bureau of Land Management,
Washington, D. C.

Bureau of Reclamation, "Guidelines for Implementing Principles
and Standards for Multi-objective Planning of Water
Resources", Review draft, 1972, Bureau of Reclamation,
U.S. Department of the Interior, Washington, D. C.

Burnham, J. B., "A Technique for Environmental Decision Making
Using Quantified Social and Aesthetic Values", Report No.
BNWL-1787, February 1974, Battelle Pacific Northwest
Laboratories, Richland, Washington.

Canter, L. W. et al., "An Assessment of Problems Associated
with Evaluating the Physical, Chemical and Biological

Impacts of Discharging Fill Material", Technical Report
D-77-29, December 1977, 236 pages, U.S. Army Corps of
Engineers, Waterways Experiment Station, Vicksburg,
Mississippi (prepared for WES by School of Civil Engineer-
ing and Environmental Science, University of Oklahoma,
Norman, Oklahoma).

Canter, L. W. and Reid, G. W., "Environmental Factors Affecting
Treatment Process Selection", paper presented at Oklahoma
Water Pollution Control Federation Annual Meeting, 1977,
Stillwater, Oklahoma.

Canter, L. W. and Hill, L. G., "Variables for Environmental
Quality Account, October 1977, 187 pages, Norman, Oklahoma
(report submitted to U.S. Army Engineers Waterways Experiment Station, Vicksburg, Mississippi).

Canter, L. W., Environmental Impact Assessment, 1977, 331
pages, McGraw-Hill Book Company, New York, New York.

Canter, L. W. "Environmental Impact Statements on Municipal
Wastewater Program", May 1978, Canter Associates, Inc.,
Norman, Oklahoma (draft report submitted to Information
Resources Press, Washington, D. C.)

Canter, L. W. "Supplement to Environmental Impact Assessment",
1978, 1062 pages, Canter Associates, Inc., Norman,
Oklahoma.

Canter, L. W. "Supplement to Environmental Impact Assessment",
Terrebonne Regional Sewerage Facilities", August 1976,
62 pages, report submitted to GST Engineers, Houma,
Louisiana.

Carstea, D. et al., "Guidelines for the Environmental Impact
Assessment of Small Structures and Related Activities in
Coastal Bodies of Water", MTR-6916, Rev. 1, August 1975,
The MITRE Corporation, McLean, Virginia (prepared for
U.S. Army Corps of Engineers, New York District).

Case, P. J., Edgmon, T. D., and Renton, D. A., "PUBLIC - A
Procedure for Public Involvement", Range Science Series
No. 22, June 1976, 138 pages, Range Science Department,
Colorado State University, Fort Collins, Colorado.

Central New York Regional Planning and Development Board,
"Environmental Resources Management", Report No. CNYRPDB-
RP-72-HUD-246-06, October 1972, 35 pages, Syracuse, New
York (report prepared for Department of Housing and Urban
Development, Region 2, New York, New York).

Chalmers, J. A. and Anderson, E. J., "Economic/Demographic Assessment Manual: Current Practices, Procedural Recommendations, and a Test Case," November 1977, Engineering and Research Center, U.S. Bureau of Reclamation, Denver, Colorado (prepared for Bureau of Reclamation by Mountain West Research, Inc., Tempe, Arizona).

Chalmers, J. A., "Bureau of Reclamation Construction Worker Survey," October 1977, Engineering and Research Center, U.S. Bureau of Reclamation, Denver, Colorado (prepared for Bureau of Reclamation by Mountain West Research, Inc., Tempe, Arizona).

Chase, G. H., "Matrix Techniques in the Evalution of Environmental Impacts", Ch. 10 in Blissett, M. (editor), "Environmental Impact Assessment", 1976, Engineering Foundation, New York, New York, pages 131-151.

Chen, W. W. and Orlob, G. T., "Ecologic Simulation for Aquatic Environments", OWRR-C-2044, December 1972, 156 pages, Office of Water Resources Research, U.S. Department of Interior, Washington, D. C. (prepared for OWRR by Water Resources Engineers, Inc., Walnut Creek, California).

Cheremisinoff, P. N. and Morresi, A. C., Environmental Assessment and Impact Statement Handbook, 1977, 438 pages, Ann Arbor Science Publishers, Inc., Ann Arbor, Michigan.

Chow, V. T. and Yen, B. C., "Urban Stormwater Runoff: Determination of Volumes and Flowrates", EPA/600/2-76/116, May 1976, 253 pages, Department of Civil Engineering, University of Illinois, Urbana, Illinois.

Christensen, K., "Social Impacts of Land Development", URI 15700, September 1976, 144 pages, The Urban Institute, Washington, D. C.

Christensen, S. W., Van Winkle, W. and Mattice, J. S., "Defining and Determining the Significance of Impacts--Concepts and Methods", 1975, 71 pages, Oak Ridge National Laboratory, Oak Ridge, Tennessee.

Clark, E. M. and Van Horn, A. J., "Risk-Benefit Analysis and Public Policy: A Bibliography", BNL-22285, November 1976, 81 pages, Brookhaven National Laboratory, Upton, New York.

Clark, J. R., "Environmental Assessment of Construction Activities", Unpublished MS Thesis, 1975, 192 pages, School of Civil Engineering and Environmental Science, University of Oklahoma, Norman, Oklahoma.

225

Clark, R. N., Hendee, J. C., and Stankey, G. H., "Codinvolve:
A Tool for Analyzing Public Input to Resource Decisions",
Ch. 8 (pages 145-165) in Pierce, J. C. and Doerksen, H. R.,
Water Politics and Public Involvement, 1976, Ann Arbor
Science Publishers, Inc., Ann Arbor, Michigan.

Coates, J. F., "The Role of Formal Models in Technology Assessment", Technological Forecasting and Social Change, Vol. 9
1976, pages 139-190.

Coates, J. F., "Some Methods and Techniques for Comprehensive
Impact Assessment", Ch. 9 in Blissett, M. (editor), "Envi-
ronmental Impact Assessment", 1976, Engineering Foundation,
New York, New York, pages 103-130.

Colonell, J. M., "Field Evaluation of a Predictive Model for
Thermal Stratification in Lakes and Reservoirs", OWRT-B-
201-MASS(2), January 1976, 215 pages, Water Resources
Research Center, University of Massachusetts, Amherst,
Massachusetts.

Colston, Jr., N. V., "Characterization and Treatment of Urban
Land Runoff", EPA-670/2-74-096, December 1974, 170 pages,
National Environmental Research Center, Environmental
Protection Agency, Cincinnati, Ohio.

Commonwealth Associates, Inc., "Environmental Analysis System",
Report No. R-1447, 1972, prepared for the Northern States
Power Company, Minnesota, by Commonwealth Associates, Inc.,
Jackson, Michigan.

Coomber, N. H. and Biswas, A. K., Evaluation of Environmental
Intangibles, Genera Press, Bronxville, New York, 1973,
77 pages.

Corwin, R. et al., Environmental Impact Assessment, 1975, 277
pages, Freeman, Cooper and Company, San Francisco,
California.

Crawford, A. B., "Impact Analysis Using Differential Weighted
Evaluation Criteria", 1973, in J. L. Cochrane and M.
Zeleny, editors, Multiple Criteria Decision Making,
University of South Carolina Press, Columbia, South
Carolina.

Cross, F. L., "Assessing Environmental Impact", Pollution
Engineering, Vol. 5, No. 6, June 1973, pages 34-35.

Curran Associates, Inc., Evaluation of Power Facilities: A Reviewer's Handbook, April 1974, 392 pages, U.S. Department of Housing and Urban Development, Washington, D. C. (prepared for HUD by Curran Associates, Inc., Northhampton, Massachusetts).

Curran Associates, Inc., "Guidelines for Review of Environmental Impact Statements---Vol. IV, Channelization Projects", July 1976, Northhampton, Massachusetts (submitted to U.S. Environmental Protection Agency, Washington, D. C.)

Dalkey, N. C., "The Delphi Method: An Experimental Study of Group Opinion", Memorandum RM-5888-PR, June 1969, The Rand Corporation, Santa Monica, California.

Darnell, R. M. et al., "Impacts of Construction Activities in Wetlands of the United States", EPA-600/3-76-045, April 1976, 392 pages, U.S. Environmental Protection Agency, Washington, D. C. (prepared for EPA by Tereco Corporation, College Station, Texas).

Dean, B. V. and Nishry, J. J., "Scoring and Profitability Models for Evaluating and Selecting Engineering Product," Journal Operations Research Society of America, Vol. 13, No. 4, July-August 1965, pages 550-569.

Dearinger, J. A., "Esthetic and Recreational Potential of Small Naturalistic Streams Near Urban Areas," April 1968, Water Resources Institute, University of Kentucky, Lexington, Kentucky.

Dee, N. et al., "Environmental Evaluation System for Water Resources Planning", Final report, 1972 Battelle-Columbus Laboratories, Columbus, Ohio (prepared for the Bureau of Reclamation, U.S. Department of the Interior, Washington, D. C.)

Dee, N. et al., "Planning Methodology for Water Quality Management: Environmental Evaluation System", July 1973, Battelle-Columbus, Columbus, Ohio.

Dee, N. et al., "An Assessment of the Usage of Environmental Assessment Methodologies in Environmental Impact Statements", DMG-DRS Journal (published by Design Methods Group, University of California, Berkeley, California), Vol. 9, No. 1, March 1975.

Dee, N. et al., "Literature Review to Identify Rationale for Developing Functional Relationships between Environmental Parameters and Environmental Quality," February 1973, 79 pages, Battelle-Southern Operations and Columbus Laboratories, Atlanta, Georgia (report to U.S. Army Corps of Engineers Waterways Experiment Station, Vicksburg, Mississippi).

Dickert, T. G., "Methods for Environmental Impact Assessment: A Comparison", in Dickert, T. G. and Domeny, K. R. (editors), "Environmental Impact Assessment: Guidelines and Commentary", 1974, University Extension, University of California at Berkeley, Berkeley, California.

Ditton, R. B. and Goodale, T. L., editors, "Environmental Impact Analysis: Philosophy and Methods", Proceedings of the Conference on Environmental Impact Analysis, Green Bay, Wisconsin, January 4-5, 1972, Sea Grant Publication Officer, University of Wisconsin, Madison, Wisconsin.

Duke, K. M. et al., "Environmental Quality Assessment in Multi-objective Planning," November 1977, Final Report to U.S. Bureau of Reclamation, Denver, Colorado (prepared for BuRec by Battelle-Columbus Laboratories, Columbus, Ohio).

Dunne, N. G., "Successful Sanitary Landfill Siting: County of San Bernadino, California", SW-617, 1977, U.S. Environmental Protection Agency, Cincinnati, Ohio.

Dunst, R. C. et al., "Survey of Lake Rehabilitation Techniques and Experiences:, Tech. Bulletin-75, 1974, 183 pages, Wisconsin Department of Natural Resources, Madison, Wisconsin.

Dwyer, J. G., Hatmaker, M. L. and Hewings, G. J. D., "Profile and Measurement of Regional Development Indicators for Use in the Evaluation of Water and Related Land Management Planning", May 1978, 140 pages, University of Illinois, Urbana, Illinois (prepared for U.S. Army Waterways Experiment Station, Vicksburg, Mississippi).

Eckenrode, R. T., "Weighting Multiple Criteria," Management Science, Vol. 12, No. 3, November 1965, pages 180-192.

Edwards, W., "How to Use Multi-Attribute Utility Measurement for Social Decision Making", SSRI Research Report 76-3, August 1976, 67 pages, Social Science Research Institute, University of Southern California, Los Angeles, California (prepared for Advanced Research Projects Agency, U.S. Department of Defense, Arlington, Virginia).

Eisler, R. and Wapner, M., "Second Annotated Bibliography on Biological Effects of Metals in Aquatic Environments", EPA-600/3-75-008, October 1975, 399 pages, Environmental Research Laboratory, U.S. Environmental Protection Agency, Narragansett, Rhode Island.

Ellis, S. L. et al., "Guide to Land Cover and Use Classification Systems Employed by Western Governmental Agencies," FWS/OBS-77/05, March 1978, 183 pages, Ecology Consultants, Inc., Fort Collins, Colorado (prepared for Western Energy and Land Use Team, Office of Biological Services, U.S. Fish and Wildlife Service, Fort Collins, Colorado).

Engineering Division, Scottish Development Department "Development of a Water Quality Index", Report No. ARD 3, December 1976, 62 pages, Edinburgh, Scotland.

Environmental Impact Center, Inc., "A Methodology for Assessing Environmental Impact of Water Resources Development", November 1973, PB-226 545, prepared by Environmental Impact Center, Inc., Cambridge, Massachusetts, for U.S. Department of the Interior, Office of Water Resources Research, Washington, D. C.

Environmental Protection Agency, "Water Quality Management Planning for Urban Runoff", EPA 440/9-75-004, December 1974, 220 pages, Washington, D. C.

Erickson, L. E., "Approach to Valuing Visual Pollution from Western Electricity Production," BNWL-2103, February 1977, 76 pages, Battelle Pacific Northwest Laboratories, Richland, Washington.

Fabos, J. C., "Model for Landscape Resource Assessment---Part I of the Metropolitan Landscape Planning Model (METLAND)", February 1973, Department of Landscape Architecture and Regional Planning, University of Massachusetts, Amherst, Massachusetts.

Falk, E. L., "Measurement of Community Values: The Spokane Experiment," Highway Research Record, 1968, No. 229, pages 53-64.

Fennelly, P. F. et al., "Environmental Assessment Perspectives", EPA-600/2-76-069, March 1976, 238 pages, U.S. Environmental Protection Agency, Research Triangle Park, North Carolina (prepared for EPA by GCA Corporation, Bedord, Massachusetts).

Finsterbusch, K. and Wolf, C. P., The Methodology of Social Impact Assessment, 1977, Dowden, Hutchinson and Ross Publishing Co., Stroudsberg, Pennsylvania.

Finsterbusch, K., "Methods for Evaluating Non-Market Impacts in Policy Decisions with Special Reference to Water Resources Development Projects," IWR Contract Report 77-78, November 1977, 46 pages, U.S. Army Engineer Institute for Water Resources, Fort Belvoir, Virginia (prepared for IWR by University of Maryland, College Park, Maryland).

Fischer, D. W. and Davies, G. S., "An Approach to Assessing Environmental Impacts", Journal Environmental Management, Vol. 1, No. 3, 1973, pages 207-227.

FitzPatrick, M. S. et al., "Manual for Evaluating Secondary Impacts of Wastewater Treatment Facilities", EPA-600/5-78-003, February 1978, 175 pages, U.S. Environmental Protection Agency, Washington, D. C., (prepared for EPA by Abt Associates, Inc., Cambridge, Massachusetts).

Fitzsimmons, S. J., Stuart, L. I. and Wolff, P. C., "Social Assessment Manual--A Guide to the Preparation of the Social Well-Being Account", July 1975, 279 pages, Bureau of Reclamation, Denver, Colorado (prepared for Bureau of Reclamation by Abt Associates, Inc., Cambridge, Massachusetts).

Flood, B. S. et al., "A Handbook for Habitat Evaluation Procedures", Resource Publ. 132, 1977, 77 pages, U.S. Fish and Wildlife Service, Washington, D. C.

Freeman, D. M. and Quint, J., "Coordinator's Manual---The Analysis of Social Well-Being: Procedures for Comparing Social Impacts of Proposed Resource Management Alternatives", October 1977, Department of Sociology, Colorado State University, Fort Collins, Colorado.

Frost, J. H. and Wilmot, W. W., Interpersonal Conflict, 1978, Wm. C. Brown Company Publishers, Dubuque, Iowa.

Fuhriman, D. K. et al., "Water Quality Effect of Diking a Shallow Arid-Region Lake", EPA/660/2-75-007, April 1975, 243 pages, Brigham Young University, Provo, Utah.

Gann, D. A., "Thermal Reduction of Municipal Solid Waste", 1975, 91 pages, Master's Thesis, School of Civil Engineering and Environmental Science, University of Oklahoma, Norman, Oklahoma.

Graf-Webster, E., Lubore, S. and Pfeffer, J., "Resource and
    Land Investigations (RALI) Program: Methodologies for
    Environmental Analysis, Vol. II, Utility Coridor Selec-
    tion", MTR-6740, Vol. II, August 1974, The MITRE Corpora-
    tion, McLean, Virginia (report prepared for U.S.
    Geological Survey, Raston, Virginia).

Greer, K. H., Blome, D. A. and Jones, Jr., J. E., "A Directory
    of Computerized Environmental Information Resources",
    IMMR 23-GR3-76, October 1976, 46 pages, Institute for
    Mining and Minerals Research, University of Kentucky,
    Lexington, Kentucky.

Grimsrud, G. P., Finnemore, E. J. and Owen, H. J., "Evaluation
    of Water Quality Models: A Management Guide for Planners",
    EPA/600/5-76/004, July 1976, 186 pages, Systems Control
    Inc., Palo Alto, California (prepared for EPA by Systems
    Control, Inc.)

Grooms, D. W., "A Directory of Computer Software Applications -
    Environmental, 1977", PB-270 018/5WP, September 1977, 189
    pages, National Technical Information Service, Springfield,
    Virginia.

Gum, R. L., Roefs, T. G. and Kimball, D. B., "Quantifying
    Societal Goals: Development of a Weighting Methodology",
    Water Resources Research, Vol. 12, No. 4, August 1976,
    pages 617-622.

Guseman, P. K. and Dietrich, K. T., "Profile and Measurement
    of Social Well-Being Indicators for Use in the Evaluation
    of Water and Related Land Management Planning", Misc.
    Paper Y-78-2, June 1978, 112 pages, U.S. Army Engineers
    Waterways Experiment Station, Vicksburg, Mississippi
    (prepared for WES by Texas Transportation Institute, Texas
    A and M University, College Station, Texas).

Hall, R. W., Westerdahl, H. E. and Eley, R. L., "Application
    of Ecosystem Modeling Methodologies to Dredged Material
    Research", WES-TR-76-3, June 1976, 72 pages, U.S. Army
    Engineer Waterways Experiment Station, Vicksburg,
    Mississippi.

Hammond, K. R. and Adelman, L., "Science, Values, and Human
    Judgment", Science, Vol. 194, October 22, 1976, pages
    389-396.

Hammond, K. R. et al., "Social Judgment Theory: Applications
    in Policy Formation", in Kaplan, M. F., and Schwartz, S.
    (editors), Human Judgment and Decision Processes in Applied
    Settings, 1977, Academic Press, New York, New York.

Harkness, T., "Visual Analysis Techniques: Outfitting Your Tool Box", Proceedings of Conference on Environmental Impact Analysis: Current Methodologies, Future Directions, University of Illinois, Urbana-Champaign, Illinois, 1975.

Harrison, E. A., "Bioindicators of Pollution (A Bibliography with Abstracts)", NTIS/PS-76/0868/OWP, November 1976, 194 pages, National Technical Information Service, Springfield, Virginia.

Harrison, E. A., "Bioindicators of Pollution (A Bibliography with Abstracts)", NTIS/PS-77/0993, November 1977, 243 pages, National Technical Information Service, Springfield, Virginia.

Harrison, E. A., "Ecosystem Models, Vol. 2, November 1975-November 1976", NTIS/PS-76/0904, November 1976, National Technical Information Service, Springfield, Virginia.

Haven, K. F., "A Methodology for Impact Assessment in the Estuarine/Marine Environment", UCRL-51949, October 1975, 43 pages, Lawrence Livermore Laboratory, Livermore, California (prepared for U.S. Energy Research and Development Administration, Washington, D. C.)

Heer, Jr., J. E. and Hagerty, D. J., Environmental Assessments and Statements, 1977, 382 pages, Van Nostrand Reinhold Company, Florence, Kentucky.

Hellstrom, D. I., "A Methodology for Preparing Environmental Statements", AFCEC-TR-75-28, August 1975, 217 pages, U.S. Air Force Civil Engineering Center, Tyndall Air Force Base, Florida (prepared for U.S. Air Force by A. D. Little, Inc. of Cambridge, Massachusetts).

Hetman, F., "Society and the Assessment of Technology", 1973, Organization for Economic Cooperation and Development, Washington, D. C. pages 115-139.

Heuting, R., "A Statistical System for Estimating the Deterioration of the Human Environment", in J. W. Pratt (editor), Statistical and Mathematical Aspects of Pollution Problems, 1974, Marcel Dekker, Inc., New York, New York, pages 123-132.

Highway Research Section, Engineering Research Division, Washington State University, "A Study of the Social, Economic and Environmental Impact of Highway Transportation Facilities on Urban Communities," 1968, Pullman, Washington (report prepared for Washington State Department of Highways).

232

Hill, M., "A Method for Evaluating Alternative Plans: The Goals-Achievement Matrix Applied to Transportation Plans," Ph.D. Dissertation, 1966, University of Pennsylvania, Philadelphia, Pennsylvania.

Hobbs, B. F. and Voelker, A. H., "Analytical Multiobjective Decision-Making Techniques and Power Plant Siting: A Survey and Critique", ORNL-5288 Special, February 1978, Oak Ridge National Laboratory, Oak Ridge, Tennessee.

Hornberger, G. M., Kelly, M. G. and Lederman, T. C., "Evaluating a Mathematical Model for Predicting Lake Eutrophication", VPI-WRCC-Bull.-82, September 1975, 102 pages, Water Resources Research Center, Virginia Polytechnic Institute and State University, Blacksburg, Virginia.

Hydrologic Engineering Center, "Reservoir Temperature Stratification Users Manual", January 1972, U.S. Army Engineer District---Sacramento, Davis, California.

Jain, R. K., Drobny, N. L. and Chatterjea, S., "Procedures for Reviewing Environmental Impact Assessments and Statements for Construction Projects", Report No. CERL-TR-E-73, August 1975, 24 pages, Construction Engineering Research Laboratory, U.S. Army, Champaign, Illinois.

Jain, R. K. et al., "Environmental Impact Study for Army Military Programs", Report No. CERL-IR-D-13, December 1973, 170 pages, U.S. Army Construction Engineering Research Laboratory, Champaign, Illinois.

Jain, R. K., Urban, L. V. and Cerchione, A. J., "Handbook for Environmental Impact Analysis", Interim Environmental Planning Bulletin 11, June 1976, U.S. Department of the Air Force, Washington, D. C. (prepared for USAF by the U.S. Army Construction Engineering Research Laboratory, Champaign, Illinois).

Jain, R. K., Urban, L. V. and Stacey, G. S., "Handbook for Environmental Impact Analysis", April 1974, Construction Engineering Research Laboratory, Department of the Army, Champaign, Illinois.

Jain, R. K., Urban, L. V. and Stacey, G. S., Environmental Impact Analysis, 1977, 340 pages, Van Nostrand Reinhold Company, Florence, Kentucky.

Jain, R. K. and Urban, L. V., "A Review and Analysis of Environmental Impact Assessment Methodologies", Report No. CERL-TR-E-69, June 1975, 23 pages, Construction Engineering Research Laboratory, U.S. Army, Champaign, Illinois.

Jameson, D. L., "Ecosystem Impacts of Urbanization Assessment Methodology", EPA-600/3-76-072, July 1976, 249 pages, Corvallis Environmental Research Laboratory, U.S. Environmental Protection Agency, Corvallis, Oregon (prepared for EPA by the Institute of Ecology, Utah State University, Logan, Utah).

Johnson, D. W. and Cole, D. W., "Anion Mobility in Soils: Relevance to Nutrient Transport from Terrestrial to Aquatic Systems", EPA-600/3-77-068, June 1977, 28 pages, U.S. Environmental Protection Agency, Corvallis, Oregon.

Kahneman, D. and Tversky, A., "Intuitive Prediction: Biases and Corrective Procedures", Special Issue of _Management Science_ on Forecasting Methodologies and Applications, in press.

Kane, J., Vertinsky, I. and Thomson, W., "KSIM: A Methodology for Interactive Resource Policy Simulation", _Water Resources Research_, Vol. 9, No. 1, February 1973, pages 65-79.

Kemp, H. T., "National Inventory of Selected Biological Monitoring Programs, Summary Report of Current or Recently Completed Projects, 1976", ORNL/TM-5792, October 1976, 711 pages, Oak Ridge National Laboratory, Tennessee.

Keyes, D. L., "Land Development and the Natural Environment: Estimating Impacts", URI 13500, April 1976, 128 pages, The Urban Institute, Washington, D. C.

Kibby, H. and Hernandez, D. J., "Environmental Impacts of Advanced Wastewater Treatment at Ely, Minnesota", EPA-600/3-76-082, August 1976, 30 pages, U.S. Environmental Protection Agency, Corvallis, Oregon.

Klein, G. E., "Evaluation of New Transportation Systems," in "Defining Transportation Requirements - Papers and Discussions," 1969, American Society of Mechanical Engineers, New York, New York.

Krauskopf, T. M. and Bunde, D. C., "Evaluation of Environmental Impact Through a Computer Modelling Process" in Ditton, R., and Goodale, T., (editors), "Environmental Impact Analysis: Philosophy and Methods,", 1972, pages 107-125, University of Wisconsin Sea Grant Program, Madison, Wisconsin.

Kruzic, P. G., "Cross-Impact Simulation in Water Resources Planning", IWR Contract Report 74-12, November 1974, 19 pages, U.S. Army Engineers Institute for Water Resources, Fort Belvoir, Virginia (prepared for IWR by Stanford Research Institute, Menlo Park, California).

Lacate, D. S., "The Role of Resource Inventories and Landscape Ecology in the Highway Route Selection Process," 1970, 198 pages, Department of Conservation, College of Agriculture, Cornell University, Ithaca, New York.

Lamanna, R. A., "Value Consensus Among Urban Residents," Journal American Institute of Planners, Vol. 30, No. 4, 1964, pages 317-323.

Lehmann, E. J., "Preparation and Evaluation of Environmental Impact Statements (A Bibliography with Abstracts)," NITS/PS-75-717, September 1975, National Technical Information Service, Springfield, Virginia.

Lehmann, E. J., "Water Quality Modeling, Hydrological and Limnological Systems, Vol. 1, 1964-1974 (A Bibliography with Abstracts)", NTIS/PS-76/0443/2ST, June 1976, 197 pages, National Technical Information Service, Springfield, Virginia.

Lehmann, E. J., "Water Quality Modeling, Hydrological and Limnological Systems, Vol. 2, 1975-June 1976 (A Bibliography with Abstracts)", NTIS/PS-76/0444/0 ST, June 1976, 103 pages, National Technical Information Service, Springfield, Virginia.

Leopold, L. B. et al., "A Procedure for Evaluating Environmental Impact", U.S. Geological Survey Circular 645, 1971, U.S. Geological Survey, Washington, D. C.

Lincor, J. L., Haynes, M. E. and Klein, M. L., "The Ecological Impact of Synthetic Organic Compounds on Estuarine Ecosystems", EPA-600/3-76-075, September 1976, 354 pages, Environmental Research Laboratory, U.S. Environmental Protection Agency, Gulf Breeze, Florida (prepared for EPA by Mote Marine Laboratory, Sarasota, Florida).

Liu, B. and Yu, E. S., "Physical and Economic Damage Functions for Air Pollutants by Receptors", EPA-600/5-76-011, September 1976, 160 pages, U.S. Environmental Protection Agency, Washington, D. C. (prepared for EPA by Midwest Research Institute, Kansas City, Missouri).

Lower Mississippi Valley Division, "A Tentative Habitat Evaluation System (HES) for Water Resources Planning", November 1976, U.S. Army Corps of Engineers, Vicksburg, Mississippi.

Malone, D. W., "An Introduction to the Application of Interpretive Structural Modeling", in Baldwin, M. M. (editor), Portraits of Complexity: Applications of Systems Methodologies to Societal Problems, 1975, Battelle Memorial Institute, Columbus, Ohio.

Markley, O. W. and Bagley, M. D., "Minimum Standards for Quality of Life", Report No. EPA-600/5-75-012, May 1975, U.S. Environmental Protection Agency, Washington, D. C. (report prepared for EPA by Stanford Research Institute, Menlo Park, California).

Markofsky, M. and Harleman, D. R., "A Predictive Model for Thermal Stratification and Water Quality in Reservoirs", EPA-16130-DJH-01/71, January 1971, 286 pages, Massachusetts Institute of Technology, Cambridge, Massachusetts.

Mac Crimmon, K. R., "An Overview of Multiple Objective Decision Making", 1973, in J. L. Cochrane and M. Zeleny, editors, "Multiple Criteria Decision Making", University of South Carolina Press, Columbia, South Carolina.

MacKinnon, W. J. and Anderson, L. M., "The SPAN III Computer Program for Synthesizing Group Decisions: Weighting Participants' Judgments in Proportion to Confidence", Behavior Research Methods and Instrumentation, Vol. 8, No. 4, 1976, pages 409-410.

Manheim, M. L. et al., "Community Values in Highway Location and Design: A Procedural Guide", September 1971, Urban Systems Laboratory, Massachusetts Institute of Technology, Camb idge, Massachusetts (report prepared for Highway Research Board, Washington, D. C.)

McElroy, A. D. et al., "Loading Functions for Assessment of Water Pollution from Nonpoint Sources", EPA/600/2-76/151, May 1976, 444 pages, U.S. Environmental Protection Agency, Washington, D. C. (prepared for EPA by Midwest Research Institute, Kansas City, Missouri).

McEvoy, III, J. and Dietz, T., Handbook for Environmental Planning, 1977, John Wiley and Sons, New York, New York.

McHarg, I., "A Comprehensive Highway Route Selection Method," pages 31-41 in Design with Nature, 1969, Natural History Press, Garden City, New York.

McKenry, C. E. et al., "Interstate 75---Evaluation of Corridors Proposed for South Florida", 1971, 62 pages, University of Miami Center for Urban Studies, Coral Gables, Florida (report prepared for State of Florida Department of Transportation).

Miller, III, J. R., Professional Decision-Making: A Procedure for Evaluating Complex Alternatives, 1970, 305 pages, Praeger Publishers, Inc., New York, New York.

Mitchell, A. et al., "Handbook of Forecasting Techniques", IWR Contract Report 75-7, December 1975, 316 pages, U.S. Army Engineer Institute for Water Resources, Fort Belvoir, Virginia (prepared for IWR by Center for Study of Social Policy, Stanford Research Institute, Menlo Park, California).

Moore, J. L. et al., "A Methodology for Evaluating Manufacturing Environmental Impact Statements for Delaware's Coastal Zone", June 1973, Battelle-Columbus Laboratories, Columbus, Ohio (report prepared for State of Delaware).

Morrill, R. A., "Comprehensive Resource and Environmental Management Planning", Research Report, June 1973, 87 pages, Engineering and Research Center, U.S. Bureau of Reclamation, Denver, Colorado.

Morrison, T. H., "Sanitary Landfill Site Selection by the Weighted Rankings Method", 1974, 31 pages, Master's Thesis, School of Civil Engineering and Environmental Science, University of Oklahoma, Norman, Oklahoma.

Muller, T., "Fiscal Impacts of Land Development", URI 98000, 1975, 68 pages, The Urban Institute, Washington, D. C.

Muller, T., "Economic Impacts of Land Development: Employment, Housing, and Property Values", URI 15800, September 1976, 148 pages, The Urban Institute, Washington, D. C.

National Forest Service, "Interaction Between Resources", 1973, National Forest Service, U.S. Department of Agriculture, Atlanta, Georgia.

Naval Environmental Support Office, "Data Sources for Environmental Impact Assessments (EIA's) and Environmental Impact Statements (EIS's)", NESO 20.2-015, November 1976, 223 pages, Naval Construction Battalion Center, Port Hueneme, California (prepared for NESO by ManTech of New Jersey Corporation, San Diego, California).

Nelson, K. E. and LaBelle, S. J., "Handbook for the Review of Airport Environmental Impact Statements", ANL/ES-46, July 1975, 159 pages, Argonne National Laboratory, Argonne, Illinois.

O'Connor, M. F., "The Application of Multi-Attribute Scaling Procedures to the Development of Indices of Value," June 1972, Engineering Psychology Laboratory, University of Michigan, Ann Arbor, Michigan.

Odum, E. P. et al., "Optimum Pathway Matrix Analysis Approach to the Environmental Decision Making Process---Test Case: Relative Impact of Preposed Highway Alternates", 1971, Institute of Ecology, University of Georgia, Athens, Georgia.

Odum, H. T., "Use of Energy Diagrams for Environmental Impact Statements", Tools for Coastal Zone Management, Proceedings of the Conference, Washington, D. C., February 1972, pages 197-213.

Omernik, J. M., "The Influence of Land Use on Stream Nutrient Levels", EPA-600/3-76-014, January 1976, 105 pages, Corvallis Environmental Research Laboratory, U.S. Environmental Protection Agency, Corvallis, Oregon.

Omernik, J. M., "Nonpoint Source - Stream Nutrient Level Relationships: A Nationwide Survey", EPA-600/3-77-105, September 1977, 151 pages, U.S. Environmental Protection Agency, Corvallis, Oregon.

Orlob, G. T. et al., "Wild Rivers---Methods for Evaluation," October 1970, 106 pages, Water Resources Engineers, Walnut Creek, California (report prepared for U.S. Department of the Interior, Washington, D. C.)

Ortolano, L., "Analyzing the Environmental Impacts of Water Projects", March 1973, 433 pages, Department of Civil Engineering, Stanford University, Menlo Park, California.

Ott, W. R., Proceedings of the EPA Conference on Environmental Modeling and Simulation, Held at Cincinnati, Ohio on April 19-22, 1975, EPA/600/9-76-016, June 1976, 861 pages, Office of Research and Development, U.S. Environmental Protection Agency, Washington, D. C.

Ott, W. R., "Water Quality Indices: A Survey of Indices Used in the United States", EPA-600/4-78-005, January 1978, 128 pages, U.S. Environmental Protection Agency, Washington, D. C.

Paul, B. W., "Subjective Prioritization of Energy Development Proposals Using Alternative Scenarios", (paper presented at the Joint National ORSA/TIMS Meeting, San Francisco, California, May 1977), Engineering and Research Center, U.S. Bureau of Reclamation, Denver, Colorado.

Pease, J. R. and Smardon, R. C., "Environmental Impact Assessment Project---Final Report, Analysis and Evaluation", Special Report 481, April 1977, Oregon State University Extension Service, Corvallis, Oregon.

Pendse, D. and Wyckoff, J. B., "A Systematic Evaluation of Environmental Perceptions, Optimum Preferences, and Trade-Off Values in Water Resource Analysis", September 1974, 86 pages, Department of Agricultural Economics, Oregon State University, Corvallis, Oregon (prepared for Office of Water Research and Technology, Massachusetts University, Amherst, Massachusetts).

Peterson, G. L., Gemmell, R. S. and Schofer, J. L., "Assessment of Environmental Impacts---Multidisciplinary Judgments of Large-Scale Projects", Ekistics, 218, January 1974, pages 23-30.

Phillips, R. D. and Kaune, W. T., "Biological Effects of Static and Low-Frequency Electromagnetic Fields: An Overview of United States Literature", BNWL-2262, April 1977, 40 pages, Battelle Pacific Northwest Labs., Richland, Washington.

Pikarsky, M., "Comprehensive Planning for the Chicago Crosstown Expressway," Highway Research Record, 1967, No. 180, pages 35-51.

Pikul, R., "Development of Environmental Indices", in Pratt, J. W., editor, Statistical and Mathematical Aspects of Pollution Problems, Marcel Dekker Book Company, New York, New York, 1974, pages 103-121.

Protasel, G. J., "Evaluating Natural Resource Planning," September 1977, Department of Political Science, Oregon State University, Corvallis, Oregon (report submitted to U.S. Soil Conservation Service, Washington, D. C.)

Raines, G., "Environmental Impact Assessment of New Installations", (paper presented at International Pollution Engineering Congress, Cleveland, Ohio, December 4-6, 1972), Battelle Memorial Institute, Columbus, Ohio.

Rea, R., "Handbook for Assessing the Social and Economic Impacts of Water Quality Management Plans", July 1973, Resource Planning Associates, Inc., Cambridge, Massachusetts (report prepared for Environmental Protection Agency, Washington, D. C.)

Reid, G. W., "Research to Develop Ecological Standards for Water Resources", July 1976, 304 pages, Bureau of Water and Environmental Resources Research, University of Oklahoma, Norman, Oklahoma (prepared for U.S. Office of Water Resources Research, Department of the Interior, Washington, D. C.)

Riggins, R. and Novak, E., "Computer-Aided Environmental Impact Analysis for Mission Change, Operations and Maintenance, and Training Activities: User Manual", CERL-TR-E-85, February 1976, 101 pages, Construction Engineering Research Laboratory, U.S. Department of the Army, Champaign, Illinois.

Rose, S. J., Manual for Environmental Impact Evaluation, Prentice-Hall, Inc., Englewood Cliffs, New Jersey, 1976, 232 pages.

Rosove, P. E., "A Trend Impact Matrix for Societal Impact Assessment", April 1973, 24 pages, Center for Futures Research, Graduate School of Business Administration, University of Southern California, Los Angeles, California.

Ross, J. H., "The Numeric Weighting of Environmental Interactions", Occasional Paper No. 10, July 1976, Lands Directorate, Environment Canada, Ottawa, Canada.

Ross, P. J., Spencer, B. G. and Peterson, Jr., J. H., "Public Participation in Water Resources Planning and Decision-Making Through Information-Education Programs: A State-of-the-Art Study", 1974, 54 pages, Water Resources Research Institute, Mississippi State University State College, Mississippi.

Rote, D. M. and Wangen, L. E., "A Generalized Air Quality Assessment Model for Air Force Operations", AFWL-TR-74-304, February 1975, 168 pages, Air Force Weapons Laboratory, Kirtland Air Force Base, New Mexico.

Salomon, S. N., "Cost-Benefit Methodology for the Selection of a Nuclear Power Plant Cooling System", paper presented at the Energy Forum, 1974 Spring Meeting of the American Physical Society, Washington, D. C., April 22, 1974.

240

Schaenman, P. S. and Muller, T., "Measuring Impacts of Land
Development", URI 86000, November 1974, 93 pages, The
Urban Institute, Washington, D. C.

Schaenman, P. S., "Using an Impact Measurement System to
Evaluate Land Development", URI 15500, September 1976,
106 pages, The Urban Institute, Washington, D. C.

Schanche, G. W. et al., "Pollution Estimation Factors", CERL
TR-N-12, November 1976, 26 pages, Construction Engineering
Research Laboratory, U.S. Army, Champaign, Illinois.

Schimpeler, C. C. and Grecco, W. L., "Systems Evaluation: An
Approach Based on Community Structures and Values," Highway Research Record, 1968, No. 238, pages 123-152.

Schlesinger, B. and Daetz, D., "A Conceptual Framework for
Applying Environmental Assessment Matrix Techniques",
The Journal of Environmental Sciences, July/August, 1973,
pages 11-16.

Schlesinger, B. and Daetz, D., "Development of a Procedure for
Forecasting Long-Range Environmental Impacts, Report to
the Resource and Land Investigations (RALI) Program, U.S.
Geological Survey", Report No. USGS-LI-75-007, August
1975, Department of Industrial Engineering, Stanford
University, Stanford, California (report prepared for U.S.
Geological Survey, Raston, Virginia).

School of Civil Engineering and Environmental Science and
Oklahoma Biological Survey, "Mid-Arkansas River Basin
Study---Effects Assessment of Alternative Navigation
Routes from Tulsa, Oklahoma to Vicinity of Wichita, Kansas",
June 1974, 555 pages, University of Oklahoma, Norman,
Oklahoma (report prepared for U.S. Army Engineer District,
Tulsa, Corps of Engineers).

Sewell, W. R. D., "Broadening the Approach to Evaluation in
Resources Management Decision-making", Journal of Environmental Management, Vol. 1, 1973, pages 33-60.

Shaheen, D. G., "Contributions of Urban Roadway Usage to Water
Pollution", EPA-ROAP-21 ASY-005, April 1975, 358 pages,
Environmental Protection Agency, Washington, D. C.

Sharma, R. K., Buffington, J. D., and McFadden, J. T., editors,
Proceedings of the Conference on the Biological Signifi-
cance of Environmental Impacts, NR-CONF-002 (Conference
held at the University of Michigan, Ann Arbor, Michigan,
June 4-6, 1975), U.S. Nuclear Regulatory Commission,
Washington, D. C.

241

Slovic, P., "Judgment, Choice and Societal Risk Taking", paper presented at Symposium on Judgment and Choice in Public Policy Decisions, Annual Meeting of the American Association for the Advancement of Science, Denver, Colorado, February 1977 (author's address is Devision Research, A Branch of Perceptronics, 1201 Oak Street, Eugene, Oregon 97401).

Smith, M. A., "Field Test of an Environmental Impact Assessment Methodology", Report ERC-1574, August 1974, Environmental Resources Center, Georgia Institute of Technology, Atlanta, Georgia.

Smith, M. F., "Environmental and Ecological Effects of Dredging (A Bibliography with Abstracts)", NTIS/PS-75/755, October 1975, National Technical Information Service, Springfield, Virginia.

Smith, W. L., "Quantifying the Environmental Impact of Transportation Systems", 1973, Van Doren-Hazard-Stallings-Schnake Consultants, Topeka, Kansas.

Sorensen, D. L. et al., "Suspended and Dissolved Solids Effects on Freshwater Biota: A Review", EPA-600/3-77-042, April 1977, 65 pages, U.S. Environmental Protection Agency, Corvallis, Oregon (prepared for EPA by Utah State University, Logan, Utah).

Sorensen, J., "A Framework for Identification and Control of Resource Degradation and Conflict in the Multiple Use of the Coastal Zone", Master's Thesis, 1971, Department of Landscape Architecture, University of California, Berkeley, California.

Southeastern Wisconsin Regional Planning Commission, "Land Use Transportation Study--Forecast and Alternative Plans: 1990", Plan Report 7, Vol. 2, June 1966.

Springer, M. D., "Research for the Development of Guidelines for Conducting and Analyzing an Environmental Water Quality Study to Determine Statistically Meaningful Results", Pub-37, OWRT-A-033-ARK(1), 1976, 173 pages, Water Resources Research Center, University of Arkansas, Fayetteville, Arkansas.

Stinson, D. S. and O'Hare, M., "Predicting the Local Impacts of Energy Development: A Critical Guide to Forecasting Methods and Models", May 1977, 98 pages, Laboratory of Architecture and Planning, Massachusetts Institute of Technology, Cambridge, Massachusetts.

242

Stover, L. V., "Environmental Impact Assessment: A Procedure", March 1973, 23 pages, Science Technology Vision, Inc., Pottstown, Pennsylvania.

Struss, S. R. and Mikucki, W. J., "Fugitive Dust Emission from Construction Haul Roads", Special Rep. N-17, February 1977, 53 pages, Construction Engineering Research Laboratory, U.S. Army, Champaign, Illinois.

Summers, D. A., Ashworth, C. D. and Feldman-Summers, S., "Judgment Processes and Interpersonal Conflict Related to Societal Problem Solutions", unpublished paper, 1975, Human Affairs Research Center, University of Washington, Seattle, Washington.

Swartzman, G. L. and Van Dyne, G. M., "An Ecologically Based Simulation - Optimization Approach to Natural Resource Planning", in "Annual Review of Ecology and Systematics", Vol. 3, 1972, pages 347-398.

Texas Water Development Board, "Simulation of Water Quality in Streams and Canals, Theory and Description of the AUAL-1 Mathematical Modeling System", EPA-OWP-TEX-128, May 1971, 62 pages, Austin, Texas.

Thomas, J. L., Paul, J. and Israelsen, E. K., "A Computer Model of the Quantity and Chemical Quality of Return Flow", OWRR-B-038-UTAH(1), June 1971, 100 pages, Utah Water Research Laboratory, Utah State University, Logan, Utah.

Thom, G. C. and Ott, W. R., "Air Pollution Indices---A Compendium and Assessment of Indices Used in the United States and Canada", December 1975, 164 pages, Council on Environmental Quality, Washington, D. C.

Thornton, K. W. and Lessem, A. S., "Sensitivity Analysis of the Water Quality for River-Reservoir Systems Model", WES-MP-Y-77-4, September 1976, 53 pages, U.S. Army Engineer Waterways Experiment Station, Vicksburg, Mississippi.

Thronson, R. E., "Nonpoint Source Control Guidance, Construction Activities", December 1976, 122 pages, Office of Water Planning and Standards, Environmental Protection Agency, Washington, D. C.

Toussaint, C. R. "A Method for the Determination of Regional Values Associated with the Assessment of Environmental Impacts", 1975, 219 pages, Ph.D. Dissertation, School of Civil Engineering and Environmental Science, University of Oklahoma, Norman, Oklahoma.

Troxler, Jr., R. W. and Thackston, E. L., "Effect of Meteoro-
logical Variables on Temperature Changes in Flowing Streams",
EPA/660/3-75-002, January 1975, 86 pages, Department of
Environmental and Water Resources Engineering, Vanderbilt
University, Nashville, Tennessee.

Turner, A. K. and Hausmanis, I., "Computer-aided Transportation
Corridor Selection in the Guelp-Dundas Area of Ontario",
1972, paper presented at Highway Research Board Summer
Meeting and in "Environmental Considerations in Planning,
Design and Construction", Special Report 138, Highway
Research Board, Washington, D. C.

U.S. Army Engineer District, Tulsa, Corps of Engineers, "Matrix
Analysis of Alternatives for Water Resource Development",
Draft technical paper, July 1972, Tulsa, Oklahoma.

U.S. Bureau of Outdoor Recreation, "Handbook: Applications of
Remote Sensing and Computer Techniques for Recreation
Planning", Vols. 1, 2, 3, and 4, March 1974, Bureau of
Outdoor Recreation, Washington, D. C. (report prepared for
BOR by University of Wisconsin, Madison, Wisconsin).

U.S. Bureau of the Census, "Environmental/Socioeconomic Data
Sources (Supplement to TAB A-1, Environmental Narrative",
October 1976, 169 pages, Subscriber Services Section
(Publications) Washington, D. C.

U.S. Department of the Army, "Handbook for Environmental Impact
Analysis", DA Pamphlet No. 200-1, April 1975, 155 pages,
Headquarters, Department of the Army, Washington, D. C.

U.S. Department of Transportation, "Environmental Assessment
Notebook Series", 6 volumes, 1975, U.S. Department of
Transportation, Washington, D. C.

U.S. Environmental Protection Agency, "Guidelines for Review
of Environmental Impact Statements, Vol. 3, Impoundment
Projects", Interim Final Report, July 1976, 147 pages,
Washington, D. C. (prepared for EPA by Curran Associates,
Inc., Northampton, Massachusetts).

U.S. Soil Conservation Service, Environmental Assessment Guidelines in the Federal Register, Vol. 42, No. 152, Monday,
August 8, 1977, pages 40127-40128.

Utah Water Research Laboratory, "Water Resources Planning Social
Goals, and Indicators: Methodological Development and
Empirical Test", PRWG-131-1, December 1974, 267 pages, Utah
State University, Logan, Utah (prepared for Office of Water
Research and Technology, Washington, D. C.)

Viohl, Jr., R. C. and Mason, K. G. M., "Environmental Impact
Assessment Methodologies: An Annotated Bibliography",
Exchange Bibliography 691, November 1974, Council of
Planning Librarians, Monticello, Illinois.

Vlachos, E. et al., "Social Impact Assessment: An Overview",
IWR Paper 75-P7, December 1975, 117 pages, U.S. Army
Engineer Institute for Water Resources, Fort Belvoir,
Virginia (prepared for IWR by Colorado State University,
Fort Collins, Colorado).

Vlachos, E. and Hendricks, D. W., "Secondary Impacts and Consequences of Highway Projects", DPT/TST-77/24, October
1976, 332 pages, U.S. Department of Transportation,
Washington, D. C. (prepared for DOT by Departments of
Civil Engineering and Sociology, Colorado State University, Fort Collins, Colorado).

Voorhees, A. M. and Associates, "Interim Guide for Environ-
mental Assessment: HUD Field Office Edition", June 1975,
Washington, D. C. (report prepared for U.S. Department of
Housing and Urban Development, Washington, D. C.)

Voelker, A. H., "Power Plant Siting", An Application of the
Nominal Group Process Technique", ORNL/NUREG/TM-81,
February, 1977, Oak Ridge National Laboratory, Oak Ridge,
Tennessee (prepared for U.S. Nuclear Regulatory Commission,
Washington, D. C.)

Von Gierke, H. E., "Guidelines for Preparing Environmental
Impact Statements on Noise", June 1977, 131 pages, National
Research Council, Washington, D. C.

Wakeland, W., "QSIM2: A Low-Budget Heuristic Approach to
Modeling and Forecasting", Technological Forecasting and
Social Change, Vol. 9, 1976, pages 213-229.

Walton, Jr., L. E. and Lewis, J. E., "A Manual for Conducting
Environmental Impact Studies", Report No. VHRC 70-R 46,
June 1971, 34 pages, Virginia Highway Research Council,
Charlottesville, Virginia (report prepared for Federal
Highway Administration, Washington, D. C.)

Warner, M. L. et al., "An Assessment Methodology for the Envi-
ronmental Impact of Water Resource Projects", Report No.
EPA-600/5-74-016, July 1974, Battelle-Columbus Laboratories,
Columbus, Ohio (report prepared for Office of Research and
Development, U.S. Environmental Protection Agency,
Washington, D. C.)

Warner, M. L., "Environmental Impact Analysis: An Examination of Three Methodologies", Ph.D. Dissertation, 1973, 248 pages, Department of Agricultural Economics, University of Wisconsin, Madison, Wisconsin.

Webster, R. D. et al., "The Economic Impact Forecast System: Description and User Instructions", CERL-TR-N-2, June 1976, 36 pages, Construction Engineering Research Laboratory, U.S. Army, Champaign, Illinois.

Wehr, P., Conflict Regulation, 1978, manuscript to be published by Westview Press, Boulder, Colorado.

Welsh, R. L., "User Manual for the Computer-Aided Environmental Legislative Data System", CERL-TR-E-78, November 1975, 62 pages, Construction Engineering Research Laboratory, U.S. Department of the Army, Champaign, Illinois.

Wenger, R. B. and Rhyner, C. R., "Evaluation of Alternatives for Solid Waste Systems", Journal of Environmental Systems, Vol. 2, No. 2, June 1972, pages 89-108.

Zirkle, J. D., "State-of-the-Art Highway Related Water Quality", June 1974, 13 pages, Washington State Department of Highways, Olympia, Washington.

APPENDIX A

INFORMATION ON 16 REFERENCES

FROM 1960-70 PERIOD

REFERENCE:

Bishop, A. B., Oglesby, C. H., and Willeke, G. E., "Socio-
Economic and Community Factors in Planning Urban Freeways,"
Sept., 1970, 216 pp., Department of Civil Engineering, Stanford
University, Menlo Park, Cal.

Abstract:

For those nonmonetary aspects of a highway project a
"profile" of alternatives is prepared and a list of environmental factors developed. The route with the most beneficial (or
detrimental) effect for a particular factor is set at 100 percent (or -100 percent) for that particular factor. The effects
of the alternative routes are then expressed as a percentage of
the effects of the best (or worst) for that factor. The results
for all factors considered are shown diagramatically on a scale
from -100 (worst) to +100 (best). Any alternative routes that
are clearly dominated are eliminated. Paired comparisons are
made for the remaining alternatives. Subjective decisions are
required since each factor is considered separately (there is
no categorization or grouping) and there is no ranking of factors.

Salient Features:

Factor profile concept is good (see following example of
community factor profiles).

Advantages/Limitations of Salient Features:

1. Field studies conducted --- yes
2. Practical for field use --- yes
3. Usage for various types/sizes of projects --- yes
4. Objective vs. subjective approaches --- objective
5. Reproducibility --- unknown
6. Scientifically sound features --- yes

Conclusions:

Use directly in WRAM
..Mention factor profile concept.

Example of Community Factor Profiles:

Correct decisions among freeway location alternatives must
have two parts: (1) an economy study which includes all items
that can be reduced to money terms, and (2) an analysis of all
items which cannot be stated in terms of money but which must
be weighed in the decision. The approach proposed for analyzing the indirect or community effects of (2) has been called
a "community factor profile."

The community factor profile is a graphical description
of the effects of each proposed freeway location alternative.
Figure 2 (page 66) is a highly simplified and consolidated version of such a profile for four alternative locations numbered
1, 2, 3, and 4. In this figure, each profile scale is on a
percentage base, ranging from a negative to a positive 100
percent. One hundred percent, either negative or positive, is
the maximum absolute value of the measure that is adopted for
each factor. Reduction to the percentage base simplifies scaling and plotting the profiles. The maximum positive or negative value of the measure, the units, and the time span are
indicated on the right hand side of the profile for reference.
For each alternative, the positive or negative value for any
factor is calculated as a percent of the maximum absolute value
over all alternatives and is plotted on the appropriate abscissa.
A broken line connecting the plotted points for each alternative
gives its factor profile. For the profiles, factors and measures
should be selected which are independent and will adequately
describe all important elements of community impact. Care
should be used in defining factor measures to assure that they
are not measuring the same consequences. Otherwise, in effect,
there would be "double counting" and disproportionate weight
would be given to those factors. This may result in incorrect
decisions.

In order to reduce the complexity of the diagram and, in
turn, of the decision-making process, the full set of community
factors should be reduced whenever it is possible to do so.
Two guidelines are suggested for accomplishing this: (1) eliminating all those factors that are not relevant or important to
the particular decision, and (2) eliminating all factors where
the values are substantially the same for all alternatives.
These tests must be acceptable to all parties involved in the
study.

It is expected that the profiles will be prepared for each
alternative from the viewpoint of each community interest group
and will incorporate the factors that are important to that particular group's viewpoint. A composite profile would also be
prepared for each alternative showing the total community effect
for each factor. Separate profiles for each alternative could
be made on transparent overlays to facilitate comparison.

+ + +

REFERENCE:

Bishop, A. B., "Public Participation in Water Resources Planning,"
IWR Report 70-7, 1970, U.S. Army Engineer Institute for Water
Resources, Fort Belvoir, Va.

Abstract:

    This is a good general reference source on the need and techniques for accomplishing public participation in water resources planning.

    This report has in essence been superceded by Bishop, A. B., "Structuring Communications Programs for Public Participation in Water Resources Planning," May, 1975 (see separate discussion of this report).

Salient Features:

    Describes various techniques of public participation.

Advantages/Limitations of Salient Features:

1. Field studies conducted --- yes
2. Practical for field use --- yes
3. Usage for various types/sizes of projects --- yes
4. Objective vs. subjective approaches --- not pertinent
5. Reproducibility --- unknown
6. Scientifically sound features --- yes

Conclusions:

    General reference for WRAM

+ + +

REFERENCE:

Brown, R. M., et al, "A Water Quality Index---Crashing the Psychological Barrier," Thomas, W. A. (editor), Indicators of Environmental Quality, 1970, pp. 173-182, Plenum Press, New York, New York.

Abstract:

    A general-use water quality index is proposed. This index would provide a uniform method for (1) reflecting the quality of water and (2) communicating the status of quality and changes in the status to the public.

$$WQI = \Sigma_1^n \, w_i q_i$$

    WQI = number between 0 & 100
       N = number of parameters
      q_i = quality of ith parameter; number between 0 & 100 (quality curves or functional curves are used)
      w_i = unit weight of ith parameter; 0 to 1

251

Salient Features:

    Water quality index concepts.
    Use of quality curves or functional curves.

Advantages/Limitations of Salient Features

1. Field studies conducted --- yes
2. Practical for field use --- yes
3. Usage for various types/sizes of projects --- yes
4. Objective vs. subjective approaches --- objective
5. Reproducibility --- yes
6. Scientifically sound features --- yes

Conclusions

    General reference for WRAM

    Note: This same general reference source also contains:

Pikul, R. P., Bisselle, C. A., and Lilienthal, M., "Development of Environmental Indices: Outdoor Recreational Resource and Land Use Shift," Thomas, W. A. (editor), Indicators of Environmental Quality, 1970, Plenum Press, New York, New York.

Shults, W. D. and Beauchamp, J. J., "Statistically Based Air-Quality Indices," Thomas, W. A., (editor), Indicators of Environmental Quality, 1970, pp. 199-209, Plenum Press, New York, New York.

(Neither of these articles add anything of substance to this review).

+ + +

REFERENCE:

Dalkey, N. C., "The Delphi Method: An Experimental Study of Group Opinion," Memorandum RM-5888-PR, June, 1969, The Rand Corporation, Santa Monica, Cal.

Abstract:

    The Delphi technique is a method of eliciting and refining group judgments. The rationale for the procedures is primarily the age-old adage "Two heads are better than one," when the issue is one where exact knowledge is not available.
    In the spring of 1968, a series of experiments were initiated at RAND to evaluate the procedures. The experiments were also designed to explore the nature of the information

252

processes occurring in the Delphi interaction. The experiments were conducted using upper-class and graduate students from UCLA as subjects and general information of the almanac type as subject matter. Ten experiments, involving 14 groups ranging in size from 11 to 30 members, were conducted. About 13,000 answers to some 350 questions were obtained.

The two basic issues being examined were (1) a comparison of face-to-face discussion with the controlled-feedback interaction, and (2) a thorough evaluation of controlled feedback as a technique of improving group estimates. The results indicated that, more often than not, face-to-face discussion tended to make the group estimates less accurate, whereas, more often than not, the anonymous controlled feedback procedure made the group estimates more accurate. The experiments thus put the application of Delphi techniques in areas of partial information on much firmer ground.

Of greater long-range significance is the insight gained into the nature of the group information processes. Delphi procedures create a well-defined process that can be described quantitatively. In particular, the average error on round one is a linear function of the dispersion of the answers. The average amount of change of opinion between round one and round two is a well-behaved function of two parameters-the distance of the first-round answer from the group median, and the distance from the true answer.

Another result of major significance is that a meaningful estimate of the accuracy of a group response to a given question can be obtained by combining individual self-ratings of competence on that question into a group rating. This result, when combined with the relationship between accuracy and standard deviation mentioned above, opens the possibility of attaching accuracy scores to the products of a Delphi exercise.

Salient Features:

Group judgments are elicited.

Advantages/Limitations of Salient Features:

1. Field studies conducted --- yes
2. Practical for field use --- yes
3. Usage for various types/sizes of projects --- yes
4. Objective vs. subjective approaches --- objective
5. Reproducibility --- yes
6. Scientifically sound features --- yes

Conclusions

Use directly in WRAM
..Mention in conjunction with importance weights and impact scaling.

253

REFERENCE:

Dean, B. V. and Nishry, J. J., "Scoring and Profitability Models for Evaluating and Selecting Engineering Products," Journal Operations Research Society of America, Vol. 13, No. 4, July-Aug., 1965, pp. 550-569.

Abstract:

This article describes a basic weighting-scaling checklist approach for multiple-criteria decision-making between alternatives. The weighting is accomplished by a paired-comparison technique used by the decision team. Alternatives are evaluated relative to the checklist items and choice coefficients are assigned based on a paired-comparison approach. The weighting is subjective while the scaling is more objective. This article forms one of the bases for the WRAM methodology.

Salient Features:

Weighting and scaling techniques (paired comparisons)

Advantages/Limitations of Salient Features:

1. Field studies conducted --- yes
2. Practical for field use --- yes
3. Usage for various types/sizes of projects --- yes
4. Objective vs. subjective approaches --- both
5. Reproducibility --- good for scaling, less so for weighting
6. Scientifically sound features --- yes

Conclusions:

Used in principle in WRAM.

+ + +

REFERENCE:

Dearinger, J. A., "Esthetic and Recreational Potential of Small Naturalistic Streams Near Urban Areas," April, 1968, Water Resources Institute, University of Kentucky, Lexington, Ky.

Abstract:

This technique was designed for evaluating esthetic and recreational aspects of small streams. Environmental factors, such as water quality, wildlife, and scenic views, were weighted on a scale from 1 to 5 depending on their importance for types of potential recreational uses: hiking trails, canoeing areas, etc. In evaluating a location, a rating number is established for each particular environmental factor in each use category. This number is between 1 and 10 and is determined through a set of value functions (e.g., BOD and turbidity for water quality). The weighting and rating numbers are multiplied for each factor and the results from all the factors added for each type of use. This final number is made a percentage of the number that would apply to the suitability of the location for a use if all conditions were optimum (all rating numbers equal to 10).

Salient Features:

Weighting and rating approach.

Advantages/Limitations of Salient Features:

1. Field studies conducted --- yes
2. Practical for field use --- yes
3. Usage for various types/sizes of projects --- small streams
4. Objective vs. subjective approaches --- both
5. Reproducibility --- unknown
6. Scientifically sound features --- yes

Conclusions

General reference for WRAM.

+ + +

REFERENCE:

Eckenrode, R. T., "Weighting Multiple Criteria," Management Science, Vol. 12, No. 3., Nov., 1965, pp. 180-192.

Abstract

Six methods for collecting the judgments of experts concerning the relative value of sets of criteria were compared for their reliability and time efficiency. The methods were ranking, rating, three versions of paired comparisons and a method of successive comparisons. The judgment situations used were concerned with the design of a specific air defense system, and with selecting a personnel subsystem manager for a development program. In each of these three situations six criteria were comparatively evaluated by the judges. The results of these experiments showed that there were no significant differences in the sets of criterion weights derived from collecting the judgment data by any of the methods, but that ranking was by far the most efficient method. A fourth experiment was conducted to develop baseline data on the time required to make comparative judgments vs. number of items to be judged, by the ranking method and by the simplest paired comparisons method. Ranking is increasingly more efficient than paired comparisons as the number of items to be judged increases from six to 30.

Salient Features:

Comparison of six methods for collecting the judgments of experts concerning the relative weights of multiple criteria.

Advantages/Limitations of Salient Features:

1. Field studies conducted --- yes
2. Practical for field use --- yes
3. Usage for various types/sizes of projects --- yes
4. Objective vs. subjective approaches --- both
5. Reproducibility --- unknown
6. Scientifically sound features --- yes

Conclusions:

Use directly in WRAM
..Mention availability of weighting techniques.

+ + +

REFERENCE:

Falk, E. L., "Measurement of Community Values: The Spokane Experiment," Highway Research Record, 1968, No. 229, pp. 53-64.

Abstract:

Experience in working with citizens advisory committees has shown that better communication between the citizen and professional planner is needed. To accomplish this new planning tools are needed to assess and combine more accurately intangible or difficult to define factors with tangible or easily measureable factors in preparing specific proposals. This is a pilot study and description of such a tool for determining the relative importance of four tangible and five intangible factors and a means of applying these measures of importance in selecting the most acceptable one of three hypothetical roadway solutions. The method requires the assumption that frequency of citizen preference for one factor over another is directly related to importance of that factor. It further assumes that the average measure of a set of tangible factors

256

is equal to the average measure of a set of intangible factors. Using this "equality of averages" assumption, tangible and intangible factors can be assigned a value within a common scaling system. By combining these common system values with measures of the relative importance of the factors involved, an evaluation table can be prepared which provides a total weighted score for each alternative solution.

Salient Features:

Public participation in relative weight assignments.
Example includes a weighting-scaling checklist.

Advantages/Limitations of Salient Features:

1. Field studies conducted --- yes
2. Practical for field use --- yes
3. Usage for various types/sizes of projects --- yes
4. Objective vs. subjective approaches --- both
5. Reproducibility --- unknown
6. Scientifically sound features --- yes

Conclusions:

Use directly in WRAM
..Include along with other ideas for weighting and
scaling.

+ + +

REFERENCE:

Highway Research Section, Engineering Research Division, Washington State University, "A Study of the Social, Economic and Environmental Impact of Highway Transportation Facilities on Urban Communities," 1968, Pullman, Washington, (report prepared for Washington State Dept. of Highways).

Abstract:

Three forms are to be completed for each alternative route for evaluation: one based on appearance consideration, one on sociological considerations, and one on economic considerations. Various parameters describing each of these three subject areas are listed on the respective form. In evaluating a particular route on appearance, for example, a number between 1 and 10 is assigned to each appearance parameter to describe the route's "desirability" for that parameter. The rating is to be done subjectively by the "administrator and his staff." The rating number is then multiplied by a weighting factor which has been

257

established by administrators and interested citizens prior to the route rating process; the weights are to reflect the objectives the road is intended to serve. This process is repeated for each parameter three times, as the life of the project has been divided into periods of from 0-5 years, 6-25 years, and 26-50 years--the weights and desirability rating may change with time. The combined 50 year weighted ratings for each appearance factor are aggregated to indicate the overall appearance rating. If a route has similar conditions throughout its entire length, it can be rated as one section. If not, the overall rating for a portion is multiplied by the ratio of its length to that of the entire route. Finally, the total weighted rating values on the appearance, sociological, and economic forms completed for each route are listed with construction cost and other monetary considerations on a "Route Comparison Form."

Salient Features:

Weighting-scaling technique

Advantages/Limitations of Salient Features:

1. Field studies conducted --- yes
2. Practical for field use --- yes
3. Usage for various types/sizes of projects --- yes
4. Objective vs. subjective approaches --- both
5. Reproducibility --- unknown
6. Scientifically sound features --- yes

Conclusions:

General reference for WRAM.

+ + +

REFERENCES:

Hill, M., "A Method for Evaluating Alternative Plans: The Goals-Achievement Matrix Applied to Transportation Plans," Ph.D. Dissertation, 1966, University of Pennsylvania, Philadelphia, Pa.

Abstract:

This method applies to transportation route alternatives. It is basically a simple matrix. Across one axis are specific environmental goals (decrease in air pollution, etc.); the other axis contains various land-use categories (residential districts, open space, etc.) subdivided into specific area, buildings,

258

etc. that are affected. At each subdivision-goal intersection, a plus, minus, or equals sign is used to indicate for each alternative route whether there is an increase in goal attainment, a decrease in goal attainment, or no change. A comparison between the alternatives themselves is then made at each land category-goal intersection, using the results of the more specific intersections as a basis for judgment. In other words, each alternative is first compared against the attainment of a goal for a group of specific locations, then compared against another alternative for the broader land-use category, with the basis of the latter comparison being how each alternative fares in the first comparison (in terms of the number of plus, minus, and equal signs). By examining the matrix horizontally, a comparison can be made between alternative routes in terms of one specific location for all the goals. By examining the matrix vertically, a comparison can be made in terms of one goal and all the land-use categories. Many subjective decisions are required with this method in determining both goal achievement for an alternative and the relative importance of each land-use category and each goal. Further, it is more suited to assessing the degree to which project objectives/goals are met than to assessing environmental consequences of meeting these goals/objectives.

Salient Features:

Simple matrix with goals as an element of comparison.

Advantages/Limitations of Salient Features:

1. Field studies conducted --- no
2. Practical for field use --- yes
3. Usage for various types/sizes of projects --- yes
4. Objective vs. subjective approaches --- both
5. Reproducibility --- unknown
6. Scientifically sound features --- yes

Conclusions:

General reference for WRAM.

+ + +

REFERENCE:

Leopold, L. B., "Quantitative Comparison of Some Aesthetic Factors Among Rivers," Geological Survey Circular 620, 1969, 16 pp., U.S. Geological Survey, Washington, D.C.

Abstract:

This report evaluates the aesthetic features of 12 sites in Idaho. These sites were being considered for hydroelectric power development. Two approaches were used---(1) the relative uniqueness of each site was considered in terms of 46 factors, and (2) specific comparisons were made in terms of valley and river character. Valley character was considered to be a function of width of valley, height of nearby hills, scenic outlook (views) and urbanization. River character was taken to be a function of river depth, river width and prevalence of rapids.

Salient Features:

Relative uniqueness concept and categorization of factors. Addresses aesthetics with a quantitative approach.

Advantages/Limitations of Salient Features:

1. Field studies conducted --- yes
2. Practical for field use --- yes
3. Usage for various types/sizes of projects --- yes
4. Objective vs. subjective approaches --- objective
5. Reproducibility --- yes, with basic system defined
6. Scientifically sound features --- yes

Conclusions:

General reference for WRAM.

+ + +

REFERENCE:

Miller, III, J. R., Professional Decision-Making: A Procedure for Evaluating Complex Alternatives, 1970, 305 pp., Praeger Publishers, Inc., New York, New York.

Abstract:

In this book the author offers a systematic and quantitative method of evaluating subjective judgments and presents experimental results that prove the value of his method for choosing between alternatives. Made possible by advances in operations research, statistical decision-theory, and systems analysis techniques, this significant contribution to the decision-making sciences is here outlined in step-by-step detail. Miller shows how alternatives that include "hidden" or subjective values can be taken into account in the decision process, along with considerations of manpower, material, and monetary resources

He demonstrates how to estimate the resource drain required by each alternative, how to assess the complex worth of each, and how to trade off these considerations - along with factors of risk and uncertainty - to arrive at a more responsible final decision. Detailed studies demonstrate how the procedure can actually be put to such diverse uses as selecting computer and weapon systems, assessing alternative transportation systems, and evaluating manpower needs.

Salient Features:

General information on weighting and scaling procedures.

Advantages/Limitations of Salient Features:

1. Field studies conducted --- not pertinent
2. Practicalffor field use --- not pertinent
3. Usage for various types/sizes of projects --- not pertinent
4. Objective vs. subjective approaches --- objective
5. Reproducibility --- unknown
6. Scientifically sound features --- yes

Conclusions:

General reference for WRAM.

+ + +

REFERENCE:

Orlob, G. T., et al, "Wild Rivers---Methods for Evaluation," Oct. 1970, 106 pages, Water Resources Engineers, Walnut Creek, Cal. (report prepared for U.S. Dept. of Interior, Washington, D.C.).

Abstract:

Nonmonetary and intangible values are expressed in dollars, on the premises that such values are at least equal to the economic development benefits that are foregone in favor of preservation, and that nonmonetary benefits equal between 0.25 and 2.0 times monetary benefits. Environmental values can then be subjected to the benefit-cost analysis. The assumptions made in this method are arbitrary, and no provision is made for analyzing the nonmonetary environmental impacts of development. The evaluations required are very lengthy mathematical computations.

Salient Features:

Nonmonetary and intangible values are expressed in dollars.

Advantages/Limitations of Salient Features:

1. Field studies conducted --- yes
2. Practical for field use --- yes
3. Usage for various types/sizes of projects --- yes
4. Objective vs. subjective approaches --- objective
5. Reproducibility --- unknown
6. Scientifically sound features --- yes

Conclusions:

General reference for WRAM.

+ + +

REFERENCE:

Pikarsky, M., "Comprehensive Planning for the Chicago Crosstown Expressway," Highway Research Record, 1967, No. 180, pp. 35-51.

Abstract:

Expressway planning consisted of the evaluation of 7 north-south and 4 east-west route alternatives relative to their engineering aspects, impacts upon existing communities, and otential land use improvements. Fifteen to 20 criteria were used for each of the three major groups, and relative importance weights assigned to each. Each alternative was rated 1-10 for each criteria with 10 representing a high rating for the criteria and 1 a low rating. A composite scoring system was used which consisted of summing the products of the relative importance weights and ratings. This is a weighting-scaling checklist.

Salient Features:

Weighting-scaling checklist.

Advantages/Limitations of Salient Features:

1. Field studies conducted --- yes
2. Practical for field use --- yes
3. Usage for various types/sizes of projects --- yes
4. Objective vs. subjective approaches --- objective
5. Reproducibility --- unknown
6. Scientifically sound features --- yes

Conclusions:

   General reference for WRAM.

+ + +

REFERENCE:

Schimpeler, C. C. and Grecco, W. L., "Systems Evaluation: An
Approach Based on Community Structures and Values," Highway
Research Record, 1968, No. 238, pp. 123-152.

Abstract:

   A comprehensive, weighted heirarchy of community development criteria are used to evaluate alternative transportation
system design concepts. The system is basically a weighting-
scaling checklist which includes the consideration of the probability that an objective j can be achieved if plan i is adopted.

Salient Features:

   Inclusion of probability along with weighting and scaling.

Advantages/Limitations of Salient Features:

   1. Field studies conducted --- yes
   2. Practical for field use --- yes
   3. Usage for various types/sizes of projects --- yes
   4. Objective vs. subjective approaches --- objective
   5. Reproducibility --- unknown
   6. Scientifically sound features --- yes

Conclusions:

   General reference for WRAM.

+ + +

REFERENCE:

Southeastern Wisconsin Regional Planning Commission, "Land Use
Transportation Study--Forecast and Alternative Plans: 1990,"
Plan Report 7, Vol. 2, June 1966.

Abstract:

   This methodology represents a weighting (rating) - ranking
checklist. Various environmental objectives are stated. These
are ranked in order of importance for each situation, then

263

weighted values are assigned on a direct reverse listing of the numerical importance rank. Each of the alternative projects or routes is then rated against the environmental objectives-no particular rating value system is specified. The two numbers for rating and ranking are multiplied together for each objective, and the resulting values for all the objectives are added for each alternative. These final values represent the evaluation of specific alternatives against their achievement of the objectives and can be used for comparison against each other. In this method the assignment of weights is arbitrary rather than objective. Subjective judgments are required in ranking and in the rating of alternatives against the objectives. Some measure of the relative value of alternative plans is achieved, but impact itself is not determined.

Salient Features:

Weighting-ranking checklist.

Advantages/Limitations of Salient Features:

1. Field studies conducted --- yes
2. Practical for field use --- yes
3. Usage for various types/sizes of projects --- yes
4. Objective vs. subjective approaches --- subjective
5. Reproducibility --- unknown
6. Scientifically sound features --- yes

Conclusions:

General reference for WRAM.

APPENDIX B

INFORMATION ON 34 REFERENCES

FROM 1971-73 PERIOD

REFERENCE:

Arnold, W., Young, J. and Brewer, J., "Constructing NonLinear
Dynamic Models for Socio-Environmental Decision Making: A
Methodology," Environmental Quality Series No. 11, Oct. 1972,
Institute of Governmental Affairs, University of California
at Davis, Davis, California.

Abstract:

The main purpose of this study was to present a methodology for the development of socioeconomic system submodels
which could be integrated into environmental impact studies.
The model development is based on the formalism suggested by
J.W. Forrester in several references. The so-called method
of "quasilinearization" is incorporated into the model-building
procedure in order to obtain values of unknown and important parameters. As an example, the socioeconomic system of
the Lake Tahoe Basin, on the California-Nevada State line, is
modeled and unknown parameters in the model are identified.
This example illustrates the application of the techniques
proposed in the model construction methodology.

Salient Features:

Provide bases for the development of functional curves
for socio-economic variables.

Advantages/Limitations of Salient Features:

1. Field studies conducted --- yes
2. Practical for field use --- no
3. Usage for various types/sizes of projects --- unknown
4. Objective vs. subjective approaches --- objective
5. Reproducibility --- unknown
6. Scientifically sound features --- yes

Conclusions:

General reference for WRAM

+ + +

REFERENCE:

Bagley, M. D., Kroll, C. A., and Clark, C., "Aesthetics in
Environmental Planning," EPA-600/5-73-009, Nov. 1973, 187 pp.,
U. S. Environmental Protection Agency, Washington, D. C. (pre-
pared for EPA by Stanford Research Institute, Menlo Park,
California).

Abstract:

    This report addresses the relationship of aesthetics to
environmental planning. The primary emphasis of the research
is on the man/environment interaction, with the ultimate goal
directed toward improving the understanding of aesthetic concepts and the implication of using those concepts in research
and planning activities. The historical development of the
Western concept of aesthetics is explored with the aim of
showing the relation of the concept to the particular set
of attitudes at each period, to illuminate the way in which
present concepts relate to today's world. Methodologies for
measuring or quantifying aesthectics are reviewed, as well as
a review of the state of the art of research in basic theory
for understanding the unquantifiable. A similar review of
selected planning agencies guidelines and procedures for
integrating aesthetics into the planning process is followed
with an outline of suggested future research needs.

Salient Features:

    Describes several approaches for quantifying the aesthetic
features of an area.

Advantages/Limitations of Salient Features:

    1. Field studies conducted --- yes
    2. Practical for field use --- yes
    3. Usage for various types/sizes of projects --- yes
    4. Objective vs. subjective approaches --- both
    5. Reproducibility --- yes
    6. Scientifically sound features --- yes

Conclusions:

    Use directly in WRAM
        ..Mention in conjunction with aesthetics evaluation.

+ + +

REFERENCE:

Bereano, P. L., et al, "A Proposed Methodology for Assessing
Alternative Technologies," Technology Assessment, Vol. 1,
No. 3, 1973, pp. 179-190.

Abstract:

    This report is a summary of a decision-making methodology
which could be used for assessing the environmental impacts

268

of alternatives. The ideal methodology is one which allows
comparison of all the alternatives on all relevant variables.
The methodology described herein uses an interaction matrix
which is based on several network analyses. Identified impacts
are described based on the product of their probability and
ultility. Probability denotes the likelihood of occurrence
and utility represents and assigned significance value ranging from +10 to -10.

Salient Features:

    Use of probability of an impact as an integral part of
an interaction matrix.

Advantages/Limitations of Salient Features:

    1. Field studies conducted --- yes
    2. Practical for field use --- yes
    3. Usage for various types/sizes of projects --- yes
    4. Ojective vs. subjective approaches --- objective
    5. Reproducibility --- unknown
    6. Scientifically sound features --- yes

Conclusions:

    General reference for WRAM

                        + + +

REFERENCE:

Bromley, D. W., et al, "Water Resource Projects and Environ-
mental Impacts: Towards a Conceptual Model," Feb. 1972,
Water Resources Center, University of Wisconsin, Madison,
Wisconsin.

Abstract:

    As multiobjective evaluation of water resource investments
becomes more common, it is important to develop conceptual
bases for including monetary as well as nonmonetary impacts
in the evaluation process. This is currently hampered by
the lack of a comprehensive and systematic model which permits the identification and display of the many project impacts.
And, more importantly, there is little information on the
linkage between economic activity and many environmental
impacts. A start is made by depicting natural resource use
by sector of economic activity with concentration on land
use. A simulation model is developed which will determine
acres in certain land use categories in Southern Idaho over

time without any water development. By being able to predict
land use changes with and without a project, the first step
in linking economic activity to certain environmental impacts
has been taken.

Salient Features:

Procedure for predicting changes in land use over time
both with and without a project.

Advantages/Limitations of Salient Features:

1. Field studies conducted --- yes
2. Practical for field use --- unknown
3. Usage for various types/sizes of projects --- unknown
4. Objective vs. subjective approaches --- objective
5. Reproducibility --- unknown
6. Scientifically sound features --- yes

Conclusions:

General reference for WRAM

+ + +

REFERENCE:

Bureau of Reclamation, "Guidelines for Implementing Princi-
ples and Standards for Multi-objective Planning of Water
Resources," Review draft, 1972, Bureau of Reclamation, U. S.
Department of the Interior, Washington, D. C.

Abstract:

This methodology was one of 8 identified in the interim
WRAM report (Feb, 1977). This multi-agency task force
approach is an attempt to coordinate features of the Water
Resources Council's (WRC) Proposed Principles and Standards
for Planning Water and Related Land Resources with requirements of NEPA. It develops a checklist of environmental components and categories organized in the same manner as the
WRC guidelines. The categories of potential impacts examined
deal comprehensively with biological, physical, cultural,
and historical resources and with pollution factors but do
not treat social or economic impacts. Impacts are measured
in quantitative terms where possible and also are rated subjectively on quality and human influence. In addition, uniqueness and irreversibility considerations are included where
appropriate. Several suggestions for summary tables and
bar graphs are offered as communications aids. Key ideas

incorporated in the approach include explicit identification
of the without-project environment as distinct from present
conditions and use of a uniqueness rating system for evaluating quality and human influence (worst known, average, best
known, etc.).

Salient Features:

Good listing of assessment variables for biological,
physical-chemical, esthetic and cultural environments.
A quality scale and human influence scale is suggested.

Advantages/Limitations of Salient Features:

1. Field studies conducted --- yes
2. Practical for field use --- yes
3. Usage for various types/sizes of projects --- yes
4. Objective vs. subjective approaches --- objective
5. Reproducibility --- unknown
6. Scientifically sound features --- yes

Conclusions:

Use directly in WRAM
..Mention quality scale and human influence scales.

+ + +

REFERENCE:

Central New York Regional Planning and Development Board,
"Environmental Resources Management," Report No. CNYRPDB -
RP-72-HUD-246-06, Oct. 1972, 35 pages, Syracuse, New York
(report prepared for Department of Housing and Urban Development, Region 2, New York, New York).

Abstract:

This methodology employs a matrix approach to assess
in simple terms the major and minor, direct and indirect
impacts of certain water related construction activities.
It is designed primarily to measure only the physical impacts
of small water resource projects in a watershed, and is based
on an identification of the specific, small-scale component
activities that are included in any project. Restricted to
physical impacts on nine different types of watershed areas
(e. g., wetlands) and fourteen types of activities (e. g.,
tree removal), the procedure indicates four possible levels
of impact-receptor interactions (major direct, major indirect,
minor direct and minor indirect). Low to moderate resources

in terms of time, money, or personnel are required for the
methodology, due principally to its simple way of quantification (major versus minor impact).

Salient Features:

Use of interaction matrices to identify impacts and
display their relative importance.

Advantages/Limitations of Salient Features:

1. Field studies conducted --- yes
2. Practical for field use --- yes
3. Usage for various types/sizes of projects --- no
4. Objective vs. subjective approaches --- both
5. Reproducibility --- unknown
6. Scientifically sound features --- yes

Conclusions:

General reference for WRAM

+ + +

REFERENCE:

Chen, C. W. and Orlob, G. T., "Ecologic Simulation for
Aquatic Environments," OWRR-C-2044, December 1972, 156 pp.,
Office of Water Resources Research, U. S. Dept. of Interior,
Washington, D. C. (prepared for OWRR by Water Resources
Engineers, Inc., Walnut Creek, California.).

Abstract:

This report describes a general purpose model for the
simulation of aquatic ecosystem behavior. Conceptually,
the model is intended to provide a realistic representation of
the response of an aquatic environment to external stimulii,
both natural and man-induced. It presently exists in two
forms, as the "Lake Ecologic Model" suitable for investigation
of stratified lakes and reservoirs, and as the "Estuary
Ecologic Model," adaptable to shallow, vertically-mixed
estuaries. Both have been tested successfully on real systems.
    The ecological model considers the aquatic ecosystem
to be comprised of water, its chemical impurities, and various life forms, i. e., bacteria, phytoplankton, zooplankton,
fish and benthic animals. Abiotic substances derived from
air, soil, adjoining waters, and the activities of man are
inputs that, while they are resident within the system, exert

272

an influence on its life structure. Indigenous biota respond
to nutrients available for cell synthesis and to various
environmental conditions, such as light, heat, toxicants, etc.
that govern rates of growth, decay, mortality, and predation.
A natural succession up the trophic ladder may be envisioned,
whereby nutrient inputs are transformed into algal biomass,
through zooplankton to fish, and ultimately to man.

The Lake Ecologic Model is founded on a model developed
earlier for the simulation to thermal energy distributions
in stratified reservoirs. Conceptually, the model considers
the lake to be idealized as a one-dimensional system of
horizontal slices. Mass and energy transfers can take place
along the vertical axis in this system and the response can
be followed in space and time by solving the appropriate
set of mass or energy balance equations. Boundary conditions
are imposed according to the natural hydrologic and meteorologic circumstances and/or the operational controls on the
impoundment.

The Estuary Ecologic Model is designed according to
the conceptual scheme used by WRE in its development for EPA
of a hydrodynamic model for shallow estuaries. Conceptually
the system is envisioned as being comprised of a network of
one-dimensional channels (links) and volume elements (nodes).
A set of mass transfer equations is written for nodes in
the system and a solution is obtained by a step-forward
explicit technique. Advective flows and diffusive properties
of the estuary are previously determined by a companion
hydrodynamic simulator. Estuarial systems that may be simulated with the model include those with tributary rivers,
embayments, portions of shallow ocean area, and a variety of
sources and sinks of water and quality constituents. The
model package includes the hydrodynamic model and an ecologic module that are closely coupled to provide a complete
representation of estuarial behavior.

Salient Features:

Ecosystem models are presented for lakes and estuaries.

Advantages/Limitations of Salient Features:

1. Field studies conducted --- yes
2. Practical for field use --- no
3. Usage for various types/sizes of projects --- not
   applicable
4. Objective vs. subjective approaches --- objective
5. Reproducibility --- unknown
6. Scientifically sound features --- yes

Conclusions:

General reference for WRAM

273

REFERENCE:

Commonwealth Associates, Inc., "Environmental Analysis System," Report No. R-1447, 1972, prepared for the Northern States Power Company, Minnesota, by Commonwealth Associates, Inc., Jackson, Michigan.

Abstract:

This methodology describes a weighting-scaling checklist useful for fossil fuel power plant site selection. Weighting is accomplished by the assignment of importance, and linear proportioning based on maximum impact is used for scaling. This checklist for evaluating environmental impact is further developed by adding the adaptability and flexibility of a computer. The computer can modify the weighting operations as often as necessary in response to new thinking.

Salient Features:

Techniques for weighting and scaling of impacts.

Advantages/Limitations of Salient Features:

1. Field studies conducted --- yes
2. Practical for field use --- yes
3. Usage for various types/sizes of projects --- yes
4. Objective vs. subjective approaches --- objective
5. Reproducibility --- unknown
6. Scientifically sound features --- yes

Conclusions:

General reference for WRAM

+ + +

REFERENCE:

Coomber, N. H., and Biswas, A. K., Evaluation of Environmental Intangibles, Genera Press, Bronxville, New York, 1973, 77 pages.

Abstract:

This study was undertaken to consider the possibility of accurate assessment of the values of environmental intangibles. If values comparable with those produced for other commodities by normal market mechanics can be adduced, a large obstacle will have been removed from accurate project appraisal and benefit-cost analysis. This study has not attempted to derive new techniques, a task which seems to be as unnecessary as it is impracticable, but has concentrated on existing methods. This in itself embodies the conclusion that some currently adopted techniques possess considerable merit and may be modified for more accurate functioning. This study fell naturally into three phases, focussing on individual contributions to the state-of-the-art: (1) the historical and economic background of evaluatory techniques and their present adaptability to benefit-cost analysis, (2) and the classification and review of techniques for the economic evaluation of environmental intangibles, (3) and the classification and criticism of non-monetary evaluatory and comparative techniques.

Salient Features:

Provides general discussion of systematic evaluation of environmental intangibles.

Advantages/Limitations of Salient Features:

1. Field studies conducted --- not applicable
2. Practical for field use --- not applicable
3. Usage for various types/sizes of projects --- not applicable
4. Objective vs. subjective approaches --- objective
5. Reproducibility --- unknown
6. Scientifically sound features --- yes

Conclusions:

General reference for WRAM

+ + +

REFERENCE:

Crawford, A. B., "Impact Analysis Using Differentially Weighted Evaluation Criteria," 1973, in J. L. Cochrane and M. Zeleny, editors, Multiple Criteria Decision Making, University of South Carolina Press, Columbia, South Carolina.

Abstract:

This paper contains a summary description of a method of analyzing alternative plans or operations using multiple evaluative criteria. The paper has two parts. The first describes the main features of the method itself; the second discusses its application in an analysis of the value

275

impacts of several highway corridor alternatives. The method of evaluation is designed to do the following: (1) to produce a numeric measure of the extent to which each of the alternatives under evaluation impacts either positively or negatively on each evaluative criterion, thus providing a basis for analyzing the value trade-offs that would be involved in a decision among these alternatives, (2) for each alternative, to analyze which consequences and groups of consequences have the most serious impacts, thus providing the designer with a basis for modifying or improving proposed plans, (3) given the relative weights assigned to the evaluative criteria by a given reference public, to produce a numeric measure of the extent to which each alternative impacts either positively or negatively on (a) each weighted evaluative criterion and (b) the entire set of weighted criteria, thus providing the decision maker with a more complete analysis of the trade-offs involved within and among the alternatives, and (4) given alternative weighting schemes (assigned by different reference publics), to compare the worth indices achieved by alternative plans, in order to aid the decision maker in identifying a "best overall" course of action.

Salient Features:

Weighting-scaling checklist for evaluation of impacts of alternatives.

Advantages/Limitations of Salient Features:

1. Field studies conducted --- yes
2. Practical for field use --- yes
3. Usage for various types/sizes of projects --- yes
4. Objective vs. subjective approaches --- objectives
5. Reproducibility --- unknown
6. Scientifically sound features --- yes

Conclusions:

General reference for WRAM

+ + +

REFERENCE:

Dee, N., et al, "Environmental Evaluation System for Water Resources Planning," Final report, 1972, Battelle-Columbus Laboratories, Columbus, Ohio (prepared for the Bureau of Reclamation, U. S. Department of the Interior, Washington, D. C.).

Abstract:

This methodology was one of 8 methodologies identified in the interim WRAM report (Feb., 1977). It is a weighting-scaling checklist methodology. It was designed for major water resource projects, but many parameters used are also appropriate for other types of projects. Seventy-eight specific environmental parameters are defined within the four categories ecology, environmental pollution, aesthetics, and human interest. The approach does not deal with economic or secondary impacts, and social impacts are only partially covered within the human interest category. Parameter measurements are scaled by converting to a common base of environmental quality units through specified graphs or value functions. Impacts can be aggregated using a set of preassigned weights of relative importance. The approach emphasizes explicit procedures for impact measurement and evaluation and should therefore produce highly replicable results. Both spatial and temporal spects of impacts are noted and explicitly weighted in the assessment. Public participation, uncertainty, and risk concepts are not considered. An important idea of the approach is to highlight key impacts via a "red flag" system.

Salient Features:

Weighting-scaling checklist with a good listing of bio-logical, physical-chemical, esthetic and cultural variables.

Advantages/Limitations of Salient Features:

1. Field studies conducted --- yes
2. Practical for field use --- yes
3. Usage for various types/sizes of projects --- yes
4. Objective vs. Subjective approaches --- objective
5. Reproducibility --- yes
6. Scientifically sound features --- yes

Conclusions:

Use directly in WRAM
..Describe functional curves and ranked pairwise comparison technique.

+ + +

REFERENCE:

Dee, N., et al, "Planning Methodology for Water Quality Management: Environmental Evaluation System," July 1973, Battelle-Columbus, Columbus, Ohio.

Abstract:

This methodology of impact assessment can be classified
as a weighting-scaling checklist although it also contains
elements of matrix and network approaches. Areas of possible
impacts are defined by a hierarchical system of 4 categories
(ecology, physical/chemical, aesthetic, social), 19 components,
and 64 parameters. An interaction matrix is presented to
indicate which activities associated with water quality treatment projects generally impact which parameters. The range of
parameters used is comprehensive, excluding only economic
variables. Impact measurement incorporates two important
elements. A set of ranges is specified for each parameter to
express impact magnitude on a scale from zero to one. The
ranges assigned to each parameter within a component are then
combined by means of an environmental assessment tree into a
summary environmental impact score for that component. The
significance of impacts on each component is quantified by a
set of assigned weights. A nte impact can be obtained for
any alternative by multiplying each component score by its
weight factor and summing across components. Because of its
explicitness, the methodology possesses only minor ambiguities
and should be highly replicable. Because the environmental
assessment trees are developed specifically for water treatment facilities, the methodology cannot be adapted to other
types of projects without reconstructing the trees, even though
the parameters could be useful as a simple checklist. See
following example for more information.

Salient Features:

Weighting-scaling checklist based on relevant matrices
and networks.
Ranges of scale values.
Concepts of "environmental assessment trees" to account
for interrelationships among assessment variables.

Advantages/Limitations of Salient Features:

1. Field studies conducted --- yes
2. Practical for field use --- yes
3. Usage for various types/sizes of projects --- yes
4. Objectives vs. subjective approaches --- objective
5. Reproducibility --- yes
6. Scientifically sound features --- yes

Conclusions:

Use directly in WRAM
..Describe "environmental assessment tree" concept
and ranges of scale values.

278

Example of Methodology:

(The following information is from Burchell, R. W., and Listokin, D., "The Environmental Impact Handbook," 1975, 239 pp., Center for Urban Policy Research, Rutgers - The State University, New Brunswick, New Jersey - Burchell and Listokin based their information on Dee, N., et al, "Planning Methodology for Water Quality Management Environmental Evaluation System," July 1973, Battelle-Columbus Laboratories, Columbus, Ohio).

1. Four major categories of information are included as shown in Table B-1. The four categories include 19 components, and the 19 components include 64 parameters.
2. Importance index values based on 100 units are assigned to each category, component and parameter in Table B-1. Assigned by interdisciplinary team.
3. Scaling of values for each of 64 parameters accomplished by a "range" approach, with 1 indicating the best environmental quality and 0 indicating the worst environmental quality. Two examples will be cited:
   (a). The dissolved oxygen index is

Range	Parameter Measurement (ppm)	Parameter Quality Index
1	0<DO<2	0.0
2	2<DO<5	0.2
3	5<DO<7	0.7
4	7<DO	1.0

   (b) The wooded shoreline index is based on the assumption that a shoreline bordered by trees and shrubs is more pleasing than one which is not.

Range	Parameter Measurement	Parameter Quality Index
1	no trees	0.0
2	some trees	0.5
3	half trees	0.8
4	predominantly trees	1.0

4. A unique part of the methodology is the use of an "environmental assessment tree." Specifically, the scores of the parameters are aggregated into nineteen components with nineteen network trees which have been constructed to translate the relationship between the good and the bad values on individual parameters into good and bad values for a set of parameters. Fig. 3 (page 83) is a reproduction of part of the Aquatic Species and Populations Assessment Tree. To obtain the environmental assessment one first determines the range of the vegetation parameter, and then

279

TABLE B-1

Battelle Environmental Evaluation System
for Water Quality Management

I.24 ECOLOGY	III.24 AESTHETICS
6 Terrestrial Species and Populations	4 Land
Vegetation	Surface Configuration
Browsers and Grazers	Land Appearance
Small Game Animals	Alignment of Stream,
Pests	Reservoir and Estuary
6 Aquatic Species and Populations	Shoreline
Vegetation	Geological Surface
Fish	Material
Waterfowl	3 Air
Pests	Odor
6 Terrestrial Habitats and Communities	Visual
Rare and Endangered	Sound
Species	6 Water
Species Diversity	Flow
6 Aquatic Habitats and Communities	Clarity
Rare and Endangered	Water Level
Species	Floating Material
Special Diversity	5 Biota
II.34 PHYSICAL/CHEMICAL	Wooded Shoreline
8 Biochemical Water Quality	Terrestrial Animals
Dissolved Oxygen	Aquatic Life
Inorganic Phosphate	Vegetation
Inorganic Nitrogen	4 Man-Made Structures
Fecal Coliform	Architectural Design
6 Chemical Water Quality	Structures
Hazardous Materials	Compatibility with
Total Dissolved Solids	Other Structures and
pH	Natural Environment
6 Physical Water Environment	Planting and Site Design
Basin Hydrologic Loss	2 Composition
Frequency of Extreme	Composite Effect
Flows	Unique Composition
Temperature	IV.18 SOCIAL
Turbidity	5 Environmental Interests
4 Air Quality	Recreational Accessibility
Particulate Matter	Recreation Activities
Reactive Hydrocarbons	Educational/Scientific
Sulfur Oxides	Historical/Cultural
Nitrogen Oxides	6 Health and Safety
	Accident Prevention
	Buffer Zone Development
	Facilities Location
	System Overload

8 Land Use
  Location of Interceptors
  Reserve
    and Treatment Facili-
    ties
  Soil Erosion
  Solid Waste Disposal
    Controls
2 Noise Pollution
  Frequency of Disturbing
    Noise
  Intensity of Disturbing
    Noise

7 Community Well-Being
    Community Involvement
    Population Served by
      Sewers
    Community Treatment
      Participation

follows the arrow to the next parameter box (waterfowl). The
same dichotomy is offered at the next parameter (pests), depending upon the answer to the initial parameter. After following
several more branches on the tree, a last branch will intersect
the environmental quality scale and provide a score for the component. For example, parameter ratings of 3 in vegetation,
4 in waterfowl, 3 in pests, and 3 in fish may be followed by
the dashed lines to an assessment of 0.8 along the tree. The
advantages of the assessment tree are that it is simple to
use, requires less precise data about individual parameters,
and places the single parameter in the context of the real-
world interrelationships among similar variables. The disadvantage of the assessment tree approach is the further loss
of information about individual parameters.

5. Other important characteristics of methodology:
    (a) Major impacts ("red flags") are defined by a change
         of two or more ranges, e. g., 4 to 2, or 3 to 1, or
         1 to 3, etc. A red flag could be the basis for pro-
         ject rejection.
    (b) User must weigh impacts in terms of their long and
         short term importance.
    (c) Public participation is encouraged.

+ + +

REFERENCE:

Environmental Impact Center, Inc., "A Methodology for Assess-
ing Environmental Impact of Water Resources Development,"
Nov. 1973, PB-226 545, prepared by Environmental Impact Center,
Inc., Cambridge, Mass., for U. S. Department of the Interior,
Office of Water Resources Research, Washington, D. C.

Abstract:

        This methodology was one of 8 methodologies identified
in the interim WRAM report (Feb, 1977). It is a descriptive
checklist with no impact weighting or scaling. Environmental
impacts of water resource projects are assessed with a dynamic
simulation model for forecasting regional economic and demographic changes and their interactions with water supply and
water quality over time. The model was applied to the Massachusetts portion of the Connecticut River Basin. Modular
sectors were developed to forecast regional population and
industrial levels, intra-regional land use patterns, and
recreational activities. These are linked to a water sector
which models stream flows, water supply withdrawals and consumption, and water quality in terms of dissolved oxygen and
carbonaceous and nitrogenous oxygen demand. Water quality is
based on both point wasteloads from domestic and industrial
sources and dispersed source wasteloads from urban runoff.

A final module represents biological activities in a stream, including algal concentrations and fish populations.

The water sector uses information on the amount and distribution of land uses to forecast water withdrawal and comsumption, and point- and dispersed source wasteloads for each reach in the river system of the region. Water quality is estimated in terms of dissolved oxygen and carbonaceous nitrogenous oxygen demand. Steady-state conditions are assumed, with base flows and temperature specified exogenously. The transient water quality impacts of dispersed source wastes are estimated in a submodel by superimposing a storm on the assumed steady-state conditions. Wastewater management plans may be evaluated by specifying outfall locations, treatment levels, and service areas for proposed wastewater systems. The water sector can also be used to estimate the impacts of flow augmentation and interbasin transfers of water. The recreation sector uses information on socioeconomic characteristics, the amount of existing recreational land, and facilities (including competition among different sites) and water quality to forecast recreational visits in the region and extent of recreation-supported employment. Recreational activities are subdivided into fishing, boating, swimming, and sightseeing. The riverine ecosystem is modeled in the biology sector in terms of three trophic levels: algae, zooplankton, and fish. Biological activities are, of course, dependent upon water quality in the reach, including both nutrient and dissolved oxygen concentrations. The biology and recreation sectors interact through fishing.

Salient Features:

Impact prediction information for certain biological and physical-chemical variables.

Advantages/Limitations of Salient Features:

1. Field studies conducted --- yes
2. Practical for field use --- yes
3. Usage for various types/sizes of projects --- yes
4. Objective vs. subjective approaches --- objective
5. Reproducibility --- unknown
6. Scientifically sound features --- yes

Conclusions:

Use directly in WRAM
..Mention dynamic simulation model.

REFERENCE:

Fischer, D. W. and Davies, G. S., "An Approach to Assessing Environmental Impact," Journal of Environmental Management, Vol. 1, No. 3, 1973, pp. 207-227.

Abstract:

This methodology consists of the use of three matrices. The first is for evaluation of environmental baseline conditions, the second is the identify potential impacts on important environmental factors, and the third is a decision matrix for the evaluation of alternatives. The concepts used are similar to the Leopold interaction matrix.

Salient Features:

Use of series of three matrices in defining environmental setting, identifying impacts and summarizing the features of alternatives.

Advantages/Limitations of Salient Features:

1. Field studies conducted --- yes
2. Practical for field use --- yes
3. Usage for various types/sizes of projects --- yes
4. Objective vs. subjective approaches --- objective
5. Reproducibility --- unknown
6. Scientifically sound features --- yes

Conclusions:

Use directly in WRAM
..Describe matrix concepts.

+ + +

REFERENCE:

Hydrologic Engineering Center, "Reservoir Temperature Stratification Users Manual," January 1972, U. S. Army Engineer District---Sacramento, Davis, California.

Abstract:

This computer program is intended for application to the design and planning problems involving consideration of multi-level intake structures. The program simulates the vertical distribution of water temperature within a reservoir and estimates the mean monthly release temperature through each level of intake.

This program is useful for evaluation of the thermal portion of a project's environmental impact. Program input information includes inflow, outflow, evaporation, precipitation, radiation, and average air temperature.

Salient Features:

Mathematical model for reservoir temperature stratification.

Advantages/Limitations of Salient Features:

1 Field studies conducted --- unknown
2. Practical for field use --- yes
3. Usage for various types/sizes of projects --- not pertinent
4. Objective vs. subjective approaches --- objective
5. Reproducibility --- yes
6. Scientifically sound features --- yes

Conclusions:

General reference for WRAM.

+ + +

REFERENCE:

Jain, R. K., et al, "Environmental Impact Study for Army Military Programs," Report No. CERL-IR-D-13, December 1973 170 pages. U. S. Army Construction Engineering Research Laboratory, Champaign, Illinois.

Abstract:

This system involves computer techniques to identify potential environmental impacts from nine functional areas of Army activitites on eleven broad environmental categories. The nine functional areas are construction; operation, maintenance and repair; training; mission change; real estate; procurement; Army industrial activities: research, development, test and evaluation; and administration and support. Each of these functional areas has a number of additional basic activities. Examples of basic activities in the construction functional area include clearing trees, removing broken concrete, back-filling foundations, curing bituminous pavement, cleaning used concrete forms, installing insulation, and landscaping sites. A total of approximately 2,000 basic activities are identified in the nine functional areas. The environment is divided into 11 areas, including ecology, health science, air quality, surface water, ground water, sociology, economics, earth science, land use, noise, and transportation.

Within each of these categories, additional parameters are defined. Aproximately 1,000 specific environmental factors are defined for the 11 environmental categories. On this basis, it is possible to have a checklist which addresses the impact of approximately 2,000 basic Army activities on 1,000 environmental factors.

The computer system is used to identify potential impacts associated with various types of activities. In a sense, this method is similar to a computerized interaction matrix. It is considered herein as a descriptive checklist because each of the environmental factors is described in detail, with information given on actual measurement and data interpretation. The system codes each interaction. into one of four categories. The first category indicates that the potential impact must be assessed every time the activity is carried out; the second indicates that the impact is usually present, but may be omitted depending upon individual circumstances; the third indicates that the impact arises in a small but predictable number of cases, and it should be considered as to its presence in the individual circumstance; and finally, if there is no indication of potential impact this means that normally there is no impact upon the particular factor by the activity under consideration.

Salient Features:

    Extensive consideration of construction phase impacts.
    Good description of selected assessment variables (called attributes in the methodology).

Advantages/Limitations of Salient Features:

1. Field studies conducted --- yes
2. Practical for field use --- yes
3. Usage for various types/sizes of projects --- system focused on military projects as opposed to civil works projects.
4. Objective vs. subjective approaches --- objective
5. Reproducibility --- yes
6. Scientifically sound features --- yes

Conclusions:

    General reference for WRAM

+ + +

REFERENCE:

Kane, J., Vertinsky, I., and Thomson, W., "KSIM: A Methodology for Interactive Resources Policy Simulation," Water Resources Research, Vol. 9, No. 1, February 1973, pp. 65-79.

Abstract:

        The study develops a simulation procedure (KSIM) that
describes complex interaction of both hard and soft variables
while not requiring mathematical simulation in its use. Further, KSIM is touted as easily modified and totally flexible.
The KSIM approach utilizes geometric concepts and an interaction
matrix. KSIM is a cross-impact simulation technique used to
better forecast and assess long-range requirements and impacts
of water resource development alternatives. The technique
provides a tool to interface broad planning issues with detailed
dynamic models so that more effective use can be made of planning resources. Both qualitative and quantitative data can be
used---a unique characteristic. KSIM combines a small group
workshop procedure with a mathematical forecasting model and a
computer program to generate changes over time in a few significant planning variables. The method helps to identify planning
needs, develop models, and test the consequences of policy
actions. The technique requires expert leadership and access
to a computer. A KSIM computer program is available.
        KSIM presents a mathematical means of articulating and
visualizing what people sense to be the relationships among
a number of interacting variables. As a simulation tool, it
combines expert opinions with analytical computing techniques
to analyze relationships among broadly defined variables in
environmental and socio-economic systems. The technique enables
a team of people, first, to define and structure a set of variables describing a perceived problem and then, using an interactive computer program, to calculate and display the changes in
the variables over time. By observing the changes and then
making modifications and refinements, the team develops a model
of the problem situation. With the model, individuals can test
various alternatives and review and improve their understanding
of the problem. Like all simulations, KSIM seeks to establish
"if-then" relationships; however, KSIM has the distinctive
feature of accommodating subjective or intuitive concepts as
well as quantitative data.

Salient Features:

        Focuses attention on cross-impacts of water resources
development projects.

Advantages/Limitations of Salient Features:

        1.   Field studies conducted --- yes
        2.   Practical for field use --- no
        3.   Usage for various types/sizes of projects --- yes
        4.   Objective vs. subjective approaches --- objective
        5.   Reproducibility --- unknown
        6.   Scientifically sound features --- yes

Conclusions:

General reference for WRAM

+ + +

REFERENCE:

Leopold, L. B., et al, "A Procedure for Evaluating Environmental Impact," U. S. Geological Survey Circular 645, 1971,
U. S. Geological Survey, Washington, D. C.

Abstract:

This is an open-cell matrix approach indentifying 100 project actions and 88 environmental characteristics or conditions.
For each action involved in a project, the analyst evaluates
the impact on every impacted environmental characteristic in
terms of impact magnitude and significance. These evaluations
are subjectively determined by the analyst. Ecological and
physical-chemical impacts are treated comprehensively, social
and indirect impacts are not addressed. The approach was not
developed in reference to any specific type of project and may
be broadly applied with some alternations. It is chiefly valuable as a means of identifying project impacts and as a display format for communicating results of an analysis.

Salient Features:

Use of interaction matrix to identify and visually display potential impacts.

Advantages/Limitations of Salient Features:

1. Field studies conducted --- yes
2. Practical for field use --- yes
3. Usage for various types/sizes of projects --- yes
4. Objective vs. subjective approaches --- objective
5. Reproducibility --- unknown
6. Scientifically sound features --- yes

Conclusions:

General reference for WRAM

+ + +

REFERENCE:

MacCrimmon, K. R., "An Overview of Multiple Objective Decision
Making," 1973, in J. L. Cochrane and M. Zeleny, editors, "Multiple
Criteria Decision Making," University of South Carolina Press,
Columbia, South Carolina. 288

Abstract:

This is a general paper which discusses the literature on multiple objective and multiple attribute decision-making. The approaches which are available are discussed under the headings of (a) weighting methods, (b) sequential elimination methods, (c) mathematical programming methods, and (d) spatial proximity methods.

Salient Features:

Literature review on multiple objective and multiple attribute decision making.

Advantages/Limitations of Salient Features:

1. Field studies conducted --- not pertinent.
2. Practical for field use --- yes
3. Usage for various types/sizes of projects --- yes
4. Objective vs. subjective approaches --- objective
5. Reproducibility --- unknown
6. Scientifically sound features --- yes

Conclusions:

General reference for WRAM

+ + +

REFERENCE:

Manheim, M. L., et al, "Community Values in Highway Location and Design: A Procedural Guide," September 1971, Urban Systems Laboratory, Massachusetts Institute of Technology, Cambridge, Massachusetts (report prepared for Highway Research Board, Washington, D. C.).

Abstract:

Coordination between an interdisciplinary location study team and community groups is used in identifying impacts, the interests affected by the impacts, and appropriate representatives for those interests. An impact matrix is devised for each affected interest to describe each alternative and corresponding impacts. The information contained in the matrix may be qualitative, pictorial, or numerical. It is the responsibility of the location team to use this information in assisting a politically responsible official to make a decision on the proper course of action.

289

Salient Features:

Use of interaction matrix for identification and visual display of impacts.

Advantages/Limitations of Salient Features:

1. Field studies conducted --- yes
2. Practical for field use --- yes
3. Usage for various types/sizes of projects --- yes
4. Objective vs. subjective approaches --- objective
5. Reproducibility --- unknown
6. Scientifically sound features --- yes

Conclusions:

General reference for WRAM

+ + +

REFERENCE:

Markofsky, M. and Harleman, D. R., "A Predictive Model for Thermal Stratification and Water Quality in Reservoirs," EPA-16130-DJH-01/71, Jan. 1971, 286 pp., Massachusetts Institute of Technology, Cambridge, Massachusetts.

Abstract:

Modifications are made on a one-dimensional analytical thermal stratification prediction method to include the time required for inflowing water to reach a dam face. A one-dimensional water quality model is developed which incorporates the internal flow pattern predicted for a stratified reservoir from the temperature model. The water quality model is designed to predict the concentration of particular water quality parameters in the outflow water as a function of time. It is tested by comparisons with measurements of outlet concentrations resulting from pulse injections of a conservative tracer into a laboratory reservoir. The application of the mathematical model to a field case of practical interest is demonstrated by solving the coupled set of water quality equations for B. O. D. and D. O. predictions in Fontana Reservoir. It is concluded that the model is capable of predicting the effect of reservoir impoundments on water quality.

Salient Features:

A thermal stratification model is described.

Advantages/Limitations of Salient Features:

1. Field studies conducted --- yes
2. Practical for field use --- unknown
3. Usage for various types/sizes of projects --- unknown
4. Objective vs. subjective approaches --- objective
5. Reproducibility --- unknown
6. Scientifically sound features --- yes

Conclusions:

General reference for WRAM

+ + +

REFERENCE:

Moore, J. L., et al, "A Methodology for Evaluating Manufacturing Environmental Impact Statements for Delaware's Coastal Zone," June 1973, Battelle-Columbus Laboratories, Columbus, Ohio (report prepared for State of Dalaware).

Abstract:

This methodology employs a network approach, linking a list of manufacturing-related activities to potential environmental alterations to major environmental effects and finally to human uses affected. The primary strength of the set of linked matrices is its utility in displaying cause-condition-effect networks and tracing secondary impact chains. Such networks are useful primarily for identifying impacts, and the issues of impact magnitude and significance are addressed only in terms of high, moderate, low, or negligible damage. As a result of these subjective evaluations, the approach would have low replicability as an assessment technique.

Salient Features:

Stepped or linked matrices to display interrelationships between impacted assessment variables.

Advantages/Limitations of Salient Features:

1. Field studies conducted --- yes
2. Practical for field use --- yes
3. Usage for various types/sizes of projects --- yes
4. Objective vs. subjective approaches --- objective
5. Reproducibility --- unknown
6. Scientifically sound features --- yes

Conclusions:

General reference for WRAM

+ + +

REFERENCE:

Morrill, R. A., "Comprehensive Resource and Environmental
Management Planning," Research Report, June, 1973, 87 pages,
Engineering and Research Center, U. S. Bureau of Reclamation,
Denver, Colorado.

Abstract:

This report records the research, conceptual studies, and
the applications of the fundamental methods of hierarchical
decomposition-multi-level analysis to planning for comprehensive resource and environmental management. The report contains some useful diagrams depicting the interrelationships
of factors for a land resource plan, water resource plan,
energy resource plan, mineral resource plan, natural environment resource plan, socioeconomic resource plan and human
resource plan. Some possible quantitative measures useful in
defining quality of life are shown in Table B-2.

Salient Features:

Presentation of hierarchical information on various categories of the environment and their associated variables.
Suggested quantitative measures for defining the quality
of life.

Advantages/Limitations of Salient Features:

1. Field studies conducted --- unknown
2. Practical for field use --- yes
3. Usage for various types/sizes of projects --- yes
4. Objective vs. subjective approaches --- objective
5. Reproducibility --- unknown
6. Scientifically sound features --- yes

Conclusions:

General reference for WRAM

TABLE B-2
POSSIBLE QUANTITATIVE MEASURE OF VALUES
RELATED TO QUALITY OF LIFE

NEEDS	SOME POSSIBLE MEASURES
Physiological	Life span and cause of death
	Living area/capita
	Energy usage/capita to run "servant machines"
	Number of appliances/family
	Calories/capita/day
	Value of housing/family
	Birth rate and birth control products/adult
	Waste products/capita
	Medical and consumer product sales related to biological needs
	Various disease incidence-of-occurrence, health care
Safety	Per capita savings and investments
	Employment statistics
	Economic stability
	Crime rate
	Court actions
	Accident rates
	Government structure and budgets
	Community services organizations
	Protective services and budgets
	Mental patients/class or disorder
	Purchases of security devices and related consumer products (alarms, handguns, fire extinguishers, locks, etc.)
Social	Divorce race/family
	Adoption races/family
	Mobility races
	Social organization memberships
	Service organization membership
	Number of "Community Leaders"
	Altruistic and theologic organizations
	Social classified book sales
	Group and community recreation activities
	Social unrest and crimes
	"Gripe" articles in media
	Mental disorders of social nature
Esteem	Purchases of award devices (medals, trophies, etc.)

Number of "famous" people
Athletic events
Income levels/avg.
Recognized outstanding accomplishments
Letters to the editor/capita
Membership in professional organiza-
    tions
Media articles/awards
Mental disorders/self-esteem
Classified book sales
Respect for leaders and government
Consumer product sales/self-esteem
Accident rates

Creative and
Esthetic

Art supply sales
Production of art objects
Number of artists and authors
Art, literature, and philosophy organ-
    izations
Awards for outstanding works
General beauty of urban area
Advanced work in colleges and Univer-
    sities
Class attendance/adult education
Commodity purchases esthetics
Classified book sales
Housing value improvement purchases
Theater, orchestra, and other cultural
    community support
Recreational facilities and usage

Self-
Actualization

"Retreat" attendance
Superior works and achievements
Number of world famous people
Production of art, literary, and
    philosophical works
Attendance in graduate and postgrad-
    uate courses and seminars
Outstanding research activities
Classified book sales of "higher
    level" literature
Number of centers of excellence, founda-
    tions, etc.
The quality of cultural activity
The quality of leadership in government,
    industry, business, etc.
Evidence of rational concern for all
    levels of human needs
The quality of the environment

REFERENCE:

O'Connor, M. F., "The Application of Multi-Attribute Scaling
Procedures to the Development of Indices of Value," June 1972,
Engineering Psychology Laboratory, Univ. of Michigan, Ann Arbor,
Mich.

Abstract:

   Using procedures developed in the study of multidimensional utility analysis, two indices of water quality are
developed. One index describes the quality of a surface body
of raw water which will be used to sustain a fish and wildlife population. A second index describes the quality of a
surface body of raw water which will be treated as is necessary
and used as a public water supply. Since the first use involves mainly the health of the wildlife population whereas the
second use involves human health and also economic and aesthetic considerations, it is anticipated that if the use to which
the water will be put is important enough to merit a separate
index, these two indices should assign very different numbers
to samples of water. The multi-attribute scaling procedures
were applied to this task by assessing, from water quality engineers, (1) judgments about which variables should be included
in the index, (2) the type of rule for combining the variables,
(3) the relative impartance weights of the different variables,
and (4) a curve describing the functional relation between
water quality and each variable.
   Water quality indices were obtained for two specific purposes -- for "public water supply" and for "fish and wildlife."
The experimenter used a modified Delphi procedure for obtaining
consensus among the engineers for each of the indices. Even
after the applications of the Delphi procedure, the engineers
disagreed on the importance weights, so a sensitivity analysis
applied the different indices to actual measurements on samples
of river water. This analysis indicated that the disagreement
about the weights was not crucial to the measurement of water
quality. In fact, a major conclusion of this research is that
the multi-attribute scaling procedures are sufficiently robust
so that, while great car should be used in determining the
purpose for which the index will be used and in selecting variables for inclusion, relatively little time and effort need be
invested in resolving small differences among quality functions
and among relative weights.

Salient Features:

   Two water quality indices are described.

Advantages/Limitations of Salient Features:

1. Field studies conducted --- yes
2. Practical for field use --- yes
3. Usage for various types/sizes of projects --- yes
4. Objective vs. subjective approaches --- objective
5. Reproducibility --- unknown
6. Scientifically sound features --- yes

Conclusions:

Use directly in WRAM
..Mention two indices

+ + +

REFERENCE:

Odum, E. P., et al, "Optimum Pathway Matrix Analysis Approach to the Environmental Decision Making Process --- Test Case: Relative Impact of Preposed Highway Alternates," 1971, Institute of Ecology, University of Georgia, Athens, Georgia.

Abstract:

This methodology incorporates a weighting-scaling checklist of 56 environmental components. Measurable indicators are specified for each component. The actual values of alternative plan impacts on a component are normalized and expressed as a decimal of the largest impact (on that one component). These represent scale values. These normalized values are multiplied by a subjectively determined weighting factor, which is the sum of a weight for initial effects plus 10 times a weight for long-term effects. The methodology is used to evaluate highway project alternatives, and the components listed are not suitable for other types of projects. A wide range of impact types is analyzed including land-use, social, aesthetic, and economic impacts.

The lower replicability of the analysis produced by using subjectively determined weighting factors is compensated for by conducting several passes at the analysis and incorporating randomly generated error variation in both actual measurements and weights. This procedure provide a basis for testing the significance of differences in total impact scores between alternatives. The procedures for normalizing or scaling measured impacts to obtain commensurability and testing of significant differences between alternatives are notable features of potential value to other impact analyses and methodologies.

296

Salient Features:

This weighting-scaling checklist includes an error term to allow for misjudgment in the assignment of importance weights.

Advantages/Limitations of Salient Features:

1. Field studies conducted --- yes
2. Practical for field use --- yes
3. Usage for various types/sizes of projects --- yes
4. Objective vs. subjective approaches --- objective
5. Reproducibility --- unknown
6. Scientifically sound features --- yes

Conclusions:

Use directly in WRAM
..Describe error term concept.

REFERENCE:

Odum, H. T., "Use of Energy Diagrams for Environmental Impact Statements," Tools for Coastal Zone Management, Proceedings of the Conference, Washington, D. C., Feb. 1972, pp. 197-213.

Abstract:

Odum proposed the use of energy diagrams for describing the impacts associated with various project types. Energy circuit diagrams may have advantages for organizing information, for improving presentations, and ultimately, for giving understanding and prediction. The energy diagram shows the flows of all energies in the system, keeping track of the main components of the system such as the plants, animals, chemical processes, reservoirs of resource storage, flows of information, and outside actions that cause change. Energy diagrams have been utilized to predict the impacts for a marine meadows ecosystem located near Fort Myers, Florida. The steps in preparing an environmental impact statement using energy diagrams are summarized in Table B-3. Although the concepts embodied in the use of energy diagrams are scientifically valid, two primary difficulties are associated with the use of this impact assessment methodology: (1) Many of the processes, and particularly the rates of change in the processes, are simply unknown, and, (2) The use of a system such as this requires a high degree of technical sophistication as well as back-up resources such as computer facilities.

297

Table B-3:   Steps in Making an Environmental Impact Statement
             Using Energy Diagrams

1. List the main properties of the system believed
   to be important in its operation and/or to man.
   These are the parts of the system sometimes
   called state variables. They are the tanks of
   model or associated with tanks.

2. Make a list of the outside causal forces and
   energy sources including the proposed new ones
   associated with plans and actions of man.
   These are called forcing function and are represented as circles.

3. Connect the symbols for forcing functions on
   the left to the components of the system with
   causal energy flows using appropriate intersection functions.

4. Each function has a different symbol

   The intersections are additive when two properties
     may be used interchangeably.
   The intersections are multiplicative when both
     are different and required.
   The intersections are switching when there are
     thresholds of action that are either on or off.
   The intersections are integrative and cumula-
     tive when there are storages that receive
     inflows and outflows developing balance between
     them.
   The intersections are autocatalytic, feeding
     storage back to act multiplicatively on the
     inflow, when the module represents some self-
     maintaining activity such as organisms,
     industries, and cities.
   One intersection type has the property of level-
     ing intself due to a circular recycling of
     some material which is limited. This is
     called the Michaelis Menton property after
     its discoverers in biochemistry.

5. Having identified the pathways, try to put
   numbers on them to gain perspectives on
   importance and times involved for effects.
   Estimate the main effects believed to result
   in the system from the change through visual
   estimation of the effects of the change in

298

or diminishing flows that converge and diverge within the diagram.

6. Having identified the pathways and compartments most likely to be involved in the proposed change, develop a simplified diagram that includes the main change and the essence of the system in few enough modules to make simulation feasible.

7. Run a simulation to test the simpler version to determine if there are unexpected patterns emerging from the network not previously recognized in the diagrams or in experiences. Whereas the simpler model cannot simulate the real complexity, it can identify effects and complications. For example, the system may show if there is a tendency to oscillate or if effects are counter intuitive (go up when you expect them to go down, etc.).

8. Sum the total energy values including those covered by money and those of nature not covered by money flows. Use these energy flow values in overall value calculations.

9. Write general English accounts to go with the diagrams to lead the reader to the points of main consideration in examining propositions for change.

Salient Features:

Use of energy diagrams to predict ecosystem changes.

Advantages/Limitations of Salient Features:

1. Field studies conducted --- yes
2. Practical for field use --- no
3. Usage for various types/sizes of projects --- unknown
4. Objective vs. subjective approaches --- objective
5. Reproducibility --- unknown
6. Scientifically sound features --- yes

Conclusions:

General reference for WRAM

+ + +

REFERENCE:

Ortolano, L., "Analyzing the Environmental Impacts of Water Projects," March 1973, 433 pp., Dept. of Civil Engineering, Stanford Univ., Menlo Park, Cal.

Abstract:

The study was aimed at developing and testing a structured, systematic methodology for the identification, description, measurement and display of the environmental impacts associated with water resources development activities. However, it does not deal with the question of the relative worth or benefits and costs associated with these impacts. The contents include: a legal analysis of the requirements of Section 102 (2) (c) of the National Environmental Policy Act of 1969; a review of selected materials relevant to environmental impact assessment; environmental impacts associated with reservoir projects; the 1971 Congressional Hearings on stream channelization - an aid to environmental impact identification; chemical and biological impacts of dredging and spoil disposal; impacts induced by water projects providing flood control and recreation; ecological, visual and cultural impacts; practical concerns in environmental impact analysis; and a case study for projects in Carmel Valley, California.

Salient Features:

Discussion of general impacts associated with water resources projects.

300

Advantages/Limitations of Salient Features:

1. Field studies conducted --- not applicable
2. Practical for field use --- not applicable
3. Usage for various types/sizes of projects --- not applicable
4. Objective vs. subjective approaches --- not applicable
5. Reproducibility --- not applicable
6. Scientifically sound features --- yes

Conclusions:

General reference for WRAM

+ + +

REFERENCE:

Pikul, R., "Development of Environmental Indices," in Pratt, J. W., editor, Statistical and Mathematical Aspects of Pollution Problems, Marcel Dekker Book Company, New York, New York, 1974, pp. 103-121.

Abstract:

An index approach to environmental assessment is used. The author presents an initial formulation of environmental indices in 14 environmental classes. A method of ranking indices while taking cost and value considerations into account is discussed. The assessment of impact is facilitated by tracking and analyzing the behavior of these indices. Each mathematical index is analyzed according to factors of impact, utility, value, cost, and importance.

Salient Features:

Use of indices to describe environmental setting and assess potential impacts.

Advantages/Limitations of Salient Features:

1. Field studies conducted --- yes
2. Practical for field use --- yes
3. Usage for various types/sizes of projects --- unknown
4. Objective vs. subjective approaches --- objective
5. Reproducibility --- unknown
6. Scientifically sound features --- yes

Conclusions:

General reference for WRAM

301

REFERENCE:

Raines, G., "Environmental Impact Assessment of New Installations," (paper presented at International Pollution Engineering Congress, Cleveland, Ohio, Dec. 4-6, 1972), Battelle
Memorial Institute, Columbus, Ohio.

Abstract:

An interaction matrix is used to identify impacts of concern. The matrix is similar in concept to the Leopold interaction matrix. Presumably, a matrix would be used for each
alternative under consideration. Value functions are used to
scale the anticipated impacts of alternatives. Value functions
are based on the scientific or technological judgement of a
professional specialist (s). A value function essentially
expresses the relationship between a set of assessed or calculated environmental impact quantities and the degree of acceptability or desirability or the levels. An example of a
value function graph is given in Figure 4 (page 88) to help
illustrate the procedure used. Cost to the environment, increasing in the positive direction, is selected for the ordinate axis and an arbitrary scale of 0 to 10 units is used.
For convenience the units are designated environmental cost
units (ECU's), and an ECU value of 10 is defined as indicative
of a "clearly unacceptable" environmental cost. The assessed
or calculated environmental impact quantity (cost), which is
to be translated into ECU's, is placed along the abscissa.
Absolute quantities may be used to determine the scale, or as
in the figure, the quantities may be normalized with respect
to a reference quantity. In either case, the value that would
represent a "clearly unacceptable" impact (cost) to the environment must be declared. This reference limit, then, is
equivalent to a value of 10 on the ECU scale.
Weighting factors are used to reflect the relative importance of identified impacts. Weighting factors reflect
subjective judgements. Many procedures can be used in arriving
at the set of weighting factors, from the considered opinion
of a single person, through a vote at a town hall meeting, to
an exhaustive, iterative, consensus of many qualified persons
(i.e., the Delphi approach), or ideally to the comprehensive
application of absolute criteria. In practice each ECU value
obtained from application of the value functions will be
multiplied by its weighting factor, and then all products will
be summed to arrive at a total environmental cost number.
This system has been applied to nuclear reactor site
selection. A total of 46 factors (impacts) were identified,
and value functions were developed for each. The set of required weighting factors was developed under the limits imposed by two conditions: first, the weighting factor for

302

each item reflects the assigned importance of that item relative to all the other items in the list, i.e., no items beyond the 46 already identified were considered and an absolute rating system was not used. Therefore, the total value of all weighting factors adds up to 46. Second, the importance or weighting values were to apply to nuclear power reactor sites in general rather than to a specific facility in particular. The weighting factors were developed by an opinion or judgement poll of twenty-four members of the Battelle-Columbus staff who have been involved in environmental systems studies. Their technical backgrounds include economics, environmental engineering, acoustics, chemistry, chemical engineering, biology, limnology, and ecology.

Salient Features:

Weighting-scaling checklists.
Use of functional curves to translate environmental impact quantities into environmental cost units.

Advantages/Limitations of Salient Features:

1. Field studies conducted --- yes
2. Practical for field use --- yes
3. Usage for various types/sizes of projects --- yes
4. Objective vs. subjective approaches --- objective
5. Reproducibility --- unknown
6. Scientifically sound features --- yes

Conclusions:

Use directly in WRAM
    ..Mention as example of weighting and scaling.

+ + +

REFERENCE:

Schlesinger, B. and Daetz, D., "A Conceptual Framework for Applying Environmental Assessment Matrix Techniques," The Journal of Environmental Sciences, July/August, 1973, pp. 11-16.

Abstract:

This article discusses a conceptual framework for environmental impact assessment matrices. It is shown that, if properly applied, an environmental assessment matrix can embody all relevant aspects of the environment potentially affected by some significant project, as well as the magnitude

of each impact, the importance of these effects, their dura-
tions and even their interrelationships and probabilities.
As an adjunct to consideration of these factors of alternative
proposals, the matrix technique can be used to indicate sensitivity or bounds of the solution, and act as a guide to
mitigating measures that might be required. Various proposed
matrix techniques are examined and evaluated with respect to
this conceptual framework.

Salient Features:

Compares sevel matrix approaches for impact assessment.

Advantages/Limitations of Salient Features:

1. Field studies conducted --- unknown
2. Practical for field use --- yes
3. Usage for various types/sizes of projects --- yes
4. Objective vs. subjective approaches --- objective
5. Reproducibility --- unknown
6. Scientifically sound features --- yes

Conclusions:

General reference for WRAM

+ + +

REFERENCE:

Sorensen, J., "A Framework for Identification and Control of
Resource Degradation and Conflict in the Multiple Use of the
Costal Zone," Master's Thesis, 1971, Department of Landscape
Architecture, University of California, Berkeley, California.

Abstract:

A network approach (stepped or linked matrices) is presented as a guide to the identification of impacts. Several
potential uses of the California coastal zone are examined
through networks relating uses to casual factors (project
activities) to first-order conditions changes to second- and
third-order condition changes and finally to effects. The
major strength of the approach is its ability to identify the
pathways by which both primary and secondary environmental
impacts are produced. Because the preparation of the required
detailed networks is a major undertaking, the approach is presently limited to some commercial, residential, and transportation uses of the California costal zone for which networks
have been prepared. An agency wishing to use the approach in

other circumstances might develop the appropriate networks for reference in subsequent environmental impact assessments.

Salient Features:

Presentation of networks (stepped or linked matrices) for impact identification.

Advantages/Limitations of Salient Features:

1. Field studies conducted --- yes
2. Practical for field use --- yes
3. Usage for various types/sizes of projects --- yes
4. Objective vs. subjective approaches --- objective
5. Reproducibility --- unknown
6. Scientifically sound features --- yes

Conclusions:

General reference for WRAM

+ + +

REFERENCE:

Stover, Lloyd V., "Environmental Impact Assessment: A Procedure," March 1973, 23 pages, Science Technology Vision, Inc., Pottstwon, Pa.

Abstract:

The methodology which is described is basically a weighting-scaling checklist with variations based on linear proportions of impacts. The basic weighting value is calculated based on an Environmental Impact Index (EII), which is equal to the initial impact (arbitrarily assigned value ranging from +5 to -5) plus the future impact (arbitrarily assinged value ranging from +10 to -10) times the length of time in years the significant environmental function is affected. The scale value is calculated based on linear proportioning relative to the maximum impact for an alternative. The scale values are called Alternative Proportional Values (APV). The product of the EII values and the APV's yields functional impact values (FIV's) which can be used to compare alternatives. This methodology is similar in concept to the Odum Optimum Pathway Matrix.

Salient Features:

Weighting-scaling checklist.

Advantages/Limitations of Salient Features:

1. Field studies conducted --- unknown

305

2. Practical for field use --- yes
3. Usage for various types/sizes of project --- yes
4. Objective vs. subjective approaches --- yes
5. Reproducibility --- unknown
6. Scientifically sound features --- yes

Conclusions:

General reference for WRAM

+ + +

REFERENCE:

Swartzman, G.L., and Van Dyne, G.M., "An Ecologically Based
Simulation - Optimization Approach to Natural Resource
Planning," Annual Review of Ecology and Systematics, Vol. 3,
1972, pp. 347-398.

Abstract:

This article presents a systematic discussion of an
ecological modelling procedure and highlights advantages and
limitations. The simulation - optimization approach is oriented to the multiple use of wild lands and natural resource
planning.

Salient Features:

Good discussion of ecological modelling for natural resource planning.

Advantages/Limitations of Salient Features:

1. Field studies conducted --- yes
2. Practical for field use --- no
3. Usage for various types/sizes of projects --- yes
4. Objective vs. subjective approaches --- objective
5. Reproducibility --- unknown
6. Scientifically sound features --- yes

Conclusions:

General reference for WRAM

+ + +

REFERENCE:

Texas Water Development Board, "Simulation of Water Quality

306

in Streams and Canals, Theory and Description of the QUAL-1
Mathematical Modeling System", EPA-OWP-TEX-128, May 1971, 62
pp., Austin, Texas.

Abstract:

The report presents the theory and description of the
QUAL-1 Mathematical Modeling System which is a set of inter-
related quality routing models for predicting the temporal and
spatial distribution of temperature, bio-chemical oxygen demand and dissolved oxygen, and conservative minerals within a
segment of a river basin. The governing differential equation
is solved by an implicit-finite-difference technique under the
assumption that advection along the longitudinal axis of the
stream is the primary mode of transport. Model application
results are presented.

Salient Features:

Models plus examples are presented for water quality impact prediction.

Advantages/Limitations of Salient Features:

1. Field studies conducted --- yes
2. Practical for field use --- yes
3. Usage for various types/sizes of projects --- n/a
4. Objective vs. subjective approaches --- objective
5. Reproducibility --- yes
6. Scientifically sound features --- yes

Conclusions:

General reference for WRAM

+ + +

REFERENCE:

Thomas, J. L., Paul, J. and Iraelsen, E. K., "A Computer Model
of the Quantity and Chemical Quality of Return Flow," OWRR-B-
038-UTAH(1), June 1971, 100 pp., Utah Water Research Laboratory, Utah State University, Logan, Utah.

Abstract:

A hybrid computer program is developed to predict the
water and salt outflow from a river basin in which irrigation
is the major water user. A chemical model which predicts the
quality of water percolated through a soil profile is combined
with a general hydrologic model to form the system simulation

307

model. The chemical model considers the reactions that occur in the soil, including the exchange of calcium, magnesium, and sodium cations on the soil complex, and the dissolution and precipitation of gypsum and lime. The six common ions of western waters, namely calcium (Ca(++)), Magnesium (Mg(++)), Sodium (Na(+)) Sulfate (SO4(=)), Chloride (Cl(-)), and Bicarbonate (HCO3-) are considered in the study. The model is tested on a portion of the Little Bear River Basin in northern Utah. The model successfully simulates measured outflows of water and each of the six ions for a 24-month period.

Salient Features:

Water quality model for irrigation return flow.

Advantages/Limitations of Salient Features:

1. Field studies conducted --- yes
2. Practical for field use --- yes
3. Usage for various types/sizes of projects --- yes
4. Objective vs. subjective approaches --- objective
5. Reproducibility --- unknown
6. Scientifically sound features --- yes

Conclusions:

General reference for WRAM

+ + +

REFERENCES:

U.S. Army Engineer District, Tulsa, Corps of Engineers, "Matrix Analysis of Alternatives for Water Resource Development", Draft technical paper, July 1972, Tulsa, Oklahoma.

Abstract:

Despite the title, this methodology can be considered a weighting-scaling checklist under the definitions used here since, although a display matrix is used to summarize and compare the impacts of project alternatives, impacts are not linked to specific project actions. The approach was developed to deal specifically with reservoir construction projects but could be readily adapted to other project types. This methodology was one of 8 methodologies identified in the interim WRAM report (Feb., 1977).
    Potential impacts are identified within three broad objectives: environmental quality, human life quality, and economics. For each impact type identified, a series of factors

308

is described, indicating possible measurable indicators. Impact magnitude is not measured in physical units but by a relative impact system. This system assigns the future state of an environmental characteristic without the project a score of zero; it then assigns the project alternative possessing the greatest positive impact on that characteristic a score of plus five or for negative impact, minus five. All other alternatives are assigned scores between zero and five by comparison. The raw scores thus obtained are multiplied by weights determined subjectively by the impact analysis team. Like the Georgia optimum pathway matrix approach, the Tulsa methodology tests for the significance of differences between alternatives by introducing error factors and conducting repeated runs. The major limitations of the approach, aside from the required computerization, are the lack of clear guidelines on exactly how to measure impacts and the lack of guidance on how the future no-project state is to be defined and described in the analysis.

The key ideas in the Tulsa approach include reliance on relative rather than absolute impact measurement, statistical tests of significance with error introduction, and specific use of the no-project conditions, as a base line for impact evaluation.

Salient Features:

Has good list of variable for EQ, SWB, and RD accounts.
Weighting-scaling checklist used for evaluation of alternatives; includes statistical testing of results.

Advantages/Limitations of Salient Features:

1. Field studies conducted --- yes
2. Practical for field use --- yes
3. Usage for various types/sizes of projects --- yes
4. Objective vs. subjective approaches --- objective
5. Reproducibility --- unknown
6. Scientifically sound features --- yes

Conclusions:

Use directly in WRAM
..Describe concepts of impact scaling and statistical testing.

+ + +

REFERENCE:

Wenger, R. B., and Rhyner, C. R., "Evaluation of Alternatives

for Solid Waste Systems," <u>Journal</u> <u>of</u> <u>Environmental</u> <u>Systems</u>,
Vol. 2, No. 2, June 1972, pp. 89-108.

Abstract:

A method is presented which incorporates environmental,
social and engineering factors into the selection of a solid
waste system from among several alternatives. The methodology
is basically a weighting-scaling checklist. A stochastic
procedure takes account of the inherent uncertainty in the
quantitative values assigned to subjective criteria (weighting)
and for the uncertainty in impact values (scaling). This
method is similar in concept to the Odum optimum pathway matrix.
An example is included which illustrates the method for solid
wastes systems evaluation.

Salient Features:

A stochastic computer procedure is used to account for
uncertainty in the weighting and scaling checklist procedure
for evaluation of solid waste system alternatives.

Advantages/Limitations of Salient Features:

1. Field studies conducted --- yes
2. Practical for field use --- yes
3. Usage for various types/sizes of projects --- yes
4. Objective vs. subjective approaches --- objective
5. Reproducibility --- yes
6. Scientifically sound features --- yes

Conclusions:

Use directly in WRAM (specific)
..Mention stochastic computer procedure

310

APPENDIX C

INFORMATION ON 16 REFERENCES

FROM 1974 PERIOD

REFERENCE:

Adkins, W. G., and Burke, Jr., D., "Social, Economic, and
Environmental Factors in Highway Decision Making," Research
Report 148-4, 1974, Texas Transportation Institute, Texas A
and M University, College Station, Texas (Report prepared for
Texas Highway Department in cooperation with the Federal Highway Administration, U.S. Department of Transportation, Washington, D.C.).

Abstract:

The Adkins-Burke methodology is a scaling checklist using
a plus five to a minus five rating system for evaluating impacts.
The approach was developed to deal specifically with the evaluation of highway route alternatives. Because the bulk of parameters used relate directly to highway transportation, the
approach is not readily adaptable to other types of projects.
The parameters are broken down into the categories transportation, environmental, sociological, and economic impacts. Environmental parameters are generally deficient in ecological considerations. Social parameters emphasize community facilities
and services. Route alternatives are scored plus five to minus
five in comparison to the present state of the project area,
not the expected future state without the project. Since the
approach uses only subjective relative estimations of impacts,
the data, manpower, and cost requirements are very flexible.
An interesting feature is the summarizing of the number as well
as the magnitude of plus and minus ratings for each impact
category. The number of pluses and minuses may be a more
reliable indicator for alternative comparison since it is less
affected by the arbitrariness of subjective scaling. These
summarizations are additive and thus implicitly weigh all
impacts equally.

Salient Features:

Scaling checklist with algebraic additions of scaled
impacts.

Advantages/Limitations of Salient Features:

1. Field studies conducted---yes
2. Practical for field use---yes
3. Usage for various types/sizes of projects---satis-
   factory as long as alternatives are similar in
   type
4. Objective vs. subjective approaches---objective
5. Reproducibility---unknown
6. Scientifically sound features---yes

Conclusions:

   General reference for WRAM

                    + + +

REFERENCE:

Alabama Development Office, State Planning Office, "Environmental Impact Assessment by Use of Matrix Diagram", June 1974,
19 pp., Montgomery, Alabama.

Abstract:

   The methodology has a simple matrix for use in environmental impact assessment. Three positive (+3, +2, +1) and
three negative (-3, -2, -1) impacts can be shown along with
no change (0). Summation of rows and columns is suggested.
See attached matrix (Fig. C-1).

Salient Features:

   Good ideas for use of simple interaction matrix.

Advantages/Limitations of Salient Features:

   1. Field studies conducted---yes
   2. Practical for field use---yes
   3. Usage for various types/sizes of projects---yes
   4. Objective vs. subjective approaches---objective
   5. Reproducibility---unknown
   6. Scientifically sound features---yes

Conclusions:

   General reference for WRAM

                    + + +

REFERENCE:

Alden, H.R., "Environmental Impact Assessment: A Procedure
for Coordinating and Organizing Environmental Planning",
Technical Publication No. 10, December 1974, 32 pages,
Thorne Ecological Institute, Boulder, Colorado.

Abstract:

   An environmental impact assessment leading to environmental planning is perceived to consist of the following 4
steps: (1) coordination and communication; (2) environmental resource inventory; (3) evaluation of environmental

impacts resulting from proposed alternative land uses; and
(4) recommendations to avoid or mitigate environmental impacts. A ranking checklist approach is used for Step 3.
Emphasis is given to ecological relationships between soils,
hydrology and vegetation and other environmental components.

Salient Features:

Ranking checklist; inclusion of descriptive information
on ecological relationships.

Advantages/Limitations of Salient Features:

1. Field studies conducted---yes
2. Practical for field use---yes
3. Usage for various types/sizes of projects---yes
4. Objective vs. subjective approaches---yes
5. Reproducibility---unknown
6. Scientifically sound features---yes

Conclusions:

General reference for WRAM

+ + +

REFERENCE:

Battelle-Columbus Laboratories, "A Methodology for Assessing
Environmental, Economic, and Social Effects of Dredge Spoil
Disposal on Marsh and Upland Areas", Draft report, 1974,
Battelle-Columbus Laboratories, Columbus, Ohio (Report pre-
pared for U.S. Army Engineer Waterways Experiment Station,
Corps of Engineers, Vicksburg, Mississippi).

Abstract:

This methodology is one of 8 methodologies described in
the interim WRAM report (February 1977). The primary orientation of this descriptive checklist methodology is toward
dredging projects. The methodology includes 84 assessment
variables, with 18 in the physical-chemical category, 16 in
the ecological category, 16 in the aesthetic category, 19 in
the economic category and 15 in the social category. The
variables are well described in terms of measurement units
and evaluation. Information is provided on the technical
aspects of impact prediction for many of the 84 assessment
variables.

315

Instructions

1) Identify all actions (located across the top of the matrix) that are part of the proposed project.
2) Under each of the proposed actions place a value at the interaction with each item on the side of the matrix if an impact is possible. A zero may be used when no impact is expected. Positive and negative values from one to three are to be used where impact is expected. Positive values indicate a beneficial impact and negative values indicate a detrimental impact. The number 1 indicates a minor impact, 2 indicates a more serious impact which may need consideration, and 3 indicates a major impact which will require special planning.
3) Having completed the matrix, all rows and columns which contain values should be added and these sums entered in the COMPUTATIONS space.
4) A text should accompany the completed matrix. This text should be a discussion of the rows and columns which received high numerical values. In addition, those individual boxes with high numerical values should be examined.

			MODIFICATION OF REGIME							LAND TRANSFORMATION AND CONSTRUCTION							
			Alteration of ground cover	Alteration of surface water hydrology	Alteration of groundwater hydrology	Erosion control	Noise and vibration	Residential sites and buildings	Commercial sites and buildings	Industrial sites and buildings	Airports	Highways and bridges	Transmission lines	Pipelines	Barriers	Canals	Dams and Impoundments
PHYSICAL AND CHEMICAL CHARACTERISTICS	EARTH	Mineral Resources															
		Construction Material															
		Landform															
		Soils															
	WATER	Surface															
		Underground															
		Quality															
		Temperature															
		Recharge															
	ATMOSPHERE	Quality															
	PROCESSES	Floods															
		Erosion															
		Deposition															
		Stability															
BIOLOGICAL CONDITIONS	FAUNA	Terrestrial															
		Aquatic															
	FLORA	Terrestrial															
		Aquatic															
CULTURAL FACTORS	LAND USE	Wilderness															
		Wetlands															
		Forestry															
		Grazing															
		Agriculture															
		Residential															
		Commercial															
		Industrial															
		Recreation															
	HUMAN INTEREST	Scenic qualities															
		Historial or archaeological sites and objects															
	CULTURAL STATUS	Cultural patterns															
		Health and Safety															
		Employment															
		Population Density															
	OTHERS																
COMPUTATIONS																	

CHARACTERISTICS AND CONDITIONS OF THE ENVIRONMENT

ACTIONS WHICH MAY CAUSE ENVIRONMENTAL IMPACT

	RESOURCE EXTRACTION				PROCESSING					CHANGES IN TRAFFIC				WASTE EMPLACEMENT						CHEMICAL TREATMENT		ACCIDENTS			OTHERS	COMPUTATIONS
	Surface excavation	Subsurface excavation	Clear cutting and other lumbering	Well drilling and fluid removal	Agriculture	Energy generation	Industrial processing	Product storage – covered	Product storage – uncovered	Land transportation	Air transportation	Water transportation	Communications	Landfill	Emplacement of tailings, spoil, overburden	Liquid effluent discharge	Septic tanks	Deep subsurface disposal	Cooling water discharge	Stack and exhaust emission	Fertilization	Herbicides	Pesticides, Insecticides	Explosions	Spills	Operational failure		

Figure C-1:   MODEL MATRIX FOR ENVIRONMENTAL IMPACT ASSESSMENT

317

Salient Features:

Good descriptive checklist for dredging projects; some impact prediction information is included.

Advantages/Limitations of Salient Features:

1. Field studies conducted---no
2. Practical for field use---yes
3. Usage for various types/sizes of projects---sizes only.
4. Objective vs. subjective approaches---objective
5. Reproducibility---unknown
6. Scientifically sound features---yes

Conclusions:

Use directly in WRAM
..Mention descriptive checklist and impact prediction information.

+ + +

REFERENCE:

Battelle-Pacific Northwest Laboratories, "Columbia River and Tributaries -- Environmental Assessment Manual", May 1974, 429 pages, Richland, Washington (prepared for North Pacific Division, U.S. Army Corps of Engineers, Portland, Oregon).

Abstract:

This report contains a review of environmental assessment methodologies and a good comparison of the advantages and limitations of numerical and subjective approaches. The desirable characteristics of a methodology include that it be comprehensive, concise, understandable, versatile, accurate and economical. The selected methodology uses a matrix to identify potential impacts and then a descriptive checklist is used. An extensive bibliography is included for specific assessment criteria, data collection, and data sources in the Columbia River and Tributaries area. (See following comparison of numerical and subjective approaches)

Salient Features:

Good descriptive checklist.

Good discussion of numerical versus subjective approaches in environmental impact assessment.

Advantages/Limitations of Salient Features:

1. Field studies conducted---yes
2. Practical for field use---yes
3. Usage for various types/sizes of projects---yes
4. Objective vs. subjective approaches---objective
5. Reproducibility---unknown
6. Scientifically sound features---yes

Conclusions:

Use directly in WRAM
..Mention comparisons of numerical and subjective
approaches.

+ + +

Comparison of Numerical and Subjective Approaches

A numerical comparison of environmental effects consists, in
general, of

- determining the actual effects for each alternative;

- converting the magnitude of each effect into a numerical value selected from an arbitrary scale of numbers
  designed to cover all magnitudes from zero to the
  maximum possible (e.g., a value of 0 might mean no
  effect, a value of 10 might mean maximum possible
  effect);

- selecting a second number from another arbitrary
  scale designed to describe the importance of each
  type of effect (e.g., and effect on salmon might be
  given a value of 1.0 and an effect on golden eagles
  might be given a value of 8.0 because it is an endangered species);

- multiplying and/or adding these "magnitude" and
  "importance" factors to obtain a numerical value
  indicating the overall merit of each effect; and

- adding the "merit" factors for an alternative to
  obtain a total numerical value for that alternative.
  The total numerical values for the several alternatives then are compared to determine which is the
  best alternative.

Advantages and disadvantates of numerical methods are listed
in Table 19 (page 98). The primary advantages of numerical

methods are uniformity of application and completeness. They
are uniform in application because they have a standard evaluation procedure. A systematic method is used for determining
numerical values for each effect and the overall numerical
ranking for each alternative.

They are complete because the procedure requires evaluation
of every conceivable environmental effect (assuming that all
possible effects have been identified and included in the
evaluation procedure).

The primary disadvantages of numerical evaluations are high
costs, high probability of structured conclusions, a lack of
uniformity in the subjective analyses, and low understand-
ability.

High cost can result from the need to evaluate a large number
of environmental effects. A numerical "magnitude" and "importance" factor must be developed for each of up to 100
types of environmental effects. Each effect must be quantified and a numerical value determined by a subjective reason-
ing process. Use of some methods requires development of
"evaluation" curves for each environmental parameter before
the numerical values used in the comparison can be determined.
These "evaluation" curves show the relationship between an
environmental condition (e.g., oxygen concentration in a water
body) and the "magnitude" factors used in the comparison.

Structured conclusions could result from the use of "evaluation"
scales or curves for determining numerical ratings. Development of the curves is costly and time consuming. Once a set
of such curves is developed for one action, there is the
possibility that this same set of curves would be used for
other actions with significantly differenct conditions. Use
of curves developed for one location at another location
could result in incorrect numerical rating values.

The subjective analyses used in development of the numerical
factors also cause a lack of uniformity among evaluations by
different assessment teams. Development of the evaluation
curves and importance factors requires the same type of subjective decisions as are used in subjective comparisons of
alternatives.

The results of numerical systems generally are hard to understand, particularly if composite numerical values are used.
The general public will not understand why one alternative
is better than the other until the actual reasons are explained. Such explanations may be particularly difficult if
an alternative with one obvious large impact is rated more

320

desirable than another alternative with numerous small (and possibly not obvious) impacts. There is also the danger that the general public will be suspicious of the numerical system because of the possibilities that (1) the numbers were manipulated to provide the desired answer or (2) the importance factors used in the evaluation are not representative of the opinions of the general public--that they represent the opinions of a group of "technical" experts from out-of-town.

A subjective comparison of environmental effects consists of:

- determining the actual effects for each alternative

- converting the effects to common units, if such a method of conversion is available

- comparing subjectively the overall effects of the various alternatives to determine their relative ranking

Subjective comparison can be made by either a single individual, an assessment team, a sample of a large population, or an entire population. An example of the last is an environmental choice that is decided by a vote of the general population.

Most environmental reports and environmental impact statements currently being issued use subjective comparisons. Typical examples are environmental reports by utilities relative to construction of nuclear reactors and transmission lines, environmental impact statements by the Corps of Engineers for water development actions and environmental reports by highway departments in conjunction with highway construction.

The primary advantage of subjective comparisons is simplicity. The reasons for a judgment are stated and subject to public scrutiny and criticism. The importance of each effect is stated and emphasis can easily be placed on the most important effects.

Because of the simplicity of a subjective comparison, it also is easily adapted in complexity and cost to the nature of the actions being evaluated. There are no rigid requirements that an elaborate evaluation procedure be used for all assessments. If it is apparent that there are few or no significant effects, the assessment can be adjusted accordingly.

The primary disadvantages of subjective comparisons are the lack of uniformity in subjective analyses and non-uniform consideration of the various types of environmental effects. Because social values and analytical capability vary widely among individuals, subjective rankings of several alternatives for an action probably would differ if made by different persons. These differences in opinion generally can be reduced by making decisions a team effort. When a reasonable amount of team effort does not resolve differences of opinion, consideration should be given to presenting more than one opinion in the final assessment report. Readers are likely to benefit from being aware of persistant divergent judgments when they exist. Because fixed procedures and assessment factors are not used for evaluation of the alternative.

+ + +

REFERENCE:

Bender, M. and Ahmed, S.B., "Index of the Composite Environment (ICE): A Basis for Evaluating Environmental Effects of Electric Power Generating Plants in Response to NEPA", Report No. ORNL TM-4492, February 1974, 77 pages, Oak Ridge National Laboratory, Oak Ridge, Tennessee.

Abstract:

A method of evaluating the environmental impacts of electric power generating plants that can be correlated with economic analysis is discussed in this report. The impacts, having no common set of measurement units are quantified by using an index of the composite environment (ICE) to measure the environmental effects. The ICE values can be varied by using engineering alternatives as a means of controlling potential damage when the environmental effects warrant amelioration. A monetary benefit-cost analysis is performed in parallel with the ICE by using busbar electric power costs as the value basis and varying these costs by selecting engineering alternatives. The ICE values and the benefit-cost values are paired to show the incremental monetary effect of a change in the ICE resulting from the use of an alternative. The result is an economic quantification of the ICE that can be used to satisfy requirements of the National Environmental Policy Act. The ICE is oriented to the needs of regulatory agencies that must provide detailed environmental impact statements to show how environmental effects have been assessed.

Salient Features:

Concept of relating an index of the composite environment (ICE) to economic differences between alternatives.

Advantages/Limitations of Salient Features:

1. Field studies conducted---yes
2. Practical for field use---unknown
3. Usage for various types/sizes of projects---unknown
4. Objective vs. subjective approaches---objective
5. Reproducibility---yes
6. Scientifically sound features---yes

Conclusions:

General reference for WRAM

+ + +

REFERENCE:

Burnham, J.B., "A Technique for Environmental Decision Making Using Quantified Social and Aesthetic Values", Report No. BNWL-1787, February 1974, Battelle Pacific Northwest Laboratories, Richland, Washington.

Abstract:

A four-phase study was designed for the evaluation of social, economic and environmental tradeoffs in the analysis of nuclear plant siting options. The results of the first phase of this work are reported here. A method was devised for combining social values with techno-economic values. This technique requires that community judgments be measured on the same plant design criteria that are independently quantified by experts on a technical basis. The social values are used as a weighting factor for the techno-economic values.

Social psychologists examined a number of environmental statements, intervenors' statements, and environmental guidelines to determine the significant criteria to be used in analyzing nuclear plant options. Eight criteria were devised in this task: economics, water quality, air quality, animal/plant life, cultural/recreational, health/safety, aesthetics, and land use. Subsequent studies showed that these criteria could be reduced to seven by eliminating land use. A questionnaire survey was developed using three cooling design options (once-through, natural draft cooling tower, and cooling lake) on each of two sites chosen as test examples. The survey was administered to three separate Seattle groups: environmentalists, high school students and businessmen. A total of 192 respondents participated and their responses had remarkably similar patterns. The environmentalists were generally less in favor of nuclear plants than businessmen and the high school students were between the two.

323

The survey was designed to measure the respondents direct weighting of the eight criteria by asking respondents to rank each criteria in order of importance. The relative weights of the criteria were also measured indirectly by rating each criterion (on a scale of one to seven) for each option and also making an overall judgment of the acceptability of each design option.

The ability to perform objective quantification of the criteria discussed above is a basic premise of the derived method. Each of the design/site options must be rated for each of the criteria. Since this analysis is to be done by technologists or economists, the methods can be complex up to the point the methodology becomes burdensome. Two of the criteria, aesthetics and land use, were examined with the goal of deriving a method for quantifying these effects. In the case of the aesthetics a method was successfully developed. Fundamental equations were derived expressing the relationships between viewscape quality and its basic components: intactness, vividness, and unity. Similarly, the relationships between aesthetic impact, population and change in viewscape quality were described. The mechanics of making the analysis of a given design on a given site are described. A technique is explained for deciding the number of viewpoints to be used in determining a viewscape, and the structural impact on each viewpoint, and for combining these measurements into an index of aesthetic impact. The study of the quantification of land use showed that this criterion was accurately defined by the other seven criteria.

Salient Features:

Public involvement in assigning importance weights to decision factors.

Procedure for systematically addressing the aesthetic features of an area.

Advantages/Limitations of Salient Features:

1. Field studies conducted---yes
2. Practical for field use---unknown
3. Usage for various types/sizes of projects---not applicable
4. Objective vs. subjective approaches---objective
5. Reproducibility---unknown
6. Scientifically sound features---yes

Conclusions:

General reference for WRAM

REFERENCE:

Jain, R.K., Urban, L.V., and Stacey, G.S., "Handbook for Environmental Impact Analysis", April 1974, Construction Engineering Research Laboratory, Department of the Army, Champaign,
Illinois.

Abstract:

Recommended procedures for use by Army personnel in preparing and processing environmental impact assessments (EIA's)
and EIS's are presented. The types of actions addressed are
related to military activities. An interaction matrix is
used to generate a checklist of assessment variables and impacts which should be addressed. Descriptive information is
provided for many assessment variables. The problems of determining relative importance and severity of impacts and of
providing a single number to indicate total environmental
impact (thereby masking the distribution of the impact among
its attributes) are avoided by assuming that each attribute
is of equal importance.

Salient Features:

Good listing of assessment variables for military activities.

Advantages/Limitations of Salient Features:

1. Field studies conducted---yes
2. Practical for field use---yes
3. Usage for various types/sizes of projects---not
   oriented to civil works projects
4. Objective vs. subjective approaches---objective
5. Reproducibility---unknown
6. Scientifically sound features---yes

Conclusions:

General reference for WRAM

+ + +

REFERENCE:

Kruzic, P.G., "Cross-Impact Simulation in Water Resources
Planning", IWR Contract Report 74-12, November 1974, 19 pp.,
U.S. Army Engineers Institute for Water Resources, Fort
Belvoir, Virginia (prepared for IWR by Stanford Research
Institute, Menlo Park, California).

Abstract:

KSIM is a simulation procedure for structuring and analyzing relationships among broadly defined variables in large
socioeconomic systems. It was originally developed by Kane
at the University of British Columbia to allow decision makers
to (1) accommodate a mix of hard data and intuitive judgment
and (2) test alternative planning options efficiently by:

.Exploring how a range of likely futures may shape a
 plan or, in turn, be subsequently modified by a plan

.Examining how various changes, such as in public preference, could affect plans.

The steps in the KSIM procedure are depicted in Figure 5
(page 99). The key step is the cross-impact matrix to identify
the impact of one variable upon another. The variable labels
are listed as row and column headings of a table. A basic
assumption is that when one variable changes, a second variable
may be completely unaffected, or may be encouraged or inhibited.
To show this, during the initial phase of KSIM the variables
are assigned cross-impact values of (0) for unrelated, (+)
for encouraged, or (-) for inhibited. Completing the cross-
impact matrix in this way provides the initial structure for
the model. Refinements are made by assigning numerical values
to these preliminary cross-impact estimates. In summary, KSIM
can be especially helpful in first stage planning, in identifying needs, and in articulating planning objectives. KSIM is
also valuable as a future oriented, quantitative technique to
display the implications of individual attitudes, orientations,
and perceptions of an issue or project at hand.

Salient Features:

Cross-impact matrix for impact identification and prediction; similar in concept to stepped matrix.

Advantages/Limitations of Salient Features:

1. Field studies conducted---yes
2. Practical for field use---yes
3. Usage for various types/sizes of projects---yes
4. Objective vs. subjective approaches---objective
5. Reproducibility---unknown
6. Scientifically sound features---yes

Conclusions:

Use directly in WRAM
..Mention availability for impact identification and
  prediction.

REFERENCE:

Pendse, D. and Wyckoff, J.B., "A Systematic Evaluation of
Environmental Perceptions, Optimum Preferences, and Trade-Off
Values in Water Resource Analysis", Sept., 1974, 86 pp., Dept.
of Agricultural Economics, Oregon State University, Corvallis,
Oregon (prepared for Office of Water Research and Technology,
Massachusetts University, Amherst, Massachusett).

Abstract:

    The study reported here was undertaken as a part of a
general research project related to: 1) development of methodology to value intangible benefits by determining intensity
of satisfaction of users of water resource projects; and 2)
development of procedures for incorporation of such values in
the benefit-cost analysis of water resource projects. The
particular technique utilized and reported here is the Priority
Evaluator. The Priority Evaluator Technique (PET) was found
to have considerable potential for overcoming two deficiencies
common to many other "direct approach", techniques, i.e.: 1)
failure to obtain trade-off patterns; and 2) failure to estimate
the economic value of non-market goods. PET is capable of
providing information on: 1) the preferences of respondents
with respect to environmental goods; 2) the value that people
attach to environmental goods; 3) trade-off patterns; and 4)
the direction and magnitude of changes preferred.
    The proposed Cascadia Dam on the South Santiam River in
Western Oregon provided a relevant and timely problem for a
large scale experimentation with the PET. Cascadia is part of
a network of fourteen authorized Corps of Engineers' dams in
the Willamette Basin. The site is unique from engineering and
technical points of view and would alleviate flood damages to
agricultural land in the Santiam Valley. The specific study
objective was to ascertain trade-off values for five environmental features: floods, water recreation, scenic view, wilderness, and a historical camping and recreation park. A simulated market experiment based on the PET was the basic methodology applied. Five environmental variables (features) divided into three subsituations were depicted in black and
white drawings highlighting environmental features and/or man-
made features. Each situation was "priced" and respondents
indicated their satisfaction trade-offs under different budget
(income) conditions. The selected mix of situations that
maximized respondents' satisfaction established the relative
value of different situations.
    Three hundred residents of five communities of the Willa-
mette Basin were interviewed during June and July, 1973. The
sample included urban and rural dwellers, downstream and up-
stream residents, and respondents from nearby and distant
communities. Local respondents perceived the impact of the dam

significantly different than those from more distant areas.
Attitudes also differed significantly by age and degree of
perceived environmental concern of the respondents. A comparison between perception of preconstruction conditions and
actual choices indicated that, on the average, respondents
sought a 27 percent increase in safety from floods and a 13
percent increase in water recreational facilities in exchange
for a 19 percent reduction in the camping and recreational
park, and 18 percent deterioration of scenic view, and a 16
percent reduction in wilderness land.

Salient Features:

A public participation study is described.

Advantages/Limitations of Salient Features:

1. Field studies conducted---yes
2. Practical for field use---yes
3. Usage for various types/sizes of projects---yes
4. Objective vs. subjective approaches---objective
5. Reproducibility---unknown
6. Scientifically sound features---yes

Conclusions:

General reference for WRAM

+ + +

REFERENCE:

Salomon, S.N., "Cost-Benefit Methodology for the Selection of
a Nuclear Power Plant Cooling System", paper presented at the
Energy Forum, 1974 Spring Meeting of the American Physical
Society, Washington, D.C., April 22, 1974.

Abstract:

A weighting-scaling checklist methodology is described
which will aid in selecting cooling systems for proposed
nuclear power plants. Thirteen external socio-economic impacts (consumptive water use, impacts on aquatic life from
the intake and discharge of water---this includes mechanical
and thermal impacts, environmental costs of chemical pollutants,
land requirements and land use impacts, recreation, aesthetics,
noise, fogging and other meteorological effects, beneficial
uses of heat, materials used, power penalty from loss in
efficiency and operation, energy requirements for operation,
and uncertainty due to technological innovation) and four
direct economic factors (capital costs, annual operation and

maintenance, value of lost power per year, and present worth of generating costs) were used in the decision making process. Information on five alternatives (natural draft towers, wet-dry mechanical draft towers, spray canal, cooling pond, and once-through systems) was assembled for each decision factor.

Usage of the methodology for a particular site involves the assignment of relative weighting factors to each of the 13 external socio-economic impacts. A total of 100 weighting points are divided among the 13 impacts, although no technique for accomplishing this step is described. In order to determine scale values a reference cooling system is used. The mechanical draft evaporative cooling tower system was chosen as a reference because the EPA considers this technology as being "the best practicable control technology currently available" relative to PL92-500. For each external socio-economic impact an apprisal is made which compares the reference system to the alternatives. For a comparative appraisal to following scale values are utilized: very superior (+8), superior (+4), moderately superior (+2), marginally superior (+1), no difference (0), marginally inferior (-1), moderately inferior (-2), inferior (-4), and very inferior (-8).

Salient Features:

Weighting-scaling checklist; relative scaling based on a reference alternative is used.

Advantages/Limitations of Salient Features:

1. Field studies conducted---yes
2. Practical for field use---yes
3. Usage for various types/sizes of projects---yes
4. Objective vs. subjective approaches---objective
5. Reproducibility---unknown
6. Scientifically sound features---yes

Conclusions:

Use directly in WRAM
..Mention relative scaling based on a reference alternative.

+ + +

REFERENCE:

Schaenman, P.S. and Muller, T., "Measuring Impacts of Land Development", URI 86000, November 1974, 93 pages, The Urban Institute, Washington, D.C.

Abstract:

    This report outlines an approach to estimating the impacts
of land development on a local jurisdiction. The methodology
is a descriptive checklist containing 48 factors and indicated
units of measurement for each. Four factors deal with local
economy, 8 deal with the natural environment, 4 deal with
aesthetics and cultural values, 22 deal with public and private
services and 10 deal with housing and social conditions. The
majority of the factors would be associated with the SWB and
RD accounts in water resources development projects.

Salient Features:

    Good listing of variables and their associated measurement
units for many relevant items in the SWB and RD accounts.

Advantages/Limitations of Salient Features:

    1. Field studies conducted---yes
    2. Practical for field use---yes
    3. Usage for various types/sizes of projects---yes
    4. Objective vs. subjective approaches---objective
    5. Reproducibility---unknown
    6. Scientifically sound features---yes

Conclusions:

    Use directly in WRAM
    ..Mention types of variables included.

                        + + +

REFERENCE:

School of Civil Engineering and Environmental Science and
Oklahoma Biological Survey, "Mid-Arkansas River Basin Study---
Effects Assessment of Alternative Navigation Routes from Tulsa,
Oklahoma to Vicinity of Wichita, Kansas", June 1974, 555 pages,
University of Oklahoma, Norman, Oklahoma (report prepared for
U.S. Army Engineer District, Tulsa, Corps of Engineers).

Abstract:

    A weighting-scaling checklist methodology was used to
evaluate the environmental impacts of 9 alternatives (8 waterway locational routes and the no-action alternative) for extending waterway navigation from Tulsa to Wichita. A total
of 102 assessment variables grouped into 6 categories (biology,
physical/chemical, regional compatibility, archeology, aesthetics
and climatology were used. A total of 1000 importance points

were distributed to the categories and variables through use of the ranked pairwise comparision technique. Impact scaling was accomplished through the use of functional curves similar in concept to those in the Battelle Environmental Evaluation System. These functional curves allowed the conversion of information on assessment variables into an environmental quality scale. Composite scores for each alternative were developed by summing the products of the importance points and scale values. A stochastically selected error term was included so as to allow the importance weights to vary by $\pm 50\%$. This concept is similar to that used in the Odum Optimum Pathway Matrix. The entire methodology was computerized to allow for ease of calculation and the conduction of a sensitivity analysis.

Salient Features:

Weighting-scaling checklist which is similar in concept to the Battelle Environmental Evaluation System; an error term is included to account for subjective misjudgments.

Advantages/Limitations of Salient Features:

1. Field studies conducted---yes
2. Practical for field use---yes
3. Usage for various types/sizes of projects---yes
4. Objective vs. subjective approaches---objective
5. Reproducibility---unknown
6. Scientifically sound features---yes

Conclusions:

Use directly in WRAM
..Mention concepts and the inclusion of the error term

+ + +

REFERENCE:

Smith, M.A., "Field Test of an Environmental Impact Assessment Methodology", Rept. ERC-1574, Aug. 1974, Environmental Resources Center, Georgia Institute of Technology, Atlanta, Ga.

Abstract:

This weighting-scaling methodology was originally developed for the Georgia Dept. of Transportation by Battelle-Columbus Laboratories, Columbus, Ohio. The method is similar to the Battelle Environmental Evaluation System developed for the Bureau of Reclamation. This study applied the method to a rapid transit system project in Atlanta. A total of 68 factors

are included and grouped into four major environmental "categories": ecological factors, physical/chemical factors, aesthetic factors, and human-interest factors. Functional curves
are used and importance weights are assigned to the 68 factors.
A total of 1000 so-called "Environmental Quality Units" (EQU)
are assigned to the total environment. The weightings are
pre-set in this methodology by an interdisciplinary team of
experts. The Delphi technique, an iterative process, is
employed to reach a consensus on the optimum distribution of
the 1000 units among the factors.

Salient Features:

Weighting-scaling checklist for a rapid transit system.

Advantages/Limitations of Salient Features:

1. Field studies conducted---yes
2. Practical for field use---yes
3. Usage for various types/sizes of projects---yes
4. Objective vs. subjective approaches---objective
5. Reproducibility---unknown
6. Scientifically sound features---yes

Conclusions:

Use directly in WRAM
..Mention use of technique

+ + +

REFERENCE:

Utah Water Research Laboratory, "Water Resources Planning,
Social Goals, and Indicators: Methodological Development
and Empirical Test", PRWG-131-1, December 1974, 267 pp., Utah
State University, Logan, Utah (prepared for Office of Water
Research and Technology, Washington, D.C.).

Abstract:

A methodology for comprehensive evaluation of water
resources development and use (TECHCOM) has been developed and
partially field tested. A model of three societal goals consists of nine primary goals successively articulated into increasingly specific subgoals. Achievement of subgoals is
perceived as affected by measurable social indicators whose
values are perturbed by water resources actions. Linking
the elements of the goal taxon by connectives, results in an
evaluation system. Historical, political and philosophical
considerations of the proposed system are discussed in Part 1.

332

Part II describes the results of the Rio Grande of New Mexico test including public perception and weighing of the subgoals and goals, and development of specific connectives. Future values of 128 social indicators for five action plans for four five-year intervals to 1987 are estimated using a computerized system based on an inversion of an input-output model interacting with social and environmental indicator connectives.

Salient Features:

Assignment of relative importance weights through public participation is described.

Advantages/Limitations of Salient Features:

1. Field studies conducted---yes
2. Practical for field use---yes
3. Usage for various types/sizes of projects---yes
4. Objective vs. subjective approaches ---objective
5. Reproducibility---unknown
6. Scientifically sound features---yes

Conclusions:

General reference for WRAM

+ + +

REFERENCE:

Warner, M.L., et al, "An Assessment Methodology for the Environmental Impact of Water Resource Projects", Report No. EPA-600/5-74-016, July 1974, Battelle-Columbus Laboratories, Columbus, Ohio (Report prepared for Office of Research and Development, U.S. Environmental Protection Agency, Washington, D.C.

Abstract:

This methodology was one of 8 methodologies described in the interim WRAM report (February, 1977). This report presents materials intended for use by reviewers of environmental impact statements on major water reservoir projects. The report is prepared as a series of six related but individually referenced discussions of the following major topics:

Reservoir project planning, construction, and operation activities

- Water quality impacts of reservoir construction

- Ecological impacts of reservoir construction

- Economic, social, and aesthetic impacts of reservoir construction

- Review criteria for assessing general statement completeness and accuracy

- A review of impact assessment methodologies.

The materials presented attempt to call to the reviewer's attention important issues or potential impacts that an adequate impact statement should address. In addition, the water quality and ecological impacts sections discuss the site-specific conditions under which a given potential impact may or may not occur. The section on water quality impacts also presents a detailed comparison of mathematical models for predicting impacts on water temperature, dissolved oxygen levels, and some chemical constituents of surface waters. The sections dealing with water quality, ecological, and economic-social-aesthetic impacts include extensive citations to relevant literature the impact statement reviewer may wish to consult for further information.

As a part of the review of methodologies for environmental impact assessment, 67 statements were examined for the methodologies used. The statements were distributed as follows: Bureau of Reclamation 15, Army Corps of Engineers 22, Tennessee Valley Authority 14, Soil Conservation Service 13, and Federal Power Commission 3.

Salient Features:

Good descriptive checklist for reservoir projects;
Information is provided on the technical aspects of prediction of water quality and ecological impacts.

Advantages/Limitations of Salient Features:

1. Field studies conducted---not applicable (methodology primarily used for review)
2. Practical for field use---yes
3. Usage for various types/sizes of projects---yes
4. Objective vs. subjective approaches---objective
5. Reproducibility---unknown
6. Scientifically sound features---yes

Conclusions:

Use directly in WRAM
..Mention impact identification and prediction.

APPENDIX D

INFORMATION ON 27 REFERENCES

FROM 1975 PERIOD

REFERENCE:

Bella, D.A., "Tidal Flats in Estuarine Water Quality Analysis", EPA/660/3-75/025, June 1975, 200 pp., National Environmental Research Center, U.S.Environmental Research Center, U.S. Environmental Protection Agency, Corvallis, Oregon (prepared for EPA by Dept. of Civil Engineering, Oregon State University, Corvallis, Oregon).

Abstract:

The initial phases of the study involved mixing processes and tidal hydraulics; however, the study emphasis shifted to estuarine benthic systems as the importance of these systems became more apparent. A conceptual model of estuarine benthic systems was developed and a classification system of estuarine benthic deposits which is based on the availability of hydrogen acceptors and reactive iron was developed. Field studies demonstrated that estuarine sediments and overlying wastes could contain significant concentrations of free sulfides which are toxic to a variety of organisms. Results from experiments using extracts from benthic deposits and algal mats demonstrated a close relationship between the rate of sulfate reduction and the sulfate and soluble organic carbon concentrations. A general systems model of estuarine benthic systems was developed. A variety of activities which could contribute to significant environmental changes with estuarine benthic systems were identified.

Salient Features:

Basic information on estuarine benthic systems is presented.

Advantages/Limitations of Salient Features:

1. Field studies conducted---yes
2. Practical for field use---unknown
3. Usage for various types/sizes of projects---not applicable
4. Objective vs. subjective approaches---objective
5. Reproducibility---unknown
6. Scientifically sound features---yes

Conclusions:

General reference for WRAM

337

REFERENCE:

Bhutani, J., et al, "Impacts of Hydrologic Modification on
Water Quality", EPA-600/2-75-007, April 1975, U.S. Environmental Protection Agency, Washington, D.C.

Abstract:

This report describes the scope and magnitude of water
pollution problems caused by hydrologic modifications (dams,
impoundments, channelization, in-water construction, out-of-
water construction, and dredging). The type of pollutants
released by each class of hydrologic modification were identified, and estimates were made of the relative amounts of these
pollutants that enter surface waters as a result of project
construction. Table D-1 summarizes the relative amounts and
indicates their beneficial and adverse effects on the receiving water system. The relative quantity (or release rate) of
each pollutant type is shown as three levels: high (H),
moderate (M), and low (L). For sediment, the release rate
was estimated relative to the release rate from a predisturbed
land surface (which may have been forested, grass-covered, or
poorly vegetated) or a predisturbed benthic area. For other
types of pollutants, the quantities released were estimated
relative to the concentrations of the same type of pollutant
in urban surface runoff. These estimates of quantities and
rates were made by the authors, and were not based on field
measurements. Table D-2 indicates in greater detail the
nature of specific pollutants and the expected effect.

In addition to construction impacts, projects using
earth fill may also exhibit operational impacts. For example,
operation of dams and impoundments affects the quality of
downstream waters by several mechanisms:

Trapping and retaining sediment. This alters the
natural equilibrium of sediment downstream of reservoirs,
causing scour and erosion. Also, trapped sediment tends
with time to fill reservoirs. When accumulated sediment
is dredged out, resuspension of sediment and other
materials may produce abnormally high concentrations
that adversely affect aquatic life downstream.

Thermal stratification. Stable layers of water having
different density, temperature, chemical, and biological
makeup may be formed in reservoirs.

Decomposition of trapped organic material. Reservoirs
accumulate organic material and, upon decomposition, de-
creases in dissolved oxygen concentrations may occur.

TABLE D-1: EFFECTS OF CONSTRUCTION PROJECTS ON WATER QUALITY

CONSTRUCTION ACTIVITY	RELATIVE QUANTITY RELEASED BY CONSTRUCTION*									EFFECTS OF POLLUTANTS	
	SEDIMENT	NUTRIENTS	DISSOLVED SOLIDS	HEAVY METALS	SALINITY	BIODEGRADABLE ORGANICS	REFR. ORGANICS	PESTICIDES	OILS AND SYNTHETIC CHEMS	BENEFICIAL	ADVERSE
OUT-OF-STREAM ACTIVITIES (EARTH MOVING) • AREAL (Suburban Devm't – residences, streets, shopping centers, parking lots, public buildings; Business/Commercial Devm't; Reclamation Landfills -- tunneling spoil disposal,** dredging spoil on-land, earth dams. Construction – dams, reservoir areas, bridges.)	H	M	L	L		L	L	L	L	Sediment produced which may sustain a receptor stream at equilibrium suspended sediment load; can help remove ions in receptor water body by adsorption.	May alter the physical and biological character of the receptor water body if subjected to excessive sediment. Results in costly loss of flora and fauna, stream cross-sectional changes, altered flow regimes, and added water treatment requirements. Biostimulation of water bodies from nutrient runoff. May cause siltation of downstream reservoirs.
IN-STREAM • Dredging Operation/In-Water Channel Excavation, Stream Realignment	H	M	M	M		L	L	L	L	Suction dredging of benthal deposits may remove undesirable heavy metals and other chemical pollutants to accelerate recovery of polluted condition.	Local temporary increase in suspended sediment and turbidity with potentially damaging effects on marine life and degraded water quality for consumptive uses. Can physically remove shellfish from their habitat. Can change channel shape, ensuing scour or aggradation imposes requirements for grade control structures, concrete linings, or rip rap to stabilize the channel.

339

TABLE D-1 CONTINUED

							Beneficial Effects	Adverse Effects
Dredged Material Disposal in Water, In-water fills, Causeways, Retarding Basins, Levees, Floodwalls	H	H	M	L	L	L	May create new land for waterfowl habitats and decrease levels of insect breeding in filled-in marshes. Stream blockages provide storm water storage and trap silt, provide fish and wildlife habitat, aesthetic improvement.	Constructed channels scour heavily during flooding. Can smother marine life on bottom, destroy fin fishes, lower dissolved oxygen levels, increase turbidity thereby reducing light transmission. Change original fish and wildlife habitat. Aquatic life stressed by temperature, and chemical and biochemical equilibria changes.
Installation of Piles, Bulkheads, Dikes, Marinas	M	L	L	L	L	L		Benthic penetration and some disturbance of bottom material resuspension of sediments.
Channelization (Stream Realignment, clearing, and snagging	M	L	L	L	L	L	Improves flow efficiency and navigation. BOD lower with lower detritus.	Temporarily increases suspended sediment and turbidity. May decrease concentration time of peak runoff and increase flooding downstream. Removes obstructions used by fish for protection, food support, and breeding areas.

*H (high), M (moderate), L (low) release rates are estimated relative to expected yield from predisturbed surface on benthic area for sediment and relative to urban runoff for chemical pollutants.

**Outflow from exit considered to be a point source.

340

TABLE D-2: WATER POLLUTION FROM CONSTRUCTION ACTIVITIES---CAUSE/EFFECT MATRIX

CLASS	POLLUTANT MATERIALS	SOURCE ACTIVITIES/OCCURRENCE	QUANTITY*	EFFECTS BENEFICIAL	ADVERSE
Physical					
SEDIMENT	Inerta and organic particles; colloids; microorganisms; (Note: during transport, the sediment load comprises the suspended load plus the bed load.)	Land-Disturbing Operations: Surface-clearing, grading, excavating, trenching, stockpiling; (Note: Subsoils often have different erodibility characteristics than surface soils) Channel Modification: Dredging, waste disposal, excavation, fill, penetration of bed Cleaning Operations: Aggregate washing, cleaning of masonry surfaces, forms, and containers	H M L	May provide material to maintain a receptor stream channel in equilibrium, i.e., provide adequate suspended sediment to prohibit erosive degradation of a fluvial channel, In-stream sediment required in formation of silt-laden farmlands along flood plains and near river mouths. Fine-grain sediment helps in the removal of ions which adhere to and are transported by particulates, which settle to the bottom. Dredged material disposal may also create new land areas (for building sites, beach restoration, waterfowl habitats) and decrease vectors in marshfilling.	May exceed equilibrium suspened load of receptor stream altering many physical and biological characteristics of the channel; these include channel aggredation, silting of reservoirs, undesirable effects on marine life such as blanketing and smothering of benthic flora and fauna, altering the flora and fauna as a result of changes in light transmission and abrasion, destroying or altering the species of fish due to changes in the flora and fauna upon which the fish depend, or obstruction of their gill function. Also a need may arise for excessive treatment (sedimentation, clarification) prior to consumptive use for municipal, industrial, or irrigation purposes. Channel siltation can adversely affect its capacity to carry flood flows or support navigation and recreation. Dredged material disposal may destroy land areas (salt marshes, wildlife refuse, vegetated coverage), block flow circulation or increase vetors in the disposal area.

341

TABLE D-2 CONTINUED

CLASS	POLLUTANT MATERIALS	SOURCE ACTIVITIES/OCCURRENCE	QUANTITY	EFFECTS BENEFICIAL	ADVERSE
Chemical NUTRIENTS	Ammonia, ortho-phosphates, polyphosphates, Organic N, Organic P	Fertilization of reestablish-ed vegetal cover	L	Stimulates growth of plants and grasses on areas denuded by con-struction (especially on slopes), thereby reducing soil loss in rain storms.	Nutrients, especially from excessive application of soluble fertilizers,will be transported from new-growth surfaces at construction sites in the runoff of pre-cipitation; by then stimu-lating growth of algae and marine plants, nutrients can have adverse effects on chemical exchange processes, leading to eutrophication and lowered oxygen levels. In addition to the bio-stimulation impacts, a large concentration of unoxidized nitrogen (organic nitrogen and ammonia) could represent a significant oxygen demand in the receiving waters.
BIO-DEGRAD-ABLE ORGANICS	Submerged or float-ing brush, lumber, tree trunks or limbs, paper, fiberboard	Improper disposal of build-ing products or poor clear-ing and clean-up practices.	L	Larger submerged objects may serve as a temporary habitat of fishes. Per-mitting growth, wood chips, and similar matter to remain in place in a future inundation area will temporarily reduce out-of-stream erosive losses by serving as a precipitation energy ab-sorber and a sheet run-off retardant.	In degrading of the organics an oxygen demand is exerted on the receiving waters. The dissolved oxygen depression, or large resultant fluctua-tions in DO, can lead to death of aquatic organisms, severe changes in types and numbers of aquatic organisms, obnoxious odors, and nuisan-ces such as aesthetic im-pacts, clogging of pumps, screens, etc.

342

REFRACTORY ORGANICS/ PESTI- CIDES	Highly persistent chemicals, heat resistant, or effectively non-degradable, e.g., certain pesticides and other synthetic organics (solid construction materials and tools of poly-vinyl chloride, thermoplastic polyesters, rubber, and epoxy fibers and liquid chemicals for treatment of walls, adhesive applications crack-sealing, water-proofing, paint-ing, and curing operations.) Major categories of insecticides include the chlor-inated hydrocarbons--- complex organic molecules of C,H,Cl-- such as chlordane, malathion, DDT, and the phosphorothioates-- C,H,P. Herbicides in-clude 2,4,D and 4,5,T.	Improper care in construc-tion applications,overusage, spillage. (Note: some of these types of pollutants, particularly the solids, are expected to remain at the source or point of appli-cation, with negligible overland transport). Trend in construction in use of biocides is away from in-organics and toward syn-thetic organics for use as insecticides, herbi-cides, fungicides, and fumigants.	L Note: expected level of produc-tion is very low because most pesticides are too expensive to be wastefully applied, resulting in effic-ient or optimal usage.	Underslab and founda-tion treatment with long-lasting in-secticides, especi-ally for termite control, is an im-portant usage; herbi-cidal treatment of soil areas to remove herbaceous and woody plants that obstruct development and for weed control prior to revegetation is necessary in many construction projects.	Toxic to a wide spectrum of marine biota; can concentrate (by biomagnification) in aquatic organisms, and the effects can be transmitted through higher levels of the biological food chain up to humans. Most biocides show a tendancy to accumulate in bottom muds. Earth-moving may reexpose pesticides previously applied to a site, e.g., if used previously for agriculture.

TABLE D-2 CONTINUED

CLASS	POLLUTANT MATERIALS	SOURCE ACTIVITIES/OCCURRENCE	QUANTITY	EFFECTS BENEFICIAL	ADVERSE
DISSOLVED SOLIDS/ HEAVY METALS	Ionic Hg, Pb, Zn, Mn, Co, Cr, Ag, Cd, As, Cu, Al, Fe	Derived from construction wastes such as discarded metallic frames, ducts, pipes, wiring, beams, gypsum board; also from fuels, paints, pesticides, and other construction chemicals. Also, concrete operations produce NPS, e.g., spilled cement, washing water, curing compounds.	L	A light, distributed concrete spillage or wash disposal may act as a cementitious stabilizer to reduce soil erosion; also it will add alkalinity which could correct acid soils	When these materials weather, decompose, and disintegrate (recognizing that many of the substances such as plasterboard are only slightly soluble in water), the resultant oxides and salts dissolved in water bodies may damage or destroy aquatic organisms; also higher concentrations of certain of the dissolved solids are toxic to humans.
		Dredging activities may reintroduce and disperse within the water column dormant layers (confined by silt deposits) of heavy metals trapped in bottom sludge deposite generally originating over long time periods from point industrial sources and urban runoff	H Note: may be significant in certain sluggish rivers, lakes, or bays especially in first dredging; generally insignificant buildup would occur by the time that maintenance (repeat) dredging is undertaken	Suction dredging and disposal of undesirable chemicals in benthal deposits may accelerate recovery of polluted water bodies, in parallel with introduction of clean inflows.	Dredging may mechanically reintroduce these chemicals into waters, with subsequent diffusion and increase in undesirable impact described above.
ALKALINITY	NaCl CaCl$_2$	Produced from saline ice-removal compounds in cold climates (constuction roads), dust control on graded areas, and concrete additives (freezing-depressant additives or early strength-enhancing agents, curing compounds). Affected by hydraulic changes resulting from channelization.	L Note: minor level, depending on nature and seasonality of construction activity	Use of salt compounds allows continuation of projects throughout a greater range of climatic conditions, reduces air pollution from dust	Increased salinity of water impacts upon nature of marine life (plants and animals) indigenous to the region; quality may be degraded for municipal, industrial, or irrigation uses.

Pollutant	Sources	Release rate*		Effects
OILS AND SYNTHETIC CHEMICALS	Petroleum products such as oils, grease, tars, asphaltic materials, fuels, solvents; paints, detergents, soaps, sealants, adhesives, chemical soil stabilizers.	Introduced into soils through improper construction and maintenance practices, (such as not using adequate caution and methods in disposing of oil wastes, transporting and transferring fuels and lubricants, oil-laden rags, and degreasing compounds), and from spills, for example, from storage tanks. Spillages during routine construction and leaks from trucks and other machinery are also serious considerations. Production of water-bitumen mixtures from road paving, roofing, and water-proofing jobs can also cause NPS concern.	L	Some of these chemicals float over water, some become entrained in water--absorbed on sediment--and some dissolve in water, but all are extremely difficult to control after entering water bodies. These categories of substances impair the use of water for drinking and for contact sports because they impart persistent odors and tastes to water Some may block the transfer of air through a water--floating substance interface, suffocating aquatic plants, organisms, and fish. Some petroleum products contain organo-metallic compounds and other impurities toxic to fish and other organisms.
Biological COLIFORM	Disease-causing pathogens: soil organisms and those of human and animal origin (bacteria, fungi, viruses).	Improperly planned and managed construction sites where inadequate sanitary conditions prevail. Note: Majority of biological pollutants exist in topsoil layers where they are feed on dead organisms; however, construction often disturbs the lower subsoils.	L M Sludge from wastewater treatment plants may promote and accelerate the restoration of graded areas.	Can cause diseases in humans and animals when released or made available in water bodies.

*H (high), M (moderate), L (low) release rates are estimated relative to expected yield from predisturbed surface on benthic areas for sediment and relative to urban runoff for chemical pollutants.

345

Nitrogen supersaturation. Violent mixing of air and
water released through turboelectric generators or a
high velocity tailwash causes the water to become super-
saturated with nitrogen from the air. Nitrogen supersaturation may lead to undesirable effects on downstream
fish populations.

Surface evaporation. The large, relatively warm surface
areas of impoundments permit rapid evaporation of water,
thus increasing the concentration of salts and other
dissolved and suspended constituents in impoundment
waters.

Salient Features:

Qualitative discussion of the impacts of water resource
projects.

Advantages/Limitations of Salient Features:

1. Field studies conducted---not applicable
2. Practical for field use---not applicable
3. Usage for various types/sizes of projects---yes
4. Objective vs. subjective approaches---objective
5. Reproducibility---unknown
6. Scientifically sound features---yes

Conclusions:

General reference for WRAM

+ + +

REFERENCE:

Bishop, A.B., "Structuring Communications Programs for Public
Participation in Water Resources Planning", IWR Contract Report 75-2, May 1975, 125 pp., U.S. Army Engineer Institute
for Water Resources, Fort Belvoir, Va. (prepared for IWR by
Utah State University, Logan, Utah).

Abstract:

Most federal agencies with resource planning and management responsibilities have received both executive and legislative directives to promote broad public involvement in
their planning studies. This report is directed toward describing methods and techniques for planner-citizen communication
which will enhance the level of public participation in the
planning process and will permit citizens and planners to
work effectively together in arriving at planning decisions

346

which affect multiple local, state, and federal jurisdictions.
Specific information is included on public forums (public
hearings, public meetings, informal small group meetings, information and coordination seminars, and forums of other agencies or groups), community contacts (operating field offices,
local planning visits, and direct community representation),
and interactive group methods (workshops, charettes, and
special committees). Table 24 (page 112) summarizes the effectiveness of various communications techniques with various
publics.

Salient Features:

    Describes features of various public participation
techniques.

Advantages/Limitations of Salient Features:

    1. Field studies conducted---yes
    2. Practical for field use---yes
    3. Usage for various types/sizes of projects---yes
    4. Objective vs. subjective approaches---objective
    5. Reproducibility---unknown
    6. Scientifically sound features---yes

Conclusions:

    Use directly in WRAM
    ..Mention various public participation techniques.

+ + +

REFERENCE:

Carstea, D., et al, "Guidelines for the Environmental Impact
Assessment of Small Structures and Related Activities in
Coastal Bodies of Water", MTR-6916, Rev. 1, August, 1975, The
MITRE Corporation, McLean, VA. (prepared for U.S. Army Corps
of Engineers, New York District).

Abstract:

    This methodology was specifically developed for the pur-
pose of providing instructions on how to conduct an impact
assessment for certain projects requiring Section 404 permits.
The objective is to describe the probable environmental impacts
(physical, biological, and socio-economic) of representative
structures and common activities performed in coastal waters
of the northeastern United States. The second purpose was to
prepare procedural and technical guidelines for an effective

347

and rapid environmental assessment review of specific permit applications. The following actions/projects are addressed: riprap placement; bulkheads; groins and jetties; piers, dolphins, mooring piles, and ramp construction; dredging (new and maintenance); outfalls, submerged lines and pipes; and aerial crossings. For each of the actions/projects considered, the following areas of environmental impact are summarized: erosion, sedimentation, and deposition; flood heights and drift; water quality; ecology; air quality; noise; safety/navigation; recreation; esthetics; and socio-economics. This methodology can be defined as a descriptive checklist. Usage involves identification of the type of structure or activity to be considered. Referral is then made to a discussion of the specific activities associated with the typical structure or activity under consideration.

Salient Features:

Descriptive checklist for quantifying impacts from small coastal projects.

Advantages/Limitations of Salient Features:

1. Field studies conducted---not applicable
2. Practical for field use---yes
3. Usage for various types/sizes of projects---yes
4. Objective vs. subjective approaches---objective
5. Reproducibility---unknown
6. Scientifically sound features---yes

Conclusions:

Use directly in WRAM
.Mention availability.

+ + +

REFERENCE:

Christensen, S.W., Van Winkle, W. and Mattice, J.S., "Defining and Determining the Significance of Impacts---Concepts and Methods", 1975, 71 pp., Oak Ridge National Laboratory, Oak Ridge, Tennessee.

Abstract:

The term impact is conceptually and mathematically defined to be the difference in the state or value of an ecosystem with versus without the source of impact. Some resulting problems associated with the measurement of impacts based on comparisons of baseline and operational data are discussed

348

briefly. The concept of a significant adverse impact on a
biological system is operationally defined in terms of an
adverse impact which, according to a proposed decision-tree,
justifies rejection of a project or a change in its site,
design, or mode of operation. A gradient of increasing
difficulty in the prediction of impacts exists as the scope
of the assessment is expanded to consider long-term, far-
field impacts with respect to higher levels of biological
organization (e.g., communities or ecosystems). The analytical
methods available for predicting short-term, near-field impacts
are discussed. Finally, the role of simulation modeling as
an aid to professional judgment in predicting the long-term,
far-field consequences of impacts is considered, and illustrated with an example.

Salient Features:

    Information is presented on impact prediction and assess-
ment for the biological environment.

Advantages/Limitations of Salient Features:

    1. Field studies conducted---not applicable
    2. Practical for field use---not applicable
    3. Usage for various types/sizes of projects---not
        applicable
    4. Objective vs. subjective approaches---objective
    5. Reproducibility---not applicable
    6. Scientifically sound features---yes

Conclusions:

    General reference for WRAM

                    +   +   +

REFERENCE:

Clark, J.R., "Environmental Assessment of Construction Activi-
ties", Unpublished MS Thesis, 1975, 192 pp., School of Civil
Engineering and Environmental Science, University of Oklahoma,
Norman, Oklahoma.

Abstract:

    This thesis was orientated to construction projects and
their potential impacts on the environment. The following
selected conclusions are based on extensive literature research, on field observations and on-site interviews: (1) The
relevance and nature of construction impacts are not generally
understood within the assessment field and in the construction

industry. The development of construction impact assessment methods is very limited. Prediction models for construction emissions are adequate if judiciously applied; (2) concerning surface and groundwater quality, surface water emissions can probably be controlled by on-site containment and monitoring activities. Groundwater contamination is probably not a problem in most cases but any threat should be treated as significant; (3) concerning ecosystems, expertise is developing in the biological sciences to inventory, study and assess biota on an ecosystem level. Construction activities may be treated in a fairly straight-forward manner with regard to ecosystems due to defined temporal and spatial conditions during construction; and (4) concerning noise and vibrations, these impacts can be minimized by local regulation if intelligent enforcement is used and quieter equipment is encouraged.

Salient Features:

Good discussion of quantifying construction impacts.

Advantages/Limitations of Salient Features:

1. Field studies conducted---not applicable
2. Practical for field use---yes
3. Usage for various types/sizes of projects---yes
4. Objective vs. subjective approaches---objective
5. Reproducibility---unknown
6. Scientifically sound features---yes

Conclusions:

General reference for WRAM

+ + +

REFERENCE:

Dee, N., et al, "An Assessment of the Usage of Environmental Assessment Methodologies in Environmental Impact Statements", DMG-DRS Journal (published by Design Methods Group, University of California, Berkeley, California), Vol. 9, No. 1, March 1975.

Abstract:

Formal environmental impact assessment methodologies have been designed to identify, integrate, and interpret environmental impacts resulting from federally funded and/or regulated projects. At the present time, these formal methodologies are largely ignored by practitioners involved in preparing impact statements. Three reasons have been identified for their non-use: (1) different perspectives on the role of EIS held by the methodology developers and practitioners, (2) the limited direction provided by administrative guidelines related to EIS implementation, and (3) the pressures initiated by the political arena. These methodologies will be incorporated into the EIS process when they are (1) responsive to the needs of the preparer, (2) perceived by the EIS actors such as CEQ and proponent agencies to yield more superior information, and (3) required by CEQ or the proponent agencies.

Salient Features:

Indicates limitations on use of methodologies.

Advantages/Limitations of Salient Features:

1. Field studies conducted---not applicable
2. Practical for field use---not applicable
3. Usage for various types/sizes of projects---not applicable
4. Objective vs. subjective approaches---not applicable
5. Reproducibility---not applicable
6. Scientifically sound features---not applicable

Conclusions:

Use directly in WRAM
..Mention limitations on uses of methodologies.

+ + +

REFERENCE:

Fitzsimmons, S.J., Stuart, L.I., and Wolff, P.C., "Social Assessment Manual--A Guide to the Preparation of the Social Well-Being Account", July 1975, 279 pp., Bureau of Reclamation, Denver, Colorado (prepared for Bureau of Reclamation by Abt Associates, Inc., Cambridge, Massachusetts).

Abstract:

This methodology is basically a scaling checklist for the SWB account in water resources development projects. The structure of the SWB account is shown in Table 25 (page 114). A total of 389 variables are included in the methodology. Assessment of existing or baseline conditions involves comparison of the measured variable with appropriate regional or national data and assigning a rating as follows: AA --- above average; A --- average; and BA --- below average. The authors stress that in order to rate an impact as good or bad, something

351

must be known about the present-day characteristics of the communities themselves. For example, in one community, a more urban one, residents value growth highly. They desire more industry and new people to expand the community and its capacity to support more services. For this community the effect of more industrial employment can be rated as quite positive. In the second community, residents are very rural-oriented in their values and lifestyles and wish no growth of this type. From the perspective of this community, the same impact, the rise in industrial employment, can be rated as a negative effect. The following five values can be assigned to a given social effect: (++) very positive; (+) positive; (0) neutral; (-) negative; and (--) very negative. These ratings are not viewed as additive across evaluation categories. They do, however, provide an important and direct way of comparing social impacts for the same variable across plans.

Salient Features:

Listing of 389 assessment variables for SWB account.

Advantages/Limitations of Salient Features:

1. Field studies conducted---unknown
2. Practical for field use---no, too many variables.
3. Usage for various types/sizes of projects---yes
4. Objective vs. subjective approaches---objective
5. Reproducibility---unknown
6. Scientifically sound features---yes

Conclusions:

Use directly in WRAM
..Mention the 389 assessment variables for SWB account.

+ + +

REFERENCE:

Fuhriman, D.K., et al, "Water Quality Effect of Diking a Shallow Arid-Region Lake", EPA/660/2-75-007, April 1975, 243 pp., Brigham Young University, Provo, Utah.

Abstract:

The inflow, outflow, and in-lake water quality and quantity of Utah Lake in Central Utah was studied over a 36-month period. The work was undertaken to determine the effect of a proposed diking project on the quality and quantity of lake water and to develop a methodology for determining the effect of diking or other management practices on the quality of water in any lake

352

system. A computer simulation model was developed which is able to analyze the effect of a given management program on the water quality of the lake, particularly as related to the 'conservative salts' present. The simulation model was also used to evaluate the evaporation from the lake by use of a salt balance technique. Results of the research indicated that the diking of Utah Lake will have a positive beneficial effect upon the water quality of the lake and will also result in considerable saving of water and reclamation of valuable land.

Salient Features:

Impact prediction method is presented for salt balance in a lake.

Advantages/Limitations of Salient Features:

1. Field studies conducted---yes
2. Practical for field use---yes
3. Usage for various types/sizes of projects---yes
4. Objective vs. subjective approaches---objective
5. Reproducibility---unknown
6. Scientifically sound features---yes

Conclusions:

General reference for WRAM

+ + +

REFERENCE:

Gann, D.A., "Thermal Reduction of Municipal Solid Waste", 1975, 91 pp., Master's Thesis, School of Civil Engineering and Environmental Science, University of Oklahoma, Norman, Oklahoma.

Abstract:

A weighting-scaling checklist for evaluation of municipal solid waste incineration systems is described. The weighted rankings method was used for both weighting and scaling. The weighted rankings concepts are included in the interim WRAM report (Feb., 1977).

Salient Features:

Weighting-scaling checklist using weighted rankings technique is described.

Advantages/Limitations of Salient Features:

1. Field studies conducted---yes
2. Practical for field use---yes
3. Usage for various types/sizes of projects---yes
4. Objective vs. subjective approaches---objective
5. Reproducibility---unknown
6. Scientifically sound features---yes

Conclusions:

General reference for WRAM

+ + +

REFERENCE:

Harkness, T., "Visual Analysis Techniques: Outfitting Your
Tool Box", Proceedings of Conference on Environmental Impact
Analysis: Current Methodologies, Future Directions, University
of Illinois, Urbana-Champaign, Illinois, 1975.

Abstract:

This paper contains an annotated bibliography of visual
analysis techniques which might be useful in environmental
impact studies.

Salient Features:

Annotated bibliography of visual analysis techniques.

Advantages/Limitations of Salient Features:

1. Field studies conducted---yes
2. Practical for field use---yes
3. Usage for various types/sizes of projects---yes
4. Objective vs. subjective approaches---objective
5. Reproducibility---unknown
6. Scientifically sound features---yes

Conclusions:

General reference for WRAM

+ + +

REFERENCE:

Haven, K.F., "A Methodology for Impact Assessment in the Estua-
rine/Marine Environment", UCRL-51949, Oct., 1975, 43pp.,

Lawrence Livermore Laboratory, Livermore, Cal. (prepared for
U.S. Energy Research and Development Administration, Washington,
D.C.).

Abstract:

    Impacts on the estuarine/marine environment can be assessed
in economic terms by tracing the impact flow out of the economic
sector through the marine environment and back into the economic
sector as a result of changes in natural resources availability.
Impacts can be measured by the changes created in the economic
sector from changes in resource availability. Primary emphasis
in this report is placed on the development of an appropriate
ecological model of the estuarine environment. Two types of
models are proposed; an ecological input/output model and a
dynamic (difference equation) model. These models are described
in detail and offer good information relative to biological
impacts and inter-relationships in estuarine areas. Particular
attention is given to the San Franciso Bay system as an example
area where the models can be applied. The acceptability criteria for the two proposed models include the ability to track
lethal and sublethal, direct and indirect (foodweb), and short
and long-term effects of pollutants related to the production
and use of various energy resources. This report was prepared
for the Energy Resources and Development Administration, and
it does contain some orientation to the energy sector; however,
its primary value is in providing basic information on ecosystem
models.

Salient Features:

    Contains information on ecosystem models for impact pre-
diction.

Advantages/Limitations of Salient Features:

    1. Field studies conducted---yes
    2. Practical for field use---no
    3. Usage for various types/sizes of projects---unknown
    4. Objective vs. subjective approaches---objective
    5. Reproducibility---unknown
    6. Scientifically sound features---yes

Conclusions:

    General reference for WRAM

+ + +

REFERENCE:

Hornberger, G.M., Kelly, M.G., and Lederman, T.C., "Evaluating a Mathematical Model for Predicting Lake Eutrophication", VPI-WRRC-Bull.-82, Sept., 1975, 102 pp., Water Resources Research Center, Virginia Polytechnic Institute and State University, Blacksburg, Virginia.

Abstract:

This research project developed a mathematical model of a lake ecosystem and then tested its ability to indicate what ecological changes-in particular eutrophication- would result from changes in the physical environment. The model was developed using a digital computer. In situ enrichment experiments then were performed to assess the relationship between nutrient concentrations and the growth of phytoplankton. The investigation included an evaluation of the use of nonlinear parameter estimation in determining the model's growth constants. The model did demonstrate that it could provide useful qualitative information. Field experiments did not, however, produce data suitable for quantifying the relationship between species diversity and nutrient addition showed that a diversity index holds little promise for use as a quantitative indicator of eutrophic conditions. The field experiments and the study of parameter estimation indicate that in situ enrichment experiments will not provide adequate data for accurate determination of model parameters.

Salient Features:

A mathematical model for predicting lake eutrophication is described.

Advantages/Limitations of Salient Features:

1. Field studies conducted---yes
2. Practical for field use---unknown
3. Usage for various types/sizes of projects---yes
4. Objective vs. subjective approaches---objective
5. Reproducibility---unknown
6. Scientifically sound features---yes

Conclusions:

General reference for WRAM

+ + +

REFERENCE:

Malone, D.W., "An Introduction to the Application of Interpretive Structural Modeling", in Baldwin, M.M. (editor), Portraits of Complexity: Applications of Systems Methodologies to Societal Problems, 1975, Battelle Memorial Institute, Columbus, Ohio.

Abstract:

Interpretive Structural Modeling (ISM) refers to the systematic application of some elementary notions of graph theory to efficiently construct a directed graph, or network representation, of a complex system. This methodology is potentially useful in impact identification, prediction and importance weighting. This paper presents an introduction to the fundamental concepts and operations of the methodology and reports on the results of two exercises conducted with a group of graduate students who had minimal mathematical training. The first exercise involved the structuring of personal values and was intended to acquaint the individuals with the methodology. The second was a group exercise focusing on barriers to investment in the central city, a subject of substantive interest to the participants. The results of the exercises demonstrate the utility of the methodology for capturing and communicating individual and group perceptions regarding complex issues.

Salient Features:

Technique for impact prediction.

Advantages/Limitations of Salient Features:

1. Field studies conducted---yes
2. Practical for field use---unknown
3. Usage for various types/sizes of projects---unknown
4. Objective vs. subjective approaches---objective
5. Reproducibility---unknown
6. Scientifically sound features---yes

Conclusions:

General reference for WRAM

+ + +

REFERENCE:

Mitchell, A., et al, "Handbook of Forecasting Techniques", IWR Contract Report 75-7, Dec., 1975, 316 pp., U.S. Army Engineer Institute for Water Resources, Fort Belvoir, Virginia

357

(prepared for IWR by Center for Study of Social Policy, Stanford Research Institute, Menlo Park, California).

Abstract:

Forecasting may mean prediction, identification of possibilities, physical plausibilities or desirables for the future. Forecasting is basic to impact prediction. A recent study for the Corps of Engineers examined 150 techniques and selected and discussed 12 basic methods suitable for a wide range of technological, economic, social and environmental forecasting. The general characteristics of the 12 methods are compared in Tables 26-29 (pages 116-119). Brief descriptions of the 12 methods are a follows:

1. Trend Extrapolation

Trend extrapolation is the general name for a variety of mathematical forecasting methods all of which determine future values for a single variable through some process of identifying a relationship valid for the past values of the variables and a solution for future values. Although the technique is generally useful for only a single variable, this variable may be highly complex in that it may reflect numerous trends.

2. Pattern Identification

Forecasting methods based on pattern identification seek to recognize a development pattern in historical data and to use this often obscure pattern as the basis of forecasting future events. The method is useful both for time-series data, where more direct extrapolating methods do not work, and for interpreting numerous social trends.

3. Probabilistic Forecasting

Many phenomena for which forecasts are needed appear to change randomly within limits. Probabilistic forecasting methods use mathematical models of such phenomena. Numerical odds are assigned to every possible outcome or combination of outcomes. On the basis of such assigned odds, predictive statements are made about the future behavior of the phenomenon studied.

4. Dynamic Models

Dynamic models of complex, nonlinear systems are extremely useful for forecasting futures resulting from interacting events. The simulation model, which is usually numeric, reveals the evolution of systems through time under specified conditions of feedback. By changing equations or adding interaction trends,

358

a large number of possible futures can be explored in computer runs. Dynamic models are also helpful in gaining qualitative insight into the interactions of system elements.

5. Cross-Impact Analysis

Cross-impact analysis strives to identify interactions among events or developments by specifying how one event will influence the likelihood, timing, and mode of impact of another event in a different but associated field. Cross-impact analysis is used not only to probe primary and secondary effects of a specified event, but to improve forecasts and to generate single forecasts (or scenarios) from multiple forecasts. Cross-impact analysis is a basic forecasting tool helpful, if not essential, in most sophisticated forecasting.

6. KSIM

KSIM is a cross-impact simulation technique used to better forecast and assess long-range requirements and impacts of water resource development alternatives. The technique provides a tool to interface broad planning issues with detailed dynamic models so that more effective use can be made of planning resources. Both qualitative and quantitative data can be used-- a unique characteristic. KSIM combines a small group workshop procedure with a mathematical forecasting model and a computer program to generate changes over time in a few significant planning variables. The method helps to identify planning needs, develop models, and test the consequences of policy actions. The technique requires expert leadership and access to a computer. A KSIM computer program is available.

7. Input-Output Analysis

Input-output (I-O) analysis is a means of inter-relating industry inputs and outputs in a single model, showing the consequences to all other sectors of a specified change in one. Different models deal with the nation, with regions, with specific industries and so on. I-O analyses are of great value in quantifying changes in a region's or subregion's commodity flows and likely industrialization patterns resulting from specific projects--such as improved navigational facilities or a new recreational site.

8. Policy Capture

"Policy capture" involves building a model that, given the same information the individual has, will accurately reproduce his judgments and hence his "policies". The goal is not simply to predict or reproduce judgments accurately; rather policy capture seeks to generate descriptions of the judgmental behavior that are helpful in identifying characteristic differences between individuals. It is felt that the judgmental process can be described mathematically with a reasonable amount of success.

9. Scenarios and Related Methods

Scenerios and related methods depend upon logical, plausible, and imaginative conjectures that are most properly regarded as descriptions of potential futures rather than as probabilistic forecasts of actual futures. Such methods, like all other qualitative methods, are most often used in conjecturing about complex, little-understood social phenomena for which more rigorous quantitative forecasting methods do not exist.

10. Expert-Opinion Methods

Expert-opinion methods include the use of panels, surveys of intentions and attitudes, and Delphi polls. It is emphasized that the definition of expertise as well as the limits to its use for forecasting purposes can be considered in terms of three aspects: topic, sponsor, and other eventual users of the study's end product. Expert-opinion methods may be used either for actual forecasts or to make conjectural explorations of potential futures.

11. Alternative Futures

Alternative futures methods of forecasting emphasize what may plausibly happen rather than what is predicted to happen. Study of an array of alternative futures is helpful in setting organizational long-term goals and policies, in charting primary strategies, and in developing contingency plans. It is pointed out that a given potential development may or may not occur; if it occurs, it may happen at any of many different times and may have any of many different potential impacts. Each unique combination of these and other variables constitutes a different alternative future. Morphological analysis and divergence mapping are discussed as examples of alternative futures methods. The techniques are best adapted to mid- and long-term planning.

12. Values Forecasting

Of all the techniques for looking ahead, values forecasting perhaps holds the greatest promise while to date it has yielded the fewest practical results. People's values (priorities, opinions, attitudes, and so on) are of crucial importance in judging what public actions and policies they will support. Data on these matters can be collected through survey methods.

Forecasts of changing values usually involve clustering values into a typology and forecasting on the basis of demographic shifts or broad societal scenarios.

Salient Features:

Literature survey on forecasting techniques.

Advantages/Limitations of Salient Features:

1. Field studies conducted---not applicable
2. Practical for field use---yes
3. Usage for various types/sizes of projects---yes
4. Objective vs. subjective approaches---objective
5. Reproducibility---unknown
6. Scientifically sound featues---yes

Conclusions:

Use directly in WRAM
..Mention impact prediction usage of forecasting techniques.

+ + +

REFERENCE:

Morrison, T.H., "Sanitary Landfill Site Selection by the Weighted Rankings Method", 1974, 31 pp., Master's Thesis, School of Civil Engineering and Environmental Science, University of Oklahoma, Norman, Oklahoma.

Abstract:

A weighting-scaling checklist for sanitary landfill site selection is described. The weighted rankings method was used for both weighting and scaling. The weighted rankings concepts are included in the interim WRAM report (Feb., 1977).

Salient Features:

Weighting-scaling checklist using weighted rankings technique is described.

Advantages/Limitations of Salient Features:

1. Field studies conducted---yes
2. Practical for field use---yes
3. Usage for various types/sizes of projects---yes
4. Objective vs. subjective approaches---objective
5. Reproducibility---unknown

6. Scientifically sound features---yes

<u>Conclusions</u>:

General reference for WRAM

+ + +

<u>REFERENCE</u>:

Muller, T., "Fiscal Impacts of Land Development", URI 98000, 1975, 68 pp., The Urban Institute, Washington, D.C.

<u>Abstract</u>:

A large number of recent studies attempt to assess what the likely fiscal effects of proposed private development will be. That is, will the developments generate revenues in excess of the needed public expenditures or vice versa? The author surveys the studies of this question to determine the present state of the art and to suggest refinements aimed at improving future fiscal impact evaluation. Techniques applied in the studies reviewed range from simple, one-dimensional methods to complex econometric models. The determination of which technique to select depends on study objectives and available resources. However, since there are only limited data available based on retrospective analysis, the reliability of techniques reviewed have not yet been adequately assessed. Given the limited state of knowledge, the most effective approach is to estimate, directly by the use of surveys or indirectly from secondary sources, the likely demographic and income characteristics of new residents by type of housing. These data can be applied to estimate both revenues expected to accrue and anticipated demand for public services.

<u>Salient Features</u>:

Presentation of fiscal impact prediction technologies.

<u>Advantages/Limitations of Salient Features</u>:

1. Field studies conducted---yes
2. Practical for field use---yes
3. Usage for various types/sizes of projects---yes
4. Objective vs. subjective approaches---objective
5. Reproducibility---unknown
6. Scientifically sound features---yes

<u>Conclusions</u>:

Use directly in WRAM
..Mention under impact prediction technologies.

362

REFERENCE:

Nelson, K.E., and LaBelle, S.J., "Handbook for the Review of Airport Environmental Impact Statements", ANL/ES-46, July, 1975, 159 pp., Argonne National Laboratory, Argonne, Ill.

Abstract:

The principal objective of this report is to supply airport planners and reviewing agencies with guidelines for the technical review of airport environmental impact statements. The guidelines contain both procedural and technical guidance for the comprehensive review of air, noise, water and wastewater, solid waste, land use, hazardous materials, and ecological impacts. Information pertinent to WRAM includes a discussion of an air quality box model and three stormwater runoff models. Basically, the box model assumes that all the emission sources in a defined area are dispersed into a given volume of air (i.e., a box). This concept would be useful in assessing construction phase impacts for a water resources project. The three stormwater models which are addressed are the Urban Storm Water Runoff Model (STORM) by the Army Corps of Engineers; the Storm Water Management Model (SWMM) by the U.S. Environmental Protection Agency; and the Hydrologic Simulation Program (HSP), a proprietary model of Hydrocomp International, Inc.

Salient Features:

Air quality box model and three stormwater runoff models are described.

Advantages/Limitations of Salient Features:

1. Field studies conducted---yes
2. Practical for field use---yes
3. Usage for various types/sizes of projects---yes
4. Objective vs. subjective approaches---objective
5. Reproducibility---unknown
6. Scientifically sound features---yes

Conclusions:

General reference for WRAM

+ + +

REFERENCE:

Schlesinger, B. and Daetz, D., "Development of a Procedure for Forecasting Long-Range Environmental Impacts, Report to the

363

Resource and Land Investigations (RALI) Program, U.S. Geological Survey", Report No. USGS-LI-75-007, August 1975, Department of Industrial Engineering, Stanford University, Stanford, California (Report prepared for U.S. Geological Survey, Reston, Virginia).

Abstract:

This report presents a procedure for forecasting long-range environmental impacts of large scale projects. For present purposes, "long-range" refers to fifteen or more years, and "large scale projects" are major construction, mining, or other industrial or municipal undertakings with significant regional impacts. The overall goal of this forecasting procedure is to allow planners and managers to compare proposed development alternatives on a more uniform basis given available environmental knowledge and a set of assumptions about how a local environment will respond in the future.

The methodology entails combining a schedule of primary environmental impacts expected as a result of future activities with a matrix of environmental factor relationships. Each term in this "cross-impact" matrix relates a change in one factor in one year to a change in another factor the following year by a linear multiplier. An extended version of the matrix is proposed that contains additional terms to reflect the impact of several environmental factors changing at the same time. Thus, approximate forecasts for each of a set of environmental factors are produced that consider both direct and higher order impacts. A case study involving strip mining of coal in the northern great plains region of the United States is used to test the procedure's concept and formulation.

Salient Features:

Cross-impact matrix procedure for dealing with long-range impacts.

Advantages/Limitations of Salient Features:

1. Field studies conducted---yes
2. Practical for field use---yes
3. Usage for various types/sizes of projects---yes
4. Objective vs. subjective approaches---objective
5. Reproducibility---unknown
6. Scientifically sound features---yes

Conclusions:

Use directly in WRAM
..Mention cross-impact matrix

REFERENCE:

Sharma, R.K., Buffinton, J.D., and McFadden, J.T., editors,
Proceedings of the Conference on the Biological Significance
of Environmental Impacts, NR-CONF-002 (Conference held at the
University of Michigan, Ann Arbor, Michigan, June 4-6, 1975).

Abstract:

The following conclusions were drawn at the Conference:

(1) Definition of Biological Significance of Environmental
     Impacts
     The significance of environmental impacts can be defined
in a biological as well as in a socioeconomic context. In
the biological context, those impacts can be termed significant which, on being imposed on naturally occurring changes
in the ecosystem, modify the dynamics or hasten succession
in the communities. As such, all impacts resulting in measurable changes in indicator parameters of community dynamics
and succession (such as abundance, functional integrity,
species diversity, etc.) can be termed significant. Therefore, it follows that an impact is significant if it results
in a change that is measurable in a statistically sound sampling program and if it persists, or is expected to persist,
more than several years at the population, community, or
ecosystem level. Costs and benefits to society are taken into
consideration when a decision is made as to whether an impact
is acceptable or unacceptable in the social context.

(2) Objectives and Quality of Information

     Despite current emphasis on the ideal of collection of
ecological data which are relevant in impact analysis, much of
the research and monitoring being carried out today produce data
that are only marginally related to the evaluation of expected
impacts. More information does not necessarily mean better
assessment.

(3) Time Frame and Spatial Constraints

     The duration of preoperational and operational studies
should reflect the variability of data and expected intensity
of response due to impact. More time is needed to get a better
pulse of the system where data variability is high. Similarly,
more observations are needed to detect low-level chronic impacts
as opposed to catastrophic changes. The longer the time frame,
the more reliable the decision; however, the time frame and
spatial limitations should be decided on a site-by-site basis.
Relatively much more effort usually is allocated to data collection than to data interpretation. It is important that

365

adequate time and effort be allocated to the latter, as well.

(4) Role of Statistics

Changes in parameters of less than 50% often may not be detectable. Also, ideal statistical designs are not always applicable to impact-evaluation studies. Care should be exercised in biological interpretation of results obtained from statistical analyses. A clear definition of which parameters are relevant and what studies are necessary to detect changes is needed. If programs are designed with suitable hypotheses and adequate consideration for problems of environmental variability, need for replication, and adequate sample size, our capabilites for making predictive impact assessments will be significantly improved.

(5) The State-of-the-Art and Standardization of Techniques

In areas such as quantitative sampling gear, interpretation parameters, and assessment of assimilative capacity of ecosystems, the state-of-the-art needs substantial improvement. In other areas such as characterization of ecosystems, identification of indicator parameters, and design of impact studies, current state-of-the-art is adequate but there is not a high degree of uniformity in the approach.

(6) Species Lists and Diversity Indices

Detailed static descriptions of ecosystems such as species lists have very little value in impact assessment; however, they provide a mechanism for crude comparisons of before-and-after situations. The use of indicator species in impact assessment should be encouraged, but additional work is necessary to permit their most efficacious use. Diversity indices should be used with caution; they are not equivalent to an ultimate synthesis of information on the state of a system.

(7) Functional Stability of Communities

Insults to functional integrity of communities are likely to result in significant impacts. Qualitative changes up to a certain extent may not be significant if functional integrity is not impaired; however, it is not then certain how many species can be replaced without risking collapse of a community. Replacement of one fish species by another with similar functional value may be important in a social context because of perceived socioeconomic values.

(8) Assimilative Capacity and Compensatory Responses

Assimilative capacity is a function of inertia, resiliency, and elasticity of impacted communities. Inertia is defined as

366

the ability of a community or ecosystem to resist displacement
or disequilibrium in regard to either structure or function.
Resiliency is defined as the number of times a system can snap
back after displacement. And elasticity is defined as an ecosystem's ability to recover following displacement of structure
and/or function to a steady state closely approximating the
original. Assimilative capacity of a community should be considered and factored into the impact analysis. Compensatory
responses may be limited to the species population or may be
spread over the community impacted. Compensatory responses
are difficult to document on large systems (such as the Great
Lakes) and, as such, difficult to factor into impact analysis.
Nevertheless, certain generalizations can be included in the
analysis, e.g. for a given cohort, impacts at early stages of
life history before compensatory mechanisms have a chance to
operate are less significant than are impacts at later life-
history stages.

(9) Simulation Models

Use of simulation models is important in terms of provision of sharp focus on expected impacts and collection of relevant information in analysis of impacts. The predictive models
can evaluate assumptions where no hard data are available,
provide synthesis, and predict future impacts. Validity of
assumptions used in the models is important. However, what
is important biologically is not always mathematically tractable, and long-term predictions can be very unrealistic.

(10) Before v. After, Controlled v. Impacted

All ecosystems are dynamic and change naturally in time.
Therefore, any before-and-after comparisons should evaluate
changes as being superimposed on naturally occurring changes.
Where before-and-after comparisons are not possible, parameter
or indicator values at disturbed sites and at similar but undisturbed sites can be compared.

Salient Features:

Good summary of technical and philosophical state-of-the-
art of biological impact prediction and assessment.

Advantages/Limitations of Salient Features:

1. Field studies conducted---not applicable
2. Practical for field use---not applicable
3. Usage for various types/sizes of projects---not
    applicable
4. Objective vs. subjective approaches---objective

367

5. Reproducibility---unknown
6. Scientifically sound features---yes

Conclusions:

Use directly in WRAM
..Mention state-of-the-art summary.

+ + +

REFERENCE:

Summers, D.A., Ashworth, C.D., and Feldman-Summers, S.,
"Judgment Processes and Interpersonal Conflict Related to
Societal Problem Solutions", unpublished paper, 1975, Human
Affairs Research Center, University of Washington, Seattle,
Washington.

Abstract:

This paper describes an application of multi-dimensional
scaling to judgments about potential solutions to the overpopulation problem. The aims of the research were twofold:
(a) to identify the manner in which individuals make judgments
about the acceptability of potential solutions to the overpopulation problem, and (b) to ascertain the source of conflict (if any) between individuals when making such judgments.
In general, the results suggest that the conceptual and methodological framework employed was useful in meeting these aims.
The findings related to interpersonal conflict were in substantial agreement with previous findings--derived from quite
different judgment tasks--concerning the components of interpersonal conflict in judgment situations. Specifically, it
was found that disagreement between randomly selected pairs
was largely the result of inconsistency in the execution of
judgment policy, rather than actual policy difference. That
is, participants tended to use the dimensions in much the same
manner in making their judgments, but failed to do so in a
perfectly consistent fashion. Under such conditions, conflict
is inevitable--even though participants may hold identical
beliefs. These findings suggest that the disputes which arise
in connection with proposed solutions to some of our most
pressing problems may reflect not only different belief systems,
but also our cognitive limitations; i.e., our inability to
exercise full control over our judgment policies in complex
judgment situations.

Salient Features:

Study findings indicated that judgmental inconsistency
was likely to be a major cause of conflicts.

368

Advantages/Limitations of Salient Features:

1. Field studies conducted---yes
2. Practical for field use---unknown
3. Usage for various types/sizes of projects---yes
4. Objective vs. subjective approaches---objective
5. Reproducibility---unknown
6. Scientifically sound features---yes

Conclusions:

Use directly in WRAM
..Mention concept of finding cause of conflict as a basis
for conflict resolution.

+ + +

REFERENCE:

Thom, G.C., and Ott, W.R., "Air Pollution Indices --- A
Compendium and Assessment of Indices Used in the United States
and Canada", Dec., 1975, 165 pp., Council on Environmental
Quality, Washington, D.C.

Abstract:

This report presents the findings of a detailed survey of
air pollution indices that are presently utilized or available.
The survey included a review of the existing literature on air
pollution indices, telephone discussions with personnel from
the 55 largest air pollution control agencies in the United
States and Canada, and a case study of a three-State region
in which an attempt is being made to develop a uniform air
pollution index. These three data sources have enabled the
preparation of the most extensive compendium of air pollution
index material currently in existence. Two general types of
air pollution indices have been developed: (1) short-term and
(2) long-term. This study provides the first systematic analysis of the short-term indices that are used routinely by
local agencies and news media across the Nation to provide
the public with simple guides for assessing the severity of
local air pollution. Of the 55 metropolitan air pollution
control agencies surveyed in the United States, 33 routinely
used some form of short-term air quality index. However, it
was found that nearly all of the indices had different mathematical formulations and different meanings to the public.

Salient Features:

Concept of using an empirical index to assess existing
air quality and potential impacts.

369

Advantages/Limitations of Salient Features:

1. Field studies conducted---yes
2. Practical for field use---yes
3. Usage for various types/sizes of projects---yes
4. Objective vs. subjective approaches---objective
5. Reproducibility---yes
6. Scientifically sound features---yes.

Conclusions:

Use directly in WRAM
..Mention index

+ + +

REFERENCE:

Toussaint, C.R., "A Method for the Determination of Regional Values Associated with the Assessment of Environmental Impacts," 1975, 219 pp., Ph.D. Dissertation, School of Civil Engineering and Environmental Science, University of Oklahoma, Norman, Oklahoma.

Abstract:

This study was concerned with a determination of the applicability of a decision-making technique to the value judgment based decisions inherent in environmental impact assessment. Results of this study produced a measure of the applicability and reliability of a new tool for the environmental analyst. The decision-making technique, employed in this study, was the Delphi method of estimating, developed by the Rand Corporation, Santa Monica, California. Fourteen water pollution parameters of the Battelle-Columbus, Environmental Evaluation System, environmental assessment methodology were investigated for the proposed Aubrey Reservoir project in northern Texas. Environmental experts, representative of the central Oklahoma region of the country, via Delphic procedures, established regional values for the two judgment based decision currently necessary in environmental impact assessment. These two decisions were referred to as the weighting (determination of the relative emphasis or degree of importance each parameter is to be assigned in the assessment) and scaling (determination of the magnitude of effect resulting from a change in a parameter measure) process associated in impact evaluation. Separate Battelle Environmental Evaluation System assessments were performed employing regionally determined values. Results of these regional assessments were compared to results of an assessment based on values recommended by the Battelle research team. Comparison of these results revealed

370

that regional values were at variance with values employed by the Battelle research team and recommended for use in the Environmental Evaluation System assessment methodology for environmental impact. The Delphi method of estimating was found to be applicable to the regional determination of judgment based decisions associated with environmental impact assessment. A measure of the reliability of the Delphi Technique was obtained.

Salient Features:

Weighting and scaling of 14 water pollution parameters was established by the Delphi procedure using two separate groups of 9 experts.

Advantages/Limitations of Salient Features:

1. Field studies conducted---yes
2. Practical for field use---yes
3. Usage for various types/sizes of projects---yes
4. Objective vs. subjective approaches---objective
5. Reproducibility---yes
6. Scientifically sound features---yes

Conclusions:

Use directly in WRAM
.. Mention consensus of opinion reached by the groups.

+ + +

REFERENCE:

Troxler, Jr., R.W., and Thackston, E.L., "Effect of Meteorological Variables on Temperature Changes in Flowing Streams", EPA/660/3-75-002, Jan. 1975, 86 pp., Dept. of Environmental and Water Resources Engineering, Vanderbilt University, Nashville, Tennessee.

Abstract:

A mathematical model for predicting the change in water temperature in a flowing stream as a function of stream geometry and standard weather information was developed and tested. Five field tests were conducted on cold water released from hydro-power stations as it warmed up moving downstream over periods up to 38 hours.

Salient Features:

Mathematical model for stream temperature is presented.

371

Advantages/Limitations of Salient Features:

1. Field studies conducted---yes
2. Practical for field use---yes
3. Usage for various types/sizes of projects---yes
4. Objective vs. subjective approaches---objective
5. Reproducibility---unknown
6. Scientifically sound features---yes

Conclusions:

General reference for WRAM

+ + +

REFERENCE:

U.S. Department of the Army, "Handbook for Environmental Impact Analysis", DA Pamphlet No. 200-1, April 1975, 155 pages, Headquarters, Department of the Army, Washington, D.C.

Abstract:

This handbook presents recommended procedures for use by Army personnel in the preparation and processing of environmental impact assessments (EIA) and statements (EIS). The methodology basically consists of using an interaction matrix to identify potential impacts and generate a descriptive checklist. Examples of representative Army actions that might have a significant environmental impact are given in Table D-3 and guidance is provided in the identification of Army activities in nine functional areas: construction; operation, maintenance and repair; training; mission change; real estate; procurement; industrial activities; research, development, test and evaluation; and administration and support. Forty-six environmental attributes (assessment variables) are included in the methodology and listed in Table 30 (page 127).

Salient Features:

Definitions, measurement, and interpretation information is presented on 46 assessment variables (called environmental attributes) primarily associated with EQ account.

Advantages/Limitations of Salient Features:

1. Field studies conducted---yes
2. Practical for field use---yes
3. Usage for various types/sizes of projects---yes

372

TABLE D-3

REPRESENTATIVE ARMY ACTIONS WHICH MIGHT HAVE A SIGNIFICANT ENVIRONMENTAL IMPACT

1. Development or purchase of new type of aircraft or other mobile facilities or substantially modified propulsion system.
2. Development or purchase of new weapon system.
3. Real estate acquisition or outleases or permitting or exchange or disposal of real estate.
4. Major construction projects.
5. New installations.
6. Production, storage, relocation or disposal of chemical munitions, pesticides, herbicides and containers.
7. Use of pesticides or herbicides, when proposed for use other than in accordance with the label as registered.
8. Harvesting of timber, wildlife, etc. (significant amounts).
9. Intentional disposal of any substances in a significant quantity or on a continuing or periodic basis.
10. Mission changes and troop deployments which increase or decrease population in any area.
11. Major research and development projects and test programs associated with R&D projects.
12. Any action which, because of real, potential, or purported adverse environmental consequences, is a highly controversial subject among people who will be affected by the action, or which although not the subject of controversy, is likely to become a highly controversial subject when it becomes known to the public.
13. New, revised, or established regulations, directives, or policy guidance concerning activities that could have an environmental effect (e.g., training, construction, or mission change). Regulations, directives, or policy guidance limit any of the alternative means of performing the actions on this list. Broad programs which could indirectly affect other actions on this list (e.g., Volunteer Army Program, Energy Conservation Program, or Expansion of the Women's Army Corps).
14. Intentional disposal of any materials in the oceans or other bodies of water.
15. Large quarrying, timbering, or earth-moving operations.
16. Airfield and range operations for test or training purposes.
17. Constructing, installing, or maintaining fences or other barriers that might prevent migration or free movement of wildlife.
18. Approval of new sanitary landfills, incinerators, and sewage treatment plants and operation of existing facilities.
19. Existing or changes to master plans.
20. Construction or acquisition of new family housing over 25 units.

21. Dredging.
22. Exercises involving divisional or larger units on or off Federal property, or where significant environmental damage may occur regardless of unit sizes.
23. Exercises involving smaller units when the training involves non-Army property or there is a significant amount of heavy or noisy equipment involved.
24. New deployment or relocation or disposal of nuclear power plants.
25. Operation of existing or new government-owned production facilities.
26. Ammunition storage facilities, new or continuing operations, or transportation of ammunition.
27. Closing or limiting of areas that previously were open to public use; that is, roads or recreational areas, etc.
28. Activities that will or may increase air or water pollution or disrupt plant life on the real estate.
29. Construction on flood plains or construction that may cause increased flooding.
30. Fuel conversion or continued consumption of significant quantities of fuel in short supply.
31. Increase in energy requirements.
32. Channelization of streams.
33. New facilities for aircraft, increase in number of aircraft at existing fields, and operation of existing aircraft in significant numbers.
34. Activities in wetland areas.
35. Storage, use, and disposition of POL products.
36. Use, storage, and disposition of radioactive materials, other than as authorized in Title 10, code of Federal regulations.
37. Operation and maintenance of power-generating equipment.
38. Control of pest organisms such as birds or other animals.
39. Construction of roads, transmission lines, or pipelines.
40. Award or termination of major contracts for supplies of natural resources; e.g., coal, oil, etc.
41. Transportation and testing of chemical agents and munitions.
42. Determination of safety standards, especially quantity-safety distances.
43. Development or purchase of new types of equipment, other than mobile facilities and weapon systems.
44. Outdoor large-scale or controversial testing of newly developed systems or material.
45. Continued operation of existing facilities which are causing pollution.

4.   Objective vs. subjective approaches---objective
5.   Reproducibility---unknown
6.   Scientifically sound features---yes

Conclusions:

Use directly in WRAM
..Mention information available on the 46 assessment
variables.

+ + +

REFERENCE:

Vlachos, E., et al, "Social Impact Assessment: An Overview,"
IWR Paper 75-P7, December 1975, 117 pp., U.S. Army Engineer
Institute for Water Resources, Fort Belvoir, Virginia (pre
pared for IWR by Colorado State University, Fort Collins,
Colorado).

Abstract:

The report presents an overview of the basic assumptions,
priorities, methodological strategies and techniques, procedures of data collection, organization and analysis for
conducting social impact assessment as a part of the entire
project assessment process. The "checklist" of Table D-4
can be used as a starting point for establishing the framework of analysis and initial data, and the categories of
effects on the human community. One aspect of concern in
the SWB account is "quality of life". Some social indicators
of quality of life are shown in Figure D-1.

Salient Features:

Good listing of potential assessment variables for SWB
account.

Advantages/Limitations of Salient Features:

1.   Field studies conducted---not applicable
2.   Practical for field use---yes
3.   Usage for various types/sizes of projects---yes
4.   Objective vs. subjective approaches---objective
5.   Reproducibility---unknown
6.   Scientifically sound features---yes

Conclusions:

General reference for WRAM

374

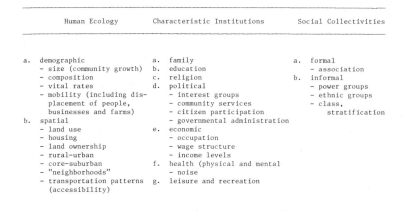

Human Ecology	Characteristic Institutions	Social Collectivities

a. demographic
  – size (community growth)
  – composition
  – vital rates
  – mobility (including displacement of people, businesses and farms)
b. spatial
  – land use
  – housing
  – land ownership
  – rural-urban
  – core-suburban
  – "neighborhoods"
  – transportation patterns (accessibility)
	a. family
	b. education
	c. religion
	d. political
	  – interest groups
	  – community services
	  – citizen participation
	  – governmental administration
	e. economic
	  – occupation
	  – wage structure
	  – income levels
	f. health (physical and mental)
	  – noise
	g. leisure and recreation
		a. formal
		  – association
		b. informal
		  – power groups
		  – ethnic groups
		  – class, stratification

TABLE D-4:   KEY STRUCTURAL VARIABLES IN HUMAN COMMUNITY

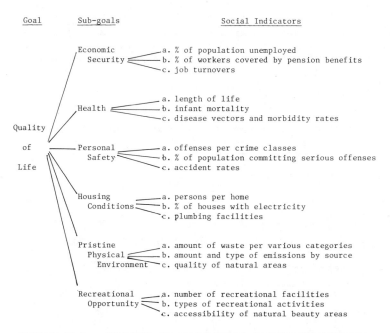

FIGURE D-1:   PROCESS OF DEVELOPING SOCIAL INDICATORS

REFERENCE:

Voorhees, A.M. and Associates, "Interim Guide for Environmental
Assessment: HUD Field Office Edition," June 1975, Washington,
D.C. (Report prepared for U.S. Department of Housing and Urban
Development, Washington, D.C.)

Abstract:

    An extensive scaling checklist approach, which also in-
corporates the concept of an interaction matrix to identify
potential impacts, has been developed for the Department of
Housing and Urban Development. All projects associated with
housing and urban development are subject to an initial
screening for the purpose of directing the evaluators to potential problem areas, highlighting the potential benefits and,
in general, organizing the total environmental assessment.
Higher level tests would be applied only in potential problem
areas; in most cases,these tests will demand particular professional expertise. The components and subcomponents of the
environment which are included in this methodology are delineated in Table 31 (page 128). The methodology utilizes a
basic interaction matrix to delineate the potential impacts of
various types of development projects on the 14 components of
the environment. Following the identifcation of potential
impacts, the HUD methodology provides additional information
on exactly how to address particular identified impacts. The
scaling system consists of the assignment of a letter grade
from A(+) to C(-). Specific information is provided on the
80 assessment variables in terms of standards/criteria/guide-
lines for assigning the scale values.

Salient Features:

    Scaling checklist with 80 assessment variables. Guidance
is provided on the assignment of "letter-scale" values for
impacts on the 80 variables.

Advantages/Limitations of Salient Features:

    1. Field studies conducted---yes
    2. Practical for field use---yes
    3. Usage for various types/sizes of projects---yes
    4. Objective vs. subjective approaches---objective
    5. Reproducibility---unknown
    6. Scientifically sound features---yes

Conclusions:

    Use directly in WRAM
    ..Mention "letter-scale" values.

APPENDIX E

INFORMATION ON 42 REFERENCES

FROM 1976 PERIOD

REFERENCE:

Adams, R. T., and Kurisu, F. M., "Simulation of Pesticide
Movement on Small Agricultural Watersheds," EPA/600/3-76/066,
Sept. 1976, 344 pp., ESL, Inc., Sunnyvale, California.

Abstract:

Simulation of Contaminant Reactions and Movement (SCRAM)
is a computer simulation designed to predict the movement of
pesticides from agricultural lands. SCRAM is composed of
deterministic submodels which describe the following physical
processes; infiltration, percolation, evaporation, runoff,
sediment loss, pesticide adsorption and desorption in the
soil profile, pesticide microbial degradation in the soil
profile, and pesticide volatilization. SCRAM predictions of
these physical processes are compared to experimental data
furnished by the Southeast Environmental Research Laboratory
in cooperation with the Southern Piedmont Conservation
Research Center. Simulated runoff for two small watersheds
(less than 3 hectares) near Athens, Georgia, agrees reason-
ably well with experimental data. Sediment loss is not as
accurately predicted. Predictions of pesticide loss in the
runoff and on the sediment are in reasonable agreement with
experimental data if allowance is made for the effects of
inaccurately predicting sediment loss.

Salient Features:

Model of pesticide movement from land is presented.

Advantages/Limitations of Salient Features:

1. Field studies conducted --- yes
2. Practical for field use --- yes
3. Usage for various types/sizes of projects --- unknown
4. Objective vs. subjective approaches --- objective
5. Reproducibility --- unknown
6. Scientifically sound features --- yes

Conclusions:

General reference for WRAM

+ + +

REFERENCE:

Boucher, W. I., and Stover, J. G., "An Annotated Bibliography
on Cross-Impact Analysis," Report 128-01-14, April 1972

(revised September 1976), The Futures Group, Glastonbury, Connecticut.

Abstract:

This bibliography provides a listing, in chronological order, of English-language publications on cross-impact analysis. The bibliography provides the user with information on the growth, applications, current status, and possible future development or uses of the technique. A total of 63 abstracts are included.

Salient Features:

Annotated bibliography of 63 references on cross-impact analysis.

Advantages/Limitations of Salient Features:

1. Field studies conducted --- not applicable
2. Practical for field use --- not applicable
3. Usage for various types/sizes of projects --- not applicable
4. Objective vs. subjective approaches --- not applicable.
5. Reproducibility --- not applicable
6. Scientifically sound features --- yes

Conclusions:

Use directly in WRAM
..Mention availability

+ + +

REFERENCE:

Canter, L. W., "Supplement to Facility Plan Report for Houma-Terrebonne Regional Sewerage Facilities," Aug. 1976, 62 pp., report submitted to GST Engineers, Houma, La.

Abstract:

A weighting-scaling checklist for selecting a waste-water treatment process is described. The weighted rankings method was used for both weighting and scaling. The weighted rankings concepts are included in the interim WRAM report (Feb. 1977).

Salient Features:

Weighting-scaling checklist using weighted rankings
technique is described.

Advantages/Limitations of Salient Features:

1. Field studies conducted --- yes
2. Practical for field use --- yes
3. Usage for various types/sizes of projects --- yes
4. Objective vs. subjective approaches --- objection
5. Reproducibility --- unknown
6. Scientifically sound features --- yes

Conclusions:

General reference for WRAM

+ + +

REFERENCE:

Case, P. J., Edgmon, T. D., and Renton, D. A., "PUBLIC-A Pro-
cedure for Public Involvement," Range Science Series No. 22,
June 1976, 138 pp., Range Science Department, Colorado State
University, Fort Collins, Colorado.

Abstract:

This report is a concept paper and user's guide for
PUBLIC, a collection of quantitative procedures designed
primarily for use by public agencies who are attempting to
heighten and improve the public input into their decision
processes. Although professional public agency administrators
recognize that public input into the decision processes of
the agency is necessary and even desirable, there is general
concern over how to utilize public input in a clear and
straightforward fashion, and also a concern about how to
maintain competent professional input simultaneously with
public input. The PUBLIC procedure outlined here attempts to
clarify the collection and analysis of public opinion data,
and also shows how such data can be utilized to examine the
correspondence between agency staff specialists and various
public opinions in such a way that professional advice and
public opinion can be more harmoniously meshed. This report
also includes a description of how to utilize the various
computer programs, which are primarily multivariate statistical techniques, included in the PUBLIC package, and a listing
of the computer programs and example problems. The programs
have been developed in American National Standards Institute
FORTRAN IV and should be operable on any computer with a
FORTRAN IV compiler.

381

Salient Features:

Public participation concepts are described

Advantages/Limitations of Salient Features:

1. Field studies conducted --- yes
2. Practical for field use --- yes
3. Usage for various types/sizes of projects --- yes
4. Objective vs. subjective approaches --- objective
5. Reproducibility --- unknown
6. Scientifically sound features --- yes

Conclusions:

General reference for WRAM

+ + +

REFERENCE:

Chase, G. H., "Matrix Techniques in the Evaluation of Environmental Impacts," Ch. 10 in Blissett, M. (editor), "Environmental Impact Assessment," 1976, Engineering Foundation, New York, New York, pp. 131-151.

Abstract:

Several types and examples of interaction matrices are described. Advantages and limitations of matrix techniques are summarized.

Salient Features:

Summarizes several examples of the use of interaction matrices.

Advantages/Limitations of Salient Features:

1. Field studies conducted --- yes
2. Practical for field use --- yes
3. Usage for various types/sizes of projects --- yes
4. Objective vs. subjective approaches --- objective
5. Reproducibility --- unknown
6. Scientifically sound features --- yes

Conclusions:

General reference for WRAM

+ + +

REFERENCE:

Christensen, K., "Social Impacts of Land Development," URI
15700, Sept., 1976, 144 pp., The Urban Institute, Washington,
D.C.

Abstract:

Proposals for land developments frequently generate
charges that the development will ruin a cohesive neighborhood. Yet decision makers often have little reliable empirical information on how proposed developments will change
residents' satisfaction with their area. This report suggests
techniques for assessing social impacts. It focuses on seven
areas in which the physical environment can affect the way
people live and interact with one another: recreation
patterns at public facilities; recreational use of informal
outdoor space; shopping opportunities; pedestrian dependency
and mobility; perceived quality of the natural environment;
personal safety and privacy; and esthetic and cultural values.
Methods of measuring impacts on different population groups
separately and of identifying alternatives that may ease any
negative impacts are recommended. The methodology which is
used is basically a descriptive checklist.

Salient Features:

Good summary of the social impacts of land development
projects.

Advantages/Limitations of Salient Features:

1. Field studies conducted --- not applicable
2. Practical for field use --- yes
3. Usage for various types/sizes of projects --- yes
4. Objective vs. subjective approaches --- objective
5. Reproducibility --- unknown
6. Scientifically sound features --- yes

Conclusions:

General reference for WRAM

+ + +

REFERENCE:

Clark, R. N., Hendee, J. C., and Stankey, G. H., "Codinvolve:
A Tool for Analyzing Public Input to Resource Decisions,"
Ch. 8 (pp. 145-165) in Pierce, J. C. and Doerksen, H. R.,

Water Politics and Public Involvement, 1976, Ann Arbor
Science Publishers, Inc., Ann Arbor, Michigan.

Abstract:

This paper describes a public participation program
developed by the U.S. Forest Service in 1972. Five main
processes are a part of any public involvement effort;
issue definition, public input collection (several techniques
should be used), analysis, evaluation and decision implementation. The relationships of these processes are shown in
Fig. 6 (page 143).
Codinvolve is the name given to the orderly and systematic transfer of information from any type of written input
to a form that is easy to summarize for review. The steps in
Codinvolve are shown in Fig. 7 (page 174). Codinvolve has been
used in over 75 studies to analyze more than 100,000 public
inputs. A case study is described in this paper.

Salient Features:

Conceptual framework and procedure for public involvement in environmental decision-making.

Advantages/Limitations of Salient Features:

1. Field studies conducted --- yes
2. Practical for field use --- yes
3. Usage for various types/sizes of projects --- yes
4. Objective vs. subjective approaches --- objective
5. Reproducibility --- unknown
6. Scientifically sound features --- yes

Conclusions:

Use directly in WRAM
..Mention concepts and approaches.

+ + +

REFERENCE:

(a) Coates, J. F., "The Role of Formal Models in Technology
Assessment," Technological Forecasting and Social Change,
Vol. 9, 1976, pp. 139-190.

Abstract:

This paper reviews the application of formal models to
each of the ten principal elements in a technology assessment.

The ten elements are shown in Fig. 8 (page144). A model is taken to be any systematic interrelationship of elements and components into a system which is intended to parallel in structure, form and function some real world system. Obviously this definition includes mental models, but it is intended primarily to focus on physical, social, biological, organizational and institutional models. The paper concludes that the application of formal models to technology assessment has been most successful in those areas where formal models have already been developed for other reasons, for example for understanding physical transport in air, water, and terrain. Formal modelling of physical systems, engineering systems, economic modelling in terms of engineering costs and economics, benefit/cost evaluations, and macroeconometric modelling are likely to continue to be central to most assessments. Relatively little or no use has been made of formal biological, psychological, or social science models.

Salient Features:

Selected impact prediction models are discussed.

Advantages/Limitations of Salient Features:

1. Field studies conducted --- yes
2. Practical for field use --- yes
3. Usage for various types/sizes of projects --- yes
4. Objective vs. subjective approaches --- objective
5. Reproducibility --- unknown
6. Scientifically sound features --- yes

Conclusions:

Use directly in WRAM
..Mention as general reference for impact prediction.

+ + +

REFERENCE:

(b) Coates, J. F., "Some Methods and Techniques for Comprehensive Impact Assessment," Ch. 9 in Blisset, M. (editor), "Environmental Impact Assessment," 1976, Engineering Foundation, New York, New York, pp. 103-130.

Abstract:

Some methods and techniques used in technology assessments and potentially useful in EIA's/EIS's are described. Methods and techniques which are briefly described include

385

Delphi, cross-impact analysis, trend extrapolation, checklists, morphological analysis, decision and relevance trees,
economic techniques, systems analysis, simulation, modeling,
physical modeling, scenarios and games, moot courts, participation techniques and technologies, survey techniques,
decision theory, scaling, brainstorming, graphics, and
judgment theory.

Salient Features:

Survey of some potential methods and techniques useful
for impact assessment is presented.

Advantages/Limitations of Salient Features:

1. Field studies conducted --- yes
2. Practical for field use --- yes
3. Usage for various types/sizes of projects --- yes
4. Objective vs. subjective approaches --- objective
5. Reproducibility --- unknown
6. Scientifically sound features --- yes

Conclusions:

Use directly in WRAM
..Mention general survey.

+ + +

REFERENCE:

Colonell, J. M., "Field Evaluation of a Predictive Model for
Thermal Stratification in Lakes and Reservoirs," OWRT-B-201-
MASS(2), Jan. 1976, 215 pp., Water Resources Research Center,
University of Massachusetts, Amherst, Massachusetts.

Abstract:

The major portion of this work was devoted to experimental investigation of the response of a reservoir to
hydrologic and meterologic influences. For this purpose an
automatic data collection system was designed and constructed.
Five meteorologic parameters (solar and long wave radiation,
mean wind speed, air temperature, and relative humidity) were
monitored. Surveillance of the thermodynamic state of the
reservoir was maintained by thermal surveys at intervals of
seven to ten days throughout the field observational season.
In addition, effort was devoted to the evaluation of a
mathematical model for prediction of the thermodynamic and
hydrodynamic behaviour of a reservoir in response to climatic
influences.

Salient Features:

Field studies to develop predictive model for thermal stratification are described.

Advantages/Limitations of Salient Features:

1. Field studies conducted --- yes
2. Practical for field use --- unknown
3. Usage for various types/sizes of projects --- yes
4. Objective vs. subjective approaches --- objective
5. Reproducibility --- unknown
6. Scientifically sound features --- yes

Conclusions:

General reference for WRAM

+ + +

REFERENCE:

Curran Associates, Inc., "Guidelines for Review of Environmental Impact Statements --- Vol. IV, Channelization Projects," July 1976, Northhampton, Mass. (Submitted to U.S. Environmental Protection Agency, Washington, D.C.).

Abstract:

This report contains a descriptive presentation of information on the primary impacts of channelization projects. It was written to provide a detailed framework for EPA's review of channelization project EIS's. It would be useful to preparers of channelization project EIS's as a descriptive checklist methodology.

Salient Features:

Contains qualitative/quantitative discussion of the primary impacts of channelization projects.

Advantages/Limitations of Salient Features:

1. Field studies conducted --- not applicable
2. Practical for field use --- not applicable
3. Usage for various types/sizes of projects --- yes
4. Objective vs. subjective approaches --- objective
5. Reproducibility --- unknown
6. Scientifically sound features --- yes

Conclusions:

        Use directly in WRAM
                ..Mention availability of descriptive checklist for
        channelization projects.

                                + + +

REFERENCE:

Darnell, R. M., et al, "Impacts of Construction Activities in
Wetlands of the United States," EPA-600/3-76-045, April 1976,
392 pp., U. S. Environmental Protection Agency, Washington,
D. C. (prepared for EPA by Tereco Corporation, College Station,
Texas).

Abstract:

        This report contains an extensive literature survey of
construction impacts on wetlands. It is a useful document as
an aid to impact identification. The primary types of construction activity which severely impact wetland environments of
the United States include: floodplain surfacing and drainage, mining, impoundment, canalization, dredging and channelizatic
and bank and shoreline construction. Each type of construction activity is attended by an identifiable suite of physical
and chemical alterations of the wetland environment which
may extend for many miles from the site of construction and may
persist for many years. In turn, each type of physical and
chemical modification has been shown to induce a derived set of
biological effects, many of which are predictable, in general,
if not in specific detail. The most environmentally damaging
effects, of construction activities in wetland areas, in order
of importance, are: direct habitat loss, addition of suspended
solids, and modification of water levels and flow regimes.
Major construction-related impacts also derive from altered
water temperature, pH, nutrient levels, oxygen, carbon dioxide,
hydrogen sulfide, and certain pollutants such as heavy metals,
radioactive isotopes, and pesticides.

Salient Features:

        Good literature survey of construction impacts on wetlands.

Advantages/Limitations of Salient Features:

        1.   Field studies conducted --- not applicable
        2.   Practical for field use --- not applicable
        3.   Usage for various types/sizes of projects --- not applica
        4.   Objective vs. subjective approaches --- objective

                                388

5. Reproducibility --- not applicable
6. Scientifically sound features --- yes

Conclusions:

    Use directly in WRAM
       .. Mention availability for impact identification.

+ + +

REFERENCE:

Edwards, W., "How to Use Multi-Attribute Utility Measurement for Social Decision Making," SSRI Research Report 76-3, August 1976, 67 pp., Social Science Research Institute, University of Southern California, Los Angeles, California (prepared for Advanced Research Projects Agency, U. S. Department of Defense, Arlington, Va.).

Abstract:

The thrust of this paper is that a public value is a value assigned to an outcome by a public, usually by means of some public institution that does the evaluating. This amounts to treating "a public" as a sort of organism whose values can be elicited by some appropriate adaptation of the methods already in use to elicit individual values. Multi-attribute utility measurement can spell out explicitly what the values of each participant (decisionmaker, expert, pressure group, government, etc.) are, show how much they differ, and in the process can frequently reduce the extent of such differences. The ten steps in the multi-attribute utility measurement technique include:
    <u>Step 1:</u> Identify the person or organization whose utilities are to be maximized. If, as is often the case, several organizations have stakes and voices in the decision, they must all be identified.
    <u>Step 2:</u> Identify the issues (i.e., decision) to which the utilities needed are relevant.
    <u>Step 3:</u> Identify the entities to be evaluated. Formally, they are outcomes of possible actions. But in a sense, the distinction between an outcome and the opportunity for further actions is usually fictitious.
    <u>Step 4:</u> Identify the relevant dimensions of value for evaluation of the entitites. Goals ordinarily come in hierarchies, but it is often practical and useful to ignore their hierarchical structure, and instead to specify a simple list of goals that seem important for the purpose at hand. It is important not to be to expansive at this stage. The number of relevant dimensions of value should be modest, for reasons that will be apparent shortly.

Step 5: Rank the dimensions in order of importance. This ranking job, like Step 4, can be performed either by an individual or by representatives of conflicting values acting separately or by those representatives acting as a group.

Step 6: Rate dimensions in importance, preserving ratios. To do this, start by assigning the least important dimension an importance of 10. Now consider the next-least-important dimension. How much more important (if at all) is it than the least important? Asign it a number that reflects that ratio. Continue up the list, checking each set of implied ratios as each new judgment is made. Thus, if a dimension if assigned a weight of 20, while another is assigned a weight of 80, it means that the 20 dimension of 1/4 as important as the 80 dimension, and so on, By the time you get to the most important dimensions, there will be many checks to perform; typically, respondents will want to revise previous judgments to make them consistent with present ones.

Step 7: Sum the importance weights, divide each by the sum. and multiply by 100. This is a purely computational step which converts importance weights into numbers that, mathematically, are rather like probabilities. The choice of a 1-to-100 scale is, of course, completely arbitrary.

Step 8: Measure the location of each entity being evaluated on each dimension. The word "measure" is used rather loosely here. There are three classes of dimensions: purely subjective, partly subjective, and purely objective. The purely subjective dimensions are perhaps the easiest; you simply get an appropriate expert to estimate the position of the entity on that dimension on a 0-to-100 scale, where 0 is defined as the minimum plausible value and 100 is defined as the maximum plausible value. Note "minimum and maximum plausible" rather than "minimum and maximum possible." The minimum plausible value often is not total absence of the dimension. A partly subjective dimension is one in which the units of measurement are objective, but the locations of the entities must be subjectively estimated. A purely objective dimension is one that can be measured non-judgmentally, in objective units, before the decison. For partly or purely objective dimensions, it is necessary to have the estimators provide not only values for each entity to be evaluated, but also minimum and maximum plausible values, in the natural units of each dimension.

Step 9: Calculate utilities for entities. The equation is:

$$U_i = \sum_j w_j u_{ij},$$

remembering that $\sum_j w_j = 100$. U_i is the aggregate utility for the ith entity. w_j is the normalized importance weight of the jth dimension of the value, and u_{ij} is the rescaled position of the ith enitiy on the jth dimension. Thus w_j is the output of Step 7 and u_{ij} is the output of Step 8. The equation, of course, is nothing more than the formula for a weighted average.

390

Step 10: Decide. If a single act is to be chosen, the rule is simple: maximize U_i. If a subset of i is to be chosen, then the subset for which $^i\Sigma_i U_i$ is maximum is best.

Salient Features:

Multi-attribute utility measurement technique for assigning importance weights.

Advantages/Limitations of Salient Features:

1. Field studies conducted --- yes
2. Practical for field use --- yes
3. Usage for various types/sizes of projects --- yes
4. Objective vs. subjective approaches --- objective
5. Reproducibility --- unknown
6. Scientifically sound features --- yes

Conclusions:

Use directly in WRAM
..Mention this technique for assigning importance weights.

+ + +

REFERENCE:

Engineering Division, Scottish Development Department, "Development of a Water Quality Index," Report No. ARD 3, December 1976, 62 pp., Edinburgh, Scotland.

Abstract:

A study was conducted from 1973-76 to examine the possibility of improving river water quality classification systems. A water quality index comprised of 10 parameters was developed. Six different formulations for developing an index were considered, with the geometric weighted index being the one of choice. The 10 parameters include DO, BOD, NH3, pH, total oxidized N, PO4(ortho), SS, temperature, conductivity and Escherichia coli. Importance weights on a relative basis were assigned to the 10 parameters, and functional curves are included for each. The functional curves are used to determine a water quality rating of from 0 to 100 for each parameter.

Salient Features:

Good discussion of concepts and development of a water quality index.

Advantages/Limitations of Salient Features:

1. Field studies conducted --- yes
2. Practical for field use --- yes
3. Usage for various types/sizes of projects --- yes
4. Objective vs. subjective approaches --- objective
5. Reproducibility --- unknown
6. Scientifically sound features --- yes

Conclusions:

Use directly in WRAM
..Mention water quality index

+ + +

REFERENCE:

Fennelly, P. F., et al, "Environmental Assessment Perspectives,"
EPA-600/2-76-069, March 1976, 238 pp., U. S. Environmental
Protection Agency, Research Triangle Park, N. C. (prepared for
EPA by GCA Corporation, Bedford, Mass.).

Abstract:

The report: (1) defines environmental ·assessment (EA)
programs and their role in energy system development; (2) indicates data requirements of an EA; (3) outlines exemplary methodologies for acquiring the necessary data; (4) serves as a technology transfer vehicle by providing background information on
environmental monitoring and modeling, which can be used in EAs;
(5) summarizes the extent, quality, applications, and location
of existing information resources which can be used in the
planning of EAs; and (6) summarizes existing or proposed standards and criteria for evaluating air, water, and land based
pollution. The report includes: waste stream characterization
and pollution identification, indirect pollution associated with
energy system development, estimating the sphere of influence of
an energy system, evaluation of environmental impact, methodology for conducting source tests, use of dispersion models,
available data banks and information sources, and existing and
proposed environmental regulations. Each topic is explored to
the degree necessary to acquaint the user with current standards, sampling and analytical techniques, and environmental models. General discussions are supplemented where possible with
specific examples in order to clarify some of the concepts
presented.

Salient Features:

Contains useful information on impact prediction for air
and water environments.

Advantages/Limitations of Salient Features:

1. Field studies conducted --- unknown
2. Practical for field use --- yes
3. Usage for various types/sizes of projects --- yes
4. Objective vs. subjective approaches --- objective
5. Reproducibility --- unknown
6. Scientifically sound features --- yes

Conclusions:

General reference for WRAM

+ + +

REFERENCE:

Grimsrud, G. P., Finnemore, E. J., and Owen, H. J., "Evalua-
tion of Water Quality Models: A Management Guide for Planners,"
EPA/600/5-76-004, July 1976, 186 pp., Systems Control Inc.,
Palo Alto, California (prepared for EPA by Systems Control, Inc.).

Abstract:

The report is designed as a handbook specifically oriented to water quality and water resources planners and
managers. It presents a large amount of basic information
concerning water quality modeling including procedures for:
model evaluation, model selection, integration of modeling
with planning activities, and contracting modeling projects.
Planners without previous experience in water quality modeling may use the information and procedures included in the
handbook to determine whether a water quality model could and
should be used in a particular planning program, and which
specific model would be cost effective. This includes a
step-by-step procedure leading to the rejection or selection
of models according to specific project needs. The handbook
discusses the implications which accompany the decision to
model, including the needs for additional labor and special-
ized technical expertise which are generated.

Salient Features:

Presents summary information on water quality models for
impact predictions.

Advantages/Limitations of Salient Features:

1. Field studies conducted --- not applicable
2. Practical for field use --- not applicable

393

3. Usage for various types/sizes of projects --- not
    applicable
4. Objective vs. subjective approaches --- not applicable
5. Reproducibility --- not applicable
6. Scientifically sound features --- yes

Conclusions:

Use directly in WRAM
        ..Mention summary information and comparison of water
quality models.

+ + +

REFERENCE:

Gum, R. L., Roefs, T. G., and Kimball, D. B., "Quantifying
Societal Goals: Development of a Weighting Methodology,"
Water Resources Research, Vol. 12, No. 4, August 1976, pp.
617-622.

Abstract:

    Water resource use is related to "social goals" in the
Techcom methodology. This is a multiobjective planning methodology developed by a technical committee of the water resource
centers of 13 western states. In the context of this system
a weighting methodology is developed to measure preferences
regarding the attainment of postulated societal goals. The
Metfessel general allocation test was used to assign importance weights to social indicators. The test utilizes as a
basis the assignment of 100 points: the subject' either actually or symbolically manipulates units of the ratio scale of
cardinal numbers, so that his manipulation of the cardinal
numbers expresses his judgments of quantitative relations among
the items of a given dimension'. More specifically, subjects
are asked to distribute or allocate 100 points simultaneously
among all stimuli in question. The results of a survey of
2500 persons each in Arizona and New Mexico indicated that
societal goals can be quantified in a manner which provides
useful information to decision makers. By developing hierarchical goals, subgoal structures and measures of the lowest
level subgoals, preference weights can be developed and used to
provide measures of the attainment of all goals and subgoals
within the hierarchical structure. The estimation of preference weights for the general public and groups of the public
is possible by the use of the Metfessel general allocation
test to obtain measures of the preference for improvement in
subgoals

Salient Features:

Method of relative importance weight assignments using public participation is described.

Advantages/Limitations of Salient Features:

1. Field studies conducted --- yes
2. Practical for field use --- yes
3. Usage for various types/sizes of projects --- yes
4. Objective vs. subjective approaches --- objective
5. Reproducibility --- unknown
6. Scientifically sound features --- yes

Conclusions:

Use directly in WRAM
    ..Mention technique of importance weight assignments.

+ + +

REFERENCE:

Hammond, K. R., and Adelman, L., "Science, Values, and Human Judgment," Science, Vol. 194, October 22, 1976, pp. 389-369.

Abstract:

This paper describes a technique for integrating social value judgments and scientific judgments in decision-making. Social value judgments involving "policy capturing" are used for assinging relative importance weights to decision factors, while scientific judgments are used for scaling each alternative relative to each decision factor. Importance weights are elicited from the general public. Scaling is accomplished via functional curves. The degree of acceptability of each alternative is equal to the summation of the product of the importance weights and scale values. A case study involving use of the technique for conflict resolution is described. The specific case involved the selection of handgun ammunition by the Denver Police Department.

Salient Features:

Public participation for conflict resolutions.

Advantages/Limitations of Salient Features:

1. Field studies conducted --- yes
2. Practical for field use --- yes
3. Usage for various types/sizes of projects --- yes
4. Objective vs. subjective approaches --- objective

5. Reproducibility --- unknown
6. Scientifically sound features --- yes

Conclusions:

Use directly in WRAM (specific)
..Mention public participation

+ + +

REFERENCE:

Harrison, E. A., "Bioindicators of Pollution (A Bibliography
with Abstracts), "NTIS/PS-76/0868/OWP, Nov. 1976, 194 pp.,
National Technical Information Service, Springfield, Va.

Abstract:

The bibliography cites abstracts relating to the use
of microorganisms, animals, plants, and fishes to detect
air and water pollution. Some of the organisms discussed
are algae, bacteria, aquatic plants, oysters, snails, clams,
insects, annelida, amphibians, beaver and fungi. This updated
bibliography contains 189 abstracts, 22 of which are new entries
to a previous edition.

Salient Features:

189 abstracts of bioindicators of pollution are presented.

Advantages/Limitations of Salient Features:

1. Field studies conducted --- yes
2. Practical for field use --- yes
3. Usage for various types/sizes of projects --- yes
4. Objective vs. subjective approaches --- objective
5. **Reproducibility --- unknown**
6. Scientifically sound features --- yes

Conslusions:

Use directly in WRAM
..Mention availability of information on bioindicators.

+ + +

REFERENCE:

Harrison, E. A., "Ecosystem Models, Vol. 2, November, 1975 -
November, 1976," NTIS/PS-76/0904, Nov., 1976, National Technical Information Service, Springfield, Virginia.

Abstract:

The preparation and use of ecosystem models are covered
in this bibliography of Federally-funded research. Models
for marine biology, wildlife, plants, water pollution, microorganisms, food chains, radioactive substances, limnology,
and diseases as related to ecosystems are included. This
updated bibliography contains 76 abstracts, all of which are
new entries to the previous edition.

Salient Features:

76 abstracts on ecosystem models are described.

Advantages/Limitations of Salient Features:

1. Field studies conducted --- yes
2. Practical for field use --- unknown
3. Usage for various types/sizes of projects --- yes
4. Objective vs. subjective approaches --- objective
5. Reproducibility --- unknown
6. Scientifically sound features --- yes

Conclusions:

Use directly in WRAM
..Mention bibliography on ecosystem models.

REFERENCE:

Jain, R. K., Urban, L. V. and Cerchione, A. J., "Handbook for
Environmental Impact Analysis," Interim Environmental Planning Bulletin 11, June 1976, U.S. Department of the Air Force,
Washington, D.C. (prepared for USAF by the U.S. Army Construction Engineering Research Laboratory, Champaign, Illinois).

Abstract:

This publication is very similar to U.S. Department of
the Army DA Pamphlet 200-1 (April, 1975). The methodology
basically consists of using an interaction matrix to identify
potential impacts and generate a descriptive checklist. The
49 environmental attributes in the methodology are in Table
36 (page 148).

Salient Features:

Definitions, measurement, and interpretation information
is presented on 49 assessment variables (called environmental

attributes) primarily associated with the EQ account.

Advantages/Limitations of Salient Features:

1. Field studies conducted --- yes
2. Practical for field use --- yes
3. Usage for various types/sizes of projects --- yes
4. Objective vs. subjective approaches --- objective
5. Reproducibility --- unknown
6. Scientifically sound features --- yes

Conclusions:

Use directly in WRAM
..Mention information available on the 49 assessment variables.

+ + +

REFERENCE:

Jameson, D. L., "Ecosystem Impacts of Urbanization Assessment Methodology," EPA-600/3-76-072, July 1976, 249 pp., Corvallis Environmental Research Laboratory, U.S. Environmental Protection Agency, Corvallis, Oregon (prepared for EPA by the Institute of Ecology, Utah State University, Logan, Utah).

Abstract:

This report provides a review of existing ecosystem models and the impacts of urbanization on natural ecosystems. It has long been recognized that infrastructure development such as highways and wastewater treatment facilities affects urbanization. The placement of trunk sewers and highways affects the pattern of development and the capacity of these systems affects the rate of development in urban areas. EPA, therefore, asked the Institute of Ecology to review the International Biological Program (IBP) biome models to determine their usefulness in predicting ecological effects associated with urbanization and, to the extent possible, to develop simplified models to make such predictions. Access to IBP information has been freely provided by various IBP offices although some of the information has not been placed in completed reports and many of the models are in active stages of development. The summaries of the modeling efforts result from the study of internal documents, conversations with a number of the ecosystem modelers, the assistance of workshop participants, and the contributions of volunteers. The results of the work showed that at this point in time there was no model, no matter how sophisticated, that could be used

to predict the ecosystem effects of urbanization. There are,
however, models which are useful in predicting specific
effects from specific perturbations. To this end, a logical
sequence (space-time analysis) of exploring the potential
ecological effects associated with various aspects of urbanization was developed.

Salient Features:

Reviews ecosystem models.and the impacts of urbanization
on natural ecosystems.

Advantages/Limitations of Salient Features:

1. Field studies conducted --- yes
2. Practical for field use --- unknown
3. Usage for various types/sizes of projects --- unknown
4. Objective vs. subjective approaches --- objective
5. Reproducibility --- unknown
6. Scientifically sound features --- yes

Conclusions:

General reference for WRAM

+ + +

REFERENCE:

Keyes, D. L., "Land Development and the Natural Environment:
Estimating Impacts," URI 13500, April 1976, 128 pp., The
Urban Institute, Washington, D.C.

Abstract:

Land development may have a critical impact on the
quality of the air, on the quality and quantity of water, on
wildlife and vegetation, and on noise levels. Such development also may be in the path of landslides and other natural
disasters or contribute to their likelihood, as when excessive paving of large areas causes rapid runoff of rain and
subsequent flooding. This report, designed primarily for
developers, planners, and others involved in the evaluation
of land developments, presents specific information on how to
predict and assess impacts on air quality, water quality and
quantity, wildlife and vegetation, and noise. Tables 37-39
(pages 151-155) show costs and reliabilities for many of the
predictive techniques. The author recommends that local jurisdictions establish specific criteria for impact assessment.
This methodology represents a good descriptive checklist
approach.

Salient Features:

Contains a good summary of impact prediction and assessment techniques for the physical-chemical and biological environments.

Advantages/Limitations of Salient Features:

1. Field studies conducted --- not applicable
2. Practical for field use --- yes
3. Usage for various types/sizes of projects --- yes
4. Objective vs. subjective approaches --- objective
5. Reproducibility --- unknown
6. Scientifically sound features --- yes

Conclusions:

Use directly in WRAM
    ..Mention prediction and assessment techniques for physical-chemical and biological environments.

+ + +

REFERENCE:

Lehman, E. J., "Water Quality Modeling, Hydrological and Limnological Systems, Vol. 1, 1964-1974 (A Bibliography with Abstracts," NTIS/PS-76/0443/2ST, June 1976, 197 pp., National Technical Information Service, Springfield, Virginia.

Abstract:

These abstracts of Federally-sponsored research cover studies on models used to describe water quality. This covers models of the chemical, physical, biological, and hydrological processes important to water quality. Included are studies on the modeling of eutrophication, nutrient removal, pollutant dispersion, stream flow, heat dissipation, limnological factors, aquifer water quality, and water runoff quality. This updated bibliography contains 192 abstracts, none of which are new entries to the previous edition.

Salient Features:

192 abstracts of models of the chemical, physical, biological, and hydrological processes important to water quality.

Advantages/Limitations of Salient Features:

1. Field studies conducted --- not applicable

400

2. Practical for field use --- not applicable
3. Usage for various types/sizes of projects --- not applicable
4. Objective vs. subjective approaches --- objective
5. Reproducibility --- not applicable
6. Scientifically sound features --- yes

Conclusions:

Use directly in WRAM
..Mention bibliography for impact prediction.

+ + +

REFERENCE:

Lehmann, E. J., "Water Quality Modeling, Hydrological and Limnological Systems," Vol. 2, 1975-June 1976 (A Bibliography with Abstracts), NTIS/PS-76/0444/0 ST, June 1976, 103 pp., National Technical Information Service, Springfield, Virginia.

Abstract:

The abstracts contain information on models used to describe water quality. This covers models of the chemical, physical, biological, and hydrological processes important to water quality. Included are studies on the modeling of eutrophication, nutrient removal, pollutant dispersion, stream flow, heat dissipation, limnological factors, aquifer water quality, and water runoff quality. This updated bibliography contains 98 abstracts, 79 of which are new entries to the previous edition.

Salient Features:

98 abstracts of models of the chemical, physical, biological, and hydrological processes important to water quality.

Advantages/Limitations of Salient Features:

1. Field studies conducted --- not applicable
2. Practical for field use --- not applicable
3. Usage for various types/sizes of projects --- not applicable
4. Objective vs. subjective approaches --- objective
5. Reproducibility --- not applicable
6. Scientifically sound features --- yes

Conclusions:

    Use directly in WRAM
        ..Mention bibliography for impact prediction.

+ + +

REFERENCE:

Liu, B., and Yu, E. S., "Physical and Economic Damage Functions
for Air Pollutants by Receptors," EPA-600/5-76-011, September
1976, 160 pp., U.S. Environmental Protection Agency, Washington, D.C. (prepared for EPA by Midwest Research Institute,
Kansas City, Missouri).

Abstract:

    This study is primarily concerned with evaluating
regional economic damages to human health, material, and
vegetation and of property soiling resulting from air pollution. This study represents a step forward in methodological
development of air pollution damage estimation. It attempts
to construct essential frameworks of the physical and economic
damage functions which can be used for calculating comparable
regional damage estimates for the several important receptors
--human health, material, and household soiling--however
tentative the damage estimates may appear to be. More
importantly, aggregate economic damage functions instrumental
for transforming the multivarious aspects of the pollution
problem into a single, homogeneous monetary unit are tenta-
tively derived and illustrated. It is hoped that these
results will be of some use to guide policymakers as they
make decisions on the implementation of programs to achieve
"optimal" pollution levels for this country. Given the
experimental nature of the methodological and statistical procedures and the degree of uncertainty associated with the
study results, a great deal of caution should be exercised in
using the products of this research. The results of this
study are potentially useable in WRAM as a basis for functional curves for air pollutants.

Salient Features:

    Has information for interpretation of air pollutant
impacts.

Advantages/Limitations of Salient Features:

    1. Field studies conducted --- not applicable
    2. Practical for field use --- not applicable
    3. Usage for various types/sizes of projects --- not
        applicable

4. Objective vs. subjective approaches --- objective
5. Reproducibility --- unknown
6. Scientifically sound features --- yes

Conclusions:

General reference for WRAM

+ + +

REFERENCE:

Lower Mississippi Valley Division, "A Tentative Habitat
Evaluation System (HES) for Water Resources Planning," Nov-
ember 1976, U.S. Army Corps of Engineers, Vicksburg,
Mississippi.

Abstract:

This is one of the 8 methodologies mentioned in the
interim WRAM report (Feb., 1977). The methodology is a
weighting-scaling checklist with primary orientation to the
Environmental Quality account for water resources projects.
The methodology defines 6 habitat types in the Lower Mississippi Valley Division area, these are: freshwater stream,
freshwater lake, bottomland hardwood forest, upland hardwood
forest, open (non-forest) lands, freshwater river swamp,
freshwater non-river swamp. Each habitat type is described
in terms of several descriptive parameters as shown in
Tables 40 through 45 (pages 156-161). A critical component
of the HES system is the use of functional curves for each
of the identified parameters. Each curve was developed to
transform raw data, collected during the environmental
assessment phase of planning, into an index value between 0.0
(undesirable) and 1.0 (desirable). Each parameter is
assigned a weight which accounts for its relative importance
in describing habitat quality. The habitat types, parameters,
functional curves and importance weights were identified and
assigned in a joint study effort between about 20 biologists
from the Lower Mississippi Valley Division and the Waterways
Experiment Station. The product of the quality index and
importance weight yields a weighted score for each parameter.
These scores are summed and a final value is calculated which
represents the quality of that particular habitat. This procedure is repeated to arrive at an estimate of the quality of
each major habitat type occurring within the project area for
each alternative plan. The effects of various alternative
plans of development can then be compared by applying the
final values to the acreages of habitats for each alternative
considered.

Salient Features:

Weighting-scaling checklist using habitat approach is
presented.

Advantages/Limitations of Salient Features:

1. Field studies conducted --- yes
2. Practical for field use --- yes
3. Usage for various types/sizes of projects --- yes
4. Objective vs. subjective approaches --- objective
5. Reproducibility --- unknown
6. Scientifically sound features --- yes

Conclusions:

Use directly in WRAM

+ + +

REFERENCE:

MacKinnon, W. J., and Anderson, L. M., "The SPAN III Computer
Program for Synthesizing Group Decisions: Weighting Participants' Judgments in Proportion to Confidence," Behavior
Research Methods and Instrumentation, Vol. 8, No. 4, 1976,
pp. 409-410.

Abstract:

This paper describes the current capabilities of the
Social Participatory Allocative Network (SPAN) method of
collecting participants' judgments and synthesizing group
decisions. In particular, the SPAN III program can process
numbers expressing participants' judgments either with or
without processing secondary numbers indicating participants'
confidence in their judgments. Thus, it adds confidence
weighting to functions performed by two previous versions of
the SPAN program. The initial 1969 SPAN program processed
data obtained by permitting participants to vote both
directly for options (alternative solutions to problems, for
example) and indirectly by using other members as representatives. The program cumulated the numerical voting power
apportioned directly and also iteratively redistributed the
indirectly apportioned power according to the receivers'
voting pattern, until virtually all power had cumulated for
options. The 1973 SPAN II program introduced the processing
of numerical voting power cast by the method of magnitude
estimation. The SPAN III program incorporates these functions
of its forerunners.

404

Salient Features:

Computer program for summarizing participants' judgments on importance weighting.

Advantages/Limitations of Salient Features:

1. Field sutdies conducted --- yes
2. Practical for field use --- unknown
3. Usage for various types/sizes of projects --- yes
4. Objective vs. subjective approaches --- objective
5. Reproducibility --- unknown
6. Scientifically sound features --- yes

Conclusions:

General reference for WRAM

+ + +

REFERENCE:

McElroy, A. D., et al, "Loading Functions for Assessment of Water Pollution from Nonpoint Sources," EPA/600/2-76/151, May 1976, 444 pp., U.S. Environmental Protection Agency, Washington, D.C. (prepared for EPA by Midwest Research Institute, Kansas City, Missouri).

Abstract:

Methods for evaluating the quantity of water pollutants generated from nonpoint sources including agriculture, silver-culture, construction, mining, runoff from urban areas and rural roads, and terrestrial disposal are developed and compiled for use in water quality planning. The loading functions, plus in some instances emission values, permit calculation of nonpoint source pollutants from available data and information. Table 46 (page 162) summarizes the available information in the report. Natural background was considered to be a source and loading functions were presented to estimate natural or background loads of pollutants. Loading functions/values are presented for average conditions, i.e., annual average loads expressed as metric tons/hectare/year (tons/acre/year). Procedures for estimating seasonal or 30-day maximum and minimum loads are also presented. In addition, a wide variety of required data inputs to loading functions, and delineation of sources of additional information are included in the report. The report also presents an evaluation of limitations and constraints of various methodologies which will enable the user to employ the functions realistically.

Salient Features:

Good summary of available quantitative information on non-point source of water pollution.

Advantages/Limitations of Salient Features:

1. Field studies conducted --- yes
2. Practical for field use --- yes
3. Usage for various types/sizes of projects --- yes
4. Objective vs. subjective approaches --- objective
5. Reproducibility --- unknown
6. Scientifically sound features --- yes

Conclusions:

Use directly in WRAM
        ..Mention availability of information for impact
prediction.

+ + +

REFERENCE:

Muller, T., "Economic Impacts of Land Development: Employment, Housing, and Property Values," URI 15800, September 1976, 148 pp., The Urban Institute, Washington, D.C.

Abstract:

Land development can exert economic impacts in terms of employment, housing, and property values. Employment impact assessment involves estimating the number of jobs created by new development and the share of jobs taken by local residents; and consideration of unemployment and underemployment, employment from the regional perspective, secondary employment effects and future levels and types of employment. The information in this report represents a descriptive checklist methodology.

Salient Features:

Contains a discussion of economic impacts of land development in terms of employment, housing and property values.

Advantages/Limitations of Salient Features:

1. Field studies conducted --- not applicable
2. Practical for field use --- yes
3. Usage for various types/sizes of projects --- yes

406

4. Objective vs. subjective approaches --- objective
5. Reproducibility --- unknown
6. Scientifically sound features --- yes

Conclusions:

Use directly in WRAM
.. Mention availability of this descriptive checklist
methodology for economic impacts.

+ + +

REFERENCE:

Omernik, J. M., "The Influence of Land Use on Stream Nutrient
Levels," EPA-600/3-76-014, January 1976, 105 pp., Corvallis
Environmental Research Laboratory, U.S. Environmental
Protection Agency, Corvallis, Oregon.

Abstract:

An analysis of drainage area characteristics and stream
nutrient runoff data compiled for 473 non-point source-type
drainage areas in the eastern United States indicate that:
(1) Streams draining agricultural watersheds had, on
the average, considerably higher nutrient concentrations than
those draining forested watersheds. Nutrient concentrations
were generally proportional to the percent of land in agriculture. Mean total phosphorus concentrations were nearly
ten times greater in streams draining agricultural lands than
in streams draining forested areas. The difference in mean
total nitrogen concentrations was about five-fold.
(2) In general, inorganic nitrogen made up a larger
percentage of total nitrogen concentrations in streams with
larger percentages of land in agriculture. The inorganic
nitrogen component increased from about 27% in streams draining
forested areas to over 75% in streams draining agricultural
watersheds. The inorganic portion (orthophosphorus) of the
total phosphorus component stayed roughly at the 40% level
regardless of land use type.
(3) Differences in nutrient loads in streams associated
with different land use categories were not as pronounced as
differences in nutrient concentrations. Mean total phosphorus
export from agricultural lands was 3.7 times greater than that
from forested lands; mean total nitrogen export was 2.2 times
greater. Differences in magnitude between the relationships
of concentration to land use and export to land use appear to
be due mainly to differences in a real stream flow from
different land use types, and to a lesser degree, to differences
in the mean annual precipitation patterns and mean slope of
study areas.

Salient Features:

Contains information on nutrient runoff data compiled for 473 non-point-source-type drainage areas in the eastern United States.

Advantages/Limitations of Salient Features:

1. Field studies conducted --- yes
2. Practical for field use --- yes
3. Usage for various types/sizes of projects --- yes
4. Objective vs. subjective approaches --- objective
5. Reproducibility --- unknown
6. Scientifically sound features --- yes

Conclusions:

General reference for WRAM

+ + +

REFERENCE:

Ott, W. R., Proceedings of the EPA Conference on Environmental Modeling and Simulation, Held at Cincinnati, Ohio on April 19-22, 1975, EPA/600/9-76/016, June 1976, 861 pp., Office of Research and Development, U.S. Environmental Protection Agency, Washington, D.C.

Abstract:

This national Conference was the first of its kind to cover the state-of-the-art of mathematical and statistical models in the air, water, and land environments. This report contains 164 technical papers on environmental modeling efforts in air quality management, air and water pollutant transport processes, water runoff, water supply, solid waste, environmental management and planning, environmental economics, environmental statistics, ecology, noise, radiation, and health. The Conference was directed toward the technical and administrative communities faced with the need to make environmental decisions and predict future environmental phenomena.

Salient Features:

Summary of modeling efforts for impact prediction on the physical-chemical environment.

Advantages/Limitations of Salient Features:

1. Field studies conducted --- not applicable

408

2. Practical for field use --- not applicable
3. Usage for various types/sizes of projects --- not applicable
4. Objective vs. subjective approaches --- objective
5. Reproducibility --- unknown
6. Scientifically sound features --- yes

Conclusions:

Use directly in WRAM
..Mention summary of impact prediction methods for physical-chemical environment.

+ + +

REFERENCE:

Reid, G. W., "Research to Develop Ecological Standards for Water Resources," July 1976, 304 pp., Bureau of Water and Environmental Resources Research, University of Oklahoma, Norman, Oklahoma (prepared for U.S. Office of Water Resources Research, Dept. of the Interior, Washington, D.C.).

Abstract:

This study was oriented to the development of ecological standards to assist in the evaluation of water resources development. Two steps were undertaken in this research. The first one is the categorization of development levels of natural environment by measuring specific socio-economic factors which are capable of delineating the human modification of the ecological system. The second one is the development of the ecological standards in response to various development levels so as to reflect the human influence on the ecological system. Three levels of development were identified in this study to represent the environmental condition of the region under consideration. The least disturbed environments are designated as Level I areas. A Level I area is assigned the strictest ecological standards in order to preserve the area for the enhancement and protection of wildlife and flora communities. The Level II areas are designated by an intermediate level of human involvement in the ecological communities. Frequently, this land may be used for agricultural or recreational purposes. The standards for Level II area are designed to allow more human interaction in the environment reflecting the necessity of utilizing ecological systems in these areas to assimilate the by-products of human society or to serve as a buffer zone to alleviate the tension man imposed on his environment. Areas where large concentrations of population are located are designated as Level III environments

and the standards applied to these areas should be more
tolerant of pollutants in the ecological systems. This
tolerance should not exceed the capacity of the ecological
systems in a region to assimilate society's by-products.
Specific information on each of 12 parameters, including
justification of the standards, is contained in the report.
The limitations of the ecological standards that were developed
stem from constraints on the project's scope, data acquisition
and reliance on institutional boundaries.

Salient Features:

Twelve ecological standards are proposed.

Advantages/Limitations of Salient Features:

1. Field studies conducted --- no
2. Practical for field use --- yes
3. Usage for various types/sizes of projects --- yes
4. Objective vs. subjective approaches --- objective
5. Reproducibility --- unknown
6. Scientifically sound features --- yes

Conclusions:

General reference for WRAM

+ + +

REFERENCE:

Ross, J. H., "The Numeric Weighting of Environmental Interactions," Occasional Paper No. 10, July 1976, Lands Directorate,
Environment Canada, Ottawa, Canada.

Abstract:

This report has two aspects relevant to the WRAM methodology. A component interaction matrix is shown in Figure 9
(page 164) and a disruption matrix is in Figure 10 (page 166).
The second aspect is a procedure for checking the consistency
of importance weight assignments using paired comparisons.
The consistency procedure is described as follows:
When using this technique, an individual who has been
requested to assess a number (N) of objects is presented with
every possible combination of these objects, and asked to make
judgments as to which of each pair is favored. His decisions
are recorded in a paired-comparison matrix. An entry (C_{ij}) of
"1" in this matrix denotes that the row object i (row stimulus)
was judged as being better, or more desirable, than the column

stimulus j. Once all possible pairs have been compared, and
the decisions recorded in the matrix, the ranking of stimuli
can be readily ascertained by summing the rows of the matrix.
The stimuli are ranked in order of these row sums. An example
comparison matrix is presented as Table 47 (page 165).

The correct ordering of the stimuli in this case is 5,
6, 1, 3, 2, and 4. When the paired-comparison matrix is permuted according to the ranking derived, a characteristic
pattern appears in which the upper right portion of the
matrix is observed to be composed of 1's, and the lower left
portion of 0's. See Table 48 (page 165).

In the foregoing example, the individual making the comparisons, hereafter termed the judge, has been perfectly consistent in his judgments. It reveals that he has a clear idea
of the stimuli, and that he has a good decision rule to follow
while making the individual paired comparisons. Such is often
not the case. Inconsistent judgments are revealed by the
presence of 1's below the diagonal in the permuted matrix. In
Table 49 (page 167), for example, the preference of the judge
for 4 over 5, 5 over 1, and 1 over 4 (generally denoted 4>5,
5>1, 1>4, and termed an intransitive triad) is revealed. It
is clearly a case of inconsistent judgment and may indicate an
unclear understanding of the stimuli, or a confused or poor
decision rule. It might also indicate that one attribute of
stimulus 1 was so far superior to that of stimulus 4 that it
became the sole determinant of the choice made in that particular
comparison. The paired-comparison technique permits and identifies inconsistencies that would be lost in more traditional
ranking approaches.

The degree to which the judge has been consistent can be
determined by calculating the coefficient of consistency (K)
as follows:

$$K = 1 - \frac{24d}{n^3 - n} \qquad \text{if n is an odd number}$$

$$\text{or...} \quad K = 1 - \frac{24d}{n^3 - 4n} \qquad \text{if n is an even number}$$

where n = the number of stimuli and,
where d = the number of intransitive triads observed

The value of K equals 1.0 when d takes a value of 0.0 (i.e.,
when there are no intransitive triads), and declines to 0.0, as
d approaches the maximum number possible. The number of intransitive triads (d) can be determined by inspecting each of the
n(n-1) (n-2)/6 triads individually, but in general, it is best
to compute its value from the equation:

$$d = \frac{T \max - T}{2}$$

where T = the sum of the squared deviations of the
row sums from their theoretically expected
values, and,

411

$$T \max = \text{the maximum possible } T = \frac{n^3-n}{12}$$

The expected number of 1's in each row of the matrix, assuming that the judgments are made randomly, is $(n-1)/2$. We can now extend Table 49 (page 167) as shown in Table 50 (page 169).

$$\text{Therefore } d = \frac{17.5 - 9.5}{2} = 4$$

$$k = 1 - \frac{96}{192} = .5$$

The interpretation of K is often difficult. Inspection of the permuted comparison matrix, Table 1, reveals that only one "1" is out of place, yet the number of incorrect judgments this involves (4), is high enough to bring the coefficient of consistency well down. The statistical significance of K must be assessed by comparing d to its expected distribution. A table for this comparison developed for $n<8$ reveals that $d = 4$ is significant only at the .792 level.

The chi square distribution, to which the distribution of d tends as n increases, is used to determine the probability of finding as few as d intransitive triads in a matrix where $n>7$. Chi square is found from the equation:

$$x^2 = 8/(n-4)\left|\tfrac{1}{4}((n(n-1)\ (n-2)/6))-d+\tfrac{1}{2}\right|\pm v$$

$$\text{where } v = (n(n-1)\ (n-2))/(n-4)^2$$

In this case, the probability of x^2 is the probability that an equal, or higher value of d would be found at random, rather than the inverse - as is usually the case.

The single-judge paired-comparison matrix may be extended to a multi-judge situation by summing the comparison matrices of a number of single judges to yield a group comparison matrix (Table 51, page 169). In such a case, one could hardly expect the level of unanimity to be as perfect as with a single judge matrix. However, this very fact later permits us to convert the ranking into a matrix scale, in which the stimuli are given real values rather than ranks.

Salient Features:

Concepts of cross-impact matrix and disruption matrix; checking procedure for consistency in paired-comparison technique for importance weight assignments.

Advantages/Limitations of Salient Features:

1. Field studies conducted --- yes
2. Practical for field use --- yes
3. Usage for various types/sizes of projects --- yes
4. Objective vs. subjective approaches --- objective

5. Reproducibility --- unknown
6. Scientifically sound features --- yes

Conclusions:

    Use directly in WRAM
      ..Mention disruption matrix and checking procedure.

+ + +

REFERENCE:

Schaenman, P. S., "Using an Impact Measurement System to Evaluate Land Development," URI 15500, September 1976, 106 pp., The Urban Institute, Washington, D.C.

Abstract:

    The methodology presented in this report is basically a descriptive checklist which contains 47 assessment variables shown in Table 52 (page 170). The report contains capsule summaries of the state-of-the-art of impact evaluation for each impact area listed in Table 52. Information is included on the methodology usage in Phoenix, Arizona, Indianapolis, Indiana, and Montgomery County, Maryland.

Salient Features:

    Descriptive checklist with 47 assessment variables for land development projects.

Advantages/Limitations of Salient Features:

1. Field studies conducted --- yes
2. Practical for field use --- yes
3. Usage for various types/sizes of projects --- yes
4. Objective vs. subjective approaches --- objective
5. Reproducibility --- unknown
6. Scientifically sound features --- yes

Conclusions:

    Use directly in WRAM
      ..Mention descriptive checklist.

+ + +

REFERENCE:

Springer, M. D., "Research for the Development of Guidelines for Conducting and Analyzing an Environmental Water Quality

413

Study to Determine Statistically Meaningful Results," Pub-37,
OWRT-A-033-ARK(1), 1976, 173 pp., Water Resources Research
Center, Univ. of Arkansas, Fayetteville, Arkansas.

Abstract:

     This report presents and discusses the basic statistical
models and methods which are useful to researchers in the
field of water resources research, as well as in other fields.
These models and methods are presented from the standpoint of
type (parametric and non-parametric or distribution free) and
purpose (e.g., simultaneous comparison of several means, comparison of two or more variances, establishment of a difference between two means with a specified confidence, etc.).
The material is presented with emphasis primarily upon methodology, including the necessary assumptions upon which each
model is based. No derivations or proofs are given, since
these are found in numerous textbooks on statistics readily
accessible to the reader. Emphasis is also placed upon the
need for the researcher to determine before obtaining data
the type of statistical model and analysis required, so that
he can use that model or method which is most powerful, and
so that he will have the proper data to permit the most
efficient analysis.

Salient Features:

     Presents information for planning a statistically signi-
ficant water quality study.

Advantages/Limitations of Salient Features:

1. Field studies conducted --- not applicable
2. Practical for field use --- not applicable
3. Usage for various types/sizes of projects --- not
    applicable
4. Objective vs. subjective approaches --- objective
5. Reproducibility --- not applicable
6. Scientifically sound features --- yes

Conclusions:

     General reference for WRAM

                         + + +
REFERENCE:

Thornton, K. W. and Lessem, A. S., "Sensitivity Analysis of
the Water Quality for River-Reservoir Systems Model," WES-MP-
Y-76-4, Sept. 1976, 53 pp., U.S. Army Engineer Waterways
Experiment Station, Vicksburg, Mississippi.

Abstract:

Most total ecosystem models require extensive data sets
for initializing and calibrating the model to the prototype
system. Data collection programs, however, are expensive and
time-consuming. To obviate these constraints, the data
collection program should be guided by a knowledge of the
model sensitivity to various initial conditions and coefficients. A software program was developed for the Honeywell
600 computer system that permitted an evaluation of sensitivity
of coefficients and initial conditions in the WQRRS model.
In general the model results were more sensitive to 10%
changes in coefficients at high nutrient concentrations than
at low nutrient concentrations. The model results were quite
sensitive to a 10% change in the evaporation and dispersion
(effective diffusion) rate coefficients, biota growth, res-
piration, and temperature rate coefficients. The nutrient
regime affected the sensitivity of the half-saturation coefficients and stoichiometric equivalences. Sensitivity
analyses perform a useful function in modeling programs.

Salient Features:

Sensitivity analysis for water quality model is presented.

Advantages/Limitations of Salient Features:

1. Field studies conducted --- yes
2. Practical for field use --- unknown
3. Usage for various types/sizes of projects --- yes
4. Objective vs. subjective approaches --- objective
5. Reproducibility --- unknown
6. Scientifically sound features --- yes

Conclusions:

General reference for WRAM

+ + +

REFERENCE:

Thronson, R. E., "Nonpoint Source Control Guidance, Con-
struction Activities," Dec., 1976, 122 pp., Office of Water
Planning and Standards, Environmental Protection Agency,
Washington, D.C.

Abstract:

The basic guidance information included in this nonpoint
source control document is principally technical in nature and

415

presented in four main chapters. They include information on the identification and assessment of existing construction nonpoint source problems; analysis and procedures needed for selection of controls; descriptions of individual and systems of Best Management Practices (BMP), with a method for determining their effectiveness; and several methods for predicting potential pollution problems from future construction activities.

Salient Features:

Provides information on construction phase non-point pollution control.

Advantages/Limitations of Salient Features:

1. Field studies conducted --- yes
2. Practical for field use --- yes
3. Usage for various types/sizes of projects --- yes
4. Objective vs. subjective approaches --- objective
5. Reproducibility --- unknown
6. Scientifically sound features --- yes

Conclusions:

General reference for WRAM

+ + +

REFERENCE:

U.S. Environmental Protection Agency, "Guidelines for Review of Environmental Impact Statements, Vol. 3, Impoundment Projects," Interim Final Report, July 1976, 147 pp., Washington, D.C. (prepared for EPA by Curran Associates, Inc., Northhampton, Mass.).

Abstract:

This report contains a descriptive presentation of information on the primary impacts of impoundment projects. It was written to provide a detailed framework for EPA's review of impoundment project EIS's. It would be useful to preparers of impoundment project EIS's as a descriptive checklist methodology.

Salient Features:

Contains qualitative/quantitative discussion of the primary impacts of impoundment projects.

Advantages/Limitations of Salient Features:

1. Field studies conducted --- unknown
2. Practical for field use --- yes
3. Usage for various types/sizes of projects --- various sizes
4. Objective vs. subjective approaches --- objective
5. Reproducibility --- unknown
6. Scientifically sound features --- yes

Conclusions:

Use directly in WRAM
..Mention availability of descriptive checklist for impoundment projects.

+ + +

REFERENCE:

Vlachos, E., and Hendricks, D. W., "Secondary Impacts and Consequences of Highway Projects," DOT/TST-77/24, October 1976, 332 pp., U.S. Department of Transportation, Washington, D.C. (prepared for DOT by Departments of Civil Engineering and Sociology, Colorado State University, Ft. Collins, Colorado).

Abstract:

The identification and analysis of secondary impacts resulting from transportation improvements is not only an important part of a larger comprehensive planning effort, but also a significant and necessary requirement of existing and emerging environmental legislation. This document attempts to delineate a consistent methodological framework and describe appropriate techniques that may make possible the definition, analysis and initial evaluation of the range of secondary impacts. Such an approach entails, ideally, a delineation, display and consideration of a consistent framework which relates values, goals and social policy options to proposed highway projects within the content of technological, environmental and institutional limitations. In addition, the present study raises a series of substantive questions concerning the ramifications of highway improvements in low density, undeveloped and environmentally-sensitive regions. The report contains the following chapters: Preface/Introduction, Basic Premises, System Description, Developing Data, Analyzing System Changes, Projecting Consequences, and the Cameron Pass (a case study). The impact assessment methodology is basically an ad hoc, descriptive checklist.

Salient Features:

A thorough presentation of the secondary impacts of high-way projects.

Advantages/Limitations of Salient Features:

1. Field studies conducted --- yes
2. Practical for field use --- yes
3. Usage for various types/sizes of projects --- high-way-related
4. Objective vs. subjective approaches --- objective
5. Reproducibility --- unknown
6. Scientifically sound features --- yes

Conclusions:

General reference for WRAM

+ + +

REFERENCE:

Wakeland, W., "QSIM 2: A Low-Budget Heuristic Approach to Modeling and Forecasting," Technological Forecasting and Social Change, Vol. 9, 1976, pp. 213-229.

Abstract:

The QSIM2 model serves primarily as a pedagogical or heuristic device to facilitate brainstorming and experimentation with hypothesis. The modeling process makes use of a FORTRAN program called QSIM2, which is inexpensive to execute, operates in a conversational mode, and has many features which give non-computer-oriented people the ability to easily create, exercise, modify and store the models that they design. The user is required to conceptualize: (1) a set of variables which describe the system; and (2) a collection of functional relationships (entered as tables) which describe how each variable is affected by each of the other variables. Given their initial values, projections for the future values of the variables can be made by entering and running the model on a computer. The specific modeling process involves the following eight steps:
Step 1: Defining the problem to be solved, e.g., improving a transportation system.
Step 2: Brainstorming the pertinent variables and establishing temporal and spatial system boundaries.
Step 3: Reducing the number of variables to a managable size by elimination and aggregation.

Step 4: Identifying the variables which affect each variable. The concept of an interaction matrix is useful, with rows representing the affected variables and columns representing the affecting variables. An "X" is placed in the matrix to indicate which of the interactions are significant. In a group effort, majority vote or consensus can be used. When in doubt, an "X" is written, since the magnitude of the interaction can be made slight when it is entered in Step 8.

Step 5: Identifying auxiliary variables. Thus far in this process it has not been necessary to distinguish between state and auxiliary variables. To simplify the construction of a preliminary model, one may disregard this distinction and proceed directly to Step 6, delaying the consideration of auxiliary variables until subsequent model refinements. There are several distinctions between state and auxiliary variables. The value of state variable is indirectly influenced by the values of other variables (by means of their impact on its rate of change), whereas the value of an auxiliary variable is directly influenced by the values of other variables. In order to determine the value of a state variable at some point in time its value at previous times is required. This is not true of auxiliary variables. State variables cannot change their values instantaneously, whereas auxiliary variables can. State variables are primary and fundamental; auxiliary variables are functions of state variables.

Step 6: Assigning the "initial values" and "base rates" for the state variables. As previously mentioned, state variables are not analytic functions of the variables checked in Step 4. Their values are obtained by numerical integration of their derivatives. In the QSIM2 implementation, the Euler approximation is used: $x(t+\Delta T)=x(t)+\Delta T\dot{x}(t)$, where x is a state variable, $\Delta T=$a short time period, and $\dot{x}(t)$ is the derivative of x, $\dot{x}(t)$ is the sum (or product, if desired) of the base rate and several terms.

Step 7: Specifying the functional form of the auxiliary variables identified in Step 5 (if any). Auxiliary variables can be either a polynomial of other variables or an extension of such a polynomial. For computational reasons, the auxiliary variables must be ordered in such a fashion that each depends only on state variables and previously specified auxiliary variables.

Step 8: Obtaining the "interaction functions." Each interaction function is a detail of an interaction specified by an "X" in the matrix. If data is available, it may be possible to use statistics to get these interaction functions. Otherwise, Step 8 involves extracting the appropriate relationships from the mental models. That is, lacking data, an intuitive approach is acceptable for defining interaction functions in a heuristic model.

419

Salient Features:

Simple modeling process for impact prediction.

Advantages/Limitations of Salient Features:

1. Field studies conducted --- yes
2. Practical for field use --- yes
3. Usage for various types/sizes of projects --- yes
4. Objective vs. subjective approaches --- objective
5. Reproducibility --- unknown
6. Scientifically sound features --- yes

Conclusions:

Use directly in WRAM
..Mention as impact prediction tool.

+ + +

REFERENCE:

Webster, R. D., et al, "The Economic Impact Forecast System: Description and User Instructions," CERL-TR-N-2, June 1976, 36 pp., Construction Engineering Research Laboratory, U.S. Army, Champaign, Illinois.

Abstract:

The Economic Impact Forecast System (EIFS) uses information from the Department of Commerce (Bureau of Census and Bureau of Economic Analysis); Department of Defense; and Department of Health, Education, and Welfare to calculate for DOD projects or actions the economic impacts caused by military activities. Using export-based location quotient techniques as the basis of its predictions, EIFS estimates the impact that expenditure of federal dollars has on local businesses, households, and governments in the areas of employment, personal income, total business volume, housing revenues, housing and business investments, and government expenses. The system currently has four operational functional areas: construction, operations and maintenance, mission change, and training. As development continues, the prediction equations will be redefined and additional functional areas will be developed. EIFS is one of three computer-based data systems which comprise the Environmental Technical Information System (ETIS). It is designed to provide information for assessing the environmental impacts of an Army project or activity in compliance with the National Environmental Policy Act (NEPA). The Environmental Impact Computer

System (EICS) and the Computer-Aided Environmental Legislative
Data System (CELDS) are related systems developed at CERL.
EICS is a basis for identifying and qualifying potential
environmental impacts, and presents a broad, systematic approach
to environmental analysis. CELDS allows access to abstracts of
pertinent state and federal environmental legislation by means
of keyword and topical searches.

Salient Features:

Techniques for quantifying the economic impacts of
military activities are described.

Advantages/Limitations of Salient Features:

1. Field studies conducted --- yes
2. Practical for field use --- yes
3. Usage for various types/sizes of projects --- yes
4. Objective vs. subjective approaches --- objective
5. Reproducibility --- unknown
6. Scientifically sound features --- yes

Conclusions:

General reference for WRAM

+ + +

APPENDIX F

INFORMATION ON 38 REFERENCES

FROM 1977-78 PERIOD

REFERENCE:

Baldwin, P., "Environmental Mediation: An Effective Alternative?", Proceedings of Conference Held in Reston, Virginia, January 11-13, 1978, 1978, RESOLVE, Center for Environmental Conflict Resolution, Palo Alto, California.

Abstract:

This report summarizes an Environmental Mediation Conference held in early 1978. Seven selected case histories are summarized. The important points discussed during the Conference are summarized as follows:

(1) General

. Environmental mediation and related techniques offer promising new approaches to environmental decision-making.

. Environmental mediation is not a panacea. While in some cases mediation and related techniques may prevent protracted and expensive litigation, these methods will certainly not supplant litigation entirely. They represent a new addition to the decision-making tool kit, not a substitution for other processes.

. Environmental mediators can learn much from the experience of labor mediators, but there are important differences which preclude a wholesale transfer of methodologies.

. Conflict resolution is not an end in itself; rather, it is a means to sound environmental decision-making. Conflict is often healthy in a democratic society, and the most difficult conflicts may produce the most creative solutions.

(2) Categories of Disputes Appropriate for Mediation

. It may be both possible and necessary to develop criteria for determining what kinds of disputes lend themselves to mediation efforts.

. Two experienced mediators suggested such criteria to the conference, and one estimated that mediation, in the more formal sense, might work in approximately 10% of the disputes reviewed by his office.

. It is important to retain an attitude of flexibility and a willingness to take risks, preventing the criteria from stunting the pioneering efforts at environmental mediation.

(3)   Necessary Qualifications for Environmental Mediators

. Mediators must inspire disputants' confidence in their
integrity, competence and objectivity; recognizable credentials
may assist in obtaining this confidence.

. Training in basic mediation techniques by recognized
experts can aid the mediator and inspire the confidence of
his or her clients.

. Some believe that expertise in substantive environmental matters should also be required of mediators, given
the highly technical nature of many environmental disputes.

. An ethical code for mediators might be appropriate. It
might simply be an ethic of process-such as the promise of
a "fair discussion, with fair representation of affected
interests." The ethical code might also deal with the
question of how the mediator should enter a case.

(4)   Institutional and Funding Issues

. A large and varied list of instutional possibilities-
ranging from a network of independent mediation organizations
to a federal endowment-exists. They are not mutually ex-
clusive, and there are precedents for virtually all.

. The immediate challenge is to find financial support
that does not jeopardize the mediators' objectivity and that
will provide standby funds enabling mediators to take quick
action on disputes as they arise. A balanced mix of foundation, corporate and governmental funding, perhaps channeled
into a revolving fund, may represent the best approach.

(5)   The Time for Mediation

. Mediation in the traditional sense of the word usually
works best after the disputants have reached a point of impasse,
having given up hope for unilateral victory. The additional
pressure of a deadline may also aid the negotiating process.

. Other conflict-resolution techniques may provide help
at earlier stages, and may be effective in preventing the
polarization of the disputing parties.

(6)   The Parties to Disputes and Resolution Efforts

. Environmental disputes typically involve a number of
parties with varying interests and degrees of involvement;
the exact mix of participants varies with each case.

. Ethical and practical considerations require the broad-
est possible spectrum of legitimate participants in each
case; a seemingly successful solution could be negated by
exclusion of one or more parties in a position to block implementation.

. While some believe that the mediator should lead in
the selection of parties to the mediation process, others hold
that the disputants themselves should decide who is to be
included.

(7)   The Role of the Mediator

. Varied circumstances require ingenuity on the mediator's
part; there are no set rules for procedures he or she should
follow, and some disagreement exists over the appropriateness
of certain approaches.

. Possible roles include:
   -Creating a climate of trust and a willingness
      to negotiate on the disputants' parts;
   -Ensuring fair and adequate representation;
   -Bringing the best available environmental informa-
      tion and expertise to the discussions;
   -Breaking deadlocks by setting goals and deadlines;
   -Suggesting solutions, or alternative solutions;
   -Outlining implementation plans and helping create
      mechanisms for implementation and enforcement of
      the agreement.

(8)   Public Accessibility

. The environmental movement has led in the trend toward
public participation and visibility in decision-making; environmental mediation is one outgrowth of this trend.

. The sensitive nature of mediation efforts may preclude
full publicity and open negotiating sessions in some cases,
but individual circumstances must be the determining factor.

(9)   Future Needs in the Environmental Mediation Field

. Early experience with environmental mediation justifies
cautious optimism, and the next step is to gain additional
practical experience. Research should focus on applications
to specific cases, carefully documented to aid those interested
in alternative methods of conflict resolution.

. Training in basic mediation and conflict resolution
skills should be made available to persons in the environmental
field. Workshops, short courses and seminars might produce a

network of mediators and the foundation of a referral service.

. Increasing awareness of the mediation alternative
among industries, government agencies, developers and citizen
activists should be a major focus in the field over the next
few years. Acquainting these groups with the possibilities
of environmental mediation may also be the best way to develop
institutional and finanacial mechanisms to support mediation
efforts.

. More research is needed in efforts to prevent environmental issues from reaching the boiling point and in dispute
avoidance.

Salient Features:

The advantages and limitations of mediation for resolving
environmental disputes are discussed.

Advantages/Limitations of Salient Features:

1. Field studies conducted---yes
2. Practical for field use---yes
3. Usage for various types/sizes of projects---yes
4. Objective vs. subjective approaches---objective
5. Reproducibility---not applicable
6. Scientifically sound features---yes

Conclusions:

Use directly in WRAM
..Mention availability of concepts.

+ + +

REFERENCE:

Boesch, D.F., "Application of Numerical Classification in
Ecological Investigations of Water Pollution," EPA/600/3-77/
033, March 1977, 127 pp., Corvallis Environmental Research
Laboratory, U.S. Environmental Protection Agency, Corvallis,
Oregon (prepared for EPA by Virginia Institute of Marine
Science, Gloucester Point, Virginia).

Abstract:

Numerical classification encompasses a variety of techniques for the grouping of entities based on the resemblance
of their attributes according to mathematically stated criteria.
In ecology this usually involves classification of collections
representing sites or sampling periods, or classification of

428

species. Classification can thus simplify patterns of collection resemblance or species distribution patterns in an in-
structive and efficient manner. Procedures of numerical
classification are thoroughly reviewed, including data manipu-
lations, computation of resemblance measures and clustering
methods. Agglomerative clustering methods which distort
spatial relationships and intensely cluster are often most useful with ecological data. The usefulness of numerical classification is demonstrated for objective analysis of the data
sets resulting from field surveys and monitoring studies conducted for the assessment of effects of pollution.

Salient Features:

    Numerical classification schemes for ecological studies
of water pollution are described.

Advantages/Limitations of Salient Features:

    1. Field studies conducted---yes
    2. Practical for field use---yes
    3. Usage for various types/sizes of projects---yes
    4. Objective vs. subjective approaches---objective
    5. Reproducibility---unknown
    6. Scientifically sound features---yes

Conclusions:

    General reference for WRAM

                    + + +

REFERENCE:

Canter, L.W., et al, "An Assessment of Problems Associated with
Evaluating the Physical, Chemical and Biological Impacts of
Discharging Fill Material," Technical Report D-77-29, December
1977, 236 pp., U.S. Army Corps of Engineers, Waterways Experiment Station, Vicksburg, Mississippi (prepared for WES
by School of Civil Engineering and Environmental Science,
University of Oklahoma, Norman, Oklahoma).

Abstract:

    Fill materials can be natural (soil, rock, or sand) or man-
altered (dredged material, solid wastes, or residues), with
projects involving usage including property protection, cause-
way/roadfills, and site development. Potential environmental
impacts are regulated by permits based on Section 404 of PL
92-500. This study focused on problems associated with evaluating environmental changes resulting from fill material discharges.

A weighted-rankings technique was used to prioritize permitting (administrative) concerns and technical deficiencies.

Permitting concerns were identified by contacts with fourteen Corps offices, ten Federal agencies, and 50 state water resource agencies. Administrative/procedural needs in decreasing priority include scientific rationale for permit issuance, increased personnel and laboratory resources, increased communications, surveilance of permit compliance, and information dissemination. Testing of proposed fill material may be required to establish engineering-related properties and identify leachates and evaluate their biological impacts.

A literature survey was conducted to determine technical deficiencies. Potential physical impacts included changes in infiltration and flow regimes, destruction/alteration of natural or man-made habitats, and creation of habitats. Chemical impacts result from the release of suspended solids, organics, nutrients and toxic substances. Biological impacts range from physical barriers to fish migration to complete "smothering" of entire wetland areas. The effects of leachates on aquatic biota are complex and diverse, ranging from no measurable changes to acute toxicity. Technical research needs in decreasing priority include studies on impact quantification and modeling, construction techniques and control measures for impact minimization, verification of predicted long-term impacts, basic chemical and biological interactions and effects, applicability of dredged material disposal findings, characterization of wetlands, and magnitude fill discharge operations.

Salient Features:

Literature survey of impacts from discharging fill material is presented.

Advantages/Limitations of Salient Features:

1. Field studies conducted---no
2. Practical for field use---yes
3. Usage for various types/sizes of projects---yes
4. Objective vs. subjective approaches---objective
5. Reproducibility---not applicable
6. Scientifically sound features---yes

Conclusions:

Use directly in WRAM
..Mention potential use for impact identification.

+ + +

REFERENCE:

Canter, L.W. and Reid, G.W., "Environmental Factors Affecting
Treatment Process Selection", paper presented at Oklahoma
Water Pollution Control Federation Annual Meeting, 1977,
Stillwater, Oklahoma.

Abstract:

This paper describes a weighting-scaling technique for
evaluation of the environmental impacts of wastewater treatment processes. The weighted-rankings technique which is
used in WRAM was used in this study.

Salient Features:

A weighting-scaling technique for evaluating the environmental impacts of wastewater treatment processes is described.

Advantages/Limitations of Salient Features:

1. Field studies conducted---no
2. Practical for field use---yes
3. Usage for various types/sizes of projects---yes
4. Objective vs. subjective approaches---objective
5. Reproducibility---unknown
6. Scientifically sound features---yes

Conclusions:

General reference for WRAM

+ + +

REFERENCE:

Canter, L.W. and Hill, L.G., "Variables for Environmental
Quality Account," Oct., 1977, 187 pages, Norman, Oklahoma.
(Report submitted to U.S. Army Engineers Waterways Experiment
Station, Vicksburg, Mississippi).

Abstract:

This report contains a comprehensive list of variables to
be used in the Environmental Quality account associated with
water resources planning. Each selected variable was grouped
into either terrestrial, aquatic, air or human interface
categories. To select pertinent variables, a master list of
189 potential ones was assembled following a review of several
environmental assessment methodologies and related reports.
A total of 62 variables were include in the final selection,

and the report contains information on each in terms of definition and measurement of baseline conditions, prediction of
impacts, functional curve (where one was available or easily
developed), general remarks, and data sources. Figure 11
(page 197) displays the categories of the selected variables
The concept of the functional curve is that the potential
values for a variable can be converted to a quality index
scale with 1 representing high quality and 0 representing
low quality.

Salient Features:

   Information on measurement, impact prediction and functional curves is included on 62 assessment variables for the
EQ account.

Advantages/Limitations of Salient Features:

   1. Field studies conducted---not applicable
   2. Practical for field use---yes
   3. Usage for various types/sizes of projects---yes
   4. Objective vs. subjective approaches---objective
   5. Reproducibility---unknown
   6. Scientifically sound features---yes

Conclusions:

   Use directly in WRAM
   ..Mention variables for EQ account.

+ + +

REFERENCE:

Canter, L.W., Environmental Impact Assessment, 1977, 331 pp.,
McGraw-Hill Book Company, New York, New York.

Abstract:

   This textbook contains 13 chapters with 6 on impact
prediction and assessment, 1 on methods of impact analysis,
and 1 on public participation.

Salient Features:

   Comprehensive textbook on impact prediction, assessment
and evaluation.

Advantages/Limitations of Salient Features:

1. Field studies conducted---not applicable
2. Practical for field use---yes
3. Usage for various types/sizes of projects---yes
4. Objective vs. subjective approaches---objective
5. Reproducibility---unknown
6. Scientifically sound features---yes

Conclusions:

General reference for WRAM

+ + +

REFERENCE:

Canter, L.W., "Supplement to Environmental Impact Assessment",
1978, 1062 pp., Canter Associates, Inc., Norman, Oklahoma.

Abstract:

This Supplement to the textbook entitled Environmental
Impact Assessment contains handbook-type materials corresponding to the 13 chapters in the textbook. Six chapters in the
Supplement deal with impact prediction and assessment, 1
deals with methods of impact analysis, and 1 deals with
public participation.

Salient Features:

Comprehensive state-of-the-art summary of information on
impact prediction, assessment, and evaluation.

Advantages/Limitations of Salient Features:

1. Field studies conducted---not applicable
2. Practical for field use---yes
3. Usage for various types/sizes of projects---yes
4. Objective vs. subjective approaches---objective
5. Reproducibility---unknown
6. Scientifically sound features---yes

Conclusions:

General reference for WRAM

+ + +

REFERENCE:

Canter, L.W., "Environmental Impact Statements on Municipal Wastewater Programs", May 1978, Canter Associates, Inc., Norman, Oklahoma, (draft report submitted to Information Resources Press, Washington, D.C.).

Abstract:

This report describes a comprehensive study of 28 environmental impact statements on wastewater facility 201 plans. The EIS's were primarily prepared in late 1976 and 1977. Twenty EIS's utilized an impact assessment methodology in selecting the proposed action from the alternatives which were studied. Four decriptive checklists, 4 ranking checklists, 6 scaling checklists, 1 weighting-ranking checklist and 5 weighting-scaling checklists were used. For the 8 EIS's in which no selection methodology was identified it is possible that they were described in the Facility Plans, but not included in the EIS's.

Salient Features:

20 of 28 EIS's on wastewater facility plans used an impact assessment methodology.

Advantages/Limitations of Salient Features:

1. Field studies conducted---yes
2. Practical for field use---yes
3. Usage for various types/sizes of projects---yes
4. Objective vs. subjective approaches---objective
5. Reproducibility---unknown
6. Scientifically sound features---yes

Conclusions:

Use directly in WRAM
..Mention usage of methodologies.

+ + +

REFERENCE:

Chalmers, J.A., and Anderson, E.J., "Economic/Demographic Assessment Manual: Current Practices, Procedural Recommendations, and a Test Case," November 1977, Engineering and Research Center, U.S. Bureau of Reclamation, Denver, Colorado, (prepared for Bureau of Reclamation by Mountain West Research, Inc., Tempe, Arizona).

Abstract:

The Economic/Demographic Assessment Manual is focused on
the problems associated with projecting the population, employment, and income impacts of both the construction and the
operation phases of water resource development projects. The
manual consists of three sections: (1) Survey of Current
Practics---a large number of environmental assessments and
planning reports are reviewed. Methods currently being used
for economic and demographic analysis are described; (2) Procedural Recommendations---based partly on current practics
and partly on the professional social science literature, a
set of procedural recommendations are made for carrying out
economic/demographic assessments. Important methodological
options are identified and evaluated as they apply to the
different steps in the projection and assessment process; and
(3) Test Case---the procedural recommendations are demonstrated by applying them to a proposed desalting plant near LaVerkin,
Utah. The organization of the assessment follows the procedural
recommendations and illustrates the way in which many of the
practical problems of an actual assessment can be met.
Each of the three major sections of the manual is organized around a seven-step procedure for carrying out an economic/
demographic assessment. The seven-step procedure is shown in
Figure 12 (page 199).

Salient Features:

Descriptive checklist for addressing the economic and
demographic impacts of water resources projects.

Advantages/Limitations of Salient Features:

1. Field studies conducted---yes
2. Practical for field use---yes
3. Usage for various types/sizes of projects---yes
4. Objective vs. subjective approaches---objective
5. Reproducibility---unknown
6. Scientifically sound features---yes

Conclusions:

Use directly in WRAM
..Mention availability of this descriptive checklist.

+ + +

REFERENCE:

Chalmers, J.A., "Bureau of Reclamation Construction Worker
Survey," October 1977, Engineering and Research Center, U.S.

Bureau of Reclamation, Denver, Colorado (prepared for Bureau of Reclamation by Mountain West Research, Inc., Tempe, Arizona).

Abstract:

This study is focused on the problems associated with estimating the economic and demographic impacts arising out of project construction activities. Methodological problems and procedures are reported on in a report entitled the Economic/Demographic Assessment Manual (covered elsewhere in this literature review). The construction worker survey is an attempt to obtain empirical observations on key characteristics of Bureau of Reclamation construction workers. A survey was conducted during the summer of 1977 and was designed to determine the characteristics of construction workers and their families; the distribution of the construction force between local and nonlocal workers; the extent to which nonlocal workers were accompanied by their families; the way in which the local residences of the nonlocal workers were distributed; and, finally, to investigate the previous employment status of local workers.

Salient Features:

Economic and demographic impacts from water resources project construction are described.

Advantages/Limitations of Salient Features:

1. Field studies conducted---yes
2. Practical for field use---yes
3. Usage for various types/sizes of projects---yes
4. Objective vs. subjective approaches---objective
5. Reproducibility---unknown
6. Scientifically sound features---yes

Conclusions:

Use directly in WRAM
..Mention availability of this study.

+ + +

REFERENCE:

Dee, N., et al, "Literature Review to Identify Rationale for Developing Functional Relationships between Environmental Parameters and Environmental Quality," February 1978, 79 pp., Battelle-Southern Operations and Columbus Laboratories, Atlanta, Georgia (report to U.S. Army Corps of Engineers Waterways Experiment Station, Vicksburg, Miss.).

Abstract:

This study focused on the adaptation of "national" functional curves to the southwestern portion of the United States, namely, New Mexico. A procedure for developing functional curves included 7 steps as follows: (1) define the variable, (2) define measurement units, (3) obtain specific data points, (4) calibrate selected data points, (5) derive functional relationship, (6) test relationship, and (7) prepare a post-project audit. Regionally-oriented functional curves were developed for natural vegetation, soil erosion, waterfowl, biochemical oxygen demand, particulates, sulfur dioxide, variety within vegetation types, and non-aircraft noise.

Salient Features:

Concepts for developing functional curves are summarized.

Advantages/Limitations of Salient Features:

1. Field studies conducted---no
2. Practival for field use---yes
3. Usage for various types/sizes of projects---yes
4. Objective vs. subjective approaches---objective
5. Reproducibility---unknown
6. Scientifically sound features---yes

Conclusions:

Use directly in WRAM
..Mention concepts of functional curves.

+ + +

REFERENCE:

Duke, K.M., et al, "Environmental Quality Assessment in Multiobjective Planning," Nov. 1977, Final Report to U.S. Bureau of Reclamation, Denver, Colo. (prepared for BuRec by Battelle-Columbus Laboratories, Columbus, Ohio).

Abstract:

This scaling checklist methodology is addressed to the Environmental Quality account used in evaluation of water resources programs and projects. The EQA Methodology has three functions that must be performed in the preparation of the Environmental Quality Account: (1) to measure the environmental effects of proposed project alternatives; (2) to evaluate the beneficial and adverse environmental effects of the proposed project alternatives, and (3) to display the results of measurement and analyses in a brief but meaningful manner. A flow diagram of these three functions is given in Figure 13 (page 200).

The environmental factors for use in the analysis are identified through use of an interaction matrix (called an environmental activity matrix) similar to the Leopold matrix. Table 57 (page 201) contains a list of potential assessment variables. The critical element in the evaluation phase is the establishment of evaluation guidelines. The guideline will be specific to the project setting and will enable the user to determine the magnitude and direction of each environmental effect. The evaluation guideline is based upon the concept of environmental potential. Each environmental factor measurement describes an element of the environment which has an optimal environmental quality. The difference between the existing quality and this optimal level is defined as the environmental potential (Figure 14, page 204). An environmental effect is defined as the difference between the future with and the future without a project plan. If the change is toward the optimum, it is beneficial (Figure 15, page 204); and if it is away from the optimum, it is adverse (Figure 16, page 204). What is defined as the optimal level of environmental quality for an environmental factor measurement varies among regions of the western United States. In some cases, the maximum quality may also be the optimal while in others it is not. The evaluation guideline is the standard that determines if the beneficial or adverse changes are significant and if there are any environmental sensitive areas (flags). The evaluation guideline is defined as the smallest change in the highest existing quality in the region that would be considered significant. The highest existing quality is defined as the best environmental quality for that factor measurement that currently exists in the region. For example, assume that the highest existing quality for dissolved oxygen in the region is 8 mg/l. If a reduction 1.5 mg/l in that stream would be considered significant, then the evaluation guideline is 1.5 mg/l. A schematic diagram of the evaluation guideline is provided in Figure 17 (page 204).

A three-step process can be used to develop evaluation guidelines for each factor measurement. It is suggested that more than one individual be involved in the development process. A consensus producing approach like the Delphi Technique might be valuable in this process. The three steps are: (1) identify the highest existing quality in the region; (2) determine the change in the highest existing quality that would be considered significant (the estimate can be based on professional judgment or the use of prediction techniques combined with professional judgment); and (3) document the rationale for the selection of the highest existing quality and the selection of the guideline. Impact display involves preparing a category

438

display and quantitative display. The purpose of the category
display is to provide an overview of the evaluation results.
The entries in a summary table are the number of environmental
factor measurements that meet each of the five evaluation
possibilities for each alternative: (1) no significant effect;
(2) significant beneficial effect; (3) significant adverse
effect; (4) beneficial flag; and (5) adverse flag. The sum
of the first three conditions will equal the total number of
factor measurements evaluated for each component for each
alternative.

Salient Features:

Scaling checklist for water resources projects; concept
of environmental potential.

Advantages/Limitations of Salient Features:

1. Field studies conducted---unknown
2. Practical for field use---yes
3. Usage for various types/sizes of projects---yes
4. Objective vs. subjective approaches---objective
5. Reproducibility---unknown
6. Scientifically sound features---yes

Conclusions:

Use directly in WRAM
..Mention concept of environmental potential.

+ + +

REFERENCE:

Dunne, N.G., "Successful Sanitary Landfill Siting: County of
San Bernadino, California", SW-617, 1977, U.S. Environmental
Protection Agency, Cincinnati, Ohio.

Abstract:

A weighting-scaling checklist was used to evaluate three
alternative landfill sites. An approach similar to the weighted
rankings technique was used to assign importance weights and
alternative scaling factors.

Salient Features:

Weighting-scaling checklist for sanitary landfill site
selection.

Advantages/Limitations of Salient Features:

1. Field studies conducted---yes
2. Practical for field use---yes
3. Usage for various types/sizes of projects---yes
4. Objective vs. subjective approaches---objective
5. Reproducibility---unknown
6. Scientifically sound features---yes

Conclusions:

General reference for WRAM

+ + +

REFERENCE:

Dwyer, J.F., Hatmaker, M.L., and Hewings, G.J.D., "Profile
and Measurement of Regional Development Indications for Use
in the Evaluation of Water and Related Land Management Planning", May, 1978, 140 pp., University of Illinois, Urbana,
Illinois (prepared for U.S. Army Waterways Experiment Station,
Vicksburg, Mississippi).

Abstract:

The accounting system presented has been developed with
three primary objectives in mind: (1) to organize the variables into a system that corresponds to the data requirements
of existing regional analysis models, (2) to provide categories
and variables which are capable of strict identification and
which are appropriate for water and related land resource
planning as outlined by the Principles and Standards, and (3)
to define variables for which data is available or easily
obtainable. A regional output disaggregation shows the economic, social, and environmental variables that are elements
of regional output or have an influence on that output. It
provides a convenient framework for inventorying the readily-
available information on stock and flow variables that are of
signigicance to regional development and output. Stock variables are those that are measured at a point in time, while
flow variables are those measured over an interval of time.
The regional output disaggregation is designed to display
several variations of the incidence of impacts and combinations
of impacts. Consequently, some impacts occur more than once
in the model but in different forms. For example, both government revenues and expenditures are shown because each may be
critical to the evaluation of a project's regional impact. For
the same reasons, direct income is considered in terms of three
categories: value of output, income by sources, and income by
type.

440

The WRAM framework (Figure 19 page 206) provides a
"balance sheet" approach to regional accounting. However,
its elements cannot be projected as entities in themselves;
they must be aggregated from projections of the stock and
flow variables in the regional output disaggregation (Figure
18 page 205). For example, the component of the WRAM framework "income increases from induced or stemming activities,"
cannot be estimated directly. Rather, direct project impacts
are used as changes in projection models that incorporate
elements of the stock and flow breakdown. These direct changes
are subjected to the income multiplier analysis within the
framework of Figure 18 (page 205) to produce total changes in
stock variables and flows such as income.

The relationship between Figures 18 and 19 is illustrated
by Figure 20 (page 207). In step I the stock and flow variables which were outlined in the regional output disaggregation (ROD) model are estimated for the pre-project situation.
Predictions of these variables under conditions without the
project are developed in step II. In step III the stocks and
flows are predicted for conditions with the project. Estimates
for with and without the project are compared to develop
estimates of project impacts (step IV). In the last step,
project impacts are aggregated into the WRAM framework. Thus
there is not a direct or 1 to 1 correspondence between the
ROD and WRAM frameworks; rather, it is an elaborate linkage
of procedures.

The primary focus of the report is on the 37 variables
listed in Figures 18 and 19. Each of the variables is defined
and described. Procedures for measurement and prediction are
also outlined, and selected data sources and references are
presented. For those variables that cannot be measured in
pecuniary terms, an illustrative hypothesized functional relationship between the variable and a quality index is presented. The hypothesized functional relationship is intended
to operationalize some of the concepts presented in the discussion of the variables.

Salient Features:

Summary of impact prediction for 37 important variables
in the Regional Development account.

Advantages/Limitations of Salient Features:

1. Field studies conducted---not applicable
2. Practical for field use---yes
3. Usage for various types/sizes of projects---yes
4. Objective vs. subjective approaches---objective
5. Reproducibility---unknown
6. Scientifically sound features---yes

Conclusions:

      Use directly in WRAM
      ..Mention availability of information for R.D. account.

+ + +

REFERENCE:

Ellis, S.L., et al, "Guide to Land Cover and Use Classification
Systems Employed by Western Governmental Agencies," FWS/OBS-
77/05, March 1978, 183 pp., Ecology Consultants, Inc., Fort
Collins, Colo. prepared for Western Energy and Land Use Team,
Office of Biological Services, U.S. Fish and Wildlife Service,
Fort Collins, Colo.

Abstract:

      This guide surveys and lists the classification systems
in use by State and Federal agencies in 18 Western States and
the Provinces of Alberta and Manitoba in Canada. The guide--
limited primarily to wildlife, land use, and terrestrial
vegetation--provides summary descriptions of classification
systems, and the data base and the techniques required to
implement these systems. System descriptions are divided into
three sections: local systems, regional and multi-regional
systems, plus some Canadian systems. Each system summary
includes the title of the system, contact person, objectives,
background, description, products and related systems.

Salient Features:

      Systematic approaches for describing the biological
setting are summarized.

Advantages/Limitations of Salient Features:

    1. Field studies conducted---yes
    2. Practical for field use---yes
    3. Usage for various types/sizes of projects---yes
    4. Objective vs. subjective approaches---objective
    5. Reproducibility---unknown
    6. Scientifically sound features---yes

Conclusions:

      General reference for WRAM

+ + +

REFERENCE:

Finsterbush, K. and Wolf, C.P., The Methodology of Social
Impact Assessment, 1977, Dowden, Hutchinson and Ross Publishing
Co., Stroudsberg, Pa.

Abstract:

This book contains a series of articles written by
different persons on various subjects related to social impact
assessment. Several articles address methodologies and
technologies for accomplishing impact prediction and assessment.

Salient Features:

Series of articles on social impact assessment.

Advantages/Limitations of Salient Features:

1. Field studies conducted---yes
2. Practical for field use---yes
3. Usage for various types/sizes of projects---yes
4. Objective vs. subjective approaches---objective
5. Reproducibility---unknown
6. Scientifically sound features---yes

Conclusions:

Use directly in WRAM
..Mention availability of book.

+ + +

REFERENCE:

Finsterbusch, K., "Methods for Evaluating Non-Market Impacts
in Policy Decisions with Special Reference to Water Resources
Development Projects," IWR Contract Report 77-78, November
1977, 46 pp., U.S. Army Engineer Institute for Water Resources, Fort Belvoir, Va. (prepared for IWR by Univ. of
Maryland, College Park, Maryland).

Abstract:

This working paper explores the as yet intractable
problem of accounting for non-market (non-monetary) impacts
in policy decisions especially in the context of water resource development projects. In the first section, 19 methods
are presented and critiqued in general terms. See Table 58
(page 209) the social impacts of water resource projects are
reviewed and related to the 19 valuation methods. In the

443

final section a number of critical issues involved in valuing non-market impacts are discussed. Work on evaluation frameworks is in a relatively primitive stage of development. All methods discussed in this paper have deficiencies and should be used cautiously. The limited achievement of the methods is to be expected because they must somehow accomplish the extremely difficult task of making interpersonal comparisons of utilities. Philosophers, economists, political theorists, and public decision-makers have been thinking about the problem for centuries and no solution is yet available. But some methods are better than other methods for various decision situations and the following review not only identifies a large number of methods but also assesses their strengths and weaknesses.

Salient Features:

This is an excellent literature review on techniques for decision-making for water resources projects.

Advantages/Limitations of Salient Features:

1. Field studies conducted---not applicable
2. Practical for field use---yes
3. Usage for various types/sizes of projects---yes
4. Objective vs. subjective approaches---objective
5. Reproducibility---unknown
6. Scientifically sound features---yes

Conclusions:

Use directly in WRAM
..Identify methods of impact assessment.

+ + +

REFERENCE:

Flood, B.S., et al, "A Handbook for Habitat Evaluation Procedures", Resource Pub. 132, 1977, 77 pp., U.S. Fish and Wildlife Service, Washington, D.C.

Abstract:

The report describes the concepts of a habitat evaluation system for measuring the effects of water development projects on fish, wildlife and related resources. This handbook was specifically written for the Meramec Park Lake project site in Crawford County, Missouri. In this handbook, six groups of animals are categorized in as many as six habitat types. They are composed principally of animals whose habitat

444

requirements are well known, easily found in literature, and occur in the project area. Animals with similar requirements were grouped in the following manner: Forest Game; Upland Game; Tree Squirrels; Terrestrial Furbearers; Aquatic Furbearers; and Waterfowl. Marsh birds, raptors, songbirds, small mammals, reptiles, and amphibians, inhabit the Meramec area but habitat criteria have not yet been developed for these groups. Habitat Types include Bottomland Hardwood, Upland Hardwood, Old Field, Pasture, Small Grain and Row Crops, and Meramec River and Riverine Habitat, An Old Field is an uncultivated or ungrazed tract; Pasture, a grazed grassland; any cultivated field is classified as Small Grain and Row Crops; and River and Riverine Habitat is the association of water, beach, and bank.

The handbook format is the same for each animal group (Evaluation Element): requirements; preferred food list; cavity-forming tree list if applicable; references; and field forms for each relevant habitat type. Exhaustive life-histories are not given; rather habitat needs (seral stages, food, cover, and reproductive requirements) are discussed. Plants are listed in decreasing order of importance as a food source for a particular species. From one to eight habitat characteristics are shown on each field form. These differ among habitat types, but relate to food, cover, and reproductive requirements. Criteria for scoring and ranges of scores are given for each habitat characteristic. The most important characteristics are scored on a 1 to 10 scale. Less important characteristics are scored on a 1 to 5 scale, permitting the weighting of characteristics.

Salient Features:

A habitat evaluation procedure for the biological environment is described.

Advantages/Limitations of Salient Features:

1. Field studies conducted---yes
2. Practical for field use---yes
3. Usage for various types/sizes of projects---yes
4. Objective vs. subjective approaches---objective
5. Reproducibility---unknown
6. Scientifically sound features---yes

Conclusions:

Use directly in WRAM
..Mention habitat evaluation procedure.

+ + +

REFERENCE:

Freeman, D.M., and Quint, J., "Coordinator's Manual --- The Analysis of Social Well-Being: Procedures for Comparing Social Impacts of Proposed Resource Management Alternatives", October 1977, Department of Sociology, Colorado State University, Fort Collins, Colorado.

Abstract:

This manual was prepared for coordinators of U.S. Forest Service public participation programs. One exercise is focused on resoloving conflicting opinions relative to Forest Service projects. Procedures for accomplishing resolution involve the assignment of importance weights to decision factors and group discussions.

Salient Features:

Practical procedure for conflict resolution.

Advantages/Limitations of Salient Features:

1. Field studies conducted---yes
2. Practical for field use---yes
3. Usage for various types/sizes of projects---yes
4. Objective vs. subjective approaches---objective
5. Reproducibility---unknown
6. Scientifically sound features---yes

Conclusions:

Use directly in WRAM
..Mention availability of procedural concepts.

+ + +

REFERENCE:

Frost, J.H., and Wilmot, W.W., *Interpersonal Conflict*, 1978 Wm. C. Brown Company Publishers, Dubuque, Iowa.

Abstract:

The book is written primarily for courses that focus on the conflict process as part of normal, on-going communication relationships. Persons interested in small groups, communication in organizations, marriage communication, male and female communication, management, counseling, and organizational development will find this book helpful as a primary text or supplement to another text. Of interst in terms of WRAM are

some suggestions for third party intervenors in conflicts.
The third party should intervene in the communication process
itself when it is apparent that the participants are not
listening to each other, or that they need help in understanding one another. Some of the rules that might be appropriate to
follow are listed on **page 210**.

Salient Features:

Practical ideas on conflict management and resolution.

Advantages/Limitations of Salient Features:

1. Field studies conducted---yes
2. Practical for field use---yes
3. Usage for various types/sizes of projects---yes
4. Objective vs. subjective approaches---not applicable
5. Reproducibility---not applicable
6. Scientifically sound features---not applicable

Conclusions:

Use directly in WRAM
..Mention availability for conflict resolution.

+ + +

REFERENCE:

Grooms, D.W., "A Directory of Computer Software Applications -
Environmental, 1977", PB-270 018/5WP, Sept., 1977, 189 pp., ·
National Technical Information Service, Springfield, Va.

Abstract:

The computer programs or the computer program documentation
which are cited in this directory have been developed for a
variety of applications in environmental studies. Software
for simulation modeling of automobile emissions, Gaussian
plumes, noise levels, radioactive hazards, water quality,
solid waste disposal, thermal pollution, and other environmental conditions are included in this directory.

Salient Features:

Abstracts of available computer programs for impact
prediction on the physical-chemical environment are described.

Advantages/Limitations of Salient Features:

1. Field studies conducted---not applicable
2. Practical for field use---yes

447

3. Usage for various types/sizes of projects---yes
4. Objective vs. subjective approaches---objective
5. Reproducibility---unknown
6. Scientifically sound features---yes

Conclusions:

Use directly in WRAM
..Mention availability of computer programs.

+ + +

REFERENCE:

Guseman, P.K., and Dietrich, K.T., "Profile and Measurement
of Social Well-Being Indicators for Use in the Evaluation of
Water and Related Land Management Planning," Misc. Paper
T-78-2, June 1978, U.S. Army Engineers Waterways Experiment
Station, Vicksburg, Mississippi (prepared for WES by Texas
Transportation Institutes, Texas A and M University, College
Station, Texas).

Abstract:

This report defines the specific concerns of the social
well-being objective of water resources planning by presenting
a listing of variables that are relevant for social well-being
impact assessment of a water project. The listing of variables
and their categorization are shown in Figures 21 through 26
(pages 213-214). The following information is included in the
report for each listed variable: definition and measurement
of baseline conditions, prediction of impacts, idealized
functional curve and rationals, remarks, data sources and
references. A total of about two pages is devoted to each
variable in the report.

Salient Features:

Information on measurement, impact prediction and functional curves is included on 50 assessment variables for the
SWB account.

Advantages/Limitations of Salient Features:

1. Field studies conducted---not applicable
2. Practical for field use---yes
3. Usage for various types/sizes of projects---yes
4. Objective vs. subjective approaches---objective
5. Reproducibility---unknown
6. Scientifically sound features---yes

Conclusions:

    Use directly in WRAM
    ..Mention availability for SWB account.

+ + +

REFERENCE:

Hammond, K.R., et al, "Social Judgment Theory: Applications in Policy Formation", in Kaplan, M.F., and Schwartz, S. (Editors), Human Judgment and Decision Processes in Applied Settings, 1977, Academic Press, New York, New York.

Abstract:

    Techniques for conflict resolution involving weighting and scaling are described. A case study involving the reduction of conflict in labor-management negotiations is described.

Salient Features:

    Weighting and scaling as a means for conflict resolution is described.

Advantages/Limitations of Salient Features:

    1. Field studies conducted---yes
    2. Practical for field use---yes
    3. Usage for various types/sizes of projects---yes
    4. Objective vs. subjective approaches---objective
    5. Reproducibility---unknown
    6. Scientifically sound features---yes

Conclusions:

    Use directly in WRAM
    ..Mention techniques for conflict resolution.

+ + +

REFERENCE:

Harrison, E.A., "Bioindicators of Pollution (A Bibliography with Abstracts)", NTIS/PS-77/0993, November 1977, 243 pp., National Technical Information Service, Springfield, Virginia.

Abstract:

    The bibliography from 1964 to November 1977 cites abstracts relating to the use of microorganisms, animals, plants, and

449

fishes to detect air and water pollution. Some of the organisms discussed are algae, bacteria, aquatic plants, oysters, snails, clams, insects, annelida, amphibians, beaver and fungi. This updated bibliography contains 243 abstracts, 54 of which are new entries to the previous edition.

Salient Features:

54 new abstracts of bioindicators of pollution are presented.

Advantages/Limitations of Salient Features:

1. Field studies conducted---yes
2. Practical for field use---yes
3. Usage for various types/sizes of projects---yes
4. Objective vs. subjective approaches---objective
5. Reproducibility---unknown
6. Scientifically sound features---yes

Conclusions:

Use directly in WRAM
..Mention availability of information on bioindicators.

+ + +

REFERENCE:

Heer, Jr., J.E., and Hagerty, D.J., Environmental Assessments and Statements, 1977, 382 pp., Van Nostrand Reinhold Company, Florence, Kentucky.

Abstract:

This volume explains required contents of impact statements, criteria for determining when a statement is needed, various methods for quantitative and qualitative assessment of environmental impact, and steps peripheral to actual preparation of the statement. It provides comprehensive information on organizing personnel into an assessment team, communicating with the public, and achieving a prompt and meaningful review of the prepared statement.

Salient Features:

General Overview of impact statement preparation.

Advantages/Limitations of Salient Features:

1. Field studies conducted---not applicable
2. Practical for field use---yes

3. Usage for various types/sizes of projects---yes
4. Objective vs. subjective approaches---objective
5. Reproducibility---not applicable
6. Scientifically sound features---yes

Conclusions:

General reference for WRAM

+ + +

REFERENCE:

Hobbs, B.F., and Voelker, A.H., "Analytical Multiobjective
Decision-Making Techniques and Power Plant Siting: A Survey
and Critique", ORNL-5288 Special, February 1978, Oak Ridge
National Laboratory, Oak Ridge, Tennessee.

Abstract:

This report explores the use of multiobjective techniques in power plant site selection. Its purpose is to act
as a primer for groups faced with the difficult task of site
selection and unfamiliar with the total range of practical
decision techniques now available. Although special emphasis
is placed on power plant siting, the techniques discussed are
applicable to a much broader range of planning decisions and
are commonly employed in other fields such as water resource
planning. The discussion of the contents of this report will
be in accordance with 3 sections or general steps: (1)
choosing and structuring siting factors, (2) desirability
scaling and (3) amalgamation of siting factors.

(1) Choosing and Structuring Siting Factors

Alternative sites can be described in terms of factors
created from a number of plant impact and site characteristics
(I&Cs). Three general rules can assist in selecting and
organizing I&Cs in any particular siting study. They are:
organize I&Cs into logical hierarchical groups, eliminate
unimportant I&Cs, and consider only those I&Cs that differ
between alternative sites. Criteria for judging the soundness
of each I&C group making up a level of the hierarchy include
the following: each group of I&Cs should be comprehensive,
no duplication should occur within a group, and each group
should have a minimum of complexity and division. In general,
the value judgments made in selecting I&Cs are extremely important to any siting study and should receive more systematic
attention than has generally been the case. Once I&Cs are
defined and quantified, they must be transformed into abstract
measures of desirability.

451

(2) Desirability Scaling

Many alternative techniques exist for transforming a physically measured I&C into a factor measured in units of desirability or site suitability. This report groups these techniques into four categories, based on the level of measurement of the resulting desirability. The four levels of measurement are:

.Categorical: Sites are assigned to categories such as acceptable or unacceptable (often called "nominal" in the literature).

.Ordinal: Sites are rank ordered. No arithmetic operations are allowed with factors scaled in this way.

.Interval: Sites are assigned values from a continuous scale without a fixed zero point, wherein the differences between values are meaningful. Values on this scale can be added, subtracted, and weighted only.

.Ratio: Sites are assigned values from a continuous scale with a fixed zero point, wherein the differences between numbers are meaningful. All arithmetic operations with the site values are allowed. The zero point is nonarbitrary; therefore, the type of statement "X is so many times as much as Y" becomes meaningful.

The transformation of I&Cs into desirability can result in information loss. For instance, when I&Cs whose physical measurements are intervally or ratio scaled are transformed into categories of acceptable or unacceptable, some knowledge of how the I&Cs relate to one another is lost. Eight methods for transforming I&Cs into intervally and ratio-scaled desirability are described in the report. They range in sophistication from a simple judgmental decision of where an I&C physical measurement fits on a scale of desirability to complex procedures involving the use of "lotteries".

(3) Amalgamation of Siting Factors

Once each I&C has been transformed into a siting factor expressed in terms of desirability, it is necessary to determine the suitability of each site by combining a number of desirabilities (a suitability vector). Formal techniques for determining relative suitability from a vector of desirabilities are known as amalgamation techniques. Several of the more popular amalgamation techniques are as follows;

.Exclusion screening is a technique that uses factors scaled categorically as acceptable and unacceptable.

452

All factors can be considered at once, or the alternatives can be screened one factor at a time until the
remaining set of sites is deemed sufficiently small.
The basic problem with exclusionary screening is that
only rarely are sites either acceptable or unacceptable;
there is usually a gradation among sites. By limiting
the site selection process to this method, important
trade-offs between factors and subtle degrees of
differences among sites will be ignored.

.The conjunctive-ranking approach is a method that
screens out all unacceptable sites in every factor
except one. The last factor (an ordinally scaled
factor) is then used to rank the remaining sites. The
highest ranked site is selected.

.The weighting-summation technique evaluates sites by
use of the following formula:

$$\text{site suitability} = \sum_{i=1}^{n} W_i F_i$$

where W_i is the weight for factor i (f_i).

A few important assumptions underlie this method. All
factors must be intervally or ratio scaled, and each
weight must be ratio scaled and represents the relative
importance of change in its factor.

There are a number of methods for selecting weights,
some more theoretically valid than others. These
methods fall into two categories:

   .Client explicated, which queries the various
    groups concerned with the site selection de-
    cision for inter-factor value judgments to
    derive weights, and

   .observer-derived, which uses multiple regression
    to calculate weights. Factor levels for each
    site are regressed against the overall evaluation
    of each site supplied by various groups.

 Observer-derived methods are relatively straight-
forward. However client-explicated methods are quite
varied. Rating is one of the simplest client-explicated
weighting methods, requiring the decision maker to rate
only the importance of each factor. The requirements
for ratio-scaled weights and for the correct type of
weight importance are seldom verified by those using
the rating approach. Client-explicated methods that

ensure theoretically valid weights by virtue of their
design are the indifference trade-off, Churchman-
Ackoff, and decision analysis techniques. Each has
its advantages and disadvantages. The indifference
trade-off approach is the simplest to use; but the
Churchman-Ackoff procedure, though more time consuming,
provides numerous checks on weight choices. Decision
analysis is the only approach using lotteries; it is
therefore the one technique that incorporates the
decision maker's attitudes toward risk. There is
little empirical evidence that one procedure provides
better or even different weights than the others.

Procedures that use groups to determine weights appear
to offer many advantages. The two most commonly used
structured group approaches are the Delphi and the
nominal group process technique. Such procedures help
to clarify areas of value conflict and ensure a more
comprehensive perspective.

The goal attainment and goal programming methods are
other amalgamation methods that use intervally scaled
factors. They choose the site that minimizes a
function of the differences between the factor levels
and the goals for the factors. The setting of goals,
however, is likely to be difficult and arbitrary in
siting studies.

A procedure that has been applied in water resource
project evaluations is the power-law model, which uses
the following formula:

$$\text{site suitability} = \prod_{i = 1}^{n} F_i^{b_i}$$

where b_i is the weight for factor (F_i). The power-
law model is inferior to the weighting-summation
method because it (1) requires ratio-scaled factors,
(2) sometimes does not consider trade-offs between
factors, and (3) necessitates the use of observer-
derived techniques for setting weights.

Salient Features:

Summary of multiobjective decision-making techniques is
presented.

Advantages/Limitations of Salient Features:

1. Field studies conducted---yes
2. Practical for field use---yes

454

3. Usage for various types/sizes of projects---yes
4. Objective vs. subjective approaches---objective
5. Reproducibility---unknown
6. Scientifically sound features---yes

Conclusions:

Use directly in WRAM
..Mention summary of techniques.

+ + +

REFERENCE:

Jain, R.K., Urban, L.V., and Stacey, G.S., Environmental
Impact Analysis, 1977, 340 pp., Van Nostrand Reinhold Company,
Florence, Kentucky.

Abstract:

This guide to EIA/EIS methodology covers the whole
spectrum of environmental characteristics-intangible areas
such as sociology, economics and aesthetics-as well as the
more obvious areas of air and water quality and ecology. The
book shows how to determine which environmental attributes
will be affected by a project, and how to identify and measure
in advance the impact on the attributes. Forty-nine biophysical and socioeconomic parameters are described in terms
of their importance, magnitude and overall relationship to
the environment. For each attribute the book discusses the
activities that affect it, measurement of variables, collection and evaluation of data, special conditions and limitations, and possible secondary effects. The information
contained in this book is similar to U.S. Department of the
Army (1975) and Jain, Urban and Cerchione (1976).

Salient Features:

Impact prediction and assessment information is presented
on 49 assessment variables (called environmental attributes).

Advantages/Limitations of Salient Features:

1. Field studies conducted---yes
2. Practical for field use---yes
3. Usage for various types/sizes of projects---yes
4. Objective vs. subjective approaches---objective
5. Reproducibility---unknown
6. Scientifically sound features---yes

Conclusions:

      Use directly in WRAM
      ..Mention availability.

+ + +

REFERENCE:

Johnson, D.W. and Cole, D.W., "Anion Mobility in Soils:
Relevance to Nutrient Transport from Terrestrial to Aquatic
Systems", EPA-600/3-77-068, June 1977, 28 pp., U.S. Environ-
mental Protection Agency, Corvallis, Oregon.

Abstract:

      Nutrient transport from terrestrial to aquatic eco-
systems is strongly mediated by soil chemical interactions.
Ions deposited on or biologically released within the soil
can enter into a variety of exchange and precipitation reactions prior to (or instead of) entering aquatic ecosystems.
This report reviews the current knowledge of soil anion
adsorption reactions and their effects on leaching, and
suggests a simple model, based on anion production and
adsorption considerations, to predict and explain nutrient
transport. The relationship of this approach to that based
on cation production and adsorption is discussed.

Salient Features:

Nutrient transport from terrestrial to aquation systems is
described.

Advantages/Limitations of Salient Features:

    1. Field studies conducted---yes
    2. Practical for field use---yes
    3. Usage for various types/sizes of projects---yes
    4. Objective vs. subjective approaches---objective
    5. Reproducibility---unknown
    6. Scientifically sound features---yes

Conclusions:

      General reference for WRAM

+ + +

REFERENCE:

McEvoy, III, J., and Dietz, T., Handbook for Environmental
Planning, 1977, John Wiley and Sons, New York, New York.

Abstract:

    This book presents a practical overview of the strategies
and methods available for predicting and assessing the social
consequences of environmental change. The book examines such
topics as legal requirements for impact analysis; population
estimation and projection techniques; land use impacts; transportation impacts; sociocultural impacts; economic methods
for impact analysis; and the organization and presentation of
impact information. Included in the volume are introductory
discussions of available data sources, analysis techniques
ranging from the simple to the complex, examinations of case
studies and hypothetical examples, and checklists for impact
identification.

Salient Features:

    Prediction and assessment of socioeconomic impacts.

Advantages/Limitations of Salient Features:

    1. Field studies conducted---yes
    2. Practical for field use---yes
    3. Usage for various types/sizes of projects---yes
    4. Objective vs. subjective approaches---objective
    5. Reproducibility---unknown
    6. Scientifically sound features---yes

Conclusions:

    Use directly in WRAM
    ..Mention availability for socioeconomic impact pre-
      diction and assessment.

+ + +

REFERENCE:

Omernik, J.M., "Nonpoint Source-Stream Nutrient Level Relationships; A Nationwide Survey", EPA-600/3-77-105, September
1977, 151 pp., U.S. Environmental Protection Agency, Corvallis,
Oregon.

Abstract:

    National Eutrophication Survey (NES) data for a nationwide
collection of 928 nonpoint source watersheds were studied for
relationships between macro-drainage area characteristics
(particularly land use) and nutrient levels in streams. Both
the total and inorganic forms of phosphorus and nitrogen concentrations and loads in streams were considered. For both

457

nationwide and regional data sets, significant correlations
were found between general land use and nutrient concentrations in streams. Mean concentrations were considerably
higher in streams draining agricultural watersheds than in
streams draining forested watersheds. The overall relationships and regionalities of the relationships and interrelationships with other characteristics are illustrated
cartographically and statistically. Two methods are provided for predicting nonpoint source nutrient levels in
streams; one utilizing mapped interpretations of NES nonpoint source data and the other, regional mathematical
equations and mapped residuals of these equations. Both
methods afford a limited accountability for regional
characteristics.

Salient Features:

Nonpoint sources of nutrients from National Eutrophication Survey are summarized.

Advantages/Limitations of Salient Features:

1. Field studies conducted---yes
2. Practical for field use---yes
3. Usage for various types/sizes of projects---yes
4. Objective vs. subjective approaches---objective
5. Reproducibility---unknown
6. Scientifically sound features---yes

Conclusions:

General reference for WRAM

+ + +

REFERENCE:

Ott, W.R., "Water Quality Indices: A Survey of Indices Used
in the United States", EPA-600/4-78-005, January 1978, 128 pp.,
U.S. Environmental Protection Agency, Washington, D.C.

Abstract:

This study documents the extent to which water quality
indices currently are being used in the United States. It
reviews the indices published in the literature and surveys
the States and interstate commissions to determine: (1) which
agencies are using indices, (2) the type of index being used,
(3) the purpose of its use, and (4) the attitudes of agency
personnel toward indices. One-fifth of the State and interstate agencies (12 out of 60 agencies) were classified as

users of water quality indices. Of the 51 State agencies
(including the District of Columbia), 10 States (20 percent)
were classified as index users. The National Sanitation
Foundation Index was the most commonly used index, accounting
for 7 of the 12 index users. The remaining agencies use
Harkins' index or various user-developed indices. A total
of 16 additional States and 1 interstate commission indicated
that they are planning to evaluate indices for possible
future application, or are developing or evaluating indices
at the present time; these were classified as "potential
users". Six new indices have been developed by water pollution control agencies.

Salient Features:

    Summary of state-of-the-art of water quality index
usage in the United States.

Advantages/Limitations of Salient Features:

    1. Field studies conducted---yes
    2. Practical for field use---yes
    3. Usage for various types/sizes of projects---yes
    4. Objective vs. subjective approaches---objective
    5. Reproducibility---unknown
    6. Scientifically sound features---yes

Conclusions:

    Use directly in WRAM
    ..Mention concepts of index.

                    + + +

REFERENCE:

Paul, B.W., "Subjective Prioritization of Energy Development
Proposals Using Alternative Scenarios," (paper presented at
the Joint National ORSA/TIMS Meeting, San Francisco, Cal.,
May 1977), Engineering and Research Center, U.S. Bureau of
Reclamation, Denver, Colorado.

Abstract:

    A weighting-scaling checklist was used to prioritize
127 potential energy development projects of the U.S. Bureau
of Reclamation.

Salient Features:

    Weighting-scaling checklist used to prioritize potential
projects.

459

Advantages/Limitations of Salient Features:

1. Field studies conducted---yes
2. Practical for field use---yes
3. Usage for various types/sizes of projects---yes
4. Objective vs. subjective approaches---objective
5. Reproducibility---unknown
6. Scientifically sound features---yes

Conclusions:

General reference for WRAM

+ + +

REFERENCE:

Protasel, G.J., "Evaluating Natural Resource Planning",
September 1977, Department of Political Science, Oregon
State University, Corvallis, Oregon (report submitted to
U.S. Soil Conservation Service, Washington, D.C.).

Abstract:

This paper describes both theory and methodology associated with measuring public preferences and priorities relative
to water resources projects. The Q methodology of rank ordering of individual preferences is described. This can be used
to assign importance weights to assessment variables.

Salient Features:

A public participation technique for importance weighting
is described.

Advantages/Limitations of Salient Features:

1. Field studies conducted---yes
2. Practical for field use---yes
3. Usage for various types/sizes of projects---yes
4. Objective vs. subjective approaches---objective
5. Reproducibility---unknown
6. Scientifically sound features---yes

Conclusions:

Use directly in WRAM
..Mention public participation technique.

+ + +

460

REFERENCE:

Stinson, D.S. and O'Hare, M., "Predicting the Local Impacts
of Energy Development: A Critical Guide to Forecasting
Methods and Models", May 1977, 98pp., Laboratory of Architecture and Planning, Massachusetts Institute of Technology,
Cambridge, Mass.

Abstract:

     Models forecasting second-order impacts from energy
development vary in their methodology, output, assumptions,
and quality. As a rough dichotomy, they either simulate
community development over time or combine various submodels
providing community "snapshots" at selected points in time.
Using one or more methods--input/output models, gravity
models, econometric models, cohort-survival models, or coefficient models -- they estimate energy-development-
stimulated employment, population, public and private service
needs, and government revenues and expenditures at some
future time (ranging from annual to "average year" predictions)
and for different governmental jurisdictions(municipal, county,
state, etc.). Underlying assumptions often conflict, reflecting their different sources -- historical data, comparative data, surveys, and judgments about future conditions.
Model quality, measured by special features, tests, export-
ability and usefulness to policy-makers, reveals careful and
thorough work in some cases and hurried operations with
insufficient in-depth analysis in others.

Salient Features:

     Has good summary matrix which shows contents of 33 tech-
niques relative to inputs, outputs and processes. The 33
projection methods (techniques) are organized and discussed
(summarized) according to employment (basic and secondary),
population (total and sub-groups), service impacts (housing,
education services, water and sewerage, other public services
and retail services), and public revenues (taxes) and expenditures.

Advantages/Limitations of Salient Features:

     1. Field studies conducted---yes
     2. Practical for field use---yes
     3. Usage for various types/sizes of projects---yes
     4. Objective vs. subjective approaches---objective
     5. Reproducibility---unknown
     6. Scientifically sound features---yes

461

Conclusions:

    Use directly in WRAM
    ..Mention impact prediction information.

+ + +

REFERENCE:

U.S. Soil Conservation Service, "Environmental Assessment
Guidelines," Federal Register, Vol. 42, No. 152, Monday,
August 8, 1977, pp. 40127-40128.

Abstract:

    These guidelines are for SCS personnel to use in their
preparation of environmental assessments and impact statements. Useful ideas are included on the need for and working
functions of an interdisciplinary team. Impact assessment
methodologies which are included are interaction matrices,
networks, and a scaling checklist. See Figure F-1 for an
example of a network for an impoundment.

Salient Features:

    Discussion of interdisciplinary team; network for an
impoundment.

Advantages/Limitations of Salient Features:

1. Field studies conducted---yes
2. Practical for field use---yes
3. Usage for various types/sizes of projects---yes
4. Objective vs. subjective approaches---objective
5. Reproducibility---unknown
6. Scientifically sound features---yes.

Conclusions:

    General reference for WRAM

+ + +

REFERENCES:

Voelker, A.H., "Power Plant Siting: An Application of the
Nominal Group Process Technique", ORNL/NUREG/TM-81, February,
1977, Oak Ridge National Laboratory, Oak Ridge, Tennessee
(prepared for U.S. Nuclear Regulatory Commission, Washington,
D.C.).

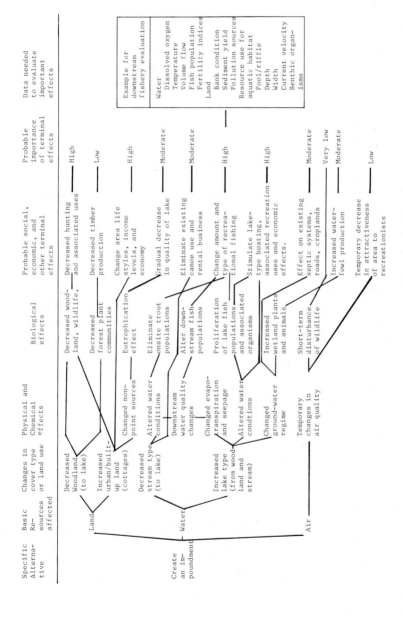

FIGURE F-1: AN EXAMPLE OF A NETWORK DIAGRAM FOR ANALYZING PROBABLE ENVIRONMENTAL IMPACTS

Abstract:

The application of interactive group processes to the problem of facility siting is examined by this report. Much of the discussion is abstracted from experience gained in applying the Nominal Group Process Technique, an interactive group technique, to the identification and rating of factors important in siting nuclear power plants. The Nominal Group Process Technique (NGT) was developed by Andre Delbecq and Andrew Van deVen in 1968. It was derived from social-psychological studies of decision conferences, management-science studies of aggregating group judgments, and social-work studies of problems surrounding citizen participation in program planning. It has gained wide acceptance in health, social service, education, industry, and government organizations. Basically, it consists of four steps: (1) nominal (silent and independent) generation of ideas in writing by a panel of participants, (2) round-robin listing of ideas generated by participants on a flip chart in a serial discussion, (3) discussion of each recorded idea by the group for the purpose of clarification and evaluation, and (4) independent voting on priority ideas, with group decision determined by mathematical rank-ordering. This report concludes that the application of interactive group process techniques to planning and resource management will effect the consideration of social, economic, and environmental concerns and ultimately lead to more rational and credible siting decisions.

Salient Features:

Nominal Group Process Technique for group assignment of relative importance weights to decision factors is described.

Advantages/Limitations of Salient Features:

1. Field studies conducted---yes
2. Practical for field use---yes
3. Usage for various types/sizes of projects---yes
4. Objective vs. subjective approaches---objective
5. Reproducibility---unknown
6. Scientifically sound features---yes

Conclusions:

Use directly in WRAM
..Mention technique as a means of assigning importance weights.

+ + +

REFERENCE:

Von Gierke, H.E., "Guidelines for Preparing Environmental
Impact Statements on Noise", June 1977, 131 pp., National
Research Council, Washington, D.C.

Abstract:

Guidelines are proposed for the uniform description and
assessment of the various noise environments potentially requiring an Environmental Impact Statement for Noise. In
addition to general, audible noise environments, the report
covers separately high-energy impulse noise, special noises
such as ultrasound and infra-sound, and the environmental impact of structure-borne vibration. Whenever feasible and
practical, a single-number noise impact characterization is
recommended, based on the new concept of level-weighted
population: i.e., the summation over the total population of
the product of each residential person times a weighting
factor that varies with yearly day-night average sound level
outside the residence of that person. A sound-level weighting
function for general impact and environmental degradation
analysis is proposed, based on the average annoyance response
observed in community response studies; this weighting
function is supplemented by an additional weighting function
at higher noise environments to quantify the potential of
noise-induced hearing loss and general health effects. The
evaluation of the environmental impact of vibration is derived from existing or proposed ISO standards. The report
explains and justifies the procedures selected and gives
examples of their application.

Salient Features:

Noise impact prediction and assessment is described.

Advantages/Limitations of Salient Features:

1. Field studies conducted---yes
2. Practical for field use---yes
3. Usage for various types/sizes of projects---yes
4. Objective vs. subjective approaches---objective
5. Reproducibility---unknown
6. Scientifically sound features---yes

Conclusions:

Use directly in WRAM
..Mention noise impact prediction and assessment.

+ + +

465

REFERENCE:

Wehr, P., <u>Conflict Regulation</u>, 1978, manuscript to be
published by Westview Press, Boulder, Colorado.

Abstract:

This manuscript provides a comprehensive discussion of
conflict regulation based on the studies and personal experiences of the author. Chapter 2 summarizes models and
techniques for conflict regulation. Chapter 6 is specifically
oriented to regulating environmental conflict based on an
actual case study in Colorado. Appendix A contains a list
of organizations engaged in conflict regulation training,
education and research.

Salient Features:

Comprehensive information on conflict management and
resolution.

Advantages/Limitations of Salient Features:

1. Field studies conducted---yes
2. Practical for field use---yes
3. Usage for various types/sizes of projects---yes
4. Objective vs. subjective approaches---objective
5. Reproducibility---unknown
6. Scientifically sound features---yes

Conclusions:

Use directly in WRAM
..Mention availability for conflict resolution.

+ + +

APPENDIX G

Abstracts of References
Not Meeting Entrance Criteria

A. 1960-70 PERIOD

REFERENCE:

Belknap, R.K. and Furtado, J.G., "Three Approaches to Environmental Resource Analysis," November 1967, Landscape Architecture Research Office, Harvard University, Cambridge, Mass.

Abstract:

This report examines three approaches for identifying, analyzing and evaluating the natural and man-made resources that comprise the physical environment. The approaches were developed by C. Angus Hills, Philip H. Lewis, Jr., and Ian L. McHarg. All three individuals have recognized needs for more comprehensive thinking by economists, planners, public officials and others who are influencing or making decisions about the development of the environment. The approaches are compared on: (1) their identification of spatial and environmental patterns beyond single factor analysis and simple spatial location, (2) their identification and evaluation of key elements and forces that affect the quality of the environment, (3) their review of analysis material for incorporation in the planning process, and (4) their treatment of the environment as an entity.

+ + +

REFERENCE:

Klein, G.E., "Evaluation of New Transportation Systems," in "Defining Transportation Requirements - Papers and Discussions," 1969, American Society of Mechanical Engineers, New York, N.Y.

Abstract:

This technique was designed to evaluate systems in terms of economic and social factors; the method could possibly be applied to environmental factors. A utility index similar to the "value functions" used in the Battelle environmental evaluation system (1972) is employed. Instead of one function defining the quality state, two functions representing the upper and lower limits are presented. The evaluator is allowed to make a decision somewhere between the two extremes. Specific criteria used in establishing the functions are placed on the horizontal axis, with the point chosen by the evaluator corresponding on the verticle axis to a 0-10 utility scale. Zero on the utility scale represents the best situation, ten the worst, and the utility index for each factor is translated directly into dollar figures. This dubious procedure is intended to put actual dollar signs on intangible

469

values, with the total evaluation based on relative costs and
benefits among alternatives.

+ + +

REFERENCE:

Lacate, D.S., "The Role of Resource Inventories and Landscape
Ecology in the Highway Route Selection Process", 1970, 198
pages, Department of Conservation, College of Agriculture,
Cornell University, Ithaca, New York.

Abstract:

Highway route alternatives are compared and the optimum
route selected based on a subjective analysis of "resource
inventories." A resource inventory is simply the process of
collecting data on a particular factor of social, economic, or
environmental concern. The information produced by the resource inventories is aggregated in a series of overlay maps;
thus, the method is actually the same as the McHarg method.
Only four overlay maps are prepared in the case study presented.
The first displays the various land uses; the second, type and
intensity of farming; the third, soils; and the last, localized
historic, cultural, and environmental values.

+ + +

REFERENCE:

Lamanna, R.A., "Value Consensus Among Urban Residents",
Journal American Institute of Planners, Vol. 30, No. 4, 1964,
pp. 317-323.

Abstract:

Priority areas of concern are identified by means of
responses to a sample survey. Persons interviewed are presented with a list of potential concerns and are asked to
weight elements according to importance on a scale from one
to three, three being most important. This method does not
insure a sound basis for indicated preferences and determines
only probable areas of lesser or greater impacts, not the
extent of impact itself.

+ + +

REFERENCE:

McHarg, I., "A Comprehensive Highway Route Selection Method",
pp. 31-41 in Design with Nature, 1969, Natural History Press,
Garden City, New York.

Abstract:

The McHarg approach is a system employing transparencies
of environmental characteristics overlaid on a regional base
map. Eleven to sixteen environmental and land use characteristics are mapped. The maps represent three levels of the
characteristics, based upon "compatibility with the highway".
This approach is basically noncomputerized and its basic value
is as a method for screening alternative project sites or
routes. Within this limited use, it is applicable to a variety
of project types. Limitations of the approach include its
inability to quantify as well as identify possible impacts
and its implicit equal weighting of all characteristics
mapped.

+ + +

B.   1971-73 PERIOD

REFERENCE:

Arthur D. Little, Inc., "Transportation and Environment:
Synthesis for Action: Impact of National Environmental Policy
Act of 1969 on the Department of Transportation", July, 1971,
Vol. 3 (Options for Environmental Management), prepared for
office of the Secretary, Department of Transportation,
Washington, D.C.

Abstract:

This is less a complete methodology than an overview
discussion of the kinds of impacts that may be expected to
occur from highway projects and the measurement techniques
that may be available to handle some of them. A quite
comprehensive list of impact types and the stages of project
development at which each may occur are presented. As broad
categories, the impact types identified are useful for other
projects as well as for highways. The approach suggests
the separate consideration of an impact's amount, effect
(public response), and value. Some suggestions are offered
for measuring the amount of impact within each of seven
categories: noise, air quality, water quality, soil erosion,
ecologic, economic, and sociopolitical impacts.

+ + +

REFERENCE:

Baker, R.W., and Gruendler, J.D., "Case Study of the Milwaukee-Green Bay Interstate Corridor Location", 1972, paper
presented at Highway Research Board Summer Meeting and in

"Environmental Considerations in Planning, Design and Construction", Special Report 138, Highway Research Board,
Washington, D.C.

Abstract:

    A computer-oriented selection process was used to simul-
taneously weigh the social, economic, and environmental
factors of a large area to determine the most acceptable
corridor for a transportation facility. Relative weights
were assigned to the variables in the selection process. The
general methodology is similar to a computerized McHarg
technique.

+ + +

REFERENCE:

Bureau of Land Management, "Environmental Analysis", Working
Draft, 1973, 126 pages, Bureau of Land Management, Washington,
D.C.

Abstract:

    This is an approach to environmental assessment that
uses an environmental analysis worksheet that is both flexible and open. The suggested environmental elements to be
considered are listed in an environmental digest. Impacts
are evaluated on a scale of low-medium-high, and positive-
negative. Accompanying remarks are an integral part of the
ongoing worksheet process.

+ + +

REFERENCE:

Cross, F.L., "Assessing Environmental Impact", Pollution
Engineering, Vol. 5, No. 6, June 1973, pp. 34-35

Abstract:

    A brief discussion of interaction matrices and their
use in evaluating alternatives is presented.

+ + +

REFERENCE:

Ditton, R.B., and Goodale, T.L. editors, "Environmental Impact Analysis: Philosophy and Methods", Proceedings of the
Conference on Environmental Impact Analysis, Green Bay,

Wisconsin, January 4-5, 1972, Sea Grant Publication Office,
University of Wisconsin, Madison, Wisconsin.

Abstract:

These proceedings contain the papers presented at a
2-day conference held in 1972. The papers reflect the first
2 years of practice under the requirements of NEPA.

+ + +

REFERENCE:

Fabos, J.G., "Model for Landscape Resource Assessment - Part 1
of the Metropolitan Landscape Planning Model (METLAND)",
February 1973, Department of Landscape Architecture and
Regional Planning, University of Massachusetts, Amherst, MA.

Abstract:

The development and application of a landscape resource
assessment model designed to estimate landscape change, both
positive and negative, caused by urbanization in the Boston
metropolitan region since 1945 are described. The model
incorporates the quantitative assessment techniques for
estimating water quality, the use of questionnaires and
matrices, mapping of value change isopleths, and other submodels for parameter evaluations. This is only the first step;
a second step is planned that will provide planners with a
model for land-use allocation and land-use activity management.

+ + +

REFERENCE:

Hetman, F., "Society and the Assessment of Technology,"
1973, Organization for Economic Cooperation and Development,
Washington, D.C., pp. 115-139.

Abstract:

Procedural steps for technology assessments developed in
three separate studies are described. The steps used in the
experimental studies of the U.S. National Academy of Engineering, the Mitre Corporation in work supported by the Office of
Science and Technology, and the Japanese Ministry of International Trade and Industry are described. The steps used
in these three studies are similar in concept to appropriate
environmental impact assessment procedures.

+ + +

REFERENCE:

Krauskopf, T.M., and Bunde, D.C., "Evaluation of Environmental Impact Through a Computer Modelling Process", in Ditton, R. and Goodale, T. (editors), "Environmental Impact Analysis: Philosophy and Methods," 1972, pp. 107-125, University of Wisconsin Sea Grant Program, Madison, Wisconsin.

Abstract:

This methodology employs an overlay technique via computer mapping. Data on a large number of environmental characteristics are collected and stored in the computer on a grid system of 1 km² cells. Either highway route alternatives can be evaluated by the computer (by noting the impacts on intersected calls) or new alternatives may be generated via a program identifying the route of least impact. The environmental characteristics used are rather comprehensive, particularly as regards land-use and physiographic characteristics. Although the methodology was developed and applied to a highway setting, it is adaptable, with relatively small changes in characteristics examined, to other project types with geographically well-defined and concentrated impacts. Because the approach requires considerable amounts of data on the project region, it is not practical for the analysis of programs of broad geographical scope. The estimation of impact importance is done through specification of subjective weights. Because the approach is computerized, the effects of several alternative weighting schemes can be readily analyzed.

+ + +

REFERENCE:

McKenry, C.E. et al., "Interstate 75 - Evaluation of Corridors Proposed for South Florida", 1971, 62 pages, University of Miami Center for Urban Studies, Coral Gables, Florida (report prepared for State of Florida Department of Transportation).

Abstract:

An ad hoc interdisciplinary panel of experts was convened to consider the qualitative advantages and disadvantages of proposed routes, making a recommendation based on a consensus judgment. Subunits of the panel prepared written reports of probable impacts in their area of expertise. These reports were then discussed in a series of deliberative sessions, and agreement on a recommendation was reached.

+ + +

REFERENCE:

National Forest Service, "Interaction Between Resources",
1973, National Forest Service, U.S. Department of Agriculture,
Atlanta, Georgia.

Abstract:

This methodology represents a qualitative discussion of
the interactions between forest resources.

+ + +

REFERENCE:

Rea, R., "Handbook for Assessing the Social and Economic
Impacts of Water Quality Management Plans", July 1973,
Resource Planning Associates, Inc., Cambridge, Massachusetts
(report prepared for Environmental Protection Agency,
Washington, D.C.).

Abstract:

These studies propose a system for environmental assessment that is definable in two discrete components - impact
identification and impact evaluation. The methodology relies
heavily on input from regional planning agencies and community
groups. In the impact identification process objectives, by-
products, short-term requirements, and long-term requirements
are considered. The authors state that due to the large
number of impact cells to be scrutinized, priorities for in-
depth analysis should be resolved by the contractor with
major input from resource planning agencies. Tables and
charts present a summary view of the findings in readily
understandable form.

+ + +

REFERENCE:

Rosove, P.E., "A Trend Impact Matrix for Societal Impact
Assessment," April 1973, 24 pp., Center for Futures Research,
Graduate School of Business Administration, University of
Southern California, Los Angeles, California.

Abstract:

This report describes the concept of a trend impact
matrix for analyzing societal trends and presenting them to
policy-makers. The trend impact matrix is similar in concept
to the Leopold interaction matrix.

475

REFERENCE:

Sewell, W.R.D., "Broadening the Approach to Evaluation in
Resources Management Decision-Making", Journal of Environmental Management, Vol. 1, 1973, pp. 33-60.

Abstract:

The task of evaluation in resource management decision-
making is becoming increasingly complex. More and more it
is becoming necessary to consider proposals for resource
development in terms of their broad social, environmental
and institutional consequences, as well as their economic
and financial effects. Increasingly, the region or the
nation rather than the local area is the appropriate area
unit for evaluation. With the aid of a descriptive model
of the policy-making process, this article examines the
extent to which present procedures for evaluation are able to
provide the data that decision-makers require at various
stages of that process. It shows that while considerable
progress has been made in the past decade in developing tools
for evaluation, there remain important weaknesses in this
connection. These weaknesses stem in part from the incapacity
to identify and measure certain effects, notably aesthetics,
other intangibles, and future values, and in part from institutional biases towards some strategies rather than others.
The author suggests that many of these weaknesses might be
overcome through the acceleration of social science research
in the resources management field, and particularly in the
following five areas: the identification of the nature and
magnitude of resources problems and of the demands for
resources-related goods and services; the delineation of
alternative strategies for dealing with resources problems;
hindsight reviews of projects and policies; examination of
alternative ways of identifying public views; and development
of more sophisticated techniques for taking account of
multiple objectives, multiple strategies, and a wide range
of values. The article concludes with a list of specific
types of studies that might be undertaken in connection with
each of these areas.

+ + +

REFERENCE:

Smith, W.L., "Quantifying the Environmental Impact of Transportation Systems", 1973, Van Doren-Hazard-Stallings-Schnake
Consultants, Topeka, Kansas.

Abstract:

The Smith approach, as developed for highway route selection, is a checklist system based on the concepts of probability
and supply-demand. The approach attempts to identify the alternative with least social cost to environmental resources and
maximum social benefit to system resources. Environmental resources elements are agriculture, wildlife conservation, interference, noise, physical features, and replacement. System
resources elements are aesthetics, cost, mode interface, and
travel desires. For each element, categories are defined and
used to classify zones of the project area. Numerical probabilities of supply and demand are then assigned to each zone
for each element. These are multiplied to produce a probability of least social cost (or maximum social benefit).
These least social cost probabilities are then multiplied
across the elements to produce a total for the route alternative under examination. The approach is tailored and perhaps
limited to project situations requiring comparison of alternatives. The range of environmental factors examined is very
limited, but presumably it could be expanded to cover more
adequately ecological, pollution, and social considerations.

+ + +

REFERENCE:

Turner, A.K., and Hausmanis, I., "Computer-Aided Transportation Corridor Selection in the Guelp-Dundas Area of Ontario",
1972, paper presented at Highway Research Board Summer Meeting
and in "Environmental Considerations in Planning, Design and
Construction", Special Report 138, Highway Research Board,
Washington, D.C.

Abstract:

A review of both graphical and computer-aided techniques
for highway route selection is presented. Different importance weights were assigned to factors in the study and a
computer-aided mapping technique was used to select an optimum route. The general methodology is similar to a computerized McHarg technique.

+ + +

REFERENCE:

Walton, Jr., L.E., and Lewis, J.E., "A Manual for Conducting
Environmental Impact Studies", Report No. VHRC 70-R 46, June
1971, 35 pages, Virginia Highway Research Council, Charlottesville, Virginia (report prepared for Federal Highway Administration, Washington, D.C.).

Abstract:

    The report develops methodologies for measuring the
anticipated environmental impact of proposed highways at the
conceptual, location and design planning stages. An interdisciplinary team approach is recommended. The research
emphasizes the systematic collection and evaluation of data
on various types of impacts, including those related to
community facilities (churches, hospitals, and parks), relocation of people and businesses, employment, noise, air
pollution and historic sites. Worksheets, utilizing monetary values and other suggested weights, are presented for
evaluating the anticipated impact. The results of the
weighting scheme are summarized for each type of impact in
an environmental ratio worksheet. The suggested weighting
scheme tends to penalize proposed routes which display certain
characteristics such as: division of a neighborhood, demo-
lition of hospitals or historic sites, and potential employment losses to the community. The report also provides a
suggested list of key individuals and agencies (such as
pastors, school principals, planning directors, and employment
commissions) which should be interviewed and with whom possible
impact results may be discussed.

+ + +

REFERENCE:

Warner, M.L., "Environmental Impact Analysis: An Examination
of Three Methodologies", Ph.D. Dissertation, 1973, 248 pages,
Department of Agricultural Economics, University of Wisconsin,
Madison, Wisconsin.

Abstract:

    This research suggests bases for the evaluation and
further development of methodologies used to prepare impact
statements. Three methodologies are critically analyzed.
They are: the "Leopold approach," suggested by Luna B.
Leopold, and others, the "Battelle approach," developed at
Battelle's Columbus Laboratories for the U.S. Bureau of
Reclamation, and the "WRC approach," contained in the "Proposed Principles and Standards for Planning Water and Related
Land Resources" of the U.S. Water Resources Council. Specific
criteria for methodology evaluation are developed within the
areas of: technical ecological content, practical applicability, and political utility. These criteria are designed
to emphasize a "full-disclosure law" interpretation of NEPA.
The methodologies are examined using each set of criteria in
turn. To provide a more concrete setting for this analysis,
a test case involving a proposed U.S. Bureau of Reclamation

water resources development project in Southwest Idaho was used. Data collection consisted of a point-by-point comparison of criteria and related desirable characteristics to each methodology. These data are analyzed for overall methodological conformance to the criteria to yield conclusions on the strengths and weaknesses of the methodologies. For political utility criteria, conclusions are based upon a model and theory of the Federal reclamation project policy-making process. None of the 12 entrance criteria are met. The three methodologies which were studied are treated separately in this literature review.

+ + +

C. 1974 PERIOD

REFERENCE:

Agency for International Development, "Environmental Assessment Guidelines Manual", September 1974, Agency for International Development, Department of State, Washington, D.C.

Abstract:

A very brief, simple checklist methodology is presented following each of the following AID project types: agricultural development (including range management), irrigation systems, dams (and water impoundments), power plants and transmission (fossil-fueled, nuclear-fueled, hydroelectric, and geothermal), municipal utilities (water supply, sewerage, solid waste and storm drainage), roads and highways (including railroads), airports, ports and harbors (including dredging), urban development and renewal (including housing, schools, hospitals, etc.), telecommunications, tourism, mining and extraction (including concentrating and smelting), and manufacturing. Each checklist addresses resource linkages, physical aspects, socio-cultural aspects and public health aspects.

+ + +

REFERENCE:

Bennington, G., Lubore, S., and Pfeffer, J., "Resource and Land Investigations (RALI) Program: Methodologies for Environmental Analysis, Vol. I, Environmental Assessment", MTR-6740, Vol. I, August, 1974, The MITRE Corporation, McLean, Virginia (Report prepared for U.S. Geological Survey, Reston, Virginia).

Abstract:

This report reviews selected methodologies used or proposed for environmental impact assessment. Pertinent methodologies are included elsewhere in this literature review.

+ + +

REFERENCE:

Brown, P.J., "Toward a Technique for Quantifying Aesthetic Quality of Water Resources", Report on Contract No. DACW 31-72-C-0060, October 1974, 100 pp., Institute for Water Resources, Fort Belvoir, VA (prepared for IWR by Utah State University, Logan, Utah).

Abstract:

The report contains the proceedings of a colloquium which was held in Park City, Utah on 16-18 October 1972 to explore various means of incorporating aesthetic considerations into the water resources planning process. The conference brought together a multi-disciplinary group of experts in the field of natural aesthetics in order to design a strategy to examine and develop the aesthetic opportunity sector of the straw man model. The straw man is heavily oriented toward computerized analysis, hence quantifying the aesthetic effects of water resource development alternatives was a primary topic of discussion during the conference. The report focuses on aesthetics and water resources development.

+ + +

REFERENCE:

Colston, Jr., N.W., "Characterization and Treatment of Urban Land Runoff", EPA-670/2-74-096, December, 1974, 170 pp., National Environmental Research Center, Environmental Protection Agency, Cincinnati, Ohio.

Abstract:

Urban land runoff from a 1.67 square-mile urban watershed in Durham, North Carolina, was characterized with respect to annual pollutant yield. Regression equations were developed to relate pollutant strength to hydrograph characteristics. Urban land runoff was found to be a significant source of pollution when compared to the raw municipal waste generated within the study area. On an annual basis, the urban runoff yield of COD was equal to 91 percent of the raw sewage

yield, the BOD yield was equal to 67 percent, and the urban
runoff suspended solids yield was 20 times that contained in
raw municipal wastes for the same area. Downstream water
quality was judged to be controlled by urban land runoff 20
percent of the time (i.e., the pounds of COD from urban land
runoff was approximately 4½ times the pounds of COD from
raw sewage). It is conceivable that critical water quality
conditions are not typified by the 10-year, 7-day low flow,
but by the period immediately following low-flow periods
when rainfall removes accumulated urban filth into the receiving watercourse, greatly increasing the pollutant load
while not substantially increasing water quantity. Specific
urban land use did not appear to influence the quality of
urban land runoff. The applicability and effectiveness of
plain sedimentation and chemical coagulation of urban land
runoff was evaluated. Plain sedimentation was found to
remove an average of 60 percent of the COD, 77 percent of
the suspended solids, and 53 percent of the turbidity.
Cationic polyelectrolytes and inorganic coagulants were found
to provide significant residual removal increases over plain
sedimentation. Alum was judged the best coagulant and produced average removals of COD, suspended solids, and turbidity
of 84, 97, and 94 percent, respectively.

+ + +

REFERENCE:

Curran Associates, Inc., "Evaluation of Power Facilities:
A Reviewer's Handbook", April 1974, 392 pp., U.S. Department
of Housing and Urban Development, Washington, D.C., (prepared for HUD by Curran Associates, Inc., Northampton, Mass.).

Abstract:

The handbook identifies and discusses the positive and
negative impacts of power facilities on regional and local
areas. The emphasis is on assisting planners in developing
the local perspective of evaluation and to prepare them for an
active participatory role in decision-making. In order that
the comprehensive aspects of power facilities be fully explored, breadth rather than depth is emphasized. It thus
serves as a primer addressed to planners, citizens and public
agencies with the intent of imparting an objective and un-
biased understanding of the major issues involved in the
planning, design, licensing, construction, operation, and
regulation of generation and transmission facilities. It
further analyzes and summarizes the mass of regulatory legislation in everyday language, and identifies opportunities
for participation of comprehensive planners in the licensing
and regulatory procedures. The handbook is also designed to

assist review of Environmental Impact Statements from the local perspective.

+ + +

REFERENCE:

Dickert, T.G., "Methods for Environmental Impact Assessment: A Comparison", in Dickert, T.G., and Domeny, K.R. (editors), "Environmental Impact Assessment" Guidelines and Commentary", 1974, University Extension, University of California at Berkeley, Berkeley, California.

Abstract:

Three analytic functions (impact identification prediction and evaluation) are used to classify environmental impact assessment methodologies. Some methodologies have all three functions while others have one or two. Less than ten methodologies are mentioned, and they are included elsewhere in this literature review.

+ + +

REFERENCE:

Dunst, R.C., et al., "Survey of Lake Rehabilitation Techniques and Experiences", Tech. Bulletin-75, 1974, 183 pp., Wisconsin Department of Natural Resources, Madison, Wisconsin.

Abstract:

Excessive eutrophication of lakes is a serious international problem. There has been a great need for a comprehensive information source usable in developing future rehabilitation/protection programs. The state-of-the-art review represents an attempt to delineate the accomplishments of lake restoration-related activities worldwide. Information was acquired through an extensive mail survey (about 8,000 entries), cooperation of several international journals/ newsletters, and a systematic literature search including foreign as well as domestic materials. The contents of the report consist of five major divisions: (1) identification, description and present utility of the various techniques; (2) compilation and description of individual past and/or ongoing restoration experiences (almost 600 accounts); (3) project methodology; (4) name and address of people providing pertinent information (over 300 respondents); and (5) literature references (more than 800 documents).

+ + +

REFERENCE:

Environmental Protection Agency, "Water Quality Management
Planning for Urban Runoff", EPA 440/9-75-004, December 1974,
220 pp., Washington, D.C.

Abstract:

The manual is designed to provide technical assistance
to state and local water quality management planners to enable them to quantify within reasonable limits the urban
non-point water pollution problem in a local planning area
without extensive data generation, and make a preliminary
evaluation of cost effective abatement and control practices.
Procedures are prescribed for several levels of input, each
requiring more self-generated data, with increasingly sophisticated results. The manual provides a guide to data generation for abatement design, and includes a state-of-the-art
and an extensive bibliography on urban storm water runoff.
The manual contains five principal sections: (1) the
section on the assessment of urban runoff quantity and quality,
provides analytical procedures to predict quality, quantity
and rate of runoff resulting from street surface contaminant
removal by specified storm events; (2) example problems are
presented to demonstrate the concepts and analytical procedures; (3) the section on miscellaneous sources of urban
runoff pollution considers sources of runoff such as urban
irrigation and snowmelt; (4) methods for treatment, abatement and ultimate disposal of urban runoff are discussed and
general criteria are provided for an evaluation of the water
pollution potential of urban runoff; (5) the state-of-the-
art section provides background information regarding major
relevant studies conducted in numerous geographical locations
since 1936. Emphasis is, however, placed upon recent studies.

+ + +

REFERENCE:

Graf-Webster, E., Lubore, S., and Pfeffer, "Resource and Land
Investigations (RALI) Program: Methodologies for Environmental
Analysis, Vol. II, Utility Corridor Selection", MTR-6740, Vol.
II, August 1974, The MITRE Corporation, McLean, Virginia
(Report prepared for U.S. Geological Survey, Reston, Virginia).

Abstract:

This volume reviews methodologies which are being employed
for the selection of environmentally suitable corridors for
the placement of utility lines. Included is an identification
of legislative constraints together with trends in legislation

dealing with utility line location. The volume concludes
with an annotated bibliography of documents dealing with
utility corridor selection techniques; environmental, economic,
engineering, technical and institutional factors and considerations affecting corridor selection; and selected utility
corridor studies which have employed the latest methodologies
for selecting corridors and rights-of-way for utility lines.

+ + +

REFERENCE:

Heuting, R., "A Statistical System for Estimating the Deterioration of the Human Environment", in J.W. Pratt (ed.),
Statistical and Mathematical Aspects of Pollution Problems,
1974, Marcel Dekker, Inc., New York, New York, pp. 123-132.

Abstract:

    An innovative approach to environmental impact is pre-
sented. The author measures deterioration in the environment as decreased availability of functions of an environmental
component. Such a decrease would be the manifest result of
competition of functions. Hence in assessment, one should
analyze where competition of functions takes place, thus
tagging a deleterious effect. The author sees this competition taking on quantitative, spatial, and qualitative aspects.

+ + +

REFERENCE:

Peterson, G.L., Gemmell, R.S., and Schofer, J.L., "Assessment
of Environmental Impacts - Multidisciplinary Judgments of
Large-Scale Projects", Ekistics, 218, January 1974, pp. 23-30.

Abstract:

    This methodology was used to evaluate alternative
regional wastewater management systems for the Chicago and
south end of Lake Michigan area. A judgmental method for
evaluating the impacts of complex and large-scale physical
systems is described. It is based upon a simplifying linear
model of the impact process. The method is intended for
application to situations in which scientific analysis of
the actual impact process is not feasible. The linear model
allows the impact problem to be dissected into many specific
questions that can be presented to experts for judgmental
response. It is also design-interactive, in that the
evaluation is repeated several times. After each iteration,

redesign recommendations are transmitted to the system de-
signers, who attempt to make appropriate modifications prior
to the next round of evaluation.

+ + +

REFERENCE:

Ross, P.J., Spencer, B.G., and Peterson, Jr., J.H. "Public
Participation in Water Resources Planning and Decision-
Making Through Information-Education Programs: A State-of-
the-Art Study," 1974, 54 pp., Water Resources Research
Institute, Mississippi State University, State College,
Mississippi.

Abstract:

    The purpose was to explore the state of the art of
activities to inform and educate the public regarding water
resources programs. This objective was sought through (1)
a critical and systematic review of literature, including
both published and unpublished technical and scientific
documents, and (2) a study of information/education programs
of agencies involved in various levels of water resources
planning and management in the state of Mississippi. The
implications of the research for planning effective educational/
informational programs are discussed. Specific recommendations
are made.

+ + +

REFERENCE:

U.S. Bureau of Outdoor Recreation, "Handbook: Applications of
Remote Sensing and Computer Techniques for Recreation Planning",
Vols. 1,2,3 and 4, March 1974, Bureau of Outdoor Recreation,
Washington, D.C. (Report prepared for BOR by University of
Wisconsin, Madison, Wisconsin).

Abstract:

    This environmental assessment system is unique in its
remote sensing data gathering and its computer-generated overlays. Statistical methods for sampling the project area
(divided into cells for study by random sampling) are documented. A total impact index (II) is calculated for each of
the cells and compared to the expected impact (EI) on each.

+ + +

REFERENCE:

Viohl, Jr., R.C. and Mason, K.G.M., "Environmental Impact
Assessment Methodologies: An Annotated Bibliography", Ex-
change Bibliography 691, November 1974, Council of Planning
Librarians, Monticello, Illinois.

Abstracts:

Abstracts of over fifteen environmental impact assessment
methodologies are presented. The authors indicate that the
literature paints an assessment methodology as a system that
incorporates value considerations in the analysis of environmental, economic, aesthetic, social and cultural impacts, both
direct (primary) and indirect (secondary). This analysis must
be one which is not so quantitative as to attenuate the importance of parameters not readily quantifiable. Further, a
methodology must be one which not only continuously integrates
and complements the planning process but also synthesizes and
defines changing values and attitudinal constraints. The
methodologies are covered individually in the literature
review.

+ + +

REFERENCE:

Zirkle, J.D., "State of the Art Highway Related Water Quality",
June, 1974, 13 pp., Washington State Department of Highways,
Olympia, Washington.

Abstract:

Basic assumptions (establishment of existing quality,
determination of regulatory water quality, identification
of desired quality, definition of special uses, and the
expenditure determined in the public interest) in any water
quality program are reviewed, and the tools to improve water
quality and the design features that will accommodate such
tools are described. Design phase provisions must include the
utilization of every opportunity to adjust the highway alignment for favorable water quality. Drainage adjustments must
be made which would improve water quality for highway runoff.
Settling basins or detention ponds are described which can be
multipurpose units and could be temporary or permanent devices.
A standard catch basin which would provide a sump below the
outlet for settleable solids is another feature of drainage
design. The basin is equipped with baffles to prevent short-
circuiting of flow and proper establishment of the retention
time. A retention time of 2 hours allows suitable settlement

characteristics. The treatment plant directed basically
toward biological treatment is also outlined. In the area
of design treatments, slope stabilization is important to
reducing erosion and water pollution. Ditch or channel
stabilization may be achieved with use of matting checks or
wiers formed from concrete or wood as well as gravel or rock.
Stepped slope treatment, the selection of suitable plant
species, the farming of right of way are other aspects discussed. Attention is drawn to the need for alertness to
sensitive issues, the establishment of the order of work,
the restriction of operating time to accommodate special
biological conditions, and the use of restricted methods.
Bid items for temporary measures, force account time, and
the provision of adequate right of way are other aspects
covered. The need is indicated for aggressive leadership,
education, staff communication, and improved state of the
art studies in cost effective treatments to water pollution.

+ + +

D. 1975 PERIOD

REFERENCE:

Bascom, S.E., et al, "Secondary Impacts of Transportation and
Wastewater Investments: Research Results," EPA/600/5/75-013,
July 1975, 225 pp., U.S. Environmental Protection Agency,
Washington, D.C. (prepared for EPA by Environmental Impact
Center, Inc., Newton, Mass.).

Abstract:

The report presents the results of original research on
the extent to which secondary development can be attributed
to highways and wastewater treatment and collection systems,
and what conditions under which causal relations appear to
exist. Case studies of recent development trends were made
in four metropolitan regions: Boston, Massachusetts, Denver,
Colorado, Washington, D.C., and Minneapolis-St. Paul, Minnesota.
Data for the four metropolitan regions were analyzed using
econometric techniques and simulation modeling.

+ + +

REFERENCE:

Burchell, R.W., and Listokin, D., "The Environmental Impact
Handbook," 1975, Center for Urban Policy Research, Rutgers-
The State University of New Jersey, New Brunswick, New Jersey.

Abstract:

This Handbook contains a description checklist methodology which is primarily directed toward proposed actions involving housing. There is a good qualitative discussion of how to predict and assess impacts on/of the environment. The contained checklist is not as complete as those found in other housing impact assessment methodologies.

+ + +

REFERENCE:

Corwin, R., et al, Environmental Impact Assessment, 1975, 277 pages, Freeman, Cooper and Company, San Francisco, California.

Abstract:

This book contains 8 chapters written by 6 different individuals. Chapter headings include: Impact Assessment---Origin, Operation and Outlook; Environmental Science---Perspectives and Methods; Assessing Social and Economic Impacts; Warm Springs Dam---A Case Study of Social and Economic Impacts; The Law of Environmental Impact Assessment; How to Prepare an EIS; Making the Process Work; and Tools for EIS---A Practical Appendix.

+ + +

REFERENCE:
Eisler, R., and Wapner, M., "Second Annotated Bibliography on Biological Effects of Metals in Aquatic Environments," EPA-600/3-75, 008, October, 1975, 399 pp., Environmental Research Laboratory, U.S. Environmental Protection Agency, Narragansett, R.I.

Abstract:

A total of 725 references are listed on the toxicological, physiological, and metabolic influence of stable and radio-labelled chemical species of metal cations to marine, estuarine, and freshwater fauna and flora. References were annotated and subsequently indexed by metal, by taxa, and by author, in cumulative indices which encompass this volume and the initial volume in this series (Eisler, R., 1973. Annotated bibliography effects of metals in aquatic environments (No. 1-567), U.S. Environmental Protection Agency, Rept. R3-73-007; 287pp.).

+ + +

REFERENCE:

Hellstrom, D.I., "A Methodology for Preparing Environmental Statements," AFCEC-TR-75-28, August 1975, 217 pp., U.S. Air Force Civil Engineering Center, Tyndall Air Force Base, Flordia (prepared for U.S. Air Force by A.D. Little, Inc. of Cambridge, Massachusetts).

Abstract:

The purpose of this technical report is to provide instructions for Air Force field personnel in the methods for preparing enviornmental statements. The report begins with an introduction to the environment and its need for protection, followed by a brief review of the procedures which are used by the Air Force to assess and report the impacts which may result from various actions. This background material is followed by a discussion on how to establish and maintain an environmental baseline data and information system, which can be used for annual environmental assessment studies as well as specific actions for which formal environmental statements are required. The report then describes how to prepare the description of the proposed action, including construction, operations and the de-activation phases, and abnormal events which may be associated with the action. The next section deals with the descriptions of the existing environment, divided into three regimes: physical (land, air, water), biotic and human environments. The air traffic environment is treated as a separate topic. Two areas of potential impact are given special attention because of their importance to Air Force activities: (1) air quality, for which methods of making emission inventories and evaluations are discussed, and (2) noise, for which the AICUZ (Air Installation Compatible Use Zones) system is described. The report then describes how the action and the existing environment data can be merged to identify potential impacts and how to evaluate them in quantitative and qualitative terms. The remaining sections of the report deal with the other subject matter required in an environmental statement, such as the treatment of alternatives, unavoidable impacts, and use of resources.

+ + +

REFERENCE:

Jain, R.K., Drobny, N.L., and Chatterjea, S., "Procedures for Reviewing Environmental Impact Assessments and Statements for Construction Projects," Report No. CERL-TR-E-73, August 1975, 24 pages, Construction Engineering Research Laboratory, U.S. Army, Champaign, Illinois.

Abstract:

   This report illustrates procedures for reviewing EIA/EIS
for construction-related projects only. The first component of
the review procedure is a set of project screening factors
which broadly categorize construction projects by their characteristics according to extent of potential impacts. The second
component is a set of factor rating criteria used to rate projects that use the screening factors. The third component is a
set of project screening criteria based upon total factor scores.
These criteria provide a rationale to categorize construction
project impacts into three major project levels (low, medium,
and high) in terms of their total factor scores. The fourth
component is the detailed EIS review criteria for each of three
major project levels. These review criteria should be used in
conjunction with the output provided by EICS (Environmental
Impact Computer System) for the review level and controversial
attributes.

+ + +

REFERENCE:

Jain, R.K., and Urban, L.V., "A Review and Analysis of Environ-
mental Impact Assessment Methodologies," Report No. CERL-TR-
E-69, June 1975, 23 pages, Construction Engineering Research
Laboratory, U.S. Army, Champaign, Illinois.

Abstract:

   This report includes a review and analysis of 19 environmental impact assessment methodologies. The review criteria
are the same as those used by Warner and Preston in their study
of 17 methodologies. The 19 methodologies studied by Jain and
Urban include the 17 from the Warner and Preston study. Six
categories of methodologies are used (ad hoc, overlays, checklists, matrices, networks and combination computer aided. The
methodologies included in this report are addressed separately
in this literature review.

+ + +

REFERENCE:

Lehmann, E.J., "Preparation and Evaluation of Environmental
Impact Statements (A Bibliography and Abstracts)," NTIS/PS-
75/717, September 1975, National Technical Information Service,
Springfield, Virginia.

Abstract:

    The purpose of this bibliography is to present citations of
Federally-funded research covering two areas: The effectiveness
that Environmental Impact Statements have had in detering environmental degradation and aids which firms, states, and Federal agencies can use in writing Environmental Impact Statements. (Contains 60 abstracts). Pertinent references in this bibliography
are contained elsewhere in this literature review.

+ + +

REFERENCE:

Markley, O.W. and Bagley, M.D., "Minimum Standards for Quality
of Life," Report No. EPA-600/5-75-012, May 1975, U.S. Environmental Protection Agency, Washington, D.C. (Report prepared
for EPA by Stanford Research Institute, Menlo Park, California).

Abstract:

    This study addresses a number of issues of concern under
various sectors of man's environment. For each issue three
types of available information are complied; (1) public laws and
other less formal understandings that set minimum standards,
(2) objective data that reflect how well those standards are
being met, and (3) subjective data that reflect how people feel
about that aspect of the quality of their life. Man's needs
are grouped into two major areas--(1) basic needs, including
minimal life conditions necessary to meet physiological and
security needs, and (2) higher needs, to include social needs,
ego needs, and a need for self-fulfillment. Standards are being
categorized under each major need area, according to four levels
of concern, arranged in a heirarchical order; First, the existing
welfare concern--a statement of the threshold level; second,
security--standards insuring the welfare for all persons; and
finally, ability to influence---standards that allow individuals to influence threshold levels and their own access to welfare. In addition to identifying the range of minimal standards
that have been codified, this study will: (1) assess the various ways in which these standards apply to real conditions (e.g.,
social indicators and additional data), (2) identify "gaps"and
inconsistencies in existing standards that need to be remedied,
and (3) analyze the policy implications and effectiveness of
using this approach as a way to describe and improve quality of
life in the United States.

+ + +

REFERENCE:

Rote, D.M., and Wangen, L.E., "A Generalized Air Quality
Assessment Model for Air Force Operations," AFWL-TR-74-304,
February 1975, 168 pp., Air Force Weapons Laboratory, Kirtland
Air Force Base, N.M.

Abstract:

The Air Quality Assessment Model (AQAM) is designed to
serve as a generalized model that can be used to assess the
impact of Air Force operations on the air environment at the
air base level. This document constitutes the technical report to this effort and, as such, contains a discussion of
the methodologies incorporated into the computer programs for
the computation of pollutant emissions and the subsequent
dispersal of these pollutants in the ambient air. Simulation
of aircraft operations, temporal and spatial modeling of
pollutant emissions, dispersion models based on the Gaussian
plume formulation and other subjects germane to the model are
discussed. The program contains a short-term dispersion model
for hourly calculations and a climatological type model based
on the "Air Quality Display Model" for long-time average concentration calculations.

+ + +

REFERENCE:

Shaheen, D.G., "Contributions of Urban Roadway Usage to Water
Pollution," EPA-ROAP-21 ASY-005, April 1975, 358 pp., Environmental Protection Agency, Washington, D.C.

Abstract:

Street surface contaminants are deposited on roadways
from many sources within an urban area. Industrial operations,
land use activities, fallout of air pollutants, roadway usage
and other activities contribute to the loading of particulates
on urban roadways. These materials are then carried into
receiving waters by storm runoff where they constitute a
substantial portion of the overall water pollution problems
of cities. Metropolitan Washington, D.C. with its low background of industrial emissions, was the area chosen for study
of contributions of motor vehicle usage to urban roadway loading factors. Specific roadway study sites within this area
were selected so as to provide minimal interference from non-
traffic-related land use activities and thus isolate, as much
as possible, the traffic-related depositions. Motor vehicular
traffic is directly or indirectly responsible for deposition
of substantial quantities of materials on roadways in urban

areas. Significant levels of toxic heavy metals and asbestos and slowly biodegradable petroleum products and rubber are deposited directly from motor vehicles along with large quantities of particulate materials contributed indirectly by traffic. The particulates contributed indirectly by traffic are largely inorganic, but have associated with them solids and nutrients which represent a serious source of water pollutants in all metropolitan areas.

+ + +

REFERENCE:

Smith, M.F., "Environmental and Ecological Effects of Dredging (A Bibliography with Abstracts)" NTIS/PS-75/755, October 1975, National Technical Information Service, Springfield, Virginia.

Abstract:

Specific as well as general ecological and environmental effects of dredging and dredge spoil disposal are presented. Citations relate topics such as dredge spoil use in land reclamation, turbidity, effects on aquatic microbiology, fish and shell fish, and spoil disposal techniques. (Contains 136 abstracts)

+ + +

REFERENCE:

U.S. Department of Transportation, "Environmental Assessment Notebook Series," 6 volumes, 1975, U.S. Department of Transportation, Washington, D.C.

Abstract:

This Notebook Series represents a complete, descriptive checklist methodology for transportation projects. Notebook I discusses the principles of transportation planning and considerations which should be incorporated in all phases of the highway planning process. Notebook II focuses on the social impacts from highway construction, including impacts related to community cohesion, accessibility of facility and services, and displacement of people. Notebook III deals with economic impacts, including those on employment, income and business activity, residential activity, property taxes, regional and community plans and growth, and resources. Notebook IV is related to the physical impacts of highway facilities, and focuses on environmental design, aesthetics and historic values, terrestrial ecosystems, aquatic ecosystems, air quality, noise and vibration. Notebooks II

through IV provide a comprehensive list of potential impacts
of highway projects, together with workable state-of-the-art
methods and techniques for impact identification, data collection, analysis and evaluation. Notebook V describes techniques for recording, organizing and communicating pertinent
findings of the transportation planning and impact assessment
process. (Department of Transportation, 1975) Notebook VI
expands the bibliographic references contained in the previous
notebooks, and lists other data and information which may be
helpful to professionals responsible for environmental impact
assessment. Various measures to minimize potential environmental impacts are summarized in Notebook III. The categories
of measures include right-of-way design measures, replacement/
restoration measures, monetary compensation measures, planning
assistance measures, regulatory measures, and technological
measures.

+ + +

REFERENCE:

Welsh, R.L., "User Manual for the Computer-Aided Environmental
Legislative Data System," CERL-TR-E-78, November, 1975, 62 pp.,
Construction Engineering Research Laboratory, U.S. Dept. of
the Army, Champaign, Ill.

Abstract:

    The Computer-Aided Environmental Legislative Data System
(CELDS) was developed to respond to the Army's need for rapid,
easy access to environmental legislation relevant to a specific
project or activity. This system, a collection of current
federal and state environmental laws, regulations, and standards, has been developed for use by non-lawyers. Abstracts
of the legislation are written in a straightforward, narrative
style with all legal jargon and excessive verbiage removed.
These abstracts are not intended to replace the original
documents or resolve complex legal problems; their sole aim
is to provide quick access to current controls on activities
that may influence the environment, and to supply informative
data for environmental impact analysis and environmental
quality management. Legislation from 32 states and the
federal government is presently included in the system, and
work is continuing for laws of the remaining states.

+ + +

E. 1976 PERIOD

REFERENCE:

Allen, H.L., et al, "Public Law 92-500, Water Quality Analysis and Environmental Impact Assessment," NCWQ-75/100-1, April 1976, National Commission on Water Quality, Washington, D.C.

Abstract:

The Environmental Sciences sector of the National Commission on Water Quality was charged with conducting a national water quality and environmental impact assessment as part of a larger analysis of the effects of achieving or not achieving the requirements and goals of the Federal Water Pollution Control Act Amendments of 1972 (P.L. 92-500). The overall study methodology, including inherent assumptions and limitations, is outlined. A major part of the national assessment focused on 41 site-specific studies in which historical and existing water quality and environmental conditions are assessed, followed by projections of change, impacts and benefits to result from abatement of point source effluent loadings. Results and findings from these studies are collated, reviewed and summarized, both regionally and nationally, and are presented in this volume. The report also contains other special water quality and environmental assessment topics together with study appendices.

+ + +

REFERENCE:

Babcock, Jr., L.R., and Nadga, N. L., "Popex---Ranking Air Pollution Sources by Population Exposure," EPA/600/2-76-063, March 1976, 345 pp., University of Illinois Medical Center, Chicago, Illinois.

Abstract:

The report gives results of research to develop quantitative models for relating emissions of air pollutants to their effects on people, and to use the methodology for determining the relative importance of air pollution sources. The quantitative methodology for ranking the sources developed in this project includes consideration of the dispersion of air pollutants, exposure of people, and subsequent health effects. The computer model, called POPEX, consists of three submodels: dispersion, population, and health effects. The model was applied to sources of air pollution in the Chicago Air Quality Control Region. Results show that 17 of 227 categories of sources contribute nearly 80% of the total air-pollution/ population-effect problem.

REFERENCE:

Bayley, S., et al, "Energetics and Systems Modeling: A
Framework Study for Energy Evaluation of Alternative Transportation Modes in Comparison with Traditional Economic
Evaluation," June 1976, Department of Environmental Engineering
Sciences, University of Florida, Gainsville, Florida (submitted to U.S. Army Corps of Engineers under Contract DACW
17-75-0075).

Abstract:

This report presents a comparison of economic and energetic approaches for evaluating transportation systems. In
the Introduction, section I, a general discussion of economics
and energetics is presented to point out similarities, differences, advantages, and disadvantages of the two approaches.
The discussion of general energy theory, section II-A, discusses the laws of energetics, the method of comparing different types of energy flow through the concept of energy quality
and the relationship between energy and economic value.
Methods for calculating the energy value of goods and services,
the role of energy flows of natural systems in a regional or
transportation system, and spatial energy theory for determining the competitiveness of different fuel source locations are
also presented. In particular, economic benefit/cost analysis
as applied to transportation systems by the Corps of Engineers
is compared to a comparable energy benefit/cost analysis. In
order to illustrate the methodology of energetics several transportation systems are analyzed in order to calculate the energy
cost of each. Both direct fuel energies for operation and indirect fossil fuel and natural energies for goods and services
were considered. Some attempt was also made to measure the
disruption of natural systems by an existing or planned transport system. Since this report is not directed towards a particular problem or project natural system disruption was only
considered in a general way with ecological models presented
for proposed research. Approximate analyses were made for
barge transportation, railroad transportation, slurry pipelines,
and electrical transmission lines. In particular, the direct
and indirect energy costs of transporting coal were evaluated.
Energy costs per ton-mile and energy yield ratios (energy trans-
ported ÷ energy costs) are presented. Some analysis of the
direct and indirect energies associated with building barges,
towboats, and locks and dams were also attempted. In order to
show how energetics might be used at a regional scale of evaluation the problem of coal development and transportation in the
Northern Great Plains is presented in section V. Model development, mathematical analysis, computer simulation, and
energy concepts are presented in this analysis for the purpose
of illustrating energetic modeling at a regional scale.

REFERENCE:

Brandsma, M.G., and Divoky, D.J., "Development of Models for Prediction of Short-Term Fate of Dredged Material Discharged in the Estuarine Environment," WES-CR-D-76-5, May 1976, 297 pp., Tetra Tech, Inc., Pasadena, California. (prepared for Dredged Material Research Program, U.S. Army Engineer Waterways Experiment Station, Vicksburg, Mississippi).

Abstract:

The Dredged Material Research Project (DMRP) has as one of its objectives to provide more definitive information on the environmental aspects of dredging and dredged material disposal operations. This study was conducted to fill the need of that program for the capability of predicting the short-term fate of dredged material discharged in the estuarine environment. Two numerical models were developed: one for the instantaneous dumped discharge and one for fixed or moving jet discharge. The models account for land boundaries, depth variations in the estuary, ambient current variations in three dimensions and in time, and variations of ambient density profiles in time. The models are capable of tracking up to twelve classes of solid particles plus the fluid fraction of a discharge through convective descent, dynamic collapse, and passive diffusion phases. The models were developed by coupling the appropriate short-term dynamic portions of the Koh-Chang oceanic disposal model with an extensive modification of a model, originally developed by Fischer, for predicting the fate of chemical wastes in an estuary. Although the models themselves are extremely complex, the input data requirements for most cases are quite simple and should allow the first-time user to run a simple case in a few hours. The models have undergone limited testing and the results produced are physically reasonable. A program of model exercise and testing is strongly recommended, however. When the models are used in cases involving complex ambient velocities, the models will be extremely dependent on good-quality velocity data.

+ + +

REFERENCE:

Chow, V.T., and Yen, B.C., "Urban Stormwater Runoff: Determination of Volumes and Flowrates," EPA/600/2-76/116, May 1976, 253 pp., Department of Civil Engineering, University of Illinois, Urban, Illinois.

Abstract:

An investigation was made to (a) develop a method of
depth-duration-frequency analysis for precipitation events
having short return period (high frequency) for urban storm
water runoff management and control purposes; (b) develop
a new high accuracy urban stormwater runoff determination
method which when verified, can be used for projects requiring
high accuracy detailed runoff results and can also be used as
the calibration scale for the less accurate urban runoff prediction methods; and (c) compare and evaluate selected urban
storm-water runoff prediction methods. The eight methods
evaluated are the rational method, unit hydrograph method,
Chicago hydrograph method, British Transport and Road Research
Laboratory method, University of Cincinnati Urban Runoff
method, Dorsch Hydrograph Volume method, EPA Storm Water
Management Model, and Illinois Urban Storm Runoff method. The
comparison and evaluation is done by using four recorded hy-
etographs of the Oakdale Avenue Drainage Basin in Chicago to
produce the predicted hydrographs by the methods and the
results are compared with recorded hydrographs. The relative
merits of the methods are discussed and recommendations are
made.

+ + +

REFERENCE:

Clark, E.M. and Van Horn, A. J., "Risk-Benefit Analysis and
Public Policy: A Bibliography," BNL-22285, November 1976,
81 pp., Brookhaven National Laboratory, Upton, New York.

Abstract:

Risk-benefit analysis has been implicitly practiced
whenever decision-makers are confronted with decisions involving risks to life, health, or to the environment. Various
methodologies have been developed to evaluate relevant
criteria and to aid in assessing the impacts of alternative
projects. Among these have been cost-benefit analysis, which
has been widely used for project evaluation. However, in
many cases it has been difficult to assign dollar costs to
those criteria involving risks and benefits which are not
now assigned explicit monetary values in our economic system.
Hence, risk-benefit analysis has evolved to become more than
merely an extension of cost-benefit analysis, and many methods
have been applied to examine the trade-offs between risks and
benefits. In addition, new scientific and statistical techniques have been developed for assessing current and future
risks. The 950 references included in this bibliography are
meant to suggest the breadth of those methodologies which have

been applied to decisions involving risk.

+ + +

REFERENCE:

Greer, K.H., Blome, D.A., and Jones, Jr., J.E., "A Directory
of Computerized Environmental Information Resources," IMMR
23-GR3-76, October 1976, 46 pp., Institute for Mining and
Minerals Research, University of Kentucky, Lexington, Ky.

Abstract:

This directory presents a selected listing of computerized
environmental information resources. A description of each
resource, along with a listing of functions and services, subjects embraced, publications available, and a mailing address,
is included. Subject areas are diverse and include such topics
as pesticides, air pollution, soil data, energy, noise, ocean-
ography,nuclear science and water, among others.

+ + +

REFERENCE:

Hall, R.W., Westerdahl, H.E., and Eley, R.L., "Application of
Ecosystem Modeling Methodologies to Dredged Material Research,"
WES-TR-76-3, June 1976, 72 pp., U.S. Army Engineer Waterways
Experment Station, Vicksburg, Mississippi.

Abstract:

The report addresses the applicability of physical and
mathematical ecosystem modeling methodologies to environmental
problems associated with dredging and disposal operations.
Three categories of physical models are discussed: Bioassays,
microcosms, and scaled ecosystem models. Mathematical models
can be divided into a number of classes, such as those predicting the effect of allochthonous loadings on the dissolved
oxygen budget, determining the partitioning and dynamics of
chemical constituents, predicting excessive eutrophication
and nuisance algal blooms due to high nutrient loadings, and
simulating biological population dynamics and ecological
interactions.

+ + +

REFERENCE:

Kemp, H.T., "National Inventory of Selected Biological Monitoring Programs, Summary Report of Current or Recently Completed

Projects, 1976," ORNL/TM-5792, October 1976, 711 pp., Oak
Ridge National Lab., Tenn.

Abstract:

The inventory has resulted in establishment of a series
of data bases containing biological monitoring information
of varying types, namely, directory of investigators, record
of projects received from mail questionnaire, detailed description of selected biomonitoring projects, and bibliographic citations supporting the projects received. This
report contains detailed descriptions of selected biomonitoring projects organized on a state-by-state basis and
with appropriate indices.

+ + +

REFERENCE:

Kibby, H. and Hernandez, D.J., "Environmental Impacts of Advanced Wastewater Treatment of Ely, Minnesota," EPA-600/3-76-
082, August 1976, 30 pp., U.S. Environmental Protection Agency,
Corvallis, Oregon.

Abstract:

The results presented in this report give an indication
of the pollutants that would be generated and the resources
consumed in operating a treatment facility similar to the one
at Ely, Minnesota. The study analyzes not only the facility
itself, but also those industries that supply products to the
treatment plant. It was found that the total energy requirement of the advanced wastewater treatment plant was 50×10^6
Btu/million gallons of water treated.

+ + +

REFERENCE:

Lincer, J.L., Haynes, M.E., Klein, M.L., "The Ecological Impact
of Synthetic Organic Compounds on Estuarine Ecosystems,"
EPA-600/3-76-075, September 1976, 354 pp., Environmental
Research Laboratory, U.S. Environmental Protection Agency,
Gulf Breeze, Florida (prepared for EPA by Mote Marine Labora-
tory, Sarasota, Florida).

Abstract:

This report concerns the presence and effects of pesticides (i.e., insecticides, herbicides, fungicides, and so
forth) and industrial toxicants in the estuarine ecosystem.

500

The industrial toxicants which are included refer primarily
to polychlorinated biphenyls, byphthalate esters, polychlorinated terphenyls, chlorinated dibenzodioxins and di-
benzofurans. There are over 700 references cited in this
report. The literature covers the last decade, with emphasis
for the latter five years which are primarily in the 1970's.
The report is organized into sections, with the first one
describing the characteristics of synthetic organic compounds
in estuarine ecosystems in terms of persistance, bio-accumu-
lation, bio-magnification, and metabolism. Another section
describes the presence of synthetic organic compounds in
estuaries in terms of general considerations and data as
well as geographic distribution. Another major section deals
with the toxicological effects of synthetic organic compounds
on estuarine life, with this section addressing pesticides
and industrial toxicants followed by general concerns relative
to synergism and modifying effects at the community and ecosystems levels.

+ + +

REFERENCE:

Naval Environmental Support Office, "Data Sources for Environ-
mental Impact Assessments (EIAs) and Environmental Impact
Statements (EISs)," NESO 20.2-015, November 1976, 223 pp.,
Naval Construction Battalion Center, Port Hueneme, California.
(prepared for NESO by ManTech of New Jersey Corporation, San
Diego, California).

Abstract:

This 1976 document identifies sources of information for
environmental impact assessments/environmental impact statements being prepared by or for the U.S. Navy. It is a practical
document that suggests points of contact and sources of information for various environmental factors. A modest bibliography is included on general sources of information.

+ + +

REFERENCE:

Riggins, R. and Novak, E., "Computer-Aided Environmental
Impact Analysis for Mission Change, Operations and Maintenance,
and Training Activities: User Manual," CERL-TR-E-85, February
1976, 101 pp., Construction Engineering Research Laboratory,
U.S. Department of the Army, Champaign, Ill.

Abstract:

   The Environmental Impact Computer System (EICS), developed
by the U.S. Army Construction Engineering Research Laboratory,
helps planners efficiently identify primary and secondary
impacts of their proposed projects or activities and suggests
ways to mitigate these impacts. This manual is designed to
assist Army personnel in assessing EICS for three of the nine
functional areas of Army activity: mission change, operations
and maintenance, and training. The manual defines new terminology and provides a step-by-step outline for obtaining and
using the system's output. Included in the instructions are
designation of activity categories and activity descriptions
for the three functional areas. Input forms necessary for
obtaining EICS output and instructions for their completion
are provided. These forms include filter questions which help
the user reduce output to more site-and project-specific
information. The manual discusses in detail procedures necessary for using EICS output for environmental impact assessment and outlines the steps for preparing a proper and complete EIA/EIS. The EICS will save its users time and money by
eliminating unnecessary library and field research.

+ + +

REFERENCE:

Rosen, S.J., Manual for Environmental Impact Evaluation,
Prentice-Hall, Inc., Engelwood Cliffs, New Jersey, 1976,
232 pp.

Abstract:

   This book represents an assortment of descriptive ideas
regarding environmental impact evaluation. Its primary orientation is toward procedural concerns regarding EIS preparation
as opposed to substantive information for inclusion. Emphasis
is also given to general project planning as well as the incorporation of public participation. Practical suggestions are
contained for preparing both draft and final EIS's.

+ + +

REFERENCE:

Schanche, G.W., et al, "Pollution Estimation Factors,"CERL
TR-N-12, Nov., 1976, 26pp., Construction Engineering Research
Laboratory, U.S. Army, Champaign, Ill.

Abstract:

This document identifies pollutant-generating activities
resulting from the operation of military facilities and vehicles
and when possible, develops pollutant estimation factors. The
report consists of three parts based on the class of pollutants
being estimated. Chapter 2 contains examples of how to use air
pollutant emission factors and identifies Army-relevant portions
of Compilation of Air Pollutant Emission Factors. Chapter 3
contains factors for estimating solid waste composition and
quantity. Chapter 4 contains factors for estimating wastewater composition and quantity. Estimation factors contained
in Chapters 3 and 4 are based on data from the literature.

+ + +

REFERENCE:

U.S. Bureau of the Census, "Environmental/Socioeconomic Data
Sources (Supplement to TAB A-1, Environmental Narrative,"
October 1976, 169 pp., Subscriber Services Section (Public-
ations), Washington, D.C.

Abstract:

This handbook was compiled to assist the U.S. Air Force
in preparing its environmental impact statements. It provides
numerous data source suggestions ranging from local sources to
Federal, with emphasis on data available from the Census Bureau.
The handbook is divided into four parts. Part one provides an
introduction to the Census Bureau and other Federal data sources
as well as to potential local data resources. Part two suggests
various research approaches and includes exercises for selecting the most appropriate census report and statistical table.
Part three indicates where specific information may be found,
and part four presents a detailed guide to census data and
programs. These are categorized by general topics such as demographic, economic, housing, and government.

+ + +

F.   1977-78 PERIOD

REFERENCE:

Bockrath, J.T., Environmental Law for Engineers, Scientists
and Managers, McGraw-Hill Book Company, Inc., New York, N.Y.,
1977, 359 pp.

Abstract:

This is an excellent book dealing with numerous concerns relative to environmental law. Specific chapters are included on the National Environmental Policy Act, Federal Statutory Control of Water Pollution, and Air Pollution Control. The chapter on NEPA is well-written and contains specific information on court decisions and their influence on the policies and procedures for preparing and reviewing environmental impact statements.

+ + +

REFERENCE:

Brown, L.R., "Estimate of Maximum Level of Oil Innocuous to Marina Biota as Inferred from Literature Review," CGR/DC-9/77, April 1977, 20 pp., Mississippi State University, Starkville, Mississippi.

Abstract:

The objective of this study was to derive an estimate of the maximum level of oil which can be considered harmless to the marine biological community based on the current state-of-the-art as determined through review and interpretation of the literature. Overall nearly 2,000 individual articles relating to oil pollution were examined. One hundred and thirty-five of the most germane of these articles are listed as references.

+ + +

REFERENCE:

Cheremisinoff, P.N., and Morresi, A.C., Environmental Assessment and Impact Statement Handbook, 1977, 438 pp., Ann Arbor Science Publishers, Inc., Ann Arbor, Michigan.

Abstract:

This book includes chapters on the National Environmental Policy Act, the environmental impact statement, environmental assessment, environmental methodology, air quality impact, impact on water resources, solid waste-noise-economics, oil spill impact, nuclear power, radio-active waste treatment practices, petroleum refinery environmental assessment, and environmental assessment of the rubber industry.

+ + +

REFERENCE:

Erickson, L.E., "Approach to Valuing Visual Pollution from Western Electricity Production," BNWL-2103, February 1977, 76 pp., Battelle Pacific Northwest Labs., Richland, Washington.

Abstract:

This paper outlines an approach to valuing visual pollution from electric power plants. The differences between public-good pollution externalities, such as these aesthetic damages, and other market failures are discussed. Approaches generally used to value externalities are briefly described. The approach used relies heavily on an earlier application of bidding games to estimate people's willingness to pay for abatement of emissions from the Four Corners fossil-fuel power plant in northwestern New Mexico. The results of these surveys were used here to estimate the value of visual pollution from electric power plants for residents of and visitors to the Four Corners Air Quality Control Region, as a function of power plant emissions in that region. The approach presented here for the Four Corners region is structured so that replication for other air quality control regions is relatively easy. Preliminary results of this procedure for all of the air quality control regions in the Western Systems Coordinating Council area are presented. Visual pollution damages from electric power plants to residents of and recreational visitors to these western regions are estimated to total more than $100 million annually by 1985. These damages are expected to occur unless additional pollution controls are implemented, even if these subject populations do not increase.

+ + +

REFERENCE:

Fitzpatrick, M.S., et al, "Manual for Evaluating Secondary Impacts of Wastewater Treatment Facilities," EPA-600/5-78-003, February 1978, 175 pp., U.S. Environmental Protection Agency, Washington, D.C. (prepared for EPA by Abt Associates, Inc., Cambridge, Massachusetts.)

Abstract:

This manual describes procedures for assessing secondary impacts of wastewater treatment facilities. The manual guides the user through this impact assessment process by describing EPA policy and regulations governing analysis of these impacts; approaches to refine and improve existing projections of amount, type and location of projected growth in a service area; and the range of potential secondary impacts and alternative

approaches for impact assessment. Application of projection
and impact assessment approaches are provided for various
levels of sophistication, consistent with analysis capabilities
and available resources. The manual also provides EPA Regional
Reviewers with a convenient framework for evaluating quality
of local analyses of secondary impacts and an analytic basis
for imposing any needed special conditions. This manual is
a tool for planners and engineers preparing impact assessments,
it does not supplant regulations which govern impact assessment
processes. The manual considers only secondary impact assessment. Measures to mitigate these impacts have not been considered in the manual but should, of course, be implemented
where the impact warrants. Fourteen areas of secondary impacts
are covered in the manual, categorized into four groups:
Media impacts (e.g., ambient noise levels); Sensitive Environmental Area Impacts (e.g., floodplains); Unique Area Impacts
(e.g., parklands); and Secondary Economic Impacts (e.g.,
impacts on property values).

+ + +

REFERENCE:

Kahneman, D., and Tversky, A., "Intuitive Prediction: Biases
and Corrective Procedures," Special Issue of <u>Management</u>
<u>Science</u> on Forecasting Methodologies and Applications, in
press.

Abstract:

    Intuitive forecasts are based on the following notions.
First, most predictions and forecasts contain an irreducible
intuitive component. Second, the intuitive predictions of
knowledgeable individuals contain much useful information.
Third, these intuitive judgments are often biased in a predictable manner. Hence, the problem is not whether to accept
intuitive predictions at face value or to reject them, but
rather how they can be debiased and improved. This paper
presents an approach to elicitation and correction of intuitive forecasts. This approach is applied to two tasks that
experts are often required to perform in the context of forecasting and in the service of decision making: the prediction
of values and the assessment of confidence intervals. The
analysis of these judgments reveals two major biases: non-
regressiveness of predictions and overconfidence. Both
biases are traced to people's tendency to give insufficient
weight to certain types of information, e.g., the base-rate
frequency of outcomes and their predictability. The corrective
procedures described in this paper are designed to elicit from
the expert relevant information which he would normally
neglect, and to help him integrate this information with his

intuitive impressions in a manner that respects basic principles of statistical prediction.

+ + +

REFERENCE:

Pease, J.R., and Smardon, R.C., "Environmental Impact Assessment Project---Final Report, Analysis and Evaluation," Special Report 481, April 1977, Oregon State University Extension Service, Corvallis, Oregon.

Abstract:

Local participation in small project design and decision-making is described. The demonstration projects are included.

+ + +

REFERENCE:

Phillips, R.D., and Kaune, W.T., "Biological Effects of Static and Low-Frequency Electromagnetic Fields: An Overview of United States Literature," BNWL-2262, April 1977, 40 pp., Battelle Pacific Northwest Labs, Richland, Washington.

Abstract:

Results are reviewed from a number of studies on the biological effects of static and low frequency electromagnetic fields on animals. Based on a long history of experience with electric fields by the utility industry, it appears that intermittent and repeated exposures to strong 60 Hz electromagnetic fields from present power transmission systems have no obvious adverse effect on the health of man. It has been recognized recently that this belief must be tested by carefully designed and executed experiments under laboratory conditions where precise control can be exercised over co-existing environmental factors. A number of studies have been initiated in response to this need to evaluate possible effects from both acute and chronic exposures.

+ + +

REFERENCE:

Slovic, P., "Judgment, Choice and Societal Risk Taking," paper presented at Symposium on Judgment and Choice in Public Policy Decisions, Annual Meeting of the American Association for the Advancement of Science, Denver, Colorado, February 1977 (author's address is Decisions Research, a Branch of Perceptronics, 1201 Oak Street, Eugene, Oregon 97401).

Abstract:

This paper describes some of the social aspects of risk assessment. The author concludes that we are not well-equipped, either individually or collectively, for making decisions about risky activities.

+ + +

REFERENCE:

Sorensen, D.L., et al, "Suspended and Dissolved Solids Effects on Freshwater Biota: A Review," EPA-600/3-77-042, April 1977, 65 pp., U.S. Environmental Protection Agency, Corvallis, Oregon (prepared for EPA by Utah State University, Logan, Utah).

Abstract:

It is widely recognized that suspended and dissolved solids in lakes, rivers, streams, and reservoirs affect water quality. In this report the research needs appropriate to setting freshwater quality criteria or standards for suspended solids (not including bedload) and dissolved solids are defined by determining the state of our knowledge from a critical review of the recent literature in this field. Although some 185 journal articles, government reports, and other references were cited herein, there is a dearth of quantitative information on the response of freshwater biota, especially at the community level, to suspended and dissolved solids. The major research need was defined as the development and/or application of concepts of community response to suspended and dissolved solids concentrations and loads. These concepts need to be applied especially to the photosynthetic, the microfauna, and macrofauna levels. Fish studies are of lower priority since more and better research has been reported for these organisms. In addition, the role of suspended solids in transporting toxic substances (organics, heavy metals), aesthetic evaluation of suspended solids in aquatic ecosystems, and dissolved solids in drinking water, and economic aspects of dissolved solids in municipal-industrial water were defined as research needs.

+ + +

REFERENCE:

Struss, S.R. and Mikucki, W.J., "Fugitive Dust Emissions from Construction Haul Roads," Special Rep. N-17, February 1977, 53 pp., Construction Engineering Research Laboratory, U.S. Army, Champaign, Ill.

Abstract:

The results of both model and field studies indicate
that soil water potential is statistically significant in the
determination of dust emissions from construction haul roads.
Also significant are the speed and weight of the vehicles
using the road and the road's soil type. The number of soils
studied was insufficient to conclusively state which soil
property most accurately determines its dusting characteristics;
however, for the two soil types tested (Gooselake clay and
Drummer silty clay loam), plastic limit was the best indicator.

+ + +

AUTHOR INDEX

Burchell, R.W., and Listokin, D., 102, 223, 279, 487
Burnham, J. B., 12-14, 16, 33, 50, 91, 95, 96, 223, 323

Canter, L. W., (1976), 12, 13, 44, 55, 130, 138, 142, 224, 380
Canter, L. W., (1977), 9, 10, 12, 13, 15, 16, 19, 185, 192, 195, 224, 429, 432
Canter, L. W. and Reid, G. W., 12, 13, 15, 45, 185, 192, 195, 224, 431
Canter, L. W., and Hill, L. G., 9, 13, 21, 23, 29, 32, 185, 192, 195, 197, 224, 431
Canter, L. W., et al., 10, 19, 185, 190, 192, 223
Canter, L. W., (Supplement 1978), 7, 9, 10, 12, 13, 15, 16, 19, 185, 192, 433
Canter, L. W., (1978), 9, 10, 12, 13, 15, 16, 17, 19, 186, 192, 195, 196, 224, 434
Carstea, D., et al., 8, 10, 11, 39, 40, 103, 109, 111, 224, 347
Case, P. J., Edgmon, T. D. and Renton, D. A., 16, 50, 130, 138, 142, 224, 381
Central New York Planning and Development Board, 10, 12, 14, 37, 70, 77, 81, 224, 271
Chalmers, J. A. and Anderson, E. J., 9, 15, 33, 34, 40, 41, 186, 192, 195, 196, 199, 225, 434
Chalmers, J. A., 10, 33-35, 186, 192, 195, 196, 225, 435
Chase, G. H., 10, 14, 38, 131, 138, 225, 382
Chen, W. W. and Orlob, G. T., 10, 11, 30, 70, 77, 81, 225, 272
Cheremisinoff, P. N. and Morresi, A. C., 184, 186, 225, 504
Chow, V. T. and Yen, B.C., 129, 131, 225, 497
Christensen, S. W., Van Winkle, W., and Mattice, J. S., 11, 14, 31, 103, 109, 111, 225, 348
Christensen, K., 9, 10, 34, 131, 138, 142, 225, 383
Clark, E. M. and Van Horn, A. J., 129, 131, 225, 498
Clark, J. R., 11, 27, 103, 109, 111, 225, 349 (1975)
Clark, R. N., Hendee, J. C. and Stankey, G. N., 16, 50, 131, 136, 138, 142, 143, 226, 383
Coates, J. F., (1976-A), 11, 14, 19, 20, 131, 136, 138, 141, 142, 144, 226, 384
Coates, J. F., (1976-B), 14, 19, 20, 131, 138, 141, 142, 226, 385
Colonell, J. M., 9, 11, 27, 131, 138, 142, 226, 383
Colston, Jr., N. V., 89, 91, 226, 480
Commonwealth Associates, 12-14, 42, 70, 77, 81, 226, 274
Coomber, N. H. and Biswas, A. K., 14, 18, 70, 77, 81, 226, 274
Corwin, R., et al., 102, 104, 226, 488

516

Phillips, R. D. and Kaune, W. T., 184, 189, 239, 507
Pikarsky, M., 12, 13, 14, 42, 63, 65, 67, 239, 262
Pikul, R., 8, 25, 73, 79, 81, 239, 301
Protasel, G. J., 12, 16, 51, 189, 194, 218, 239, 460

Raines, G., 8, 10, 12, 13, 14, 25, 43, 73, 79, 81, 87, 88,
    239, 302
Rea, R., 73, 76, 240, 475
Reid, G. W., 14, 31, 134, 140, 142, 240, 409
Riggins, R. and Novak, E., 129, 135, 240, 501
Rosen, S. J., 129, 135, 240, 502
Rosove, P. E., 73, 76, 240, 475
Ross, P. J., Spencer, B. G. and Peterson, Jr., J. H., 89,
    92, 240, 485
Ross, J. H., 12, 14, 38, 45, 47, 135, 140, 142, 163-167, 169,
    240, 410
Rote, D. M. and Wangen, L. E., 102, 106, 240, 492

Salomon, S. N., 12, 13, 14, 41, 44, 55, 92, 96, 99, 100,
    240, 328
Schaenman, P. S., 9, 14, 40, 41, 135, 140, 142, 168, 241,
    413
Schaenman, P. S., and Muller, T., 8, 10, 21, 22, 92, 96,
    100, 241, 329
Schanche, G. W., et al., 129, 135, 241, 502
Schimpeler, C. C. and Grecco, W. L., 12, 13, 14, 42, 63, 66,
    67, 241, 263
Schlesinger, B. and Daetz, D., (1973), 10-14, 37, 73, 79,
    81, 241, 303
Schlesinger, B. and Daetz, D., (1975), 10, 11, 38, 39, 106,
    110, 111, 241, 363, 122
School of Civil Engineering and Environmental Science and
    Oklahoma Biological Survey, 8, 12-14, 44, 46, 92, 96,
    100, 241, 330
Sewell, W. R. D., 73, 76, 241, 476
Shaheen, D. G., 102, 106, 241, 492
Sharma, R. K., Buffington, J. D. and McFadden, J. T., 11,
    14, 31, 32, 106, 110, 111, 122, 241, 365
Slovic, P., 184, 189, 242, 507
Smith, W. L., 73, 76, 242, 476
Smith, M. A., 12, 13, 44, 46, 93, 96, 242, 331, 101
Smith, M. F., 102, 106, 242, 493
Sorensen, J., 10, 37, 74, 79, 81, 242
Sorensen, D. L., et al., 184, 189, 242, 304, 508
Southeastern Wisconsin Regional Planning Commission, 12-14,
    42, 63, 66, 67, 242, 263

SUBJECT INDEX

Advanced wastewater treatment plant, 500
Aerial crossings, 39, 111, 348
Aesthetics, 65, 76, 77, 95, 254, 260, 268, 324
Agency for International Development, 479
Air quality assessment model, 492
    box models, 27, 110, 363
    display model, 492
    indices, 24, 125, 369
Alternative choice coefficients, 60
Alternative futures, 20, 116, 117, 118, 119, 121, 360
Alternative proportional values, 305
APRAC, 152
Arizona, 147
    Pheonix, 168, 413
Assessment variables, 4, 6, 17, 21, 22, 23, 29, 30, 33, 36,
    38, 39, 40, 41, 42, 43, 45, 46, 47, 48, 52, 57, 58, 60,
    64, 68, 69, 75, 76, 77, 78, 89, 93, 94, 95, 100, 101, 102,
    108, 110, 126, 129, 137, 140, 147, 168, 184, 191, 192,
    194, 197, 198, 199, 286, 315, 325, 352, 372, 374, 413,
    432, 438, 448, 455
Assimilative capacity, 124
Atlanta, 331
Atmospheric dispersion models, 150, 151
Aubrey reservoir, 126, 370
Auto-qual, 153

Battelle environmental evaluation system, 44, 96, 101, 126,
    331, 370
Bioindicators, 25, 26, 194, 396, 450
Biological indices, 24
    setting, 442
    significance, 122, 365
Brainstorming, 141, 386
Bulkheads, 39, 111, 348

California coastal zone, 304
    highway model, 151
Carmel Valley, California, 300
Cascadia Dam, 327
CEQ Regulations, 17, 48, 113
Channelization, 28, 30, 32, 138, 142, 300, 338, 387
Check lists, 36, 52, 141, 386, 477, 479

521

Utah, Park City, 480
Utah Lake, 352, 353

Values forecasting, 20, 116-119, 121, 360
Visual analysis techniques, 33, 109, 354
Visual pollution, 505

Washington, D.C., 487
Wastewater facility plans, 19, 192, 196, 434
    treatment and collection systems, 487
    treatment plants, 48
    treatment process, 45, 192, 380, 431
    treatment projects, 81
Water quality index, 24-26, 65, 139, 146, 194, 251, 252,
    391, 392, 459
    indices, 24, 79, 86, 218, 295, 458
    models, 29, 139, 150, 153, 393, 415
Water Resources Council, 76, 270, 478
Waterway navigation, 101, 330
Waterways Experiment Station, 48, 51, 55, 150, 403
Weighted rankings technique, 44, 60, 109, 353, 361, 430, 431,
    439
Weighting, 41, 42, 112
Weighting and rating approach, 255
Weighting-ranking checklists, 17, 35, 41, 42, 196, 263, 264,
    434
Weighting-scaling, 17, 24, 35, 41, 42
Weighting-scaling checklist, 43-45, 47, 48, 65, 68, 77, 79,
    80, 86, 87, 96, 99, 100, 109, 140, 150, 193, 194, 196,
    254, 257, 262, 274, 276-278, 296, 297, 303, 305, 308,
    309, 328-331, 353, 361, 380, 403, 404, 439, 459
Weighting-scaling methodology, 331
Weighting-scaling techniques, 258, 431
Weighting summation technique, 453
Weighting techniques, 256
Willamette Basin, 327
WRAM, 3, 5, 7, 17, 21, 23, 26, 29, 32, 33, 35, 36, 38, 40,
    45-47, 51, 52, 55-57, 66-69, 76, 80, 84, 86, 87, 89, 93,
    96, 101, 107, 111, 136, 141, 150, 163, 184, 195, 206, 208,
    210, 249, 251-264, 267-278, 282-286, 288-292, 296, 297,
    300, 301, 303-310, 314, 315, 318, 319, 323-326, 328-334,
    337, 346-357, 361-364, 368-372, 374, 376, 379-389, 391-
    410, 413-418, 420, 421, 428-437, 439-451, 455-460, 462,
    464-466